D1608088

STUDIES IN COMMUNICATION

VOLUME 4

Communication and Culture:
Language Performance, Technology, and Media
Selected Proceedings from the Sixth
International Conference on Culture
and Communication, Temple University, 1986

Edited by

SARI THOMAS

Temple University

A Volume in the Series
COMMUNICATION AND INFORMATION SCIENCE
Melvin J. Voigt, series editor

ABLEX Publishing Corporation
Norwood, New Jersey 07648

Library of Congress Cataloging-in-Publication Data

International Conference on Culture and Communication (6th : 1986 :
   Temple University)
      Communication and Culture : language, performance, technology, and
   media : selected proceedings from the Sixth International Conference
   on Culture and Communication / edited by Sari Thomas and William A.
   Evans.
         p. cm. — (Studies in communication ; v. 4) (Communication
   and information science)
      Includes bibliographical references.
      ISBN 0-89391-497-5
      1. Communication and culture—Congresses. I. Thomas, Sari, 1949–XX.
   II. Evans, William A., 1923–XXXX. III. Title. IV. Series.
   V. Series: Studies in communication (Norwood, N.J.) ; v. 4.
   P91.I57   1986
   302.2—dc20   89-17536
                                                                 CIP

Printed in the United States of America.

ABLEX Publishing Corporation
355 Chestnut Street
Norwood, New Jersey 07648

Contents

PART **VIII**   **RETHINKING COMMUNICATION POLICY**

RICHARD COLLINS

32   The Internationalization of TV Entertainment   317
MURIEL G. CANTOR AND JOEL M. CANTOR

33   France Confronts the New Media: Issues in National
Communications and Cultural Policy   325
JAMES MILLER

34   Participant Observation and the Study of African Broadcast
Organizations   342
LOUISE M. BOURGAULT

     AUTHOR INDEX   355

     SUBJECT INDEX   363

Introduction

The International Conference on Culture and Communication is unlike most other scholarly meetings. Its schedule is not fixed; meetings are held every 2 or 3 years. This irregularity is, in part, related to the fact that the ICCC is not bound to a professional organization. The negative side of this lack of affiliation is that there is neither standing funds nor staff to orchestrate a large conference—and the Conference *has* grown from 180 participants in 1979 to 1500 in 1986. The more positive side of being organizationally unaffiliated is that the Conference's boundaries are fluid and, thus, not determined by preordained divisions, ideologies, or agenda items. While the ICCC solicits material within broadly articulated categories (communication theory/research methodology and philosophy of social science/interpersonal interaction/ government, industry, and culture/communication and ideology/mass media and acculturation/art as cultural artifact), there is no guaranteed scheduling of any one of these areas; an attempt is made to present the most intriguing work submitted. As a result, the emphases of particular meetings shift in relation to the quality of the papers proposed.

What I have suggested above may imply that the ICCC is without structure or particular goals, but to infer this would be inaccurate. In operating the Conference, there is indeed a hidden agenda consisting of three interrelated elements. First, it is hoped that the majority of featured papers deal with information processes as contextualized (or, at least, applicable in the context of) macrosocial theory. Second, the ICCC is committed to taking some chances on provocative, nonmainstream perspectives, methodological alternatives, and budding theories. Third, the Conference actively seeks scholars outside as well as within the discipline of communication.

While this "agenda" generally makes for an exciting meeting, it *does* create certain problems in compiling a selected anthology *from* that meeting. Sometimes the quality or depth of the work is uneven as a result of our attempt to foray into theretofore relatively uncharted areas. Also, edited volumes are "supposed to be" thematically coherent, and yet the breadth of the ICCC often mitigates against narrow focus. Thus, in selecting articles for a volume, there must be an attempt to develop context as well as interesting content. Of the more than 300 papers delivered at the 1986 meeting, eight broad "subject matters" emerged that might constitute reading sections for this new volume.

The first two parts address "language" from very different perspectives. Part I, "Language and Politics," is concerned with power and ideology through verbal discourse. The authors in this the section analyze different issues by (sometimes radically) different means. Keyan Tomaselli, Eric Loew, and Ruth Tomaselli confront the issue of government language in crisis situations, particularly how a government's rhetorical efforts may work to control social unrest. Nancy Nelson and, next, Catherine Ann Collins regard myth and metaphor as central in the public construction of meaning with respect to news and public address. Kevin M. Carragee studies a newsmagazine's symbolic construction of foreign developments. In both historical and theoretical frameworks, Carl R. Bybee and Kenneth Hacker analyze how journalistic language produces meaning and legitimizes power. Finally, Richard Buttny and J. Louis Campbell analyze the discourse of a welfare interview and show how established power is sustained in interpersonal interaction. The inclusion of this last article in this section is used, in part, to indicate that, in many contexts, the line drawn between mass and interpersonal communication is rather arbitrary.

Part II, "Sociolinguistics," deals again with language, but this time more in the context of interpersonal discourse and more in terms of *linguistic* issues themselves. Laura Miller investigates the importance of the listener in an analysis of oral narrative, while Asli G. Gokhan analyzes Turkish proverbs to show how metaphor functions in interaction. Patricia Johnson probes the inference process in a study of second-language learners interpreting conversational utterances. Following this work in sociolinguistics, Part III, "Performance as Cultural Reflection," picks up on related issues of folk art, lore, and ritual. Becky M. Mulvaney examines the relationship between social conditions, popular music, and dance, and Sally Ann Ness finds latent messages about social structure in traditional dance forms. Inga E. Treitler describes the linkages between individual narrative, myth, and the social construction of beliefs and values.

Generally more modern forms of ritual are considered in Part IV, "Sales, Promotion, and Organization." This part opens with Thomas E. Harris' theoretical exploration of organizations as myth- and communication-reliant cultures. Next, Audrey Korelstein and Neil Weinstock examine the music-video industry from the perspective of the anthropology of commodities and consumption. Mark Sanford provides heretofore academically unavailable insight into the strategies employed by agents in sales interactions. With specific attention to convenience stores, Frank Nevius examines the role of consumer goods and product-placement in the commercialization process. Lastly, Stephen Prince takes an historical look at an ostensibly Marxist style of film editing that has become a mainstay in U.S. advertising.

Part V explores "Technology in Its Social Context." Although it is not uncommon to find scholarly proclamations of "radical" change as induced by the advent of a "new" communication system, Gwenyth Jackaway's examination of public reaction to the emergence of television indicates that patterns of reaction to "new" technology may be "old." A.D. Coleman discusses social change that follows the introduction of an "invisible" technology—the lens, and Jeffrey Kittay suggests new ways of using the insights of McLuhan to investigate the emergence of prose. How language and interaction patterns are affected by computers is the subject of Richard D. Heyman's article.

The final three parts in this volume concern issues in mass communication. Part VI, "Mass Media and Socialization," explores some new issues alongside of older issues with new perspectives. One newer concern appears in Sue Brower's description of the social uses of television-related gossip. In reanalyzing audience effects, Alison Alexander and Virginia H. Fry examine the strategies by which individuals derive and construct meanings from television programming. Next, Paul J. Traudt reanalyzes differential effects by examining the role of mass media in the social construction of ethnicity, while Ali R. Zohoori investigates media use as both an instrument of and a result of socialization. Finally, Karl Erik Rosengren and Bo Reimer attempt to forward the theory of Cultivation Analysis as applied to media influence on individual and cultural values.

Part VII, "Sex, Gender, and Family," examines the symbolic construction of particular social roles and images in the mass media. Stephen Prince and Paul Messaris provide provocative evidence concerning the issue of violence against women—evidence that should cause a reexamination of certain arm-chair based assumptions about mass-media sexism. While female role-portrayals have recently been a somewhat standard research concern, Jonathan D. Tankel and Barbara Jane Banks discuss changes and continuities in *male* roles on television. Marion W. Weiss examines new television portrayals of the family, focusing on messages about traditional values and family stability. Barbara G. Cox and David W. Seaman analyze relational stages and movement between these stages as portrayed in recent films.

Part VIII, "Re-thinking Communication Policy," offers some fresh ideas on issues pertaining to mass-media regulation and economics. Richard Collins suggests the need for recasting familiar concepts like "competition" and "public good" in light of recent developments in world-broadcasting systems. Next, in examining the international market for television programming, Muriel G. Cantor and Joel M. Cantor present new evidence that challenges traditional notions of "media imperialism." James Miller offers a detailed account of how "new" communication technologies and markets have forced one nation, France, to rethink longstanding economic and cultural policies, and, finally, Louise M. Bourgault shows the necessity of considering cultural values and practices when studying a nation's broadcasting system.

The next ICCC is scheduled for 1989 and it is uncertain whether or not that program will reflect the same concerns as those appearing in this volume or, for that matter, the hundreds of other papers presented at the 1986 conference. However, it *is* certain that our multidisciplinary exploration into communication concerns will endure.

Sari Thomas
Director
Institute of Culture and Communication
Temple University

PART I

LANGUAGE AND POLITICS

1

Communication, Language and the Crisis of Hegemony in South Africa[1]

KEYAN TOMASELLI, ERIC LOUW, AND RUTH TOMASELLI
University of Natal, South Africa

Societies in conflict are marked by struggle between different discourses. Where governments try to rule through a balance of coercion and consent, the media and language become crucial in the job of ideological regulation. In South Africa, the government has tried to capture the entire discursive field: "That is the reality" being the phrase most often used by the State President, P. W. Botha, in his 1986 advertising campaign to try to retain the support of white readers and the international investment community (Tomaselli, 1986).

Apartheid is a politico-economic system wrought with contradictions. This chapter proposes some brief remarks on the nature of the current crisis in hegemony; and analyzes the State's response to the crisis in terms of its 'communications policy.' Particular concern here is with the use of language and the relexification of political terminology.[2]

BACKWARDS AND FORWARDS; THE STATE'S RESPONSE TO CRISES

Periods during which the State and capital have been able to induce consent or apathy from the oppressed black classes have always been followed by the use of extreme coercion during times of heightened opposition (e.g., Sharpeville, 1961; Soweto, 1976; the whole country since October 1984—see Howe, 1985).

---

[1] This study is drawn from a larger research project undertaken by the CCSU during 1986. Where not specifically referenced, language examples have been drawn from video recordings of SABC-TV News between August 1985 and September 1986; and reports in the *Sunday Tribune*, *Sunday Star*, *Sunday Times*, *Mercury*, *Daily News*, *Weekly Mail*, *New Nation*, *Financial Mail*, *The Star*, and *Rapport*. No attempt has been made to reference all the cases of semantic repetition, because the terms dealt with were recurrent in South African political discourse during the study period.

We would like to thank Susan Regnard for her critique of an earlier version of this chapter and the Human Sciences Research Council for making available a grant to enable the senior author to present the chapter at the Culture and Communication Conference. The outcome is solely the responsibility of the authors.

[2] The capping of racial terms is an example of the rhetoric of apartheid where race is made into a noun rather than an adjective.

South Africa has been facing a crisis in capitalist accumulation since the early 1970s (Clarke, 1978; Legassick, 1974), and more particularly since the 1976 Soweto disturbances (Saul & Gelb, 1981). The ruling National Party is itself divided at Cabinet level and the myth of Afrikaner unity no longer binds the 'nation' (see *Financial Mail*, November 11, 1985, pp. 36–38). The government appears to be immobilized by a fear of the extreme right-wing political parties (the Reconstituted National Party and Conservative Party) and the neo-Fascist paramilitary movement (the Afrikaner Resistance Movement).[3]

On the Left, the State has tried to smash the United Democratic Front (UDF) and the Azanian Peoples Organization (AZAPO) and the National Forum (NF) during the two states of emergency it declared in 1985 and 1986, respectively. The UDF is a nonracial coalition of about 800 smaller affiliated organizations representing localized community, church, educational, student, and trade union groups which have adopted the ANC Freedom Charter as their political credo. The Azanian People's Organization (AZAPO) is an outgrowth of the Black Consciousness movement of the 1960s heralded by Steve Biko. The NF is also composed of an affiliation of smaller organizations (e.g., AZAPO) and represents a Left–populist alliance.

The two movements—the UDF and AZAPO—are challenged by bantustan-based political organizations. One such organization, Inkatha, even operates outside its Zulu bantustan base in Natal, and through its paramilitary wing tries to enforce a Zulu nationalism throughout the province and in parts of the Transvaal. Inkatha, and its leader Gatsha Buthelezi, has allied itself with capital and the verligtes within the white hegemony, but against certain other Bantustan leaders who have accepted 'independence' from Pretoria. In some of the other bantustans such as the Transkei, Ciskei, Boputhatswana, Kwa-Ndebele, and Venda, the rural comprador-bourgeoisie have acted on behalf of the central State in a more compliant manner.

In the past the State was able to ensure hegemony over whites by ideological means, and over the mass of black workers and lumpenproletariat chiefly by coercion. In an effort to contain political and economic instability in the urban areas of 'white' South Africa since the late 1970s, the State, as the guardian of the welfare of capital in general, set out to forge a coalition between the dominant white classes and the 'coloured,' 'Indian,' and black middle classes. The result has been the racially tiered tricameral parliament, set up in 1983. However, far from containing opposition to apartheid, the elections held for the tricameral parliament provided a point of massive mobilization to resistance on numerous fronts. One result was a shifting strategy of resistance, and a growing sophistication among members of the emerging counterhegemony, since the early 1980s. Street protests simply attracted police quirts and bullets. In their wake has come resistance through *organization*: community, student, church, civic, womens', media, cultural, and a variety of other localized bodies sprang

---

[3]All these parties and movements are breakaways from the ruling National Party.

up across the country. Black and nonracial trade unionism had been building since 1974, and the State is thus now faced with a growing degree of sophisticated opposition which, although organizationally fragmented, is fairly ideologically cohesive. Increasingly, the resistance to apartheid has taken on a class character. The UDF coalesced out of these organizational dynamics in August 1983.

The State is being squeezed on all sides as its hegemonic crisis deepens. It is faced with the demands of capital, particularly English-dominated capital[4] to 'liberalize' its policies (*Weekly Mail*, January 1986) as the State is no longer in a position to secure even the basic conditions for the reproduction of capital (except in the gold mining industry). A chronic depression and massive unemployment co-exists with a 16%–20% rate of inflation. A crisis in confidence among the business classes has resulted in a 'brain drain' (Legassick, 1985).

Consumer boycotts by blacks of white-owned businesses have considerably increased the already accelerated rate of bankruptcy. Rent boycotts by 300,000 households spanning 38 black townships has caused the State to lose R250 million so far (Jochelson, 1985, p. 15). Hundreds of thousands of black and colored schoolchildren have been boycotting classes and in many cases have seized the initiative in many areas in opposing apartheid (Gardner, 1986, p. 57). Apart from the obvious disruptions this will have on the future workforce, it has led to the occupation of numerous black townships by both the police and the defence force. The result has been the smashing of parental, teacher, and school authority. In the place of family security a fragile township political culture has developed, precariously held together by an emerging system of street and area committees controlled by the 'comrades' who ally themselves with the UDF and ANC (*Weekly Mail*, January 1986, p. 4) A number of these areas became *de facto* 'liberated zones' (*Weekly Mail*, March 1986, pp. 6–7).

State responses have been erratic, confused, and contradictory. The Security Police and SA Defense Force (SADF) have occupied black townships, black schools, and some universities. In some cases the police have been fuelling conflicts within these areas by arming and abetting conservative elements of the black working class and by providing them with cover to attack UDF, AZAPO, and comrade groupings. By this means, the previously intractable community of Cape Town's Crossroads squatter camp was broken up and forced to relocate to the government-designated black area of Kyalitsha (Cole, 1986).

Tens of thousands of people have been detained and scores tortured during the past 2 years. During the first State of Emergency (1985–86), police detained UDF and AZAPO leaders. As this had limited effect on the nature and extent of

---

[4]*English capital* refers to capital owned by English-speaking South Africans. South African English capital and multinational corporation capital were previously integrated into the South African hegemony to a large extent. But since mid-1985 these fractions have been increasingly peripheralized.

resistance (*Weekly Mail*, March 1985, pp. 14–15; March 1986, pp. 14–15), during the Second State of Emergency, declared on June 12, 1986, the police concentrated on grassroots community and trade union organizers, outspoken clergy, journalists, student activists, and the various anticonscription organizations. Meetings of scores of organizations were banned and 'political' funerals were subject to severe restrictions (Schlemmer, 1986).

COMMUNICATION AND CONTROL

Since 1979 the State has tried to redefine the language of control. Until mid-1985, the State was able to legitimize its role to the Western world and white South Africans through continually updating a semantic lexicon which elicits a preferred reading of 'reform' and political evolution in South Africa. Internally, this lexicon has been naturalized through Afrikaner Nationalist control of broadcasting, Afrikaans language newspapers, the educational system and the Afrikaans Churches (Tomaselli, Williams, Steenveld, & Tomaselli, 1986). Internally, there was also some attempt to 'sell' the ruling hegemony to black South Africans. The Army Civic Action (Burgersake) programme attempted to 'sell' the idea to black South Africans that the military were their 'friends' and were to 'protect' everybody from communism (*Paratus*, 1985, p. 2). The Civic Action propagandists, however, lacked one important component: a 'sellable' message which black South Africans could believe. Externally, attempts have been made to convince the world of the sincerity of the South African government through the employment of foreign PR companies and the illegal activities of the previous Department of Information. The latter secretly funded large-scale advertising in the foreign press, attempted to buy controlling interests in numerous American newspapers and television stations, and set up *The Citizen* newspaper in South Africa after it had failed to acquire SA Associated Newspapers through a front company. The Department was closed down when the illegal activities of its employees were exposed by the English-language press in 1978 and 1979 (Rees & Day, 1980).

The closure of the Department of Information had significant political effects. Simultaneously with P. W. Botha's reformist policies came a shift in approach by the quasi-State research bodies. The study of 'intergroup' or 'intercultural' relations/communication became a major research focus amongst Afrikaans university academics and the Human Sciences Research Council (Marais & Dreyer, 1982; Main Committee, 1985). The concern was with intercultural communication which seeks ways to 'bridge' the cultural/race gap while retaining racial/cultural distance (see, e.g., Du Preez, 1985; Weich, 1982; Groenewald & Wepener, 1983). The hidden agenda of this kind of work is that the 'group character' of South African society should be endorsed in a more 'humane' manner.

A parallel area of research concerns the 'foreign image' of South Africa and the idea of a 'communications policy' (*Rapport*, September 15, 1985; Nofke,

1985; Vorster, 1986; de Wet, 1985). The two strands—communication policy and foreign image—interlock at the point of diplomacy. These ideas were not, however, immediately adopted by the government. The exploits and exposure of the previous Department of Information remained an embarrassment, and other means were used to try to persuade the world that apartheid was not as bad as some would infer.

New Name Apartheid

Significantly, the government rejected the HSRC Main Report on Intergroup Relations (1985) which argued that 'communication' in the absence of 'reform' through 'joint decision making' (i.e., across 'groups') was insufficient to reduce tensions "in a deeply divided society" (Marais, 1985, 1986, p. 64). This Report was a belated acknowledgement that the fundamental stresses of our society could no longer be hidden under semantic categories. In the past, apartheid was punted as the *solution* to 'intergroup differences'; now, (old style) apartheid has been declared dead, as 'an outdated concept,' a soiled relic of the early British colonial administrations such as the Native policies of Shepstone and Milner (P. W. Botha in Rubicon II in *Cape Times*, February 1, 1986, p. 19). Since the term has taken on extremely negative connotations, particularly in the foreign media, the government has attempted to exorcise it from South African political discourse. Dressed up in the *avant garde* liberal vernacular of democracy, the State President and cabinet ministers now talk of *negotiation, minority rights, free enterprise, devolution of power, freedom, the right to own property, de-regulation, privatisation*, and so on in the face of its actions to the contrary. By colonizing liberal discourse, the State had hoped to render apartheid structures invisible through introducing a new set of terms in conjunction with certain legislative rearrangements.

As a term, *Apartheid* has had many forebears (e.g., *segregation*) and just as many subsequent derivatives and mutations. A new terminology of substitutive and associative phrases has been developed, such as: *influx control, separate development, plural relations, vertical differentiation* (as opposed to *horizontal differentiation*), *ideal dispensation, separate freedoms, national self-determination, multicultural co-operative existence, multinationalism, multi-culturalism, own kind of development (eiesoortige ontwikkeling), own affairs* (as opposed to *general affairs*), *good neighbourliness, community development* (with the stress on communiti*es*/peopl*es*); *consocialism*, and the term *canton system*, is even being used.

Clearly, a process of relexification is at work here. As each term takes on perjorative overtones, new 'cleansed' terminology is engineered to replace it. In the example of apartheid, euphemism fulfills two associated functions: the need to dissociate the previous term from negative connotations (*separate development* for *baaskap* (white supremacy); *plural relations* for *apartheid*), and the need to reinforce/manufacture positive connotations (separate *development*; separate *freedoms*). The purpose of this relexification is to conceal the inherent contradictions subsumed in the term, and, by so doing, obscure the relations of power and domination. This is done by foregrounding the positive aspects of the terms while minimizing the negative aspects. The rate at which relexification has taken place since 1976 is indexical of the seriousness of the crisis of legitimacy facing the State.

A second example will help to illustrate the point. The present Department of Co-operation and Development has had many previous names: Department of Native Affairs, Department of Non-European Affairs, Department of Bantu Administration, and Department of Plural Relations. Notice how, in the latest title, 'Co-operation' and 'Development' both have positive connotations, and no mention is made of the fact that this Department is concerned with repressive control relating to one (i.e., black) race group only (Janks, 1986).

When the nationalists came to power in 1948, rural Africans lived in what was known as *African reserves* or, more colloquially, *the reserves*. Under the Verwoerdian system of Grand Apartheid, these were relabeled as *bantustans*. As this term has taken on a pejorative connotation, it has progressively been replaced by *homelands* and *our national states* (which exemplifies a certain residual colonial mentality among white South Africans). In an attempt to legitimize apartheid ideologically, these *states* were catapulted into *constitutional development* which would move from a message of *self-government* to *independence*. In keeping with this strategy, which was self-consciously based on the postcolonial model of *independence* experienced throughout Africa, the bantustans progressively moved from being *homelands* to *national states*, then *self-governing national states*, and, ultimately, *independent national states*. At the present time, several bantustans are considered as self-governing national states, while four are *independent* (Transkei, BophuthaTswana, Venda, and Ciskei, collectively referred to by the State media as the 'TBVC countries').

The 'TBVC countries' are also occasionally referred to as *neighbouring states*, a term which is also used to label Swaziland, Lesotho, Botswana, Zimbabwe, Mozambique, and Angola. This semantic ambiguity works to legitimate further the concept of sovereignty manufactured for these territories. Both the *independent* and the *non-independent* territories are joined in a *confederation of states*, or a *constellation of states*, of which South Africa is part, thus imparting a spurious *international* identity of these territories to white South Africans if nobody else.

Relexification is one way of redefining the ideological ground. The same effect can be achieved by syntactical methods, in which the negative connotations of a term are exorcised by simply omitting, rather than backgrounding them. Thus the word *group* often is, in South Africa, used as a short-hand for *racial group*, dropping the overt reference to the apartheid basis of the *grouping*. Hence our earlier criticism of the idea of *intergroup relations* as an object of study. Consider, for example this statement by the Minister of Co-operation and Development:

> Without group security and group protection we cannot bring about acceptable reform. (*The Star*, February 7, 1986)

In a recent television interview on West German television, the State President, P. W. Botha, totally ommited any reference to apartheid, or any of its synonyms:

> (interviewer): Looking at your country, there is a very strong polarisation in SA of those who want change and those who want to preserve apartheid by all means— where is your position?
>
> PWB: I don't think you are right saying that there is a confrontation or polarisation between those who want to preserve *that which is in the past*, and those who want *reform*. . . . A small minority of people cling to *the far past*, yes, but they are a small minority. (*Financial Mail*, September 5, 1986, pp. 57–61; emphasis added)

Not only does Botha skirt the issue of labelling *apartheid*, but, by reformulating it as 'that which is in the past,' and then qualifying it as something belonging to the 'far past,' he tries to absolve the present State from responsibility for apartheid structures. At the same time, he juxtaposes the 'past' with the 'present,' in which the interviewer's 'change' is re-defined as 'reform.' Reform implies maintenance and is incompatible with 'change'. The interviewer asks for his position on *change*: Botha offers him a reformed, renamed, updated version of an essentially *unchanged* apartheid. Thus Botha is able to shift the question in a way which naturalizes the relations of domination and semantically *displaces* the historical struggles with regard to apartheid away from the National Party, the State, and the government.

The argument presented by the government is that the world has misinterpreted what is meant by apartheid. So consistently and effectively have antiapartheid movements appropriated the term that the State has had to exorcise it from its own discourse. The first attempt to 'kill' the word occurred in the then Minister of Co-Operation and Development's (Piet Koornhof) 'Apartheid is dead' speech, made in June 1979 in Washington, D.C. This was followed by the National Party's 1981 election manifesto, which attempted to discredit the hostile liberal discourse against racism by counter arguing that:

> The National Party has never accepted the antiquated, simplistic and racist approach that South Africa consisted of a White minority and a Black majority. (This sentence reappeared in PW Botha's 'Rubicon I' speech in August 1985.)

By continually substituting new words and obscured contexts for apartheid, the government hoped to determine the preferred readings of different audiences: insiders, who would, like the psychologist's inkblot, see what they wanted to see (no change) in apartheid (Graaf, Urbasch, & Doria, 1986); and outsiders who would believe that apartheid was indeed being dismantled. The State has overplayed its attempts at semantic engineering, an acknowledgement contained in Rubicon I, but which is at the same time used to shift the blame for inadequate reform onto antiapartheid critics themselves:

> To find solutions have been impeded and frustrated because of different interpretations of the terminology that we use to describe our particular form of democratic solutions. (Address to NP Congress, Durban, August 17, 1986)

A society in crisis is a society in which contradictions become increasingly opaque. Marx has suggested that "a society cannot exist without forging a representation of its unity" (Thompson, 1984, p. 25). Semantic engineering is only one way of dealing with the crisis in legitimacy. It is not by any means the only way. An important strand in the creation of ideological hegemony is the definition of a common enemy—the 'them' against which the 'we' can unite. Thus the threat of Soviet imperialism is used by the State as an effective rallying point. Much of the blame for the present predicament is thus shifted to external factors (the Soviets, communism, Marxism, the ungodly evil of those who wish to destroy Christian civilization, the ANC who are 'defined' as being 'outside', as the 'enemy') which are jointly and severally responsible for industrial strikes, rent and trade boycotts, the rejection of Bantustan 'independence' and 'constitutional developments.' At no point has the government shown any willingness to see how central apartheid policies have been in creating the problems it now finds itself faced with, though its spokesmen have, at times, admitted placing too great an emphasis on the 'differences' between 'communities' in terms of legislative measures (Tomaselli et al., 1986, p. 106).

However, the previously incontestable meanings no longer entirely persuade apartheid critics. Discursive authorizations and repitions are in themselves insufficient to ensure the dominance of apartheid discourse. Each time the State President addresses a public or televisual audience, he is struggling to find a code in which his preferred meaning will be *the* dominant, most frequently decoded, one. Detractors on both sides of the ideological spectrum have penetrated the 'naturalness' of the code and have deconstructed the common sense on which it is based. The contradictions are pinprick sharp, and language has become an increasingly important site of struggle (Tomaselli, 1986).

National Security, the Media, and Political Violence

A parallel area of State-sanctioned research to that of intergroup relations has been concerned with the idea of a *communications policy*, particularly in as far as it influences the image of South Africa abroad. The soothing sounds of diplomatic noise have been substituted for the blunt and uncompromising political discourse of the 1960s and 1970s. The infiltration of the SABC (and Afrikaans universities to a lesser extent) by Foreign Affairs personnel has resulted in an alliance of universities, the State, and some advertising agencies offering ways of 'improving' South Africa's image abroad. The assumption is, of course, that the country has a 'bad' press and that the crisis of hegemony facing South Africa can be rectified by improving the performance of some superstructural elements without much fundamental adjustment to the economic base (see Nofke, 1985, p. 33).

Official thinking on the reporting of political violence rests on two distinct sources: (a) counterinsurgency arguments about the State's need for psychological warfare strategies; and (b) generalized assertions about the causal links between popular imagery and social violence, or the 'contagion effect.' In terms of the former, an important contribution to the debate as far as South African defence strategy is concerned has been the counterrevolutionary ideas developed by the *guerre revolutionaire* school of French writers, drawing on their Vietnamese and Algerian experiences. Briefly stated, their position is that the nature of warfare has changed since World War Two; modern warfare is characterized by insurgency tactics, and is not won on the battlefield but rather in the hearts and minds of the population. This is psychological warfare, and is fought on two fronts: externally through diplomacy, and internally through boosting the morale of our 'own' side into believing that they can win, and that they want to win; and demoralizing the enemy by making them think victory is impossible. This is achieved through the selective dissemination of information, and through the exclusion of information which will damage the cause (Beaufre, 1973; Kelly & Brown, 1970; Kitson, 1970).

In applying this to a media policy, Clutterbuck (1981) addresses the question of "how, in a liberal democracy, we can ensure that television and the press do not become allies of terrorism and other forms of political violence" (p. xi). The result has been a gross overestimation of the power of the media, and a failure to understand how 'unsellable' the apartheid (or whatever it is called) message is to the majority of South Africans. Further, the 'hearts and minds' exercise has very little application to human rights. It is a policy being conducted mainly at the ideological idealist level, and rarely intersects with conditions on the ground (see NUSAS, 1982; *Resister* and End Conscription Campaign publications).

MEDIA MANAGEMENT AND MEDIA REPRESSION

A Bad Case of Publicity: Drowning in the Rubicon

Control the government once had over preferred readings in National Party political discourse came apart when the State President addressed the world from the National Party congress held in Durban in August 1985. The State President threatened the world against 'pushing us too far.' He established an 'us/them' conflict, arguing that 'reasonable people' supported the National Party. All others, including a local English-language press that had until then energetically supported his 'reformist' initiatives, were 'the enemy' (Alison-Broomhead, Chetty, Daran, & Savage, 1986). Within hours of the speech, the rand collapsed, the stock market fell, pressure for sanctions increased, and the English-language press representing South African English capital, in particular, vented its unbridled anger. Even the American State Department was taken aback, and complained about the need to 'decode' Botha's terminology. International monopoly capital and local businessmen responded by purchasing full pages in the national press demanding an end to apartheid (these included the American Chamber of Commerce, representing 76 signatories, Mobil,

Rank Xerox, and a grouping of civil rights activists supporting Bishop Desmond Tutu and signed by Joan Baez and other celebrities).

At the same time, the State was extremely perturbed by the massive amount of negative publicity South Africa received abroad during the first State of Emergency. Various ad hoc efforts at restraining the media were undertaken, but the bottom line remained, that, where there were graphic incidents of violence, civil disobedience, and a concomitantly violent repression and police response, foreign newsmen would continue to file reports, photographs, and television footage.

The press, particularly the foreign press, became the scapegoats who were seen as responsible, not only for reporting the almost daily violence, but also, by extension, for causing or at least exacerbating it. Government sources frequently claimed that many cases of unrest incidents were sparked off, or aggravated, by the presence of cameras. By September 1985 the relationship between the State and foreign correspondents was distinctly strained. "There is no doubt that reports emanating from South Africa are unfair and creating the wrong impression of the situation here", stated Louis Nel, then Deputy Minister of Foreign Affairs, (now Deputy Minister of Information in the office of the State President) (*EP Herald*, September 24, 1985). State policy thus became geared to improving the 'negative image' of the country in the world media. Controlling the media was seen to be the solution to the 'problem.'

The 'communications gap,' as conceptualized by the State and some academics, has two dimensions to it: (a) The inability to convey a believable message that 'reform' was seriously being undertaken. This was exemplified in the failure of the 'Rubicon' speech; and (b) A perception on the part of the government that the coverage of the 'unrest' by foreign journalists acted as a catalyst for further violence on the part of activists who 'played up for the cameras,' and, more importantly, sensationalized the crisis in the country.

The crisis of legitimation led to the establishment of a Bureau For Information in September 1985, with the express aim of improving the country's overseas image. The mechanisms for achieving this ranged from media "repression" to media "management". The establishment of the Bureau should be seen as an attempt at the latter, though we shall argue that its initial purpose has been subverted to that of repression (Heard, 1986, p. 7) The Bureau seems to have adopted but trivialized Vorster's (1981, p. 44) ideas on using the 'pen' and the 'sword' simultaneously "as an instrument to provide peace and understanding." Recently, Vorster suggested that the Bureau is not able to fullfil a 'professional communication role' because the State is ignoring the government's 'communications' advisors (Vorster, 1986, p. 19).

During the first half of 1986, the Bureau seems to have played a fairly low-keyed role, devoting most of its energy to the orchestration of 'information campaigns' designed to publicise the State President's 'reform initiatives.' Double-page spread advertisements were placed in all the major dailies and some 50 regional papers, punting the sentiments expressed in Botha's opening speech to parliament in January 1986 ("We have outgrown the outdated concept of apartheid"). A second campaign was undertaken in April to launch the new identity documents, which became necessary in terms of the 'demise' of 'influx control' legislation, now euphemistically referred to as 'an orderly urbanisation strategy' (Cilliers, 1986).

The Bureau also published several booklets and pamphlets. Some, for instance A NEW BEGINNING, PARTNERS IN TERROR and LET'S BUILD AND WORK IN PEACE, were edited transcripts of the State President's various speeches. By far the most controversial booklet has been TALKING TO THE ANC, which sets out the history of the ANC from the State's perspective, and uses many quotes from the ANC to (mis)illustrate its policy on revolution, violence, and the links with the SA Communist Party. The notoriety of the booklet rests largely on the only legally published photograph of Nelson Mandela since his incarceration 25 years ago. The demand for the booklet was so great that the entire print-run of 70,000 was distributed within 2 weeks of publication. Many of these went to black readers, who "want to read ANC statements which could previously not be published and obtain a copy of the good quality photograph of Nelson Mandela featured in the booklet" (*Sunday Tribune*, June 15, 1986). The book has subsequently been republished, but that photograph has been replaced with an innocuous longshot of an ANC gathering of the 1950s.

A more recent project of the Bureau has been the production of a 'peace song,' for a reputed and unprecedented R1.5 million production fee. The effort has been a dismal failure: not only has it raised the ire of counterideologues who argue that the contributing pop stars have prostituted their art, but conservative whites have protested against the apparent squandering of their taxes. The final irony has been that the State-owned South African Broadcasting Corporation has refused to give the song airtime, claiming that it is not a pop song but a commercial, and, as such, the Bureau should purchase airtime (*Sunday Times* September 28, 1986).

The establishment of the Bureau For Information, then, should be examined against the background of the expectations of a "brand new, streamlined Department of Information managed by experts" (*Die Burger*, quoted in *The Mercury*, September 16, 1985). Less expected, however, was the vehemence with which the Bureau has acted as a censoring and repressive agency, a role which has come to be associated with the police. The Directorate of Publications, which was pursuing a more sophisticated course, has been marginalized. At present, the Bureau is reportedly appointing advertising and PR agencies in South Africa's major cities to promote the government's image on a regional basis. This move follows the advice of Vorster (1986) on the use of 'professional' communication techniques derived from political advertising methods used in America.

Initially, the Bureau did not interfere in the *control* of journalists or the news media. This was left to the police and the Department of Internal Affairs. Journalists were harrassed in the course of their duties, arrested, their copy and cameras were confiscated, and several foreign journalists were deported (Stewart, 1986). From October 1985, Nel clearly supported the more hardline approach against the media, while still concentrating the Bureau's efforts on 'positive approaches' to news manipulation. With the declaration of the second State of Emergency, however, the Bureau took on an overtly *control* type approach. Armed with the most restrictive Emergency regulations yet placed on the South African media, including six 'definitions' of a subversive statement, the Bureau was able to take ascendency over all other sources of news relating to what is euphemistically known as 'unrest-related incidents,' or, more generally, the 'security situation' (Tomaselli & Tomaselli, 1986). In September 1986 the Bureau announced that it would only reply to written and telexed queries from the media.

The takeover was so complete, and so sudden, that it took many journalists, editors, and large sections of the South African public by surprise. Yet for the assiduous reader of editorial and political commentary over the previous 10 months, the move was predictable and expected (see Tomaselli, 1985; Muller, Tomaselli, & Tomaselli, 1985). 'Communications experts' in Afrikaans universities have been vociferous on the establishment of a 'communications strategy' (e.g., de Wet, 1985). These academic responses reflect the State's reading of black protest, where resistance is seen to occur because the 'benefits' of apartheid have not been communicated clearly enough to them. The problem is either simplistically conceived of as a 'communications gap,' or, increasingly, that the "legitimacy crisis" was caused by "Whites" who have initiated reform in the absence of "joint decision making, negotiation, bargaining, etc." with "Blacks" (Marais, 1986; Main Committee, 1985).

'Reform' thus remains 'group' oriented and separatist. It is an attempt to mobilize the power of the media and the legislature to redesign the image of apartheid in nonethnic and seemingly neutral 'free enterprise' terms in response to the crisis of capital accumulation that has beset the country since the mid-1970s. The appropriation of liberal discourse has failed to conceal deepset, historically derived racial and class agendas. Semantic engineering and control of the media are no longer adequate weapons in persuading international investors of the stability and potential of South Africa as a site of profit taking. 'Communication' was never intended to operate in South Africa in terms of democratic ideals, but rather as a means to engineer cultural, political, and social perspectives best suited to foster the most efficient conditions for the reproduction of capital and the privilege of the capitalist, mainly white, classes.

REFERENCES

Alison-Broomhead, M., Chetty, A., Daran, D., & Savage J. (1986, July). *The visual role of the 'Rubicon' speeches as part of the 'reform' strategy.* Paper presented at the Association For Sociology in Southern Africa, University of Natal.

Beaufre, A. (1965). *An introduction to strategy.* London: Faber.

Cilliers, S. P. (1986). Demise of the Dompas: From influx control to orderly urbanisation. *Indicator SA, 4*, 95–98.

Clarke, S. (1978). Capital, 'fractions' of capital, and the State. *Captial and Class, 5.*

Clutterbuck, R. (1981). *The media and political violence.* London: MacMillan.

Cole, J. (1986). Crossroads—The destruction of a symbol. *Work In Progress, 43*, 3–9.

De Wet, J. C. (1985). Gedagtes oor die Weermag en die nuusmedia tydens weermagoptredes. *Communicatio, 11*, 55–59.

Du Preez, H. (1985). Simbole in interkulturele kommunikasie. *Communicatio, 11*, 61–68.

Gardner, M. (1986). Zones of progress: a report on the Durban Conference on the Crisis in Education, March 1986. *Perspectives in Education, 9*, 57–70.

Graaf, M., Urbasch, M., & Doria, C. (1986). *The semantic engineering of apartheid: an analysis of the discourse of South African power.* Unpublished research paper, CCSU, University of Natal, Durban.

Groenewald, H. J., & Wepener, M. (1983). Ethnosentrisme en interkulturele kommunikasie. *Communicatio, 9*, 2–8.

Heard, A. (1986). Caution is the watchword. *Index on Censorship, 15*, 7–8.

Howe, G. (1985). Cycles of civil unrest 1976/84: Triggers, targets and trends. *Indicator SA* (Political Monitor), *3*, 7–12.

Janks, H. (1986, September). *Preparing classroom materials on the relationship between language and ideology in the South African/Azanian context.* English Academy Conference, Johannesburg.

Jochelson, K., & Brown, S. (1985). UDF and AZAPO: An evaluation. *Work in Progress, 35*, 12–17.

Legassick, M. (1974). Legislation, ideology and economy in post-1948 South Africa. *Journal of Southern African Studies, 1*, 5–35.

Legassick, M. (1985). The struggle for workers' democracy. *Die Suid-Afrikaan*, (Winter), pp. 24–26.

Kelly, G. A., & Brown C. W. (Eds.). (1970). *Struggles in the state: Sources and patterns in world revolution.* New York: Wiley.

Kitson, F. (1970). *Low intensity operations.* London: Faber.

Main Committee, HSRC Investigation into Intergroup Relations. (1985). *The South African Society.* Pretoria, South Africa: HSRC.

Marais, H. C., & Dreyer, L. (1982). HSRC investigation into intergroup relations: The programme and its financing. *Communicare, 1*, 3–7.

Marais, H. C. (1985). On communication in a divided society. *Communicare, 4*, 38–43.

Marais, H. C. (1986). On communication and intergroup relations. *Communicare, 5*, 64–65.

Muller, P. (1986). The media and the security forces: Is a joint strategy possible? *Communicare, 5*, 29–33.

Muller, J., Tomaselli, K. G., & Tomaselli, R. E. (1985). *The lineage of contemporary cultural studies: A brief historical examination (seminar paper #4).* Durban, South Africa: CCSU.

Nofke, C. (1985). SUID-AFRIKA: Moet ons bly of loop. *Die Ekonoom, 1*, 32–33.

NUSAS. (1982). *Total war in South Africa: Militarisation and the apartheid state.* Cape Town, South Africa: Author.

Phillips, D. (1985). A communication strategy for speeding up the process of reform in South Africa. *Communicare, 4*, 77–79.

Rees, M., & Day, C. (1980). *Muldergate: The story of the Info scandal.* Johannesburg, South Africa: MacMillan.

Saul, J. S., & Gelb, S. (1981). *The crisis in South Africa: Class defence, class revolution.* New York: Monthly Review Press.

Schlemmer, L. (1986). Unrest: The emerging significance. *Indicator SA, 3*, 3–6.

Stewart, G. (1986). Intimidation and prosecution of journalists (South Africa). *Index on Censorship, 15*, 24–40.

Thompson, J. B. (1984). *Studies in the theory of ideology.* Oxford, England: Polity.

Tomaselli, K. G. (1986). *A contested terrain: Struggle through culture* (inaugural lecture). Durban, South Africa: Natal University Press.

Tomaselli, K. G., Williams, A., Steenveld, L., & Tomaselli, R. E. (1986). *Myth, race and power: South Africans imaged on film and TV.* Bellville, South Africa: Anthropos.

Tomaselli, R. E., & Tomaselli, K. G. (1986). Focus on the media: From news management to control. *Die Suid-Afrikaan,* (Winter), 53–55

Tomaselli, K. G., Tomaselli, R. E., & Muller, J. (Eds.). (1989). *The press in South Africa.* London: James Currey.

Vorster, P. J. (1981). Gedagtes oor kommunikasie, politiek en oorlog. *Communicatio, 7,* 40–45

Vorster, P. J. (1986). Political communication in South Africa after Rubicon: A trend towards professionalism? *Communicare, 5,* 12–28

Weich, H. (1982). Intercultural communication and the House Journal: A case study. *Communicatio, 8,* 29–34.

2

Metaphor and the Media

NANCY L NELSON

University of New Mexico

The ideal of OBJECTIVE news reporting is a fundamental value in the U.S. printed media and news-wire services. Yet news production and presentation practices systematically distort objectivity. As a result, news reporting is rarely neutral; it carries strong ideological orientations.

One of the most subtle and pervasive means by which the media shapes public perspectives and ideology is through the use of nonliteral language. Journalistic limits on time and space require the simple and efficient expression of complex ideas. Metaphor, more than any other form of figurative language, accomplishes this by associating complex ideas with common images or experiences. These associations can influence public understanding and subsequent action on important issues.

METAPHORS

Most anthropologists agree that metaphors structure new ways of perceiving through the juxtaposition of two terms from separate domains. By juxtaposing these terms we are compelled to examine them in relationship to each other (Sapir, 1977, p. 9). According to Schön, metaphors "frame" shared features, "carrying over . . . perspectives from one domain of experience to another" (1979, p. 254). It is through this process of framing that metaphor structures our concepts. They simultaneously emphasize and obscure certain aspects of a problem directing our perception of it (Lakoff & Johnson, 1980, p. 11). Moreover, framing systematically produces certain secondary metaphorical entailments which correspond to this focus. Among these entailments is a solution coherent with those aspects of the problem the metaphor highlights.

This ability to generate solutions is also the basis of the metaphor's power to direct action. Actions that fit purposefully within the definitions, inferences, and limits of a metaphor will be sanctioned by it. According to Lakoff and Johnson, such actions "reinforce the power of the metaphor to make experience coherent. In this sense metaphors can be self-fulfilling prophecies" (1980, p. 156). The truth or falsity of the metaphor itself is not at issue. Its systematic framing of terms makes the emphasized relationship and solution appear coher-

17

ent and "natural" (Crocker, 1977, p. 42). But metaphorical framing is never objective; it is rhetorical.

To illustrate how metaphors shape our concepts and direct action, consider the metaphor *love is a rose*. This particular focus might generate entailments such as:

love is beautiful	*love can hurt*
love is delicate	*love must be cultivated*
love is thorny	*love is natural*

These entailments tend to highlight the positive aspects of love, implying that it should be handled carefully and nurtured in order for it to grow. If not, love may die. In contrast, another metaphor, such as *love is war*, generates very different conceptualizations. In this case the negative aspects of love are emphasized, and appropriate actions might include developing one's defenses against it.

METAPHORS AND THE MEDIA

While metaphor is a fundamental part of our conceptual system, when used in mass communications its' potential impact is stronger, not only because the media reaches such a broad audience, but because Western culture as a whole claims "objectivism" as the basis of their journalistic practices. Moreover, the abstract nature of the media's two most important subjects, politics and economics, increases the use of figurative language. "Like all other metaphors, political and economic metaphors can hide aspects of reality. But in the area of politics and economics, metaphors matter more, because they constrain our lives" (Lakoff & Johnson, 1980, p. 236).

In printed media, metaphors tend to appear more frequently on the editorial page, but they are not limited to it. Front page news articles commonly use metaphorical language. Although various metaphors may be used to describe a particular issue by a single news source, generally one metaphorical image is used more frequently. For example, mainstream newspapers tend to employ metaphors that reflect a culture's dominant values, while other newspapers will have different priorities reflected in alternative metaphors. By framing public issues in certain ways, metaphors reinforce select social values. Moreover, the emphasis of these metaphors changes as social realities change. Descriptions of the world economy by the *New York Times*, the *Guardian*, and the *Worker's World* in 1982, and again in 1986, illustrate these points. The possibility of default on their foreign debt by Brazil, Argentina, and Mexico made the economy an important media subject both years.

In 1982, the *New York Times* discussed the economic situation in terms of an *illness*. The most commonly used metaphor implied that *the world economic body has a circulatory malady*. The *body* was evidenced in quotes such as "policy directives that get to the heart of the domestic economy" (*New York*

Times, May 31, 1982) and "the spirit of intergovenmental cooperation, which is at the heart of this institition (IMF)" (September 7, 1982). The *illness* is referred to as an "epidemic of recession" (November 25, 1982), a "planetary ailment" (October 18, 1982), and, in one case, is given this *diagnosis*: "the drastic upheavals in the circulatory system of the world's economic body left deep scars like a heart attack" (October 19, 1982).

Consistent with this image are *prescriptions for recovery*. On September 7, the *New York Times* reported that "Mexico is only the first of a long list of possible candidates for infusions of cash," and, on November 11, "the United States Government's policy is aimed at restrained recovery, because the White House fears that a robust recovery may reignite inflation," *freeing circulation* to stimulate growth and a healthy body is the solution the *Times* implies when it says that "the catch is cash flow and the cure is sound programs" (September 14, 1982), "the world economy grows when trade grows" (October 18, 1982), and "economists here express their confidence that the monetary system will survive" (September 8, 1982).

During this same period, the *Guardian* and *Worker's World* described the economy quite differently. In their metaphorical language, *the world economy is a crumbling structure*. On November 17, the *Guardian* reported that, "with the whole interdependent structure somewhat wobbly, there is an uncomfortable feeling that it may be no stronger than its weakest part," and "the shaky financial condition of Third World countries and industrial corporations is undermining confidence in the capitalist banking system." The *Worker's World* predicted that "a default would rock the foundations of the capitalist banking fraternity" (May 6, 1983), and the *Guardian* similarly said that "legitimate fears have been raised about the collapse of the financial system" (November 10, 1982).

These papers insinuate that *reconstruction* is ultimately the only solution. The *Guardian* warned of "the hazard of the rapidly increasing use of debt to speed up the realization of profits and shore up the economy" (November 10, 1982), whereas the *Worker's World* noted that the Marxian answer is the "undoing of capitalism and construction upon its ashes . . . [of] a new order" (May 6, 1983).

The differences between these metaphorical treatments of the economy correspond to the political and economic orientations of the newspapers that use them. The *New York Times's* emphasis on the economic *body's health* and *recovery* suggests our own capitalist economy. This is a *natural* and *organic* image, legitimating the concept of economic interdependence. When all its parts are working together, the body is in peak condition. The framing of this metaphor highlights economic problems in terms of a systemic malfunctioning. If blockages to circulation or distribution were removed, the economic body would be healthy and grow. This focus on distribution, or the free flow of goods, corresponds to the central principle of laissez-faire economics. The concept of a *world economic body* also stimulates a strong emotional identification. The image is our own. *Survival* is the first concern; the body cannot die. As a mainstream newspaper, the *New York Times'* use of this particular metaphor is not surprising. In fact, the solutions it prescribes were also the solutions prescribed by the Reagan administration at the time: the removal of quotas and other trade barriers.

In contrast, the metaphor used by the leftist publications highlights the faults of the system as it exists. The image of the *world economy as a crumbling structure* implies that the foundation upon which it was built is unstable. Continued expansion or building is jeopardized by this fundamental weakness. Former attempts to repair these flaws have been futile because the materials (credit) are only temporary (credit becomes debt), and do nothing to change the basic structural problems. The *Guardian* and *Worker's World* focus on questions of *building* or design corresponds to the Marxist's theoretical emphasis on production. Like the *New York Times* metaphor, this also has a strong emotional impact. In this case, the threat of collapse instills fear, but with hope of new opportunities to build a different and solid structure.

Since 1982, the *New York Times'* use of the *ailing economic body* metaphor has changed slightly. Negotiations between commercial banks, the International Monetary Fund, and debtor Latin American nations are reflected in a different image. While the *Times* continues to use primarily the *illness* metaphor, it no longer refers specifically to *circulatory problems*. References are made to "diagnosis" and "prescription" (September 5, 1986), "miracle potions," "health and growth" (August 24, 1986), "emergency infusions of capital," "rescue operations," and "global economic recovery" (June 8, 1986), but barriers to capital circulation are rarely mentioned. Instead, negotiations on the Latin American debt are evidence in a new *performance* metaphor. On August 24, 1986, the *New York Times* wrote that commercial banks "have ended another cliff-hanger in the on-and-off saga of Latin American debt," and, on March 10, that "the market will applaud their efforts to reflect the true value of their loans." In two separate articles on June 8, the *New York Times* refers to the "major players in this fragile scenario" and "the major actors in Mexico's economic drama."

Real changes in the world economic situation between 1982 and 1986 account for this change in metaphorical images. The shift in emphasis indicated by the *performance* metaphor highlights the fact that, by 1986, the debt problem was seen as involving more than one economic body. Negotiations over the Latin American debt in 1982 had resulted in a massive program of rescheduling and new loans which recycled money back to the banks as interest on prior debt. In effect, the debt burden remained solely Latin America's. By 1986, however, these policies had inflated the total Latin American debt to such proportions that it was apparent the problem had impacted upon the U.S. domestic economy. Developing countries, which are the majority of the debting nations, account for 24% of world trade (*New York Times*, September 5, 1986). United States exports to Latin America fell from approximately $20 billion a year, at the time of the first debt crisis, to $9 billion in 1984 (August 24, 1986). Senator Bill Bradley estimated that one million American jobs had been lost due to the Latin American debt (August 24, 1986). Thus, when debt negotiations came up again in 1986, there was no alternative but to share the debt burden. In March, the Cartagena group of Latin American debtor nations called for a reduction in interest rates on their foreign debts. That same month, Brazil reached a new accord with foreign lenders lowering the interest rate almost 1% on debts maturing in 1986 (March 3, 1986). These agreements demonstrate a shift in responsibility for the debt, to include the performance of the lending institutions as well as the debting nations.

Such economic changes are the basis of the *Times'* new metaphorical emphasis on *all* actors' performances in the debt crisis, and also the reason for its dropping the *circulatory malady* metaphor. Facing a record foreign debt and import/export imbalances, the Reagan administration was forced to reconsider its blanket support of free trade markets. According to the *New York Times*, the administration was "no longer willing to renounce the right to protect (U.S.) jobs and markets" (September 5, 1986). Moreover, in the latest debt negotiations some trade concessions were made by the debtor nations in exchange for the proposed interest relief policies. Mexico, for example, signed the General Agreement on Trade and Tariffs (GATT) in May. Thus, while the *New York Times* continued to use the *illness* metaphor, trade barriers and *free circulation* were no longer important issues, and this aspect of the metaphor disappeared.

METAPHOR, THE MEDIA, AND THE MESSAGE

Lakoff and Johnson argue that "virtually all major industrialized nations, whether capitalist or socialist, use the same metaphor in their economic theories and policies" (1980, p. 237). The examples used here, however, clearly contradict this statement. Metaphorical conceptualizations of the economy are very different in the mainstream U.S. press than in leftist publications. In addition, subtle metaphorical changes reflect changing social policies. The metaphorical structuring of our conceptual system is a continuous and complex process grounded in specific social contexts. Yet the media's repeated use of certain metaphors, if accepted, can create a coherence in perspective, ideology, and appropriate action. The ideological bend of a particular journalistic source may have little significance where different choices are available. When possible, we tend to buy newspapers oriented toward out own ideological perspectives. But when journalistic alternatives are limited or nonexistent, the media's use of figurative language matters more.

This is not simply an issue of state-controlled versus private, commercial media systems, while ideological opposition is generally not given access to the press in state-owned systems, the existing monopoly on privately owned media enterprises significantly limits ideological expression there too. The four major privately owned world news agencies are concentrated in three Western, industrial nations: Reuters in Britian, Agence France Presse in France, and the Associated Press and United Press International in the U.S.[1] As a result of this centralization of news sources, news flow is largely uni-directional—from the developed world to the developing. A study of 14 major Latin American newspapers showed that 90% of nonlocal news came from AP, UPI, and AFP (NACLA, 1982, p. 13), and only one-fifth of these agencies' correspondents are based in all of Latin America, Asia, and Africa (p. 14). Moreover, news gathered by Western agencies from these countries is sent to centers in London, Paris, New York, and Washington for editing, and then restransmitted to the developing countries for publication. Few horizontal lines of communication exist between these nations. Although a nonaligned news pool has been created, it cannot compete with the larger, more established agencies. The widest circulating newspapers in Latin America, for example, use independent sources generally only as supplements to the major Western news agencies.

The West's monopoly of the world's privately owned communication systems radically biases the media's representation of developing nations in two ways. Press coverage not only tends to concentrate primarily upon issues affecting U.S. and Western European interests, but its portrayal of these issues is from a Western perspective (see Hester, 1974; Mattelart, 1978; Peterson, 1980; Rosenblum, 1981; Schiller, 1976). Such a bias affects Western readers' understanding and action on these issues but, more importantly, it has the same affect on non-Western readers. Differing perspectives have far less chance of representation in developing countries, particularly when even news originating there is edited by Westerners in agency headquarters before it is published locally. While blatant biases might be removed before these articles appear in the national press, more subtle forms, such as metaphor, are often missed.

Representation of Mexico's debt negotiations in the country's daily newspaper, *Excelsior*, serves as an illustration. An article appearing on the editorial page of the *New York Times* on June 8, 1986 was published in translation on the front page of *Excelsior* the day before. In its discussion of proposals to solve the debt crisis, the U.S. version stated that

> These proposals are based on a number of unrealistic assumptions: that banks and governments have the political will and economic power to unilaterally institute them; that they can readily identify their own long-term self-interest, and that they are concerned with Mexico's best interests.

The Excelsior translation appeared without the line questioning the ability of the "governments" to identify their own self-interests. Since it was specifically the Mexican debt which was being discussed and, therefore, the capabilities of the Mexican government which appeared to be questioned, it is not surprising

---

[1] Although United Press International was purchased in June 1986 by Mario Vásquez, a Mexican businessman, its headquarters will remain in Washington. In a letter to UPI clients, he assured them that it will continue to be a "100 percent U.S. news agency" (*Newsweek International*, June 16, 1986).

that this line was edited. Nevertheless, the same article repeatedly used the *illness* metaphor to describe the debt problem, refering to "prescriptions," "urgent injections of capital," "rescue operations," "global economic recupera- tion," and "economic growth."[2] Other articles appearing in *Excelsior* from the *New York Times* news service on June 13, and from AP on June 7, similarly employed the same metaphorical image.

While *Excelsior's* own journalists used the *illness* metaphor for the debt crisis on occasion, an alternative metaphor appeared more frequently. In this case the country's economic problems were described as a *road rally*, where the driver must chart his own course, overcome obstacles, and rely on his inner strength for success. This metaphor is apparent in quotes such as "The Bank of Mexico began a whirling road," "we are passing the most profound of the depressions, from which the bottom still cannot be seen," and "it is impossible to withdraw from the velocity of inflation" (*Excelsior*, June 14, 1986). In an article on June 9, *Excelsior* stated that "a mistake at these altitudes and below the present circumstances would be fatal for the country." An editorial on June 2 metaphorically expressed the country's need for self-reliance by writing that "we are exploring the roads" and that Mexico's "history has demonstrated its self-worth and that it has a powerful internal motor. . . . It no longer wants to listen to the boisterous sounds of the street. It desires the internal harmony of popular demand that will correctly drive its energy."

The two metaphorical images used by *Excelsior* and the U.S. news agencies generate very different conceptualizations of the debt issue and corresponding solutions. Whereas the *illness* metaphor emphasizes survival of the economic system, the *road rally* metaphor portrays the economic route as undefined and unexplored. The divergence of these ideological orientations is critically impor- tant if Mexico wishes to develop independent or alternative economic solu- tions. The media's ability to subtly shape public perception of this issue could significantly influence the Mexican people's support of, or opposition to, their government's economic policies. But the imbalance in the world communica- tion structure weighs heavily on the side of foreign interests.

CONCLUSION

For the last decade, developing and industrialized nations at the United Nations Economic, Social and Cultural Organization (UNESCO) have debated the issues of press objectivity, the world communications monopoly, and private or public regulation of the media. The industrialized nations, arguing for the "free flow of information" world-wide, view a free press as vital to democratic government, and the free flow of ideas as essential to self-governing peoples. The developing nations, on the other hand, have promoted the concept of a New World Information and Communication Order, where the media is directly responsible to the people it serves and the ideas it dissemi-

---

[2]All translations in this article are by the author.

nates contribute positively to the well-being, education, and sovereign development of society. This position, in contrast to that of the industrialized nations, recognizes a direct role for the government in relation to the media. Ultimately, there is an ideological congruence between these two positions and the economic metaphors discussed previously. The parallels between the concepts of a new world economic structure and a new world information order are obvious, as is the congruence between the concept of freely circulating capital and the free flow of information. Observing the UNESCO debate, a journalist from the *London Economist* wrote:

> It was the impression of most of the delegations that the Americans wanted to secure for their news agencies that general freedom of the market for the most efficient which has been the object of all their initiatives in trade policy — that they regard freedom of information as an extension of the charter of the International Trade Organization rather than a special and important subject of its own. (NACLA, 1982, p. 6)

The UNESCO debate has died out in recent years, due much to the problems UNESCO itself is suffering. Yet the West, and the U.S. in particular, still expound on the necessity of a free and autonomous press if developing nations are to develop democratically. But the point is moot. Whether communication systems are controlled by the state or commercially, there is a direct relationship between the press and the ideological basis of the system which controls it. The media will always be biased ideologically. Objectivity is a subjective concept; our language shapes our concepts. Nevertheless, it is essential that the public be made aware of systemic factors which distort objectivity and bias reporting, and this is particularly true in a society that readily accepts the myth of an objective press and claims freedom as a fundamental cultural value. The media significantly shapes our political perspectives, and metaphor is one of its more powerful rhetorical tools.

REFERENCES

Crocker, C. (1977). The social functions of rhetorical forms. In D. Sapir & C. Crocker (Eds.), *The social use of metaphor: Essays on the anthropology of rhetoric* (pp. 33–66). Philadelphia, PA: University of Pennsylvania Press.

Hester, A. (1974). The news from Latin America via a world news agency. *Gazette, 20,* 82–98.

Lakoff, G., & Johnson, M. (1980). *Metaphors we live by.* Chicago, IL: University of Chicago Press.

Mattelart, A. (1978). The nature of communications practice in a dependent society. *Latin American Perspectives: Culture in the Age of Mass Media, 5,* 35–48.

NACLA. (1982). Report on the Americas. *Toward a new information order, 16* (4), 13.

Peterson, S. (1980). A case study of Third World news coverage by the Western news agencies and *The Times* (London). *Studies in Comparative International Development, 15,* 62–98.

Rosenblum, M. (1981). *Coups and earthquakes.* New York: Harper and Row.

Sapir, D. (1977). The anatomy of metaphor. In D. Sapir & C. Crocker (Eds.), *The social use of metaphor: Essays on the anthropology of rhetoric* (pp. 3–33). Philadelphia, PA: University of Pennsylvania Press.

Schiller, H. (1976). *Communication and cultural domination.* New York International Arts and Sciences Press.

3

Cultural Stories in the Rhetoric of U.S. Involvement in Vietnam

CATHERINE ANN COLLINS
Willamette University, Salem, OR

Can attention to narrative inform our understanding of the administrative rhetoric surrounding the Vietnam War? Rhetoric which attempts to justify actions taken on behalf of the public must frame that justification in arguments which are acceptable to the public being represented. Most of these arguments are enthymematic. That is, the arguments rely on unstated premises which are popularly accepted by the public. The purpose of this chapter is to examine the administrative rhetoric which justifies America's involvement and progress in the Vietnam War. The result will be an understanding of the archetypal stories which support enthymematic public argument. Specifically, the structure of the "Vietnam stories" will be assessed in accordance with the theories of Northrop Frye and Leslie Fiedler.

NORTHROP FRYE: NARRATIVE ARCHETYPES IN THE QUEST MYTH

In *Fables of Identity* (1963) and *Anatomy of Criticism* (1957), Frye presents a coordinating principle or central hypothesis for literary criticism. He argues that the organizing principle is the narrative. In ritual, he believes, we find the origins of narrative, and, in patterns of imagery, fragments of significance. Imagery and ritual are united in the archetypal myth of narrative—the quest myth. "In the solar cycle of the day, the seasonal cycle of the year, and the organic cycle of human life, there is a single pattern of significance, out of which myth constructs a central narrative" (Frye, 1963, p. 15). The four phases of the archetypal quest myth are played out in four literary archetypes: the romance, the comedy, the tragedy, and the satire. The particular archetype of a story depends on the phase of the quest myth depicted. Each archetype has a narrative structure which reveals the motivation for the hero's action and the consequences of that action in a particular world. In pure form, the motivation in both romance and tragedy is choosing to depend upon oneself; in comedy and irony, it is being forced to depend upon the world. In pure form, romance and comedy reap full rewards, while tragedy and irony result in failure (Cadbury, 1982).

Frye's archetypes help explain the story told by successive administrations to justify America's involvement in Vietnam. Ivie (1974) identifies the quest myth in presidential rhetoric. He argues that a vocabulary of motives exists, having a definite hierarchy with " 'right' at the pinnacle, as the primary god-term for purpose, and with 'law' and 'democracy' as secondary god-terms for agency. Only through the agencies of law and democracy can rights such as 'freedom' be made secure" (Ivie, 1974, p. 340). The quest is to secure peace, in times of war, by insisting on the preservation of America's sacred rights. Similarly, the justification for going to war is to insure other countries access to the moral and political rights which we espouse. Baritz describes this as the myth of America as a city on a hill. "In countless ways Americans know in their gut—the only place myths can live—that we have been chosen to lead the world in public morality and to instruct it in political virtue. . . . The benevolence of our national motives, the absence of material gain in what we seek, the dedication to principle, and our impenetrable ignorance were all related to the original myth of America" (Baritz, 1985, pp. 11, 13) The quest, then, is to preserve our highest ideal—American moral rights, law, democracy, freedom—the myth of America as a city on a hill. In seeing ourselves as the chosen people, choosing to depend upon ourselves is the clear motive for actions. Whether in pure or modified terms, America's quest stories will be either archetypically romance or tragedy, depending upon the consequences of our actions. We judge our actions on behalf of others as (romantic) heroic.

VIETNAM AS QUEST MYTH

Although the story of our involvement in Vietnam is told by successive administrations, there is an essential sameness in all the tellings. Kail (1973) provides a content analysis of the dominant words and themes of the official rhetoric from 1950 through 1969. His analysis, and my reading of the texts, indicate that the exportation of the American quest myth plays a prominent role in our justification for involvement. Over a period of more than 20 years we promise freedom and liberty for the people of Vietnam (later, South Vietnam) which are possible only with the adoption of our system of law and democracy. For the story to be consistent with our national self-concepts, the exportation of our "system of rights" must not serve colonialism; rather, countries must first share our beliefs and then see these values threatened.

One line of argument depicts Vietnamese society as similar to our own—sharing basic values, aspirations, and commitments. Kennedy can say, "The sacrifices that you have willingly made, the courage you have shown, the burdens you have endured have been a source of inspiration to all people all over the world" (Kennedy, 1962, p. 377). Rusk can suggest that the South Vietnamese value a lifestyle similar to our own in contrast to the North Vietnamese who, although they inherited the majority of industrial resources, "fell rapidly behind South Viet-Nam in food production, the number of children in school, and in standards of living" (Rusk, 1963b, p. 729). Thus, we conclude that the South Vietnamese share our values while the North Vietnamese hold alien values.

An alternate rationale for our involvement casts the South Vietnamese as children in need of parental guidance and support. In answering critics who point to waste and mismanagement of U.S. aid, Rusk replies, "Let us recall that we are talking about a nation which has been responsible for its own affairs for less than a decade, about a people who have had no peace since 1941 and little experience in direct participation in political affairs" (Rusk, 1963b, p. 729). Both rationales support a plot line which casts the society as weak, ineffective, and dependent for salvation on U.S. moral leadership.

The story of Vietnam, as told by the Johnson Administration, changes somewhat between 1963 and 1968, but U.S. moral leadership is affirmed through appeals to value clusters surrounding duty and courage. In 1964, Johnson argues before Congress: "Daily they (the free people of Vietnam) face danger in the cause of freedom. Duty requires, and the American people demand, that we give them the fullest measure of support" (Johnson, 1964a, p. 892). In a 1964 address, Johnson links our fundamental cultural values to the cause of peace-making: "if a nation is to keep its freedom it must be prepared to risk war . . . if one man can compel others, unjustly and unlawfully . . . then your community is not a place of peace;" that peace requires "persistent and patient effort" (Johnson, 1964b, p. 79). Finally, rightness of our cause cannot be questioned when we stand "on the side of peaceful justice, of self-determination, of human freedom" (Johnson, 1964b, p. 80). Continuing the story told by previous administrations, Johnson consistently appeals to the American version of the quest myth. He emphasizes the nation's moral duty to provide the cultural rights, the rule of law, freedom, and democracy to deserving nations. He ends his July address with an appeal to our determination to be the peace*makers* for the world: "it is with the people and not with their leaders that the final question whether the liberties and the life of this land shall be 'preserved to the latest generations' . . . our children's children will gladly remember us in the ancient phrase: 'Blessed are the peacemakers, for they shall be called the children of God' " (Johnson, 1964b, p. 81).

The preservation of our national quest and its fruition in other countries allows Nixon to say, "never in history have men fought for less selfish motives— not for conquest, not for glory, but only for the right of a people far away to choose the kind of government they want" (Nixon, 1971, p. 525). It is clear from the responses of these three Presidents that the cause is noble and that the responsibility of world freedom rests on U.S. shoulders. As in any romance story, our will and dedication will yield full rewards.

The romance demands a confrontation between the hero and the villain. When the villain troubles others, the action line for the hero must be to preserve the safety and independence of the threatened party. The Vietnamese population generally, and later the South Vietnamese, assume the role of threatened party. In the Vietnam story the villain is alternately labelled communist, aggressor, North Vietnamese, or Viet Cong. Because the Communists were already culturally defined villains, they provided the initial threat justifying American intervention.

Kail suggests that "The rhetoric of the Kennedy Administration, when compared with that which followed, was in both its quantity and content insubstantial" (Kail, 1973, p. 181). Kennedy does, however, continue the story initiated by Truman and maintained by Eisenhower, that the Vietnamese share our cultural values and, thus, need our help in resisting outside forces (Communists).

In his February 5, 1962 message to the Vietnamese, Kennedy promises, "Let me assure you of our continued assistance in the development of your capabilities to maintain your freedom and to defeat those who wish to destroy that freedom" (Kennedy, 1962, pp. 377–378). A week later, Rusk reminds the nation of the grave threat of communism in Southeast Asia, of the need to protect the Vietnamese against "Communist assaults and terror tactics," and of the likely success in vanquishing our mutual foe: "with our help, the brave and capable people of South Viet-Nam will preserve their independence and steadily eradicate the Communist infestation" (Rusk, 1963a, p. 312). The U.S. and other Western powers are heroes undertaking the job of protecting a weaker society from a powerful villain. Rust argues that the Vietnamese have "major deficiencies in training, intelligence, and mobility" (Rusk, 1963a, p. 312) which the U.S. needs to repair. The main story remains a "worldwide struggle between freedom and coercion" (Rusk, 1963b, p. 727), with Vietnam serving as one vital sector in the global battle.

For Johnson the villains became the Viet Cong, who represented the global communist threat to our quest: "the Viet Cong guerrillas, under orders from their communist masters in the north, have intensified terrorist actions against the peaceful people of South Vietnam. This increased terrorism requires increased response" (Johnson, 1964a, p. 892).

The hero's actions must be consistent with heroic principles to assure an honorable end. In this vein, Johnson proclaims: "No one should think for a moment that we will be worn down, nor will we be driven out, and we will not be provoked into rashness; but we will continue to meet aggression with firmness and unprovoked attack with measured reply. . . . Our firmness at moments of crisis has always been matched by restraint—our determination by care" (Johnson, 1964c, p. 300). Our goal has been consistent in actions throughout the world, not just in Southeast Asia, since the end of World War II. It has been, Johnson declares, a constant struggle in which we have "patiently labored to construct a world order in which both peace and freedom could flourish" (Johnson, 1964c, p. 298). In 1965 Johnson says, "We love peace. We hate war. But our course is charted by the compass of honor. We know today, as Americans have always known, that liberty has only one price—and that is eternal vigilance. That price we are able and willing to pay" (Johnson, 1965b, p. 653).

Through both Republican and Democratic administrations, the story remains essentially the same: the United States is protecting a threatened group (in need of our protection) from the villain. Any actions taken in support of that cause are heroic; any actions taken by the villains are alien and thus justify whatever response we take. The story consistently tells of a hero in control who is appropriately rewarded for persistence in a noble fight.

LESLIE A. FIEDLER: THE MYTHOLOGICAL WESTERN

Fiedler attaches pregeneric archetypes to American stories. He begins by asserting that "geography in the United States is mythological" and that Americans have defined themselves and their country topologically in terms of "a mythicized North, South, East, and West" (Fiedler, 1968, p. 16). He suggests that American literature roughly follows these four mythicized cardinal points in telling Northerns, Southerns, Easterns, and Westerns. The Northern story sees the individual fighting a hostile environment, attempting to subjugate nature. The Southern favors melodrama, as the dark side of the individual is cast out onto a scapegoat—the symbolic Black to the Southern Whitey. The Eastern "treats the return of the American to the Old World" (Fiedler, 1968, p. 19) and concludes that the old corruption has been replaced with a new clean space. Only the Western story is called by its mythicized geographical name. It is characterized by the encounter with the Indian (an alien culture) who inhabits a new kind of space ("an unhumanized vastness"). Fiedler argues, "The Western story in archetypal form is, then, a fiction dealing with the confrontation in the wilderness of a transplanted WASP and a radically alien other, an Indian—leading either to a metamorphosis of the WASP into something neither White nor Red . . . or else to the annihilation of the Indian" (Fiedler, 1968, p. 24). Of all the story forms which characterize the American experience, the Western best captures the spirit of the culture—"America equals the West" (Fiedler, 1968, p. 25). When we tell the American story, we most often tell the Western.

> It is astonishing how often American GIs in Vietnam approvingly referred to John Wayne, not as a movie star, but as a model and a standard. Everyone in Vietnam called dangerous areas Indian country. . . . They called their Vietnamese scouts who defected from the Communists Kit Carsons. These nineteen-year-old Americans brought up on World War II movies and westerns, walking through the jungle, armed to the teeth, searching for an invisible enemy who knew the wilderness better than they did, could hardly miss these connections. One after another said, at some point, something like, "Hey, this is just like a movie." (Baritz, 1985, p. 37)

VIETNAM AS MYTHOLOGICAL WESTERN

The Western begins with the confrontation between the hero and the stranger in a new and alien environment. One of the first clear references to an alien and inhospitable land is the description of Vietnam as a land of jungles and "steaming soil" (Johnson, 1965b, p. 606). Two years later, Johnson argues that Americans are making their imprint in "the fierce hills and the sweltering jungles of Vietnam" (Johnson, 1967a, p. 534). One result of the American action is to change the land of steaming soil and jungle, the tragic world of death and decay into a garden, a romantic land, "a very rich and a very fertile land" (Johnson, 1965e, p. 839)—to be accomplished through Western restoration.

Fiedler tells us, however, that the Western requires, not only confrontation between the hero and the alien land, but with the alien as well. In the Vietnam story, the alien other must be the enemy—communism in general or the North Vietnamese in particular. The enemy is alien in his use of different tactics of warfare, in the different value he places on human life, and in his rejection of the American quest myth, including our moral leadership.

Johnson's depiction of the villain as alien is consistent with the story told by previous administrations. In a Christmas message to Americans in Vietnam, Johnson declares, "It is a war of terror where the aggressor moves in the secret shadows of the nights. Murder and kidnapping and deception are his tools. Subversion and conquest are his goals" (Johnson, 1964d, p. 76). He even argues that this is a particularly alien enemy: "Instead of the sweep of invading armies there is the steady and the deadly attack in the night by guerrilla bands that come without warning, that kill people while they sleep" (Johnson, 1965d, p. 817) In 1967 Johnson characterizes the enemy's style as reminiscent of an earlier foe when he says, "Viet-Nam is aggression in a new guise, as far removed from trench warfare as the rifle from the longbow. This is a war of infiltration, of subversion, of ambush" (Johnson, 1967a, p. 535). Johnson contrasts the enemy's behavior with American civilians in Vietnam, who posses "a passionate devotion to serving humanity" a "willingness to be lonely and afraid for long periods of time" and "seek right answers in an alien culture" (Johnson, 1967b, p. 289).

In the Western story, only one set of values can survive. Because our actions are not based on selfish motives, efforts to eliminate the alien from the land are deemed appropriate, even essential. Johnson says, "We have no ambition there for ourselves. We seek no dominion. We seek no conquest. We seek no wider war" (Johnson, 1965a, p. 333). Two months later he reaffirms, "We want nothing for ourselves—only that the people of South Viet-Nam be allowed to guide their own country in their own way" (Johnson, 1965b, p. 607). Frustrated by the refusal of the the North Vietnamese to come to the bargaining table, Johnson casts them as those who "seek a solution by bullet rather than by ballot" (Johnson, 1968c, p. 899).

Johnson uses a consistent light—dark metaphor to distinguish between the actions of the alien other and the U.S. hero. He reminds the American people that "the people of South Viet-Nam must know that after the long, brutal journey through the dark tunnel of conflict there breaks the light of a happier day" (Johnson, 1965e, p. 839).

Clearly, the story of America's involvement in Vietnam is but a continuation of its long standing battle against the corruption of the old order and the efforts to establish a new covenant in a new land. Drawing an analogy between America's War of Independence and the conflict in Vietnam, Johnson says,

> But there were—and we thank God for this—enough brave men and women to bear the burden; there were enough dedicated men and women to endure year after year of war and suffering; and there were allies who stood with us all through those darkest hours until we finally prevailed. After 13 years of war and political strife, we here in America prevailed.
>
> Given that background, we ought not to be astonished that this struggle in Viet-Nam continues. We ought not to be astonished that that nation, racked by a war of insurgency and beset by its neighbors to the North, has not already emerged, full-blown, as a perfect model of two-party democracy. (Johnson, 1967b, p. 289)

American efforts to impose values on a hostile alien (whether the American Indian or the corrupt alien of the Old World) have succeeded in the past and offer hope for the current struggle.

At some point the story about Vietnam involvement changes. In September of 1967, Johnson still justifies U.S. involvement in classical Western form, but he extends the argument beyond domino theory and makes U.S. self-preservation a key justification. He refers to speeches of Eisenhower, Kennedy, and other leaders in suggesting a threat to the U.S., "So your American President cannot tell you—with certainty—that a Southeast Asia dominated by Communist power would bring a third world war much closer to terrible reality. One could hope that this would not be so" (Johnson, 1967c, p. 520).

Just as the hero in the Western story helps the town restore peace and order (the law being days away from the frontier), American Presidents sought to cast our efforts in these terms In 1961, Kennedy said, "we are neither 'warmongers' nor 'appeasers,' neither 'hard' nor 'soft.' We are Americans, determined to defend the frontiers of freedom by an honorable peace if possible, but by arms if arms are used against us" (Kennedy, 1961, p. 917). Johnson later proclaimed, "The true peacekeepers are those men who stand out there on the DMZ at this very hour taking the worst that the enemy can give. The true peacekeepers are the soldiers who are breaking the terrorist's grip around the villages of Viet-Nam" (Johnson, 1967c, p. 522).

CHANGING THE STORY OF VIETNAM

The traditional Vietnam story ceased to work in approximately 1967. If, as a nation, we received the story as a Western, did the story's failure result from the disparity between the Western's inevitable success and our prolonged losses in Vietnam? Does the Western depend on villagers who may be inept initially, but who ultimately can command the common ideals? If, as a nation, we received the Vietnam story as a romance, did the story's failure result from the heroes, American troops, who no longer could determine their own destiny? Did our actions cease being heroic when we bombed and napalmed civilians, when we defoliated the countryside?

When, on March 31, 1968, Johnson announced that he would not seek reelection, he still tried to tell the story in heroic terms. "But let men everywhere know, however, that a strong, a confident, and a vigilant America stands ready tonight to seek an honorable peace—and stands ready tonight to defend as honored cause—whatever the price, whatever the burden, whatever the sacrifices that duty may bring" (Johnson, 1968a, p. 486). When Johnson, and later Richard Nixon, continued the war to assure an "honorable peace," the form had failed.

In Frye's terms, the original Vietnam story, as told by the Administration, was a romance. Faced with a longer than expected war, with greater resistance from the aggressors, with less "growth" on the part of the South Vietnamese, the story was subtly changed from pure romance to a modified form—tragic romance. The story, structurally, located the motivation for action with the hero; but the consequence of those actions was attenuated rather than reaping full rewards—not what we had hoped for, but acceptable. As other voices told a different story about Vietnam, Johnson and then Nixon had to respond. When the public story revealed admissions of misestimatation of troop strength or public antiwar protests, the predominant story could not prevail. While the administrations attempted to continue a romance, dissonant plot episodes in the story revealed the archetype of romantic tragedy (heroic action with partial failure). When the competing stories became more prominent, the administrations' stories are interpreted as comic irony (choosing to depend upon oneself with partial failure). Structurally, then, the story moves from romance to romantic tragedy and the meaning of the Vietnam story as told by the administration changes markedly. The Romantic Western, which is attempted by successive Presidents, is less credible, because it is less able to elimate references to conflicting stories and because conflicting stories challenge the appropriateness of the cultural story form which is employed.

REFERENCES

Baritz, L. (1985). *Backfire*. New York: Ballantine Books.
Cadbury, W. (1982). Semiology, human nature, and John Ford. In W. Cadbury & L. Poague (Eds.), *Film criticism a counter theory* (pp. 69–88). Ames, IA: Iowa State University Press.
Fiedler, L. A. (1968). *The return of the vanishing American*. New York: Stein and Day.
Frye, N. (1957). *Anatomy of criticism*. Princeton, NJ: Princeton University Press.
Frye, N. (1963). *Fables of identity: Studies in poetic mythology*. New York: Harcourt Brace, Jovanovich.
Ivie, R. L. (1974). Presidential motives for war. *Quarterly Journal of Speech, 60*, 337–345.
Johnson, L. B. (1964a). 5/18 Address. *Department of State Bulletin, 50*, 891–893.

Johnson, L. B. (1964b). 7/20 Address. *Department of State Bulletin, 51*, 79–81.
Johnson, L. B. (1964c). 8/12 Address. *Department of State Bulletin, 51*, 298–301.
Johnson, L. B. (1964d). 12/23 Address. *Department of State Bulletin, 51*, 76.
Johnson, L. B. (1965a). 2/17 Address. *Department of State Bulletin, 52*, 333.
Johnson, L. B. (1965b). 4/7 Address. *Department of State Bulletin, 52*, 606–610.
Johnson, L. B. (1965c). 4/17 Address. *Department of State Bulletin, 52*, 650–654.
Johnson, L. B. (1965d). 5/4 Address. *Department of State Bulletin, 52*, 816–822.
Johnson, L. B. (1965e). 5/13 Address. *Department of State Bulletin, 52*, 838–841.
Johnson, L. B. (1965f). 7/13 Address. *Department of State Bulletin, 53*, 182–190.
Johnson, L. B. (1965g). 7/28 Address. *Department of State Bulletin, 53*, 262–265.
Johnson, L. B. (1965h). 9/27 Address. *Department of State Bulletin, 53*, 1014.
Johnson, L. B. (1967a). 3/15 Address. *Department of State Bulletin, 56*, 534–539.
Johnson, L. B. (1967b). 8/16 Address. *Department of State Bulletin, 57*, 288–290.
Johnson, L. B. (1967c). 9/29 Address. *Department of State Bulletin, 57*, 519–522.
Johnson, L. B. (1967d). 12/19 Address. *Department of State Bulletin, 57*, 33–38.
Johnson, L. B. (1968a). 3/31 Address. *Public Papers of the Presidents, I*, 170.
Johnson, L. B. (1968b). 4/1 Address. *Public Papers of the Presidents, I*, 172.
Johnson, L. B. (1968c). 8/19 Address. *Public Papers of the Presidents, II*, 452.
Johnson, L. B. (1968d). 9/9 Address. *Public Papers of the Presidents, II*, 471
Johnson, L. B. (1968e). 10/31 Address. *Public Papers of the Presidents, II*, 572.
Kail, F. M. (1973). *What Washington said.* New York: Harper and Row.
Kennedy, J. F. (1961). 11/16 Address. *Department of State Bulletin, 45*, 917.
Kennedy, J. F. (1962). 2/5 Address. *Department of State Bulletin, 46*, 377–378.
Kennedy, J. F. (1963). 9/2 Address. *Department of State Bulletin, 49*, 498–500.
Nixon, R. M. (1971). 4/7 Address. *Public Papers of the Presidents, III*, 525.
Rusk, D. (1963a). 2/13 Address. *Department of State Bulletin, 48*, 311–316.
Rusk, D. (1963b). 4/22 Address. *Department of State Bulletin, 48*, 727–732.

4

Defining a Foreign Social Movement: An Analysis of *Newsweek's* Coverage of the Solidarity Trade Union Movement in Poland

KEVIN M. CARRAGEE
Boston College

This study examines *Newsweek's* coverage of Poland, especially the news-magazine's definition of Solidarity.[1] Through a "thick description" (Geertz, 1973) of this reportage, this analysis seeks to convey the complexity of the symbolic world constructed by *Newsweek* in its coverage of Poland. Both the formal properties (e.g., the amount of reporting concerning Poland) and the thematic emphases of the coverage are explored. In addition, by comparing the magazine's definition of Solidarity with other interpretive accounts of the trade union movement, this study examines the characteristics of news as a form of social knowledge.

All reporting concerning international affairs requires some form of translation; foreign news developments need to be explored so as to make them meaningful to the American public. This is a complex process, especially when the events in question take place in a nation whose political and economic system is different from our own.

The significance of news production as a social process may be even more pronounced in the reporting of international affairs. The American press plays a decisive role in interpreting the relevance and importance of foreign events for their readers (Cohen, 1963; Batscha, 1975; Rubin, 1977). Lacking immediate contact with foreign events and issues, the American public is largely dependent on news media reports for their information on international concerns.

An analysis of *Newsweek's* coverage of Poland also has significance in a broader cultural context. Journalistic accounts of events and issues are both an institutional product and a construction of reality (Tuchman, 1978; Altheide, 1974; Epstein, 1973; Fishman, 1980). Influenced by organizational practices and procedures, news is "a way of defining and making sense of the world" (Dahlgren, 1982, p. 45).

---

[1] This research is part of a more extensive analysis of American media coverage of Solidarity. See Carragee (1985).

METHODS

Sample

This study examines *Newsweek*'s coverage of Poland from August 1, 1980 to December 13, 1981. (The union movement was initiated by the Gdansk Agreement of August 1980 and was driven underground by the imposition of martial law on December 13, 1981.) All stories concerning Poland published by *Newsweek* during this period were analyzed.

As a national medium reaching a large audience, *Newsweek* possessed the resources to provide detailed coverage of Poland. The limitation of the analysis to one media message system, while sacrificing breadth in favor of depth, allows for a comprehensive examination of news content without demanding a sampling of stories. *Newsweek* has been judged as an important part of the elite press by American foreign service officers (Davison, 1975).

Research Questions and Operational Definitions

The analysis was guided by the following major questions: How much coverage did *Newsweek* devote to Poland? How did the amount of *Newsweek*'s coverage concerning Poland compare with the amount of coverage devoted to other international regions? How were stories concerning Poland "placed" on the news agenda developed by *Newsweek*? What were the thematic emphases of *Newsweek*'s coverage of Poland?

The unit of analysis for all coding categories was the individual news story.

The *total news hole* of *Newsweek* is defined as the total number of pages in the newsmagazine's National and International sections. Cover stories are included in the measurement of the total news hole. This definition excludes the following parts of the magazine from the measurement of the total news hole: the Update section, the Periscope section, the Newsmakers page, and the back-of-the-book sections. The decision to exclude these segments restricts the analysis to the magazine's main news sections.

Newsweek's *international news hole* is defined as the total number of pages devoted to the coverage of foreign or international news. International news coverage was coded into a number of regional classifications. The coding system employed in this analysis is derived from Larson's (1982) study of international affairs coverage on American television network news. The sole change from Larson's system is a separate regional category for Poland.[2]

Another part of the inquiry concerns the thematic emphasis of *Newsweek*'s coverage. Stories concerning Poland were content analyzed for primary theme. The *dominant* theme of a news story was determined by a careful examination

---

[2]Latin America, Africa, Middle East, South Asia, Southeast Asia and the Pacific, East Asia, Eastern Europe and the Soviet Union, Western Europe, Canada, and Poland.

of the entire article. The following categories were derived from pretesting a
sample of the universe under study:

1. Soviet Intervention/Potential Response
2. Polish-Soviet Relations
3. Polish-American Relations
4. Polish Communist Party Developments
5. Government-Solidarity Conflict
6. Government-Solidarity Cooperation
7. Intra-Solidarity Developments
8. The Role of Dissident Groups within Poland
9. The Role of the Catholic Church within Poland
10. The Economy of Poland
11. The Influence of Events in Poland on Eastern Europe
12. Other.

The results of a reliability analysis indicate a high degree of reliability in the
application of the coding categories.[3]

THE AMOUNT AND PLACEMENT OF COVERAGE

Newsweek published 70 stories concerning Poland during the period of analysis, devoting 88 pages to this coverage. Seventy percent of *Newsweek* issues
from August 1980 to December 1981 included stories on Poland. Coverage was
most extensive in December 1980, when *Newsweek* devoted 16 pages to the
Polish crisis. September 1980 and April 1981 also were marked by extensive
reporting on Poland. Reportage in two of these months, December and April,
emphasized the likelihood of a Soviet military invasion, while coverage in
September examined the terms and implications of the Gdansk Agreement.

The newsmagazine's total news hole during the period of analysis was 1,633
pages, while coverage of Poland comprised 88 pages. This represents 5.4% of
the total news hole. More than 10% of the total news hole was devoted to
coverage of Poland in September 1980, December 1980, and April 1981.

Newsweek devoted 695 pages to coverage of international news; this represents 42.5% of the newsmagazine's total news hole during the period of study.
Coverage of Poland accounted for 12.7% of the international news hole from
August 1980 to December 1981. In three months, September 1980, December
1980, and April 1981, coverage of Poland as a proportion of the international
news hole exceeded 35%. These results indicate that *Newsweek*'s coverage of
Poland was extensive during the period of analysis.

---

[3]Two undergraduate students worked independently on reliability coding. Reliability coeffi-
cients were derived from the use of Scott's pi, an index of reliability which takes into account that
some coding agreement occurs by chance. Intercoder reliability was .95 for the selection of
international regions and .88 for the selection of primary themes.

To provide further context for an understanding of the extent of reportage concerning Poland, this coverage is compared with stories concerning other geographical regions. This comparison supplies insight into the "news geography" developed by *Newsweek*. It also provides a better understanding of the real extent of Polish coverage in that this reportage is now compared with a corresponding level of analysis, rather than with the total news hole or the total international news hole. *Newsweek* published 590 international news stories during the 17 months of analysis.

Table 1 compares Poland with geographical regions composed of numerous individual nations. This procedure was necessary for data reduction. Despite the fact that this method minimizes the extent of reportage concerning Poland in relation to other *regions*, Poland was the third most frequently covered area, following the Middle East and Western Europe. Coverage of the Middle East, a traditional area of American news media attention because of the tensions between Israel and Arab nations, was emphasized further during the period of analysis because of the seizure of American embassy employees by Iranian students. This dramatic story coincided with news attention to developments in Poland from August 1980 to the release of the hostages in January 1981. Despite this, during the 17 months of study, *Newsweek* provided more news stories on Poland than on any other individual nation. Consequently, while the number of stories concerning the Middle East exceeds the number of stories concerning Poland, coverage of Poland was more extensive than coverage of any single Middle Eastern nation. In terms of space devoted to news stories concerning a single nation, *Newsweek*'s coverage of Poland was exceeded only by its treatment of Iran.

By any measure, the newsmagazine's coverage of the Polish crisis was

Table 1   The News Geography of *Newsweek*

Region	Number of Stories	Percentage of Total Stories
Poland	70	11.8
Eastern Europe	28	4.7
Western Europe	122	20.6
Latin America	57	9.6
Africa	33	5.5
South Asia	12	2.0
East Asia	38	6.4
Southeast Asia	10	1.6
Middle East	161	27.2
Canada	5	0.8
Other International Concerns[4]	54	9.1

[4]*Newsweek* stories coded into this category included articles examining world hunger, nuclear proliferation and international women's issues. This category, then, includes reports on topical issues, not linked to specific geographical regions.

Table 2   The News Geography of *Newsweek's* **International Cover Stories**

Region	Number of Cover Stories	Percentage of Total Stories
Poland	2	11.7
Western Europe	1	5.8
Eastern Europe	1	5.8
Latin America	1	5.8
Middle East	9	52.9
Other	3	17.6

extensive and sustained during the period of analysis. Coverage was particularly heavy following the Gdansk strike, and during periods of intense Western concern over a Soviet military invasion of Poland.

The placement of stories is related closely to the characteristics of the news medium examined in this study. *Newsweek* is a highly structured magazine with distinct national and international sections. The international section routinely follows the national section. At times, *Newsweek* highlights foreign developments by devoting a cover story to these concerns.

An initial determination of the priority given to coverage of Poland involves an analysis of the newsmagazine's cover stories. Seventy-three issues of *Newsweek* were examined; 17 cover stories explored international developments. Table 2 examines the news geography of these stories.

The major determination concerning the priority given to coverage of Poland involved an examination of the lead story within *Newsweek's* international section. Cover stories examining foreign developments were coded as the lead story in the international section. Table 3 provides the results.

Stories concerning the Middle East most often occupied the lead position within the international section; articles concerning Poland received the second highest priority. These results are consistent with past findings concerning the amount and priority given to coverage of specific regions by *Newsweek*. In coverage of individual nations, stories concerning Poland were placed in the lead position more frequently than reports examining any other country, including Iran.

THE THEMATIC EMPHASIS OF THE COVERAGE

Table 4 provides an analysis of the thematic emphasis of *Newsweek's* stories concerning Poland. Care should be taken to place these findings in context, because individual stories were often multithematic.[5]

---

[5]As part of a more extensive analysis of *Newsweek's* coverage of Poland, stories were analyzed for the appearance of secondary themes. The results indicate that 78% of all stories concerning Poland contained at least one secondary theme. The two most extensive secondary themes were the conflicts between Solidarity and the Polish government and the likelihood of a Soviet military invasion.

Table 3   The News Geography of the Lead Story within Newsweek's International Section

Region	Number of Stories	Percentage of Stories
Poland	16	21.9
Western Europe	12	16.4
Eastern Europe	3	4.1
Latin America	5	6.8
Africa	2	2.7
East Asia	1	1.3
Middle East	28	38.3
Other	6	8.2

The three major thematic emphases, both in the number of stories and the space devoted to these stories, were the conflicts between the Polish government and Solidarity, the internal developments in the Polish Communist Party (the Polish United Workers' Party) and the likelihood of a Soviet military invasion of Poland. These three themes accounted for the thematic focus of 58.6% of all stories. *Newsweek* devoted few stories to the character of the union movement; the newsmagazine provided little coverage of Solidarity as a social movement.

Table 4 reveals the extensiveness of reportage examining the possible *external* implications of events in Poland. Stories focusing on three themes—the likelihood of a Soviet military intervention, the relationship between Poland and the U.S.S.R., and the influence of Polish events on Eastern Europe—explored the external repercussions of developments in Poland. These subjects dominated 25% of all *Newsweek* stories concerning Poland. This reportage viewed Polish developments from the perspective of superpower politics. The

Table 4   The Primary Theme of Newsweek Stories Concerning Poland

Theme	Number of Stories	Percentage of Total Stories
Soviet Intervention	11	15.7
Polish-Soviet Relations	3	4.3
Polish-American Relations	—	—
Communist Party Developments	14	20.0
Government and Solidarity Conflict	16	22.9
Government and Solidarity Cooperation	3	4.3
Intra-Solidarity Developments	7	10.0
Role of Dissident Groups	—	—
Role of Catholic Church	3	4.3
The Economy of Poland	5	7.1
Influence on Eastern Europe	4	5.7
Other	4	5.7

treatment of events in Poland became background for the foreground examination of the competing interests of the United States and the Soviet Union.

An analysis of the thematic emphasis of the coverage over time reveals a number of significant trends in the reporting. Coverage of the likelihood of a Soviet military invasion was most pronounced from December 1980 to April 1981. The May to July 1981 period was marked by a dramatic shift in coverage to reportage concerning events and issues confronting the PUWP. This was largely a product of *Newsweek*'s treatment of the Party Congress held in July 1981. Correspondingly, a sharp increase in coverage of the union's internal dynamics occurred in September and October 1981, owing to the Solidarity Congress held in these months. Prior to this period, *Newsweek* had provided little coverage of Solidarity itself despite the tremendous growth of the union in the initial period of the Polish crisis.[6]

A THICK DESCRIPTION OF THE COVERAGE

This analysis focuses on the three major emphases in the coverage: the portrayal of the conflicts between Solidarity and the Polish government; the characterization of developments within the Polish government or the PUWP; the depiction of the likelihood of a Soviet military invasion of Poland. In addition, the newsmagazine's definition of the union movement is explored.

Newsweek's Reporting on the Conflicts Between Solidarity and the Polish Government

The newsmagazine's coverage of the conflicts between the union and the Polish government was characterized by stories examining strikes and demonstrations. Throughout the period of analysis, *Newsweek* devoted considerable coverage to these protest actions. Stories chronicled: the Gdansk strike in August 1980 that led to Solidarity's formation; the nationwide warning strike in October 1980, protesting the government's delay in implementing the Gdansk Agreement; the regional strikes in January 1981, called to demand a 5-day work week; the national warning strike, held in March 1981, called in response to police violence directed against Solidarity officials; the demonstrations in August 1981 to protest food shortages; the union's third nationwide warning strike, held in October 1981; and the occupation strike in a Warsaw fire academy that immediately preceeded the imposition of martial law in December 1981.

Through its descriptions of these strikes and protests, *Newsweek* constructed a dramatic narrative on the conflicts besetting Polish society. According to *Newsweek*, the trade union movement and the government were involved in a

---

[6]By any measure, the growth of Solidarity was spectacular. By 25 November 1980, 28% of the entire adult population of Poland belonged to the union. Total membership reached more than seven million in that month.

"test of wills" (April 6, 1981, p. 51), a "protracted war of nerves" (November 10, 1980, p. 70), a "political tug of war" (October 19, 1980, p. 35), and a "game of brinkmanship" (November 2, 1981, p. 53). These conflicts held the danger that "both sides would wind up covered in blood" (September 28, 1981, p. 45).

Although *Newsweek* examined varied strikes and protests, these stories manifested similar stylistic and narrative features. Corcoran (1983, p. 307) points out that the "news magazine style stresses revealing anecdotes, colorful adjectives, startling quotations, and scene setting facts." The emphasis on the setting of scene and the establishment of atmosphere played a significant role in the reporting on strikes and demonstrations. In a story examining negotiations between striking workers in Gdansk and the government, *Newsweek* reported that

> Night was falling in Gdansk when the Polish government extended its olive branch. Deputy Prime Minister Mieczyslaw Jagielski telephoned the Lenin shipyard, the nerve center of the strikes that had paralyzed Poland's Baltic region. Quickly, three strike leaders drove to a brick villa outside town, where Jagielski gave them a hearty greeting and offered refreshments. For the next hour, the two sides probed each other on ways to settle the strike. (September 1, 1980, p. 28)

The lead sentence establishes scene and implicitly promises that more important details will follow. The paragraph demonstrates *Newsweek*'s close attention to detail: the meeting was held at a "brick villa;" Jagielski gave the workers a "hearty greeting" and offered "refreshments." These details suggest an insider's account of the meeting, and the initial paragraph indicates *Newsweek*'s ability to gain access to these accounts. The lead paragraph thus serves as an initial legitimation of the newsmagazine's interpretation of the Gdansk strike.

Attention to atmosphere and the detailed descriptions of scene help to create "prose pictures" (Gans, 1979, p. 159). According to Friedrich (1964, p. 61), the "inundation of minutiae" in a newsmagazine story is based upon the belief that "knowledge of lesser facts implies knowledge of major facts." The emphasis on detail and scene in stories on strikes and demonstrations played a part in validating the magazine's interpretive accounts of these events.

Easily structured as dramatic narratives of conflict, strike stories provided clear divisions between protagonists and antagonists. Event-oriented, timebound and discrete, stories on strikes or demonstrations offered clear divisions between winners and losers, frequently concluded with an assessment of the mood of the country and supplied an opportunity for the construction of prose pictures.

Newsweek's Reporting on the Polish Government and the PUWP

Newsweek repeatedly questioned the political legitimacy of the Polish government and the PUWP. Lacking popular support, the government and the Party were dependent on Soviet support for their survival. Both were torn by conflicts between *moderates* and *hardliners*. These terms were employed frequently, but their meaning remained problematic in the coverage.

Newsweek described Poland's geopolitical situation in sharp Cold War terms: "Nowhere is the Soviet empire more vulnerable than in Poland, long the most volatile of Moscow's client states" (September 1, 1980, p. 31). After the outbreak of labor unrest in Poland, the newsmagazine contended that "Communist Party officials viewed the Polish drama, wondering if the latest challenge to the Soviet imposed system might spread to other outposts of Moscow's East European empire" (September 8, 1980, p. 36). Because of their client status, Polish government officials were depicted as subordinate to Soviet authority. The growth of Solidarity "alarmed Warsaw's Communist rulers and stirred up their overlords in Moscow as well" (September 29, 1980, p. 35). On a visit to Moscow, Stanislaw Kania, the first secretary of the PUWP, assured his "allies and overlords" of continued loyalty (December 15, 1980, p. 39).

The newsmagazine described the Polish government as a "regime" (August 18, 1980, p. 40). In accounts of changes in the political leadership of the Party or government, officials were seldom replaced, but rather were "purged" (September 8, 1980, p. 30), "ousted" (September 15, 1980, p. 47), or "sacked" (November 9, 1981). Gierek, Kania, and Jaruzelski, in turn, were described as "the boss" of the Communist Party (August 18, 1980; April 6, 1981; October 19, 1981). This term, of course, is applied often to corrupt political or union officials in the United States and its use in the description of the Party leadership delegitimizes their authority. While these leaders reported to their overlords in Moscow, the Poles resented the "special privileges enjoyed by their Communist overlords" (February 16, 1981, p. 47).

Through the use of these polemical descriptions, *Newsweek* directly questioned the legitimacy and autonomy of the Polish government and the Polish Communist Party. These characterizations placed Solidarity's struggle for reform securely within an East-West geopolitical framework. *Newsweek*'s use of these descriptions supports the view that American news organizations often treat foreign news with less detachment than domestic news (Batscha, 1975) and that "explicit value judgments that would not be considered justifiable in domestic news appear in stories about the rest of the world, particularly from Communist countries" (Gans, 1979, p. 131).

In its coverage of the Party and the government, *Newsweek* defined Polish politics by characterizing individuals as hardliners, moderates, liberals, and reformers. The magazine described delegates to the Party's Congress as neither "conservatives or radical reformers," rather the "overwhelming majority were moderate, nonideological and eager to express their opinion" (July 27, 1981, p. 32).

Present in many news stories, these characterizations remained ill-defined. While these descriptions did distinguish between officials within the PUWP, their meaning is tied ultimately to the political context of Poland's Communist Party. One figure's moderation, for example, needs to be located within the political environment of his party. How did his *moderation* differ from another's *liberalism*? In *Newsweek*'s account, these terms derived their meaning fundamentally by their opposition to one another, and any context which may have given shape to these definitions remained underdeveloped.

At times, the difficulty in the application of these ill-defined terms became evident in the coverage; major contradictions existed in the application of these terms. In September 1980, for example, *Newsweek* described Stefan Olszowski as a "sophisticated economic reformer." In explaining why Olszowski did not assume the leadership of the Party after Gierek's resignation, the magazine reported that "Olszowski may have been too liberal for Moscow's taste" (September 15, 1980, p. 47). In another article, *Newsweek* defined Olszowski as a "reformist" (September 8, 1980, p. 35), although this reference and the earlier descriptions did not provide a context for understanding his reformist views. In sharp contrast to these characterizations, *Newsweek* later described Olszowski as a "good friend of Moscow's" and as a "hardline Politbureaucrat" (April 6, 1981, p. 51). Similarly, *Newsweek* initially described Tadeusz Grabski by noting that he and other Kania appointees were "dedicated, if reform-minded Communists—men who by and large support Kania's cooperation with Solidarity and his proposals for sweeping economic reform" (December 15, 1980, p. 42). Later, the magazine repeatedly characterized Grabski as a "hardliner." These examples illustrate the difficulty in applying general and ill-defined characterizations to leaders of a foreign political party. They represent contradictions in *Newsweek*'s coverage of the PUWP.

Newsweek's Reporting on the Likelihood of a Soviet Invasion

Frequently combined with the use of evocative metaphors to describe the consequences of a Soviet invasion, the reliance on veiled, and presumably governmental, sources for information characterized *Newsweek*'s coverage of the potential Russian military threat to Poland. Examples from a story published on December 15, 1980 are representative: "A number of lesser anomalies also alarmed the Pentagon's Polish watch," or "American crisis managers were awaiting some firmer signals of the Soviet Union's intentions."

The source of much of this information on Soviet intentions was most likely Pentagon and State Department background sessions for journalists. The reliance on veiled sources helped to validate the narrative development of stories examining the likelihood of a Soviet invasion. The characterizations of these sources affirmed *Newsweek*'s ability to provide the *private* as well as *public* record on this important concern.

The magazine's reporting concerning the potential for a Soviet invasion provides an intriguing look at the interaction between the American press and the American government. In comparison with the reporting on domestic issues, this interaction may be even more intense because of the increased journalistic dependence on information supplied by the American government owing to the relative lack of press access to other sources. The restrictions on available sources become more pronounced when dealing with "closed" political systems, for example, the Soviet Union and Poland. A detailed examination of this coverage supports Sigal's (1973) and Fishman's (1980) observation that much of the news is the product of the interaction between press and governmental bureaucracies.

Throughout the period of analysis, *Newsweek* linked events in Poland to the Soviet invasions of Czechoslovakia in 1968 and Hungary in 1956. Soviet military maneuvers were compared with 1968 military exercises which "overthrew the liberal regime of Alexander Dubcek in Czechoslovakia" (September 1, 1980, p. 29). *Newsweek* compared the Gdansk settlement with the Prague Spring of 1968, which was "crushed by Soviet tanks" (September 15, 1980, p. 50). The newsmagazine reported that a Soviet military invasion would lead to a "bloodbath unseen in Eastern Europe since Hungary 24 years ago" (September 1, 1980, p. 31).

The thematic emphasis on the likelihood of a Soviet invasion influenced the newsmagazine's treatment of the historical context of the Solidarity era. Most decisively, this emphasis made the Czech events of 1968 and the Hungarian events of 1956 the most significant historical experiences for an understanding of the Polish crisis. Conversely, this emphasis severely restricted *Newsweek's* treatment of Polish reform efforts in 1956, 1968, 1970, and 1976. The development of opposition groups in the late 1970s and the beginning of links between Polish dissident intellectuals, the Catholic Church and worker activists was ignored. As a consequence, both the general and immediate historical context of the 1980 unrest remained unexplored.

The limited reporting on past unrest in Poland ignored the continuities and discountinuities between those struggles and Solidarity's evolution. The demand for independent unions, for example, was not new. In the 1970 worker protests in Szczecin, the strike committee had demanded the creation of independent unions (Ascherson, 1981, pp. 77–79). Solidarity traced its legacy back to the earlier efforts at reform. In the program adopted at its National Congress, the union noted that its

> Social and moral protest did not occur overnight. Inherent in it was the heritage of blood shed by workers in Poznan in 1956 and on the coast in December 1970, of the 1968 students' rebellion, and the 1976 sufferings in Radom and Ursus. (Program of the Independent Self-Governing Trade Union Solidarity, 1982, p. 192)

The lack of reporting on past unrest in Poland helped to cut off Solidarity from its social roots. An historically self-conscious movement was defined in a strikingly ahistoric manner.

The immediate historical context of the 1980 worker protests also remained unexplored. The period after the 1976 strikes was marked by the establishment of links between dissident intellectuals and worker activists and by the evolution of opposition groups, including the Committee for Social Self-Defense (KOR) and The Movement for the Defense of Human and Civil Rights (ROP-CIO). Historical and sociological works have stressed the significance of this activity in setting the stage for Solidarity's growth (Raina, 1981; Brumberg, 1981; Singer, 1981; Ascherson, 1981). These interpretations of the origin of the 1980 strikes did not play a role in *Newsweek*'s coverage; the historical context that shaped the movement was ignored.

Newsweek's Definition of Solidarity

Within the magazine's account, Solidarity was defined through the coverage of its opposition to a repressive Communist state. Stories on strikes and demonstrations, for example, provided a limited definition of the movement's political character. Articles on these conflicts reflected Solidarity's commitment to political pluralism and the government's opposition to independent social and political institutions which would threaten the preeminent role of the PUWP in Polish society. This coverage, however, manifested a number of characteristics which restricted an examination of the union movement itself. Tied to discrete events, this reportage did not explore the evolution of Solidarity as a social movement, nor did it investigate the union's self-definition.

Another important element in *Newsweek*'s definition of Solidarity was the magazine's treatment of the Catholic Church's influence on the movement. In its initial stories on the Gdansk strike, *Newsweek* underscored the commitment of Polish workers to Catholicism. The magazine described the strikers as "passionately religious" and reported that "part of the public spectacle was the sight of Catholic priests hearing confessions and conducting Mass inside the strikebound factories and shipyards" (September 1, 1980, p. 28). *Newsweek* concluded that Pope John Paul's visit to Poland in 1979 "had fanned Poland's national rebellion and thrust him into the very center of his people's rebellion" (November 23, 1981, p. 74). Stories detailed the relationship between Walesa and Stefan Cardinal Wyszynski, the Church's influence on Rural Solidarity and the Pope's role in advising the labor movement.

The other salient characteristic of *Newsweek*'s coverage of Solidarity was the strong emphasis on Lech Walesa's role within the movement. According to the magazine, Walesa was the "master gamesman" of Polish politics (December 8, 1980, p. 40). In a profile of Solidarity's leader, *Newsweek* described Walesa as "an adroit politician," a "Polish folk hero," a "working class legend" (December 8, 1980, pp. 42–43). Walesa was the most frequently photographed and the most frequently quoted newsmaker in the coverage; within the newsmagazine's account, he was the central actor in the Polish drama.

Newsweek also stressed Walesa's devotion to Catholicism. He was described as a "devout Catholic" (December 8, 1980, p. 42) and the magazine noted that "one of his aides carries a large crucifix to hang on the wall wherever he speaks" (December 22, 1980, p. 48). Walesa was pictured kneeling before the Pope, holding one of his daughters in front of a painting of the Pontiff and grasping a photograph of John Paul. In this area, two distinguishing characteristics of *Newsweek*'s definition of Solidarity merged: Walesa's religious passion reflected the religious commitment of his movement.

A close examination of the coverage reveals that *Newsweek* personalized the movement through its emphasis on Walesa and, in so doing, limited reporting on Solidarity as a social movement. The union's internal debates, its hetero-geneous membership and its ideological character were neglected. This finding supports the observation by Galtung and Ruge (1965) that foreign news tends to focus on personalities rather than social forces or social processes. Similarly, Carey (1983, p. 130) criticizes American journalism for its almost exclusive attention to "the role of personalities or actors in the creation of events." This process of personalization takes on added significance in coverage of social movements, because it divorces these movements from their origin in collec-tive action.

The implications of *Newsweek*'s personalization of the movement are evident in its coverage of initiatives for workers' self-management. In a story on Solidarity's Congress, the magazine reported on the union's demand that Polish workers "have the sole power over production, profits and the hiring and firing of factory managers" (December 21, 1981, p. 55). *Newsweek* noted the union's rejection of a government plan for workers' self-management and, in a subse-quent article, detailed a compromise reached between Solidarity and the government on this issue (October 5, 1981, p. 42).

These brief references to the workers' self-management controversy repre-sent *Newsweek*'s initial treatment of this issue. The newsmagazine did not provide coverage of the gradual evolution of self-management initiatives within Solidarity. After the initial reluctance to embrace workers' councils because of past Communist Party successes in subordinating these structures to state control, the spring and summer of 1981 witnessed a growth of workers' efforts to gain control over economic production. The beginning of an interfactory "Network" of workers' self-government initiatives had formed by March, and by July it linked more than 3,000 enterprises. Ash (1983) describes these initiatives as a spontaneous movement; they were not directed by Solidarity's leadership. Although the growth of the "Network" directly threatened the PUWP's control over economic production and reflected grass roots pressure for more radical economic reforms, *Newsweek* did not report on this move-ment. Because of its emphasis on Walesa's leadership, the newsmagazine provided a top-down portrayal of Solidarity as a social movement. The base of the movement—its industrial rank-and-file—received little attention.

Given this discussion of the salient features of *Newsweek*'s portrayal of Solidarity, how does this definition compare with other interpretive accounts examining the character of this movement?

The newsmagazine's emphasis on the importance of the links between the Catholic Church and Solidarity is echoed in historical and sociological accounts of the movement (Ash, 1983; Ascherson, 1981). Not surprisingly, other ac-counts explored the influence of Walesa's leadership on Solidarity, although *Newsweek*'s portrayal exhibited a greater tendency to personalize the move-ment through a discussion of Solidarity's national chairman.

Other emphases common in other accounts examining Solidarity were largely absent in the magazine's portrayal of the labor movement. These emphases include the movement's egalitarian social values, its political pluralism, its working class origin and its relationship to socialism. Beyond its treatment of the Church's influence on Solidarity, *Newsweek* provided little coverage of the movement's political orientations.

Varied studies stress the egalitarianism of the Solidarity movement (De Weydenthal, 1981; Singer, 1981; Ash, 1983; Mason, 1984). Staniszkis (1981, p. 212), for example, describes the workers' movement as "deeply egalitarian and anti-hierarchical." The Gdansk Agreement, which included provisions demanding a redistribution of economic resources in Polish society, manifests the movement's commitment to greater economic and social equality. The program adopted by the Solidarity Congress affirmed the union's desire for egalitarianism. The program called for the elimination of wage and social inequalities between enterprises and urged that Poland's incomes policy guarantee favorable treatment for the poor. The identification of the union's egalitarian demands, so prominent in these accounts, played no part in *Newsweek*'s definition of Solidarity.

Discussion of the pluralistic influences on the evolution of Solidarity and the political tendencies within the union also played little part in *Newsweek*'s portrayal of the movement. Two statements—the first contained in a report published by the union in April 1981 and the second included in the program adopted by the union at its Congress—define the major social influences on Solidarity.

> The nation's best traditions, Christianity's ethical principles, democracy's political mandate, and socialist social thought—these are the four main sources of our inspiration. (Directions of the Operations of Solidarity, 1981, p. 147)

> When defining its aims, Solidarity draws from the values of Christian ethics, from our national traditions, from the workers and democratic traditions of the labor world. (Program of the Independent Self-Governing Trade Union Solidarity, 1982, p. 100)

The purposive decision to delete from the program a direct reference to the importance of *socialist social thought* in the evolution of the movement reveals an ambivalence within Solidarity toward an acceptance of a term long associated with the discredited Communist Party. While *Newsweek* stressed both the Church's influence on Solidarity and the union's attempt to achieve a limited form of democracy based on political pluralism, the magazine did not examine the movement's ambivalent and complex relationship to socialism.

The multiple influences on the union's development guaranteed that varied social and political tendencies were represented within Solidarity. Ash (1983, p. 284) argues that the movement "overcame some of the deepest divisions within Polish society—between town and country dwellers, between workers and intelligentsia, between the 'Two Nations' of socialists and Catholics." De

Weydenthal (1983) emphasizes the working-class origin of Solidarity and the swift expansion of that base to include professionals, intellectuals and students. In a broader context, Touraine (1983, p. 2) identifies three essential dimensions of the labor movement.

> It [Solidarity] is a workers' movement . . . but it is also a national movement and a struggle for the democratisation of society. Outside Poland, many observers try to reduce it to only one of its dimensions: for some, it is a purely working-class movement animated by socialist ideals which were deformed or destroyed by regimes having their origins in Stalinism; for others, it is above all a struggle for national liberation in the tradition of the uprisings of the eighteenth and nineteenth centuries and the Warsaw Risings of 1944. Finally, there are those who maintain that Solidarity is of particular concern to us because it appeals openly to the values of Western democracy, human rights and political pluralism. The difficulty is that all these images are in themselves correct: working-class consciousness is just as strong in Solidarity as the attachment to the figure of the Pope, and this is a national liberation movement which has sought to establish the most highly developed forms of representative democracy.

This interpretation is particularly convincing because of Touraine's detailed analysis of rank-and-file feelings toward these dimensions. These political and social tendencies within the union received scant attention in the newsmagazine's coverage.

Newsweek's limited attention to the political dimensions of the union movement became most evident in its lack of detailed coverage of the program adapted by Solidarity at its Congress. The program was an articulation of the diverse political and social traditions embraced by Solidarity. Ash (1982, p. 51–52) provides a perceptive appraisal of the program.

> Anyone who troubles to read the Solidarity programme will see that it in fact embodies a quite original mixture of ideals, goals and proposals, drawn from very diverse traditions and experience—"right," and "left" and "centre" . . . Solidarity produced a conservative - socialist - liberal programme. In culture and education, for example, it might justly be characterized as "conservative - restorationist": that is, it proposed to restore the knowledge and values which had been conserved in the Church, the family and in the preservation (unofficial and emigre) of the continuity of Polish culture, to their proper place in the schools and universities. The main political institutions which it envisaged for the "self-governing republic" were those of a classical, Western liberal democracy. But the priority it gave to equality, the welfare state, and full employment, can be characterized as "socialist."

While the program provided an opportunity to explore the political character of Solidarity, *Newsweek* did not seize this opportunity.

Nor did *Newsweek* examine the economic proposals in the program. The document stated that the "socialized enterprise should be the basic organizational unit in the economy. It should be controlled by the workers' council representing the collective" (Program of the Independent Self-Governing

Trade Union Solidarity, 1982, p. 103). This position was consistent with the increasing acceptance among Poles of the socialization of medium and heavy industry (Nowak, 1981). It also reflected the distinction between state and social control of the means of production which had been previously advanced by the "Network."

In their evaluations of the union movement, Ash (1983) and Singer (1981) contend that the concept of workers' self-management was open to varied interpretations within Solidarity. According to these accounts, some members of the union advanced proposals for workers' self-management as a means to introduce decentralized socialism, while for other self-management represented another means to free Polish society from Communist Party control. Andrzej Slowik, a Solidarity leader in Lodz, stressed the former interpretation: "There are only two possibilities: either the bureaucratic dictatorship . . . or working-class self-management socialism" (Kowalewski, 1982, p. 237). This view reflected broader sentiments in the union which explicitly defined Solidarity as a socialist movement (see the documents in MacDonald, 1981, and Persky & Flamm, 1982). These sentiments were ignored in *Newsweek*'s definition of Solidarity.

The position of the movement as a whole toward socialism—a relationship central to an understanding of the union's political character—remains a subject of debate. Solidarity's size, its rapid growth, its ability to transcend social and class divisions, its internal political pluralism, and its heterogenous membership make it difficult to sustain generalizations concerning *the* movement's ideology or its relationship to socialism. Difficulty notwithstanding, varied accounts have explored the union's political character.

Writing most of his book prior to the Solidarity Congress, Ascherson (1981, p. 229) argues that the August strikes displayed "an ambiguous attitude toward socialist theory and practice." He defines Solidarity as "asocialist" (p. 231), indifferent in its relationship to socialist theory and practice. While acknowledging the class consciousness of Polish workers, Singer (1983) laments the absence of a revolutionary socialist group within Solidarity. Potel (1982) contends that the movement lacked a coherent debate on the merits of socialism.

After noting the political pluralism in Solidarity, Ash (1982, p. 48) argues that the labor movement cannot be explained by a "single ideology or heuristic system." He concludes that Solidarity incorporated conservative, liberal democratic and socialist traditions into its program. Persky (1981) contends that the movement sought decentralized and democratic workers' control of the means of production, though many workers held ambivalent feelings toward socialist ideology because of the abuses of the "socialist" system. In one of the more detailed analyses of Solidarity's relationship to socialism, Mason (1984, p. 118) argues that the union "was working to create a society both freer and more genuinely socialist." Given the egalitarian thrust of the movement, Mason concludes that "there were strong socialist elements in the Solidarity movement and in the Program" (p. 119).

Despite their differences in evaluating Solidarity's political orientations, these accounts do provide an interpretation of the ideological tendencies within the union. In contrast, it is striking that *Newsweek* provided little discussion of the movement's political character.

CONCLUSION

Carey (1983) reminds us that journalism is a literary act. With its emphasis on scene-setting facts, with its extensive use of revealing anecdotes, with its dramatic tone, the collaboratively written newsmagazine story as a literary act adopts a "narrative point of view" in its portrayal of events and issues (Corcoran, 1983, p. 307). In a discussion of the influence of forms on the definition of reality, Jamieson and Campbell (1983, p. 39) point out that the narrative structure of news stories is "ideally suited to reporting single, dramatic events, to presenting characters (spokespersons who are quoted), to focusing on action, and to covering novel, exciting events. Conversely, it is ill suited to coverage of an idea, concept or process."

Jamieson and Campbell's observation provides a context for understanding the general characteristics of the magazine's coverage of Poland. Within its stories, *Newsweek* stressed discrete, dramatic events (strikes and demonstrations), personalities (especially Lech Walesa), and the culturally familiar. These concerns could be defined rather easily within the narrative structure of the newsmagazine's stories. Other concerns—the evolution of Solidarity as a social movement and the ideological orientations of the movement's membership—proved less amenable to such a structure.

Newsweek emphasized the culturally familiar in its stories concerning Poland; that is, the newsmagazine stressed elements within the Polish crisis which were somewhat close to the individual or social experience of its mass audience. Conversely, *Newsweek* overlooked or minimized the culturally unfamiliar, those factors removed from the individual or social experience of its audience. Thus, the newsmagazine emphasized the significance of charismatic leadership, while neglecting the historical context of events in Poland. The role of the Church in sparking Solidarity's opposition to Communist authority and the religious fervor of the Polish people received a good deal of attention, while Solidarity's working class origin and its relationship to socialism was ignored. The movement's commitment to political pluralism was stressed, while proposals for workers' control over economic production received scant attention.

In stressing the culturally familiar, *Newsweek*'s stories narrowed the ideological disharmony between the Polish workers' rebellion and contemporary American politics. By ignoring Solidarity's relationship to socialism and by neglecting demands for workers' control over the means of production, *Newsweek* avoided concerns divorced from the American political mainstream. These patterns of exclusion indicate the political dimensions of editorial selection (Gerbner, 1964; Hall, 1982).

Despite extensive coverage during a 17-month period, and despite the central role of Solidarity in demanding a restructuring of political power in Polish society, *Newsweek* devoted little coverage to the movement's evolution and character. Few stories primarily examined the labor movement and developments within the union received scant attention prior to the Solidarity Congress. These findings support claims that the American news media devote little coverage to the ideological dimensions of international affairs (Batscha, 1975).

When compared with other perspectives on Solidarity, *Newsweek*'s account offers little examination of the working class origin of Solidarity, its ability to transcend previous divisions within Polish society, its heterogeneous political orientations, its egalitarian demands and its relationship to socialism. These complex and ambiguous issues may have blurred the story's dominant and compelling framework: an independent union, aligned with the Polish Catholic Church, fighting for democracy against a repressive Communist state backed by the Soviet Union. In this sense, *Newsweek*'s coverage of Solidarity becomes a story in a dual sense. It is both a story about contemporary events in Poland and a story about the process by which international events are translated into news for the American public.

REFERENCES

Altheide, D. (1974). *Creating reality*. Beverly Hills, CA. Sage.

Ascherson, N. (1981). *The Polish August*. New York: Penguin.

Ash, T. G. (1983). *The Polish revolution: Solidarity*. New York: Charles Scribner's Sons.

Ash, T. G. (1982). The significance of Solidarity. *Survey*, 26, 49–54.

Batscha, R. (1975). *Foreign affairs news and the broadcast journalist*. New York: Praeger.

Brumberg, A. (1981). The revolt of the workers. *Dissent*, (Winter), 21–31.

Carey, J. (1983). Journalism and criticism: The case of an undeveloped profession. In M. Emory & T. C. Smythe (Eds.), *Readings in mass communication* (pp. 123–133). Dubuque, IA: Wm. C. Brown.

Carragee, K. M. (1985). *A content analysis of ABC News and Newsweek's coverage of Poland, 1980-1981*. Unpublished doctoral dissertation, University of Massachusetts at Amherst.

Cohen, B. (1963). *The press and foreign policy*. Princeton, NJ: Princeton University Press.

Corcoran, F. (1983). The bear in the back yard: Myth, ideology, and victimage ritual in Soviet funerals. *Communication Monographs, 50*, 305–320.

Dahlgren, P., with S. Chakrapani (1982). The Third World on TV News: Western ways of seeing the "other". In W. C. Adams (Ed.), *Television Coverage of International Affairs* (pp. 45–65). Norwood, NJ: Ablex Publishing Corp.

Davison, W. P. (1975). Diplomatic reporting: Rules of the game. *Journal of Communication, 25*, 138–146.

de Weydenthal, J. Porter, B., & Devlin, K. (1983). *The Polish drama: 1980-1982*. Lexington, MA: D.C. Heath.

de Weydenthal, J., (1981). Workers and party in Poland. *Problems of Communism, 30*, 1–22.

Directions of the Operations of Solidarity, the Independent Self-Governing Labor Union (1981). In *RAD Background Report (Poland) Radio Free Europe Research 5 March 1981*. Washington DC: Government Printing Office.

Epstein, E. J. (1973). *News from nowhere*. New York: Vintage Books.

Fishman, M. (1980). *Manufacturing the news.* Austin, TX: University of Texas Press.

Freidrich, O. (1964, October). There are 00 trees in Russia: The function of facts in news magazines. *Harpers,* pp. 59–65.

Galtung, J., & Ruge, M. H. (1965). The structure of foreign news. *Journal of Peace Research, 1,* 64–90.

Gans, H. (1979). *Deciding what's news.* New York: Random House.

Geertz, C. (1973). *The interpretation of cultures.* New York: Basic Books.

Gerbner, G. (1964). Ideological perspectives and political tendencies in news reporting. *Journalism Quarterly, 41,* 362–370.

Hall, S. (1982). The rediscovery of 'ideology': Return of the repressed in media studies. In M. Gurevitch, T. Bennett, J. Curran, & J. Woollacott (Eds.), *Culture, Society and the Media* (pp. 56–90). London: Methuen.

Jamieson, K. H., & Campbell, K. K. (1983). *The interplay of influence: Mass media and their publics in news, advertising, politics.* Belmont, CA: Wadsworth.

Kowalewski, Z. (1982). Solidarity on the eve. In S. Persky & H. Flamm (Eds.), *The Solidarity sourcebook* (pp. 230–240). Vancouver, Canada: New Star Books.

Larson, J. F. (1982). International Affairs Coverage on U.S. Evening Network News. In W. C. Adams (Ed.), *Television coverage of international affairs* (pp. 15–41). Norwood, NJ: Ablex Publishing Corp.

MacDonald, O. (1981). *The Polish August: Documents from the beginnings of the Polish workers' rebellion.* Seattle, WA: Left Bank Books.

Mason, D. (1984). Solidarity and Socialism. In J. Bielasiak & M. Simon (Eds.), *Polish politics: Edge of the abyss* (pp. 118–137). New York: Praeger.

Nowak, S. (1981, July). Values and attitudes of the Polish people. *Scientific American,* p. 49.

Persky, S., & Flamm, H. (Eds.) (1982). *The Solidarity sourcebook.* Vancouver, Canada: New Star Books.

Persky, S. (1981). *At the Lenin Shipyard: Poland and the rise of the Solidarity Trade Union.* Vancouver, Canada: New Star Books.

Potel, J. (1982). *The summer before the frost.* London: Pluto Press.

Program of the Independent Self-Governing Trade Union Solidarity. (1982). In *RAD Background Report (Poland), Radio Free Europe Research 16 July 1982.* Washington DC: Government Printing Office.

Raina, P. (1981). *Independent social movements in Poland.* London: Orbis.

Rubin, B. (1977). *International news and the American media.* Beverly Hills, CA: Sage.

Sigal, L. (1973). *Reporters and officials: The organization of newsmaking.* Lexington, MA: D.C. Heath.

Singer, D. (1983). Poland in Perspective. In P. Jacobson & J. Jacobson (Eds.), *Socialist perspectives.* New York: Karz Cohl.

Singer, D. (1981). *The road to Gdansk.* New York: Monthly Review Press.

Staniszkis, J. (1981). The evolution of working class protest in Poland: Sociological reflections on the Gdansk-Szczecin case. *Soviet Studies, 33,* 204–231.

Tuchman, G. (1978). *Making news: A study in the construction of reality.* New York: The Free Press.

Touraine, A., Dubet, F., Wieriorka, M., & Strzelecki, J. (1983). *Solidarity: The analysis of a social movement.* Cambridge, England: Cambridge University Press.

5

The Third Crisis in Journalism:
A Political Linguistics Perspective

CARL R. BYBEE

University of Oregon

KENNETH L HACKER

Michigan Technological University

U.S. journalism has entered a third period of crisis centering on the imminent collapse of the concept of objectivity. For the last 50 years the concept of objectivity has performed the Herculean task of reconciling free speech and profit motives within the same institution. In addition, "objectivity" has served as the linchpin in legitimating the institutional independence of journalistic practice from the state and other sources of potential influence. The concept however, is presently under attack from a startling number of vantage points, ranging from the views of language philosophers to those of news practitioners. The most damaging challenge may be the one that integrates several positions—the concept of objectivity has failed to account for the recent theoretical advances in our understanding of the processes through which meaning and knowledge are created. It has also ignored the essential political character of those processes.

If the practice of journalism is reconceptualized as the political act of meaning production, rather than the neutral act of information transmittal, the legitimating power of the objectivity concept is undermined. This makes the contradiction between free speech and profit seeking more visible. Unlike the crises in American journalism of the 1830s and the 1920s, the ideological shape of the resolution is more likely to accent authoritarian mandates which overtly manage the blossoming anarchy of meaning, rather than emphasizing the ideal necessity of free and unrestricted speech. This is done to maintain the current political, economic, and social power configurations.

To develop this argument, it is necessary to lay some conceptual groundwork concerning the nature of journalism, the meaning of political linguistic phenomena, and the nature of the crisis in an advanced capitalistic democracy. After a brief discussion of these issues, we will review two historical moments of journalistic crisis, along with resolutions for the crises, and then draw attention to the impending crisis in journalism.

CONCEPTUALIZING THE PRACTICE OF JOURNALISM

What is journalism? One answer sees journalism as the institutionalized process of news gathering and dissemination. A second response envisions journalism as discourse in a Foucaultian sense; i.e., journalism is viewed as an historically unique practice which defines itself and is legitimated as a valid practice through its interdependent activity with other historically unique institutions.

Journalism as News Reporting

The view of journalism as news writing has been reified through its inclusion into introductory American textbooks on journalism/mass communication. It has been reinforced by ritualistic celebrations by contemporary journalists, media institutions, and liberal pluralistic theories of society. This view is based on a dramatic recounting of the historicized struggle between the forces of authoritarianism and the forces of humanistic democracy over what has come to be known as free speech (Emery & Emery, 1972; Sandman, Rubin, & Sachsman, 1982). Democracy, ahistorically and vaguely defined, triumphs, of course, and the concept of free speech embedded in the natural rights of humans assumes an institutional form in the practice of journalism.

The critical moment in this drama is the attachment of the First Amendment to the U.S. Constitution. Tribute is paid to the philosophical roots of natural law and Mill's liberalism, to the supporting role played by technological developments in communication (particularly the printing press, radio, and television), and to the mixed blessings of developing capitalism. At times this has secured a needed economic base for an independent press, while at other times it has undercut the very foundations of that independence. Emery and Emery (1972, p. iii) state that journalism is "the story of man's long struggle to communicate freely with his fellow men—to dig out and interpret news, and to freely offer intelligent opinion in the marketplace of ideas." Embedded in this narrative of journalism are several interrelated and critical—yet unexamined— assumptions concerning the relationship of language and power.

The first, and perhaps most visible, assumption is that the press is or could possibly be independent of other social, economic, and political institutions. This assumption of autonomy is crucial to liberal pluralistic social theory. The concept of an independent press underpins the notion of a pluralistic democracy composed of competing interest groups vying for state favors. It does this by providing the necessary institutional form for alerting individuals and groups to issues demanding their attention, coordinating those interests and making them known (Sandman et al., 1982; Defleur & Ball-Rokeach, 1982; Kraus & Davis, 1976). The independent press is assumed to play a role as a special interest group itself, protecting its special status with respect to the constitution and commercial enterprise.

The second assumption in this dominant view is the conceptualization of journalism communication as a transporting of information from a source to a receiver (Carey & Kreiling, 1974; Gurevitch, Bennett, Curran, & Woollacott, 1982; Shannon & Weaver, 1960; Westley & MacClean, 1957). Information, or what are called "facts" in journalism, are treated as discrete bits of empirically observable reality which can be decontextualized, packaged, shipped, and re-experienced with only marginal losses in meaning.[1]

The third interrelated assumption shows contemporary American journalism grounded in logical positivism. Reality is assumed to exist out there. It is perceived accurately or inaccurately as our senses and instruments of observation allow. Objectivity of knowledge is the ideal of human understanding.

In this light, the practice of journalism is the application of the canons of empirical science to everyday understanding (Meyer, 1974). The press is assumed to be independent from other socially, politically, and economically determined institutions. It also legitimizes the daily practice of journalism as a roughly adequate process of fact gathering. Even DeFleur and Ball-Rokeach's (1982) sophisticated articulation of an interdependent media–society relationship finally becomes an ode to pluralism, since it rests on a base of logical positivism. In so doing, it does not question the relationship between what is called knowledge and the multidimensional mechanisms of power (Lukes, 1974).

Finally, there is a fourth interrelated and implicit assumption in the dominant view of journalistic practice. It is this deepest assumption which gives credibility to logical positivism and which ultimately becomes the point of departure for our counterargument. Journalists assume language to be an instrument of representation (Merrill & Odell, 1983). This view of language is rooted in the philosophy of language which Volosinov (1973) locates as being rooted in 17th and 18th century rationalism labeled the objectivist position. This position adheres to the following four propositions:

1. Language is a stable, immutable system of normatively identical linguistic forms which the individual consciousness finds ready-made and is incontestable for that consciousness.
2. The laws of language are the specifically linguistic laws of connection between signs in a given linguistic system.
3. Specifically linguistic connections have nothing in common with ideological values.
4. Individual acts of speaking are merely fortuitous refractions, variations, or distortions of normatively identical forms. There is no connection or sharing of motives between the system of language and history.

---

[1] Critics within this dominant view have been sensitive enough to recognize the need to examine, if not challenge, the criteria by which facts are gathered and disseminated. This represented, in some instances, a recognition of the intersection of values and information. However, it did not necessarily question the ideal possibility of their separation, or the underlying theory of meaning upon which the possibility rests. Bias existed, but it simply represented the degree of deviation of an informative report from objective reality (Hackett, 1984).

The primary importance of language within this dominant view is its represen- tational and technical usage. Paradoxically, the practicing journalist recognizes the fluid character of meaning associated with words, even as she or he overtly subscribes to the myth that each word is capable of capturing some essence of a reality with a stable existence.

Journalism as Discourse: The Production of Meaning

A consideration of the practice of journalism as discourse leads to a direct confrontation of the complex intersections of the social, economic, and political forces which dynamically and historically produce what we call journalism. *Discourse* refers to the active process by which a wide range of structural forces gives meaning to a particular practice at a particular moment in history (Drey- fus & Rabinow, 1983). This view of discourse is related to a fundamental concern with how meanings are mythically elevated to the status of knowledge.

Conceptualizing journalism as discourse has its roots in the complex history of the concept of ideology (see Williams, 1977; Abercrombie, 1983, for useful historical reviews of the concept). There are four aspects of ideology to which attention should be drawn. First, as Marx noted, there is the possibility of co- existing yet possibly conflicting "realities." Second, with multiple claims on reality, there must be some mechanism of expression for these claims. Third, there must be an explanation of the process by which a particular claim achieves privilege status as "truth." Fourth, it is possible that particular world views taken as "truth" advantage certain groups in society to the disadvantage of other groups. Knowledge and truth are not neutral. In short, the conceptual- ization of journalism as discourse requires a focus on the process of meaning production, rather than accepting meaning as a given. In turn, we must consider the political implications of the meaning production process, along with the social structual web which the process help sustain.

CRITIQUE OF THE OBJECTIVIST PHILOSOPHY OF LANGUAGE

The objectivist position on language, was not necessarily formulated as a reaction to the Humboldtian position of language being purely subjective and creative activity. However, it did evolve in many respects as its antithesis (Volosinov, 1973; Shapiro, 1982). The objectivist position rejected the subjecti- vist notions of language as a continuous process of creative activity, governed primarily by the laws of individual psychology, and as an instrument of personal creative expression. This rejection led to the search for a formal, socially reified system of meaning, which Saussure recognized in distinguishing the study of language as "langue," and the study of individual speech acts as "parole." To objectify the study of systems of meaning in language required a focus on the stable, supposedly rule-governed "langue," along with a discounting of the chaotic, individualistic realm of everyday speech. Saussure's move in this direction, while certainly not unique, was largely compatible with the increasingly hegemonic theoretical position of logical positivism in the social "sciences." Langue existed in correspondence to some existing reality. The powerful momentum of structuralism, which would ultimately sever this assumption of correspondence which grounded objectivist language theory in the "real" world, had been launched.

The costs of rejecting subjectivism and the theoretical embracing of langue were high. The entire realm of speech was dismissed from a philosophy-of-meaning perspective, and relegated to the study of technical expression. At stake, it was assumed, was the sophistication and skill with which one employed the langue system of meaning. Speech was performance. In addition, a whole new problematic was created and in many ways ignored or relegated to secondary importance. It concerned the difficulty of explaining how a particular word changes over time, as well as how new words are created and old ones abandoned. Moreover, the stage had been set for a theoretical drama in which the possibility of individual freedom in speech, thought, and action would be rejected. However, the philosophy of meaning which was becoming a philosophy of language had moved into an increasingly esoteric realm of academic debate and speculation. Logical positivism/empiricism had become more self-reflexive and self-legitimating. The fact that the domain of language, that supposed clear glass in the spectacles through which scientism proclaimed itself science, might actually be a multifaceted and shifting prism, was a muffled cry from the delegitimated humanities.

In many respects, it was the constant hammering away at the concept of ideology by Western marxist theorists and those studying the sociology of knowledge, which forced the question of the relativity of meaning in language back into the agenda of academic and political action groups.

A COUNTERTHEORY: LANGUAGE AS DIALOGUE

Volosinov (1973) presented a countertheory to the objectivist conceptualization of language, synthesizing the objectivist and subjectivist theories of language. The result was a theory of language as dialogue.[2]

Volosinov presented a theory of language which recognized the contribution of individual creativity while preserving the social character of meaning. This theory accounts for the process by which the meaning of a word changes over time and how value-laden meaning produces and labels truth. There are five basic propositions to Volosinov's dialogic theory of language:

---

[2]In the 1930s, Volosinov was one among many Marxist theoreticians whose work was at odds with Stalinist doctrine. His theories were consequently purged. Although his personal fate remains a mystery today, his work survived and was integrated into the theoretical activity of the Prague Linguistic Circle in the 1930s and 1940s. However, it was not until 1973 that his theory of language was translated into English. Stuart Hall (1982) and Raymond Williams (1977) are primarily responsible for introducing his work into Western critical theory.

1. The belief that language is a stable system or normatively identical forms, is merely a scientific abstraction. It is not adequate to the concrete reality of language.
2. Language is a continuous generative process implemented in the social interactions of speakers.
3. The laws of the generative process of language are not the laws of individual psychology. However, they cannot be divorced from the activity of speakers. The laws of generation are sociological.
4. Linguistic creativity does not coincide with any other type of ideological creativity. However, linguistic creativity cannot be understood apart from the ideological meanings and values that fill it. The generative process of language, as is true of any historical generative process, can be perceived as blind mechanical necessity, but it can also become "free necessity" once it has reached the position of a conscious and desired necessity.
5. The structure of an utterance is a purely sociological structure. An utterance obtains between speakers. The individual speech act is *contradictio in adjecto*.

DIALOGUE AND POWER

Lukes (1974, p.14) describes three dimensions of power. The first dimension focuses "on behavior in the making of decisions on issues over which there is an observable conflict of (subjective) interests, seen as expressed policy preferences, revealed by political participation." This widely reified view of power suggests a relatively limited role for the contribution of language to power relationships. The role of language is implicit and conceptualized in objectivist terms. Language is viewed as an instrument of information transmission, allowing for the coordination of behavior, the negotiation of decisions, and the expression of interests. The skillful use of language may facilitate the accomplishment of these technical objectives and in some cases even advantage a particular side. However, the true conflict is between the expressed subjective interests of the two groups.

The second dimension of power examines power which resides in non-decision-making and the structural forces which mobilize a certain bias into the mechanics of social and political organizations. The ability to exercise control over the parameters of debate, to define issues and nonissues, and to impede the articulation of particular grievances and/or needs are aspects of the second dimension of power. It "involves a qualified critique of the behavioral focus of the first view (qualified because it still assumes that non-decision-making is a form of decision making) and it allows for consideration of how decisions are prevented from being taken on potential issues over which there is observable conflict of (subjective) interests, seen embodied in expressed policy preferences and subpolitical grievances" (Lukes, 1974, p. 20).

The second dimension of power initiates an interest in the relationship between conceptualization and action. The study of the strategic use of language in power struggles is strongly suggested by this view. Still, language is considered within the objectivist frame as a manipulative tool for fighting specific political battles rather than a system of meaning production.

It is in Luke's (1974) third dimension of power, strongly influenced by the work of Gramsci (1971), that we see the appropriate theoretical terrain for Volosinov's dialogic theory of language. The third dimension of power focuses on "a) decision-making and control over the political agenda (not necessarily through decisions), b) issues and potential issues, c) observable (overt and covert) and latent conflict, and d) subjective and real interests" (Lukes, 1974, p.25). In each of these cases, conceptualizing language as a dialogic meaning-producing activity illuminates how, through structures of distorted and controlled dialogue, power can be subtly exerted. The traditional view of the practices of journalism, underpinned by an objectivist philosophy of language, obscures the role of journalism in the systematic exercise of political power. It thus conceals from consideration the role of journalism in the power relations which take place in Luke's third dimension.

POLITICAL LINGUISTICS

By *political linguistics*, we refer to study of the political dimensions of language which are always present. The focus of political linguistics is centered on the process of meaning production in language, and on how that production constantly provides an ideological accent to every social categorization of human experience.

THE NATURE OF CRISIS

Thus far, we have attempted to lay out the details of a shift in perspective regarding a new view of journalism and the contextual importance of that shift in terms of power mechanisms in an advanced capitalist society. What we are constructing is a political linguistics reconceptualization of journalistic practice. For help in this effort, we may turn to the work of Habermas on the mechanisms of capitalism and the concepts of public sphere and crisis.

Held (1980, p.260) summarizes the concept of public sphere discussed by Habermas in the following manner:

> Habermas refers to a "realm of social life in which something approaching public opinion can be formed." It is a sphere in which citizens can "confer in unrestricted fashion—that is, with the guarantee of freedom of assembly and association and the freedom to express and publish their opinions—about matters of general interest." It is a realm in which, in principle, political life can be discussed openly; debate prceeds in accordance with standards of critical reason and not by simple appeal to traditional dogmas and authorities (the divine right of kings, for instance). The procedures and presuppositions of free argument are the basis for the

justification of opinions. It is these conditions of argument that lend public opinion its legitimizing force: "public opinion" becomes distinguished from mere "opinion" (for example, cultural assumptions, customs, and collective prejudice.

Habermas (1974) traces the rise of the public sphere and its paradoxical incorporation into certain national constitutions in the form of protection for free speech and a free press. A separation is contrived between the realm of politics and that of private life. This separation makes political equality and democratic political dialogue seem possible, while rationalizing inequality in the economic and social spheres.

The argument that Habermas makes about the undermining of the public sphere parallels our argument about the dissolution of the legitimizing function of journalism as an agent of the public sphere. We differ from Habermas in (a) our focus on journalism as a particular institutionalized element of the public sphere in the United States, (b) our focus on language as a dialogic process of meaning construction which materially underlies the construction of the public sphere, (c) our analysis of the particular character of the shifting basis of the legitimacy of American journalism, and (d) our specification of the particular character of the crisis now unfolding in commercial American journalism.

CRISIS

Habermas (1973) theorizes that the history of capitalism is the history of crisis. He distinguishes two types of crisis: (a) an external threat to the continuation of a social system, and (b) an internal threat to a system arising from the collision of two structurally inherent but imcompatible characteristics of the system. He argues that there are four types on internal crises in the development of capitalism—economic, rationality, legitimation, and motivation. Of these four, we are primarily concerned with the crises of legitimation and motivation.

A *motivational crisis* is what Habermas describes as a situation in which the "requisite quantity" of "action-motivating meaning" is not created. He argues that motivation is generated in late capitalistic societies by the sociocultural system in two ways—civil and famililial-vocational privatism. Civil privatism demands an interest in the satisfactory functioning of the state without any real desire for significant participation in that process. Familial-vocational privatism promotes family-oriented behavior which focuses on leisure, consumption, and career ambitions of status and competition. Habermas argues that both patterns are necessary for maintenance of present capitalistic institutions, and that both are being systematically eroded. The increasing pervasiveness of the general process of rationalization (instrumental logic) has eroded traditional world views, resulting in a "loss of an interpretation of the totality of life; and the increasing subjectivizating and relativizing of morality" (Held, 1980, p. 293). Habermas has sought to support this claim through the analysis of achievement ideology, possessive individualism, and the orientation toward exchange value.

Our interest here is to examine a core institution engaged in the process of meaning production, and consider how it has maintained itself and interacted with the introduction of rational philosophy. The tendency to a motivational crisis, we argue, takes place, not only in the erosion of motivational myths, but in the erosion of the legitimating character of the machine which produces the myth. In a sense, we are arguing that the crisis of motivation can be seen as a double crisis of legitimacy: the eroded quality of systems sustaining myths, and the eroded quality of the mechanism by which the myths are created.

In this sense, we are exploring the intersection of Habermas's concept of motivational crisis and his concept of *legitimation crisis*—the crisis when the "requisite quantity" of "generalized motivations" are not produced. As he argues, when, in late capitalism, the administrative system expands into "areas traditionally assigned to the private sphere, there is a progressive demystification of the nature-like process of social fate" (Held, 1980, p.291). In a sense, we ask a very specific set of questions of a very particular and critical institution—journalism. Has there been an increasing visibility of the political character of the production of everyday reality we call news? In what ways has the structure of capitalism attempted to recover from any tendencies toward demystification? What are the implications of this struggle?

Habermas's work on internal crisis leads us to an identification of the periods in journalism history where we find the collision of two or more structurally inherent forces in the emerging institution of journalism which were incompatible. We have retrospectively identified two by drawing on the work of Schudson (1978) and Schiller (1981).

THE FIRST CRISIS: COLLAPSE OF ARISTOCRATIC CONTROL

Lippman (1920) describes the history of the press as a progression from captivity to freedom. This progression involves four stages. In the first stage, the press is operated as a monopoly controlled by an authoritarian state. In the second stage, political parties assume control of the press as an expression of their contrasting viewpoints. In the third stage, the press breaks from both the state and the political parties by enlisting the commercial support of readers to provide it with an independent economic base. In the fourth stage, the press enters an era of professional journalism, where news gathering is institutionalized and the function of news reporting and dissemination, the fostering and maintenance of public debate, is underwritten and protected by the enlistment of scientific objectivity. This development is portrayed as natural and largely inevitable.

Several points are important here. First, as Foucault notes, all history is actually a theory of the present. Lippman's description is really an application of a theory of evolution which reflects the reigning influence of a Darwinian sense of social development and commitment to logical positivism. It fails to question the relationship of language and perception. Moreover, it implies a recognition of the close association between power and knowledge, while assuming that knowledge can be dissociated from power and consequently act as an independent force in social relations.

Still, Lippman's theory can serve as a point of departure for our rereading of the history of journalism because of its insightful recognition of the key points of transition in journalistic association with the power–knowledge relationship. We may not agree with his labeling or interpretation, but we do agree with the attention he calls to the critical points in history. We focus specifically on the transition between his second and third stages. It is in the process and nature of the transition between those stages that special attention and explanation is required.

The early 1800s in American history is marked most forcibly by what Schudson (1978) describes as the emergence of a democratic market society. Although the constitution initiating a representative democracy had been written and agreed upon decades earlier, the practical matter of its implementation was a cause of experimentation and conflict. In the political arena, it was the first significant movement away from gentry rule toward mass democracy. It was also the launching of a market-based economy and its integration into economic life. The double crisis of legitimacy faced by the press was comprised of two questions—who would succeed the gentry as authorities in the production of meaning, and how would this succession be presented as reasonable and natural to the general population.

Schudson (1978) argues that the triumph of the Penny Press, which succeeded the Partisan Press, centered on its ability to challenge the moral authority of the residual aristocratic interests with the supposed justice of the market. The market was to be the guarantor of democratic values in the same way it promoted equality in the marketplace. The cost of the newspaper democratized access to the news. Additionally, the Penny Press would not impose arbitrary moral authority on advertisers, because it would accept all ads for all products. This movement was framed as an advance in the concept of free speech. Free speech was presented as the stepping stone to rational decision making by the masses. It thus made participatory democracy possible. Further, the Penny Press would focus on verifiable facts which were seen as a nonpartisan reflection on reality. From a traditional history of journalism perspective, with its uncritical treatment of language and meaning, it was possible to retell the story of the emergence of the Penny Press as a progressive liberation of unrestricted speech.

A different story comes forth when this transition is viewed as a crisis from our political-linguistics perspective. Instead of a progressive liberation of free speech, we see simply a shift in power over the production of meaning through dialogue from an aristocratic power base to an economic one. Information and knowledge are not freed from power, but the character of the new authority has receded further from view. The new rules of access are cloaked in the myth of the market. The market is offered as counterpoint to the power of the state. Facts are presented as representations of an external and verifiable reality. The basic tenets of speech as technologically mediated dialogue, however, remain unchanged. There are few authors and many readers. The active meaning-producing character of language through dialogue goes unnoticed and, consequently, continues to powerfully and invisibly disadvantage those who must speak and internalize meaning over which they have no control.

The first crisis emerged as a conflict over control of the means of knowledge production between the gentry whose economic and political power was diminishing, and the rising industrial middle class. The conflict was resolved by coupling the notion of the liberating character of the marketplace with both political democracy and the mystified concept of free speech. The independence of the press from the government would thus be celebrated.

THE SECOND CRISIS: THE RISE OF OBJECTIVITY

If the first crisis of journalism was the clash between the remnants of gentry power and the rising middle class over control of the means of meaning production, the second crisis represented a collision of class interests over a more sophisticated idea of the public sphere. Economic privilege rather than aristocratic state control was seen as the enemy.

The successful control by industrial interests over the press, whether done through direct advertising patronage or indirect collusion among powerful corporations (which now included press monopolies), threatened to crack the veneer of legitimacy of a supposedly independent press. This precipitated a motivational crisis. If the press was not independent, the flow of facts necessary for rational decision making in a democracy would cease. Perhaps more importantly, if the illusion of facts being available to any rational person was extinguished, there might be a withdrawal of general consent by the governed for existing institutional structures.

Our political-linguistics approach to the study of journalism would have predicted the onset of the crisis as the new masters of meaning production revealed their primary allegiance to the protection of capital. Lippman (1920, p. 5), referring to the growing turbulence among western democracies after World War I, called the present crisis of western democracy a "crisis of journalism." Lippman (p. 41) notes:

> So long as there is interposed between the ordinary citizen and the facts a news organization determining by entirely private and unexamined standards, no matter how lofty, what he shall know, and hence what he shall believe, no one shall be able to say that the substance of democratic government is secure.

The gross misconduct of the press in the reporting of labor/capital conflict in the early 1900s underscores Lippman's concerns.

The resolution of the crisis of the invasion of the press by the marketplace is, in Lipmann's view, the professionalization of journalism and the enshrinement of objectivity as the journalistic ideal. No shift in the fundamental power relationships within society or within journalistic practices were required. The solution to class conflict over control of the public sphere was not to democratize access, but to legitimize existing control through scientific rationality. Objectivity, as the journalistic embodiment of the logical positivist notion of science, became the unintentional but nevertheless explicit specification of the particular philosophy of language which would underpin journalistic practice into the 1980s.

The theory of language as the reflection of observable political reality had been called into question as early as 1651 by Thomas Hobbes (Hacker & Bybee, 1985). It was a theory of meaning already being refuted from several directions by Saussure (1960), Vygotsky (1986), Volosinov (1973), Mannheim (1936), and others. This theory theory of language, which could not recognize that science was an ideology—a particular ideology in service of a particular form of economic production. The theory reified the arbitrary compartmentalization of knowledge into the humanities, social sciences, and sciences. It was a theory that might allow for a relationship between knowledge and democracy, but which obscured the relationship between meaning and power.

Journalism would separate fact from value. Under the banner of objectivity, a progressive reform movement in journalism was mounted in the 1920s and 1930s. By the 1940s, we were presented with the landmark Hutchins Commission report on a social responsibility theory of the press. This theory was underpinned by an assumed objectivist theory of language.

The notion of objectivity became another layer in the mystification of the true character of the public sphere and the power–meaning relationship highlighted by the dialogic theory of language. As the photograph had come to support the scientific character of facts as representations of reality, the live formats of radio and television bolstered newspapers' reification of objectivity.

Overall, journalistic practice came out of the second crisis with new strength. Scientism, in the form of objectivity, provided a sturdy legitimizing rationale for the continued combination of free speech protections with profit seeking. This legitimization within the practice of journalism allowed journalism to sustain its role as the watchdog of institutional independence and the protector of the public sphere.

Journalism became a part of what Habermas (1973) called the primary legitimation system of advanced capitalism—technocratic consciousness. This system is based upon "the ability of groups of administrators, technicians, and politicians to guarantee a minimum level of welfare, manage the economy successfully and sustain economic growth . . . technocratic consciousness is both more and less ideological than all previous ideologies" (Habermas, 1973, p. 78). According to Habermas (1973, p. 83), it "conceals behind a facade (not of democracy) but of objective necessity, the interests of classes and groups that actually determine the functions, directions and pace of technological and social development." Questions regarding symbolic interaction and meaning production are replaced by questions that focus on purposive, rational actions. The question of language was forced aside.

THE THIRD CRISIS: UNMASKING THE THIRD PERSON

The third crisis in American journalism is now unfolding. It centers around the collapse of the concept of journalistic objectivity. In one sense, our argument seems like an old one. The traditional history of journalism is the history of free speech being constantly tested and challenged. In this sense, the current period of history is no different from any other. The forces of commercialism, the efforts of government to maximize state control, and the problems of new technologies, might appear to represent the old struggles in new clothes. However, such an interpretation is dangerously naive. It fails to recognize the character of the struggle over meaning production which we have attempted to outline. It also fails to attach enough importance to the proposition that journalistic objectivity is an historically recent intellectual invention, developed for the purpose of holding back a legitimation/motivation crisis in journalistic practice 50 years ago. If the concept of objectivity is beginning to disintegrate, the wagon carrying our present social and political structures will have lost a very important wheel.

This third crisis is particularly acute. While, previously, the concept of objectivity found validity in other areas of research and thought such as academia, those bases of support are no longer as available. In communication theory, for example, the concept of objectivity is being called into question more and more as the process of meaning and interpretation are observed and described.

The shape of this third crisis takes the following forms. There has been a collapse of the distinction between news and entertainment, driven by the profit-seeking imperative of media companies. Paradoxically, it was the concept of objectivity which legitimized the distinction between fact and fiction. It is now profit seeking which reunifies fact and fiction.

We have also seen the widespread dissemination of the advertising values of presentation, production, and targeting. Particularly in terms of presentation, advertising has been the form of mass communication which has most explicitly recognized and incorporated the insight of meaning production into its work. Its invasion into the marketing of political candidates, explicitly political viewpoints (such as Mobil Oil's advertorials and Beyond War's market-based documentaries), and even religious presentation and recruitment, demonstrates a working knowledge of a countertheory to the official hegemony of objectivity.

The rise of intentional symbolic manipulation by those in positions of power to access the means of meaning production also sheds light on the abandonment of the objectivist theory of meaning. Again, the trends and examples are numerous, from the ongoing emotional charging of the word *communist* to the struggle over and recapture of the word *black* by the civil rights movement. It can be seen in the battle between *pro-choice* and *pro-life*, between *Star Wars* and *Star Peace*, and between *Freedom Fighters* and *Contra rebels*. This symbolic warfare is becoming both more intentional and more visible. The struggles are presented regularly by the press which attempts to adhere or at least to appear to adhere, to the canons of objectivity which are called into question by these struggles.

We have also seen the amusing rise of a counterphenomenon. At the same time that symbolic struggles over meaning and framing have become more visible, various groups have attempted to subvert the conventions of objectivity in pursuit of symbolic manipulation. Consider the Christian Broadcasting Network or the Labor Institute for Public Affairs. Both have actively engaged in the production of network-like news programs which retell the news of the day from a particular ideological perspective. Each perspective is cloaked in the format and cues of objectivity, as the programs seek to legitimate their presentations and content. The illusion of objectivity has become so transparent that almost every major group engaged in politics routinely creates its own disinformation bureau. A disinformation bureau is a communication staff which churns out propaganda consistent with the group's recognition of the importance of meaning production (and management) and modeled after public relations arms of major corporations. The major corporations were the pioneers of meaning production in America. From the community rape-crisis center to the notorious Heritage Foundation, the wobbly validity of the concept of journalistic objectivity is recognized in the practices of communication.

Finally, we have seen the rise of the international New World Information Order. In its creation and attempts to articulate a philosophical basis of existence, we see wonderfully compressed the agony of practice searching for a theoretical rationale in an obsolete paradigm. The New World Information Order was born from the New World Economic Order in UNESCO. The NWEO movement marked a recognition by the Third-World nations that the rules of the world economic game, formalized in the doctrine of comparative advantage, meant that the likelihood of future economic parity among all nations was close to zero (Schiller, 1981). The future in economic development appeared to lie in the information industries. In addition, the control of the world information industries appeared to determine which nations would control the character and distribution of the all forms of economic development. Thus, economic power was seen to be inextricably linked to information control. The NWIO movement was consequently a response on the part of the Third World to investigate the nature of the current distribution of information resources, and to formulate a demand for a democratization of these increasingly visible and precious resources.

The New World Information Order attempted to articulate a theoretical basis for its demands for democratization of communication. It borrowed the theoretical premises of objectivism, particularly in terms of journalistic practice, and ended up contradicting itself. The tenets of a philosophy of meaning, grounded in logical positivism, fit poorly with a political philosophy of democracy which argues that rightfulness is determined through consensus rather than through a scientific approximation of reality.

Each of the above instances of challenges to the hegemony of journalistic objectivity, constitutes a force for the destablization of the concept's authority for legitimation.

CONCLUSIONS

We have presented an argument which asserts that journalism has entered a third crisis. This crisis entails the crumbling of the concept of objectivity. Whether in news, academics, or any other kind of careful reporting of facts, we see the third person losing the mask.

The first crisis of journalism was the collapse of political party control and the rise of the commercial press. The second crisis was the rise of positivism in journalistic practice. The third crisis is the increasing visibility of the production of meaning in journalism, and the attached issues of who controls the various facets of the production processes. The third crisis is visible everywhere. The story of Nicholas Daniloff changed daily. Bernard Kalb resigned as State Department chief spokesman because of what he called the "disinformation program" of the Reagan administration against Libya. White House press secretary Larry Speakes admits that he reinforced misleading reports and dominated the flow of news in America with his morning press briefings. Referring to the CIA plane incident in Nicaragua, Senator Patrick Leahy says that "the Administration is skating on the knife edge of credibility." Meanwhile, Jimmy Swaggart shows film footage of Moscow as he rails about the Russian tentacles which are stretching out to devour the free and Christian world. Linking humanism, academics, and child abuse together, Swaagart has citations from various publications superimposed on the television screen. At the Sixth International Conference on Culture and Communication, one could learn that television news promotions are selling anchor people in slick and sexy print and television spots, that tv news footage functions to sell the credibility of news narrative, that information graphics create a feeling of objectivity, that investigative reporters champion the causes of the oppressed while reinforcing the codes of the dominant order, and that prolonged dependence on television leads to mainstreaming and conservative thinking.

So what does the railing of Jimmy Swaggart with proofs attached to his claims have to do with the selling of anchorpeople? What does the resignation of Bernard Kalb have to do with the persuasive rhetoric of news film footage and information graphics? All of these observations point to the collapse of the concept of objectivity in American journalism. Moreover, they continue to suggest that the essence of journalism is not accurate reporting of unbiased data, but rather interpretations of data which are presented in ways that produce certain structures of meaning. Only when the fundamental shift from the representationalist to the dialogic theory of language is made by journalists will the practice of journalism be capable of closer alignment with linguistic creativity and democracy.

REFERENCES

Abercrombie, N. (1983). *Class, structure, and knowledge.* New York: New York University Press.

Bachrach, P., & Baratz, M. (1962). The two faces of power. *American Political Science Review, 56,* 947–952.

Carey, M., & Kreiling, A. (1974). Popular culture and uses and gratifications. In J. Blumler & E. Katz (Eds.), *The uses of mass communication* (pp. 225–249). Beverly Hills, CA: Sage.

DeFleur, M., & Ball-Rokeach, S. (1982). *Theories of mass communication.* New York: Longman.

Dreyfus, J., & Rabinow, P. (1983). *Michel Foucault: Beyond structuralism and hermeneutics.* Chicago, IL: University of Chicago Press.

Emery, E., & Emery, M. (1972). *The press and America.* New York: Prentice-Hall.

Gramsci, A. (1971). *Selections from the prison notebooks.* London: Lawrence and Wishart.

Gurevitch, M., Bennett, T., Curran, J., & Woollacott, J. (Eds.). (1982). *Culture, society and the media.* New York: Methuen.

Habermas, J. (1973). *Legitimation crisis.* Boston, MA: Beacon Press.

Habermas, J. (1974). The public sphere. *New German Critique, 3,* 198–210.

Hacker, K., & Bybee, C. (1985, May). *Toward an expication of political linguistics.* Paper presented to the International Communication Association, Honolulu.

Hackett, R. (1984). Decline of a paradigm? Bias and objectivity in news media studies. *Critical Studies in Mass Communication, 3,* 229–259.

Hall, S. (1982). The rediscovery of "ideology": return of the repressed in media studies. In M. Gurevitch, T. Bennett, J. Curran, & J. Woolacott (Eds.), *Culture, society and media* (pp. 56–91). New York: Methuen.

Held, D. (1980). *Introduction to critical theory.* Berkeley, CA: University of California Press.

Kraus, S., & Davis, D. (1976). *The effects of mass communication on political behavior.* University Park, PA: Pennsylvania University Press.

Lippman, A. (1920). *Liberty and the news.* New York: Harcourt, Brace and Hone.

Lukes, S. (1974). *Power: A radical view.* London: Macmillan.

Mannheim, K. (1936). *Ideology and utopia.* New York: Harcourt, Brace and World.

Merrill, J., & Odell, J. (1983). *Philosophy and journalism.* New York: Longman.

Merton, R. (1962). *Social theory and social structure.* New York: Free Press.

Meyer, P. (1974). *Precision journalism.* Bloomington, IN: Indiana University Press.

Sandman, P., Rubin, D., & Sachsman, D. (1982). *Media: An introductory analysis of American mass communication.* New York: Prentice-Hall.

Saussure, F. (1960). *Course in general linguistics.* London: P. Owen.

Schiller, D. (1979). *Objectivity and the news: The public and the rise of commercial journalism.* Philadelphia, PA: University of Pennsylvania Press.

Schudson, M. (1978). *Discovering the news.* New York: Basic Books, Inc.

Shannon, C., & Weaver, W. (1960). *The mathematical theory of communication.* Urbana, IL: University of Illinois Press.

Shapiro, M. (1982). *Language and political understanding.* New York: New York University Press.

Volosinov, V. N. (1973). *Marxism and the philosophy of language.* New York: Seminar Press.

Vygotsky, L. (1986). *Thought and language.* Cambridge, MA: The MIT Press.

Williams, R. (1977). *Marxism and literature.* London: New Left Books.

6

Discourse Direction and Power: Diverging Strategies during a Welfare Interview

RICHARD BUTTNY

Syracuse University

J. LOUIS CAMPBELL III

Pennsylvania State University

Application interviews are interesting because of the importance that participants place on language use and self-presentation. Talk during interviews is highly goal-directed; however, participants often do not share mutual goals or equal means of attaining those goals. Typically, there is an asymmetry of power and control between participants, e.g., job interviews (Jupp, Roberts, & Cook-Gumperz, 1982; Kress & Fowler, 1979; Ragan, 1983). Interviewers function as gatekeepers in the direction and allocation of institutional resources and positions (Erickson & Schultz, 1982). There are well-known structural differences between participants (interviewer and interviewee) and the corresponding rights and obligations attached to each role. While these structural differences or parameters are very real, *they must be interactionally accomplished through talk*. As Gumperz and Cook-Gumperz state, "The study of language as interaction discourse demonstrates that these parameters are not constants that can be taken for granted but are communicatively produced." In short, "We must focus on what communication does: how it constrains evaluation and decision making, not merely how it is structured" (Gumperz & Cook-Gumperz, 1982, p. 1). Decisions made from application interviews are constrained by factors external to the interview, such as economic and political realities. Communication processes which constitute the interview, are also crucial in understanding decisions and how they are justified.

In this chapter, we will examine one such setting, a welfare interview. Our focus is on the caseworker's ways of justifying her evaluation and the client's ways of challenging this evaluation. One of the most striking features of this case is the recurring or repetitive character of the discourse. We will examine the participants' procedures for presenting and evaluating problems, and how these are used as justifications or challenges. The notion of "discourse strategies" is used as a unit of analysis to explain how participants use language to achieve their ends and how these choices reflect an asymmetry of power.

WELFARE INTERVIEWS AS A LANGUAGE GAME

Perhaps the most distinguishing characteristic of welfare interviews is the practice of applicants giving accounts of their problematic circumstances before a caseworker who evaluates whether or not the case merits assistance. Given the increasing bureaucratization of social aid programs (Weed, 1979), these interviews are structured by various standardized procedures: application forms, supporting documents, submitting to an interview, being investigated, etc. To qualify for assistance, the applicant must meet certain institutional standards. Decision-making procedures are guided by various institutional rules and procedures. Caseworkers routinely expect applicants to have self-interested motives and to present their accounts of problematic circumstances to support their application (Zimmerman, 1974).

The practice of a professionally trained caseworker applying institutional criteria to a case to determine eligibility suggests an air of objectivity in decision making. However, researchers are beginning to demonstrate that such decision-making procedures of examining documents and records, listening to applicants' accounts, and conducting investigations are not entirely unambiguous and objective (Buckholdt & Gubrium, 1983; Geist & Chandler, 1984; Tompkins & Cheney, 1983; Zimmerman, 1974). Decision making involves, not only explicit institutional rules and procedures, but also tacit conventions and criteria based on cultural assumptions of the situation, appropriate ways of structuring information, and preferred ways of speaking. Those ignorant of such conventions and criteria are put at a disadvantage in attempting to attain their goals (Gumperz & Cook-Gumperz, 1982). Typically, evaluators must decide "for all practical purposes" that a "fact" has been established or that a general rule applies in a particular situation (Zimmerman, 1970).

The decisions made in a welfare interview are, in principle, subject to public accountability according to objective standards of evaluation. Thus caseworkers find it necessary to have accounts ready at hand to justify their decisions according to institutional standards (Buckholdt & Gubrium, 1983; Buttny, 1985). However, for the applicant to challenge successfully the caseworker's evaluation requires a specialized knowledge and rhetorical sophistication based on institutional assumptions (Gumperz & Cook-Gumperz, 1982).

These doubts about the objectivity of institutional decision making suggests the importance of understanding the procedures and rules which caseworkers actually use in the allocation and denial of assistance. Equally important is understanding the strategies which applicants use in presenting their case during the interview. Given that the discourse of welfare interviews is goal directed and that participants may have diverging goals and unequal participation rights (Rees, 1975), how do participants attempt to achieve their respective ends?

A welfare interview may be viewed as a particular kind of "language game" (Wittgenstein, 1953) or "speech event" (Hymes, 1972) in which participants make various "moves" (Goffman, 1976; Owen, 1981) to realize their ends. The notion of a *move* may be characterized as an interactional unit to "refer to any full stretch of talk . . . which has a distinctive unitary bearing on some set or other of the circumstances in which participants find themselves (some 'game' or other in the peculiar sense employed by Wittgenstein)" (Goffman, 1976, p. 272). A move is not isomorphic with a speaking turn, since more than one move can be made in a turn or, conversely, it may take multiple turns to accomplish a move. In the present case, moves include requesting information, giving advice, directing to other channels, justifying decisions, describing personal circumstances, challenging decisions, explaining background information, and the like.

A move may be used in conjunction with other moves in the attempt to achieve particular ends. A combined cluster of moves may be identified as a *discourse strategy*. A discourse strategy is a larger level unit of conversational organization which is comprised of various moves used in a means–end structure.

Our project here is to examine the discourse of a welfare interview. We will consider an interview in which the caseworker and client have differing evaluations of the client's case. The discourse organization of how problems are told is an especially important feature in this interview. Our focus in on the moves participants make in formulating, using, and evaluating problems as part of their discourse strategies in the attempt to achieve their ends.

MATERIALS

A film of naturally occurring interview in a state welfare agency in the Northeastern U.S. provides our materials. This filmed interview is a portion of a training film for welfare caseworkers. This film is an unedited exerpt from Frederick Wiseman's documentary, *Welfare* (1975).

There are three participants in this interview: a caseworker, an applicant and the applicant's daughter. All the participants are female; the caseworker is white and the applicant and her daughter are black. The applicant's daughter does most of the talking with the caseworker—she will be identified by the more convenient term *client*.

THE USE OF PROBLEMS AS DISCOURSE STRATEGIES

Evaluation and Challenge

The welfare interview examined here (see Appendix) involves a dispute between the caseworker and client over the applicant's qualification for assistance. The applicant's case has been previously rejected by this caseworker (line 28). Since this initial rejection, the applicant has pursued other means of support, such as applying for Social Security (line 29) and taking her husband to court for child-support payments. However, the Social Security Agency and the courts are delayed in deciding the applicant's case; consequently, the applicant is presently without a means of support, so she has returned to reapply for welfare assistance.

The following fragment from the interview will be examined for how problems are used and evaluated.

(1) FRAGMENT (lines 7–14)

> 07 CASEWORKER: It has to be in the court's hands as long as he's getting income and then he's not using it while he's in the hospital. It's for the children (.) that's the way
>
> [
>
> 08 CLIENT: What's the alternatives? What, is she gonna take checks from him if he doesn't want to give them to her? (.) What's the alternative? She's been to court, yesterday, yesterday.
>
> 09 CASEWORKER: Now wait a minute, what'd the court say?
>
> 10 CLIENT: He didn't show up, they sent out a warrant for him.
>
> 11 CASEWORKER: Well he'll show up.
>
> 12 CLIENT: But what do you want her to do if he doesn't show up? And he's got the checks and he won't give them to her.
>
> 13 CASEWORKER: The only thing that I can suggest is that you talk to the application supervisor and if you feel that you've been treated unfairly
>
> [
>
> 14 CLIENT: Of course we feel—why do you think we're back here now?

The caseworker initially evaluates the client's case as being in the court's jurisdiction (line 7). This evaluation is marked as necessary as indicated by the verb choice "It has to be in the court's hands," as well as by the justification of citing the husband's legal responsibilities. Here the caseworker draws on the institutional procedure that the courts take precedence over the welfare agency. This procedure is not verbally explained, but is the underlying assumption of the caseworker's move. In other words, without this institutional procedure of the courts taking precedence, the caseworker could not accomplish this justification.

The caseworker is simultaneously making two moves here—in evaluating that the case is in the courts' hands, she implies that the client's application is being denied. The client's response (line 8) shows that she recognizes the implied denial even though it is never explicitly stated. This recognition is displayed by the client citing various problems with the caseworker's evaluation. The client's utterances are marked as problems in that they describe negative circumstances which will result from the caseworker's evaluation. These negative circumstances include the husband not wanting to give her the checks, and already having been to court but the case being delayed. The client uses these problems as obstacles to the caseworker's evaluation. As obstacles, these problems respond to the caseworker's evaluation by challenging its appropriateness.

The client prefaces the presentation of these problems with the question, "What's the alternatives?" (line 8). The implication the client wants the caseworker to draw is that the client has no other "alternatives" for support except to receive welfare assistance. *These moves of presenting problems-as-obstacles to the caseworker's evaluation to implicate the need for welfare assistance constitutes the client's discourse strategy.*

At line 13 the caseworker displays recognition of the client's problems with the courts by suggesting that she arrange a fair hearing through the applications supervisor. This proposal allows the caseworker to continue to reject the application while simultaneously responding with a "solution" to the client's problems. These moves display that the caseworker does not accept the client's discourse strategy (that there are no other options but welfare assistance). Instead, the caseworker offers an option (consistent with bureaucratic procedures), which allows her to maintain her initial evaluation.

The caseworker's moves are to direct the client to follow institutional channels: the case is the courts' decision (line 7), or arrange a fair hearing through the applications supervisor (lines 13–15). The caseworker's moves are based on the maxim, *follow institutional procedures.* This maxim is not explicitly uttered, but rather it is the underlying assumption behind the above mentioned moves. Drawing on this maxim allows the caseworker to justify her evaluation by reference to institutional criteria, and to deny the client's reapplication. *These combination of moves grounded on the maxim, follow institutional procedures, constitutes the caseworker's discourse strategy.* We will see that this discourse strategy is used throughout the interview.

In line 12 the client again challenges the caseworker's solution by *repeating the problems* of the husband's not appearing in court as well as not wanting to give her the checks. These problems were mentioned previously (lines 6, 8, and 10). The client prefaces the presentation of problems-as-obstacles with the question, "But what do you want her do do if" these problems are not solved (line 12). This formulation is structurally similar to the preface to the problems at line 8, "What's the alternatives." These prefacing questions combined with the device, problems-as-obstacles, are used to imply that there is nothing the client can do (line 12) or that no options are left but welfare assistance (line 8). We will see that the client uses these problems-as-obstacles throughout the interview as a response to the caseworker's negative evaluation.

Negotiation.   The participants' diverging goals and corresponding discourse strategies comprise the central tension of the interview: the conflict between *the caseworker's maxim, follow institutional procedures* and *the applicant's claim that all channels have been tried.*

How do the participants attempt to manage this divergence? Returning to the above fragment we can see that the caseworker responds to the client's problems (line 9) by asking what appears to be an informational question. Note, though, that this question is oriented to "what'd the courts say" (i.e., the caseworker's preferred outcome) rather than to the client's problematic circumstances. That is, the question is not to the main point of the client's prior turn, but to an ancillary episode which the caseworker makes relevant. So the caseworker's question, in addition to requesting information, simultaneously attempts to regulate the discourse in the direction of the caseworker's proposal.

The client (line 10) answers this question in a way consistent with her discourse strategy. She answers by repeating the problem cited in her previous turn—the husband's failure to appear in court (line 8). So, while the caseworker's question attempts to regulate the discourse in accordance with her strategy, the client is able to answer by continuing to cite problems-as-obstacles. The caseworker responds (line 11) by providing a "solution" to the client's problem which works to regulate the discourse towards the court's procedures.

A welfare interview as a language game may be seen as comprised of two basic parts: (a) application or request for assistance, and (b) caseworker's evaluation, which complies with or denies the request. In applying for assistance the client presents accounts of problematic circumstances. These descriptions of problematic circumstances have different sequential implications than (b)— i.e., problems make conditionally relevant responses such as "solutions." There seems to be a mixing of sequence types in the language game: on the one hand, application–evaluation, and on the other, problem–solution. Thus, in responding to the client, the caseworker may face the competing demands of administering institutional procedures and helping the client.

These competing demands may be seen, for instance, in the caseworker's response at line 13. The caseworker displays that she is oriented to the competing demands of *providing a solution to the client's problems* as well as *applying institutional criteria to evaluate the client's application*. In short, the caseworker's response may be seen as both a solution and an evaluation. It is a "solution" in that it suggests a course of action for the client to receive assistance. And it is simultaneously an evaluation in that it continues to deny the client's original application while directing the client to the appropriate bureaucratic channel. Or it may be more parsimonious to say that the caseworker's solution is constrained by the institutional evaluation. The point here is that it is too simplistic to gloss the caseworker as merely applying institutional criteria to evaluate the client's case. The caseworker is responding to the sometime competing demands of the client's lifeworld, and following institutional criteria (Mishler, 1984).

Recurring Problems and Evaluations

Towards the end of the interview the client metacommunicates, "We're going into a vicious cycle again and I'm getting tired of it" (line 40). One of the most striking discourse features of this interview is the recurring statement of problems by the client and proposed solutions by the caseworker without any agreement between them. This recurrence of problems and solutions could be identified as a "pattern" and written as a redundancy rule from a systems theory perspective. But our concern here is to see how these moves are produced and accomplished by the participants to achieve their respective discourse strategies.

The recurrence or repetition of the discourse is accomplished by the client's challenge of the caseworker's evaluation. This suggests a third part to the basic structure of the welfare interview—the client's acceptance, or rejection and challenge of the caseworker's evaluation. The client cannot simply reject the caseworker's evaluation. Rather, the client's challenge is used in the attempt to recycle the basic evaluation sequence (Goffman, 1971; Morris, 1985). This is accomplished by making the problems relevant such that the caseworker's evaluation and solution do not alleviate them.

In recycling the sequence, the participants, of course, do not return to the beginning of the process. Rather, given the client's discourse strategy of presenting problems-as-obstacles, the client attempts to implicate a positive evaluation (i.e., the necessity of receiving assistance). But the caseworker's use of the maxim—follow institutional procedures—allows her to channel the client's problems and adhere to her original evaluation.

The problem of waiting.   Here we will examine the use of the recurring problem of waiting. The problems with waiting are cited on four occassions by the client (lines 16, 32, 42, and 48). How is the problem of waiting used as a move in a discourse strategy, and what does it tell us about the language game? The problem of waiting first appears in the following fragment.

(2) FRAGMENT (lines 15–16)
    15 CASEWORKER: She'll arrange a fair hearing
                                    [
    16 CLIENT: And in the meantime what they gonna do if they stay here, starve to death? (.) He's in the hospital, she's sick, she's got diabetes, she's got arthritis, she's got heart trouble (.) What is she supposed to do while waiting for a fair hearing? (.) Since November I've been walking around, running around with this woman.

Having to wait is displayed as a problem for the client due to her immediate needs and poor health. Not only is waiting a problem, but it is also used as grounds for challenging the caseworker's solution. The problem of waiting constitutes part of the client's discourse strategy—it challenges the prior solution, thereby attempting to recycle the evaluation process to implicate the necessity for receiving welfare assistance.

The problem of waiting appears on a second occasion as a response to the caseworker's solution "to apply for a fair hearing."

(3) FRAGMENT (lines 41–43)
    41 CASEWORKER: Well as I said before you have to apply for a fair hearing.
    42 CLIENT: Oh and how long is a fair hearing going to take? And what's she going to do in the meanwhile while she's waiting for a fair hearing? (.) She's been coming here since November.
    43 CASEWORKER: It's her responsibility to try to get

The caseworker's solution (line 41) again draws on the maxim, follow institutional procedures. This solution is presented as a directive: "you have to apply for a fair hearing." In contrast, this solution was initially proposed as an option (lines 13–15): "I can suggest that you talk to the application supervisor and if you feel." The caseworker's solution here is shorter and more direct which is characteristic of repeated utterances. The caseworker marks the utterance as repeated by the preface "Well as I said before."

The client again responds (line 42) by challenging the caseworker's solution. The client's initial question, "Oh and how long is a fair hearing going to take?", is not presented as a question-to-be-answered, but rather to implicate the problem with the solution. As such, it works as a sarcastic response. Note that the caseworker does not answer this question (though, in a different sequential environment, it would make a sensible query). The client makes the problems-as-obstacles explicit immediately after her sarcastic question. In formulating the problem (line 42), she uses similar devices to those she used at line 16, "what's she going to do in the meanwhile while waiting for a fair hearing" and "since November." Using these problems for a second time displays that the client does not feel that they were satisfactorily answered by the caseworker. The client's discourse strategy turns on the assumption that problems that cannot be solved by the client or by the caseworker's proposals demand a solution from welfare.

The problem of waiting appears for a third time in the following fragment:

(4) FRAGMENT (line 48–50)
   48 CLIENT: You told me to waiting for a fair hearing—what's she going to do in the meantime?
   49 CASEWORKER: Well you have to ask the applications supervisor to re-entertain the application.
   50 CLIENT: What do you think I'm here for now. Why am I talking to you for this?

In the first two instances the problem of waiting is used as a response to the caseworker's solution to see the applications supervisor and arrange a fair hearing. Here (line 48) the client formulates the caseworker's prior solution, "You told me to wait for a fair hearing," and the client's corresponding problem with that solution, "what's she going to do in the meantime?" This formulation of the problem displays that the client feels that the caseworker has not solved the problem of waiting. It also indicates the key assumption of her discourse strategy—that problematic circumstances which cannot be readily solved require welfare assistance.

The caseworker avoids answering this problem and refers the client to the applications supervisor (line 49). The caseworker's response displays that she does not accept the client's underlying assumption. Instead, the caseworker directs the client in how to "re-entertain the application."

This answer is clearly not what the client was asking about, as seen by the client's response of asking what the interview is about (line 50) and marked by her shouting (lines 51–52). The participants not only have diverging ends and discourse strategies, but also do not appear to agree on the very nature of what the interview is about. This exchange indicates to the client that she has been talking to the wrong caseworker.

   Responsibility.   The ascription of responsibility occurs throughout the interview. Initially, it will be examined as a response to the problems with waiting.

(5) FRAGMENT (lines 17–21)
    17 CASEWORKER: You know you're making it sound like it's my fault.
    18 CLIENT: It's not my fault either—it's not his fault, he's in the hospital—it's not her fault, she's sick. Whose fault is it?
    19 CASEWORKER: I'm telling you what they're telling me.
    20 CLIENT: Who is responsible for her (.) if her husband is sick, he's in the hospital, and she's
                [
    21 CASEWORKER: He's still on disability payments.

The caseworker responds (line 17) to the client's problem of waiting (fragment 2, line 16) with what we may call a denial of personal intent. The implicit contrast here is between her personal responsibility and the constraints she is under as a caseworker. At line 19 the caseworker, by citing membership category (Sacks, 1972), denies that her decision is based on her personal feelings toward the client; it results from job-related responsibilities. The caseworker's justification displays that she takes the client's prior turn as a blame or ascription of fault. Her response is to deny personal accountability and attribute it to her superiors in the welfare system.

The client responds to the caseworker's denial of fault by making relevant the issue of "fault" in a broader sense (line 18). The client accomplishes this by drawing on the conversational resources (Harré, 1977) of the prior two turns. The client uses the caseworker's term, *fault*, to deny fault for herself as well as for her father and mother. Also, the client uses a listing device at line 16 (e.g., a listing of ailments) to formulate a list of denials of fault at line 18. The client concludes by asking "Whose fault is it?" given the above denials of fault. In response (line 19), the caseworker draws upon her institutional constraints. The client (line 20) moves from the denials of fault to the related notion of responsibility, "Who is responsible for her." This move is crucial for the production of the client's discourse strategy—it is based on the assumption that, if no one is responsible for these problems, the only available option is welfare assistance.

The ascription of responsibility is used by both caseworker and client throughout the interview. Initially the caseworker labeled the client's husband as "legally responsible" (line 1). The client later raised the question, "Who is responsible for her" (line 20) given that it was not her "fault" for her circumstances. The client raises the question again, orienting it to the problem of waiting for a decision to be made:

(6) FRAGMENT (lines 31–33)
    31 CASEWORKER: Well Social Security is evaluating her application—that's a different thing
                [
    32 CLIENT: Okay, but meanwhile who's responsible for her?
    33 CASEWORKER: Her husband.

The client's raising the question of responsibility constitutes a version of her discourse strategy: the client is not responsible for her circumstances (line 18) and her husband "isn't meeting his responsibilities" (line 24), so, by implication, the state has to be responsible for her. The caseworker, however, does not accept this implication and contradicts the client's claim by ascribing responsibility to the husband (line 33). The caseworker accomplishes this ascription of responsibility by again drawing on the maxim, follow institutional procedures.

This sequence (fragment 6) reflects the conflicting discourse strategies. As already mentioned, the client's strategy is to show that no one is responsible for her problematic circumstances, so, by implication, the welfare agency must be responsible. On the other hand, the caseworker subsumes the case under the maxim, follow institutional procedures, so the courts can obligate the husband to meet his responsibilities. The caseworker uses the ascription of responsibility throughout the interview as part of her discourse strategy. For instance, following the client's problem of waiting, the caseworker ascribes responsibility to the client to arrange a hearing (lines 41–43). So, in labeling the husband as "legally responsible" (lines 1 and 16) and the client as responsible for arranging a fair hearing (lines 43 and 49), the caseworker is able to invoke institutional procedures and thereby disavow the power to act on the case.

The ascription of responsibility seems to be an especially strong label for participants due to its implications for action. A marked asymmetry in the participants' respective uses of *responsibility* is that the caseworker *directly ascribes responsibility* to the husband and the client, while the client *only raises it as a question with the implied answer that the state is responsible*. In addition, the caseworker can draw upon case files and upon her knowledge of institutional procedures to justify her ascriptions of responsibility. The client, in contrast, can only make an argument based on personal need and problematic circumstances. Here we see an asymmetry of specialized, bureaucratic knowledge and how it affects the linguistic options in the production of moves and discourse strategies.

CONCLUSION

Two caveats are in order here. First of all, differences based on race are not used in the above analysis. The rationale for this is that we wanted to focus on the talk itself and bracket categories of persons. The relevance of being white or black should be marked or displayed in their ways of speaking, not as an a priori category (Heritage, 1986). By way of preliminary analysis, there is some indication for marked differences by race consistent with Kochman's work on diverging communication styles between middle-class white culture and inner-city black culture (Kochman, 1981, pp. 12–15). For instance, the white caseworker appears to "talk down" to the client in repeating institutional procedures and ascribing responsibility (Erickson, 1979), and the black client displays a more expressive communicative style in showing disagreement (Kochman, 1981).

The issue of generalizability needs to be raised, given that only a single interview was examined (Jackson, 1986). This reflects the practical problems of gaining access to tape recordings which are usually confidential. While it goes without saying that more research is needed, it is important to note that the above kind of analysis focuses on a universe of moves as accomplished through language use rather than on a universe of person-attributes. The assumption here is that these discourse structures and interactional sequences are not merely features of this single case but are available as linguistic options in other welfare interviews. The advantage of doing a "close reading" of the text is that it reveals aspects of interaction and discourse organization which may not be readily visible when working with traditional methods.

It might be argued that the language game of a welfare interview reflects contemporary culture. One of the most noticeable features of the discourse of this interview is the advocacy of the client in challenging the caseworker's decision. The client is unwilling to accept the authority of caseworker as the final word. Given the bureaucratization of welfare agencies (which is indicative of the growing segmentation of everyday life), the caseworker cannot simply give aid to the applicant because she is needy; rather, she must quality for assistance according to standardized criteria. The language game of the welfare interview is based on a form of life of individual entitlements for the poor, rather than on its historical roots in charity. Thus, the client's discourse strategy can be drawn from a "vocabulary of motives" (Mills, 1940) which uses problems, not to evoke charity, but to challenge the justification of the caseworker's decision.

APPENDIX

01 CASEWORKER: He's legally responsible to take care of the children.
02 CLIENT: We know that.
03 CASEWORKER: And her as long as she's married.
                           [   ]   [
04 CLIENT: Yes   Yes (   )
05 CASEWORKER: But she went to court=
06 CLIENT: =He didn't show up
07 CASEWORKER: It has to be in the court's hands as long as he's getting income and
    then he's not using it while he's in the hospital. It's for the children (.)
    that's the way
          [
08 CLIENT: What's the alternatives? What, is she gonna take checks from him
if he doesn't want to give them to her? (.) What's the alternative? She's been to court,
    yesterday, yesterday.
09 CASEWORKER: Now wait a minute, what'd the court say?
10 CLIENT: He didn't show up, they sent out a warrant for him.
11 CASEWORKER: Well he'll show up.
12 CLIENT: But what do you want her to do if he doesn't show up? And he's got the
    checks and he won't give them to her.

13 CASEWORKER: The only thing that I can suggest is that you talk to the application supervisor and if you feel that you've been treated unfairly

[

14 CLIENT: Of course we feel—why do you think we're back here now?

15 CASEWORKER: She'll arrange a fair hearing

[

16 CLIENT: And in the meantime what they gonna do if they stay here, starve to death? (.) He's in the hospital, she's sick, she's got diabetes, she's got arthritis, she's got heart trouble (.) What is she supposed to do while waiting for a fair hearing? (.) Since November I've been walking around, running around with this woman.

17 CASEWORKER: You know you're making it sound like it's my fault.

18 CLIENT: It's not my fault either—it's not his fault, he's in the hospital—it's not her fault, she's sick. Whose fault is it?

19 CASEWORKER: I'm telling you what they're telling me.

20 CLIENT: Who is responsible for her (.) if her husband is sick, he's in the hospital and she's

[

21 CASEWORKER: He's still on disability payments.

22 CLIENT: Can she take the checks from him?

23 CASEWORKER: He's legally responsible for her support.

24 CLIENT: That's why she's taking him to court because he isn't meeting his responsibilities.

25 CASEWORKER: It's in the hands of the courts

[

26 CLIENT: The court sent her here. I have a letter from the court telling her to come here. (Client hands the letter to the caseworker and caseworker reads the letter).

27 CASEWORKER: Now this was before the case was rejected. The case was rejected on the twenty-fourth and this was given to her

[

28 CLIENT: The same day I came here—when you rejected her she had this letter.

29 APPLICANT: They told me to go here, Social Security, that's where I went.

30 CLIENT: She went to Social Security, they sent her back here. They gonna take care of her?

31 CASEWORKER: Well Social Security is evaluating her application—that's a different thing

[

32 CLIENT: Okay, but meanwhile who's responsible for her?

33 CASEWORKER: Her husband.

34 CLIENT: He's in the hospital as you very well know.

35 CASEWORKER: Well I understand he's in the hospital

[

36 CLIENT: Now what is she supposed to do?

37 CASEWORKER: The checks are coming
               [
38 CLIENT: Hold onto the checks that don't belong to her? They belong to him.
39 CASEWORKER: He has a responsibility
               [
40 CLIENT: He don't want to give them to her. We're going into a vicious cycle again and I'm getting tired of it.
41 CASEWORKER: Well as I said before you have to apply for a fair hearing.
42 CLIENT: Oh and how long is a fair hearing going to take? And what's she going to do in the meanwhile while she's waiting for a fair hearing? (.) She's been coming here since November.
43 CASEWORKER: It's her responsibility to try to get
               [
44 CLIENT: What do you think she's trying to do? (.) Why do you think she's going to court? (.) You're sending me around in a vicious cycle—I'm trying to tell you her hands are tied.
45 CASEWORKER: I'm not sending you
               [
46 CLIENT: He's sick, she is sick—who is going to take care of her?
47 CASEWORKER: I'm not sending you anywhere.
48 CLIENT: You told me to wait for a fair hearing—what's she going to do in the meanwhile?
49 CASEWORKER: Well you have to ask the application's supervisor to re-entertain the application.
50 CLIENT: What do you think I'm here for now. Why am I talking to you now for this?
51 CASEWORKER: You don't need to shout.
52 CLIENT: Well I'm gonna do some more shouting if you don't stop this. Ever since November (.) You talk about shouting—I've been trying to take care of this woman—what do you want from me? (.) Sending us around to all these places and sending us around in circles.
53 APPLICANT: Where are you supposed to go?
54 CLIENT: That's what I want to know, she said go to court—she went to court. Go to Social Security—they sent her back here (.) They're up there sitting on their behinds upstairs, that's why that can't do nothin' for nobody (.) Have you sit here all damn day—sending you all around to the courts and the courts sending you here.

REFERENCES

Buckholdt, D., & Gubrium, J. F. (1983). Practicing accountability in human service institutions. *Urban Life, 12,* 249–268.

Buttny, R. (1985). Accounts as a reconstruction of an event's context. *Communication Monographs, 52,* 57–77.

Erickson, F. (1979). Talking down: Some cultural sources of miscommunication in intercultural interviews. In A. Wolgang (Ed.), *Nonverbal behavior: Applications and cultural implications* (pp. 99–126). New York: Academic Press.

Erickson, F., & Schultz, J. J. (1982). *The counselor as gatekeeper: Social and cultural organization of communication in counselling inteviews.* New York: Academic Press.

Geist, P., & Chandler, T. (1984). Account analysis of group decision-making. *Communication Monographs, 51*, 67–78.

Goffman, E. (1971). *Relations in public.* New York: Harper & Row.

Goffman, E. (1976). Replies and responses. *Language in Society, 5*, 257–313.

Gumperz, J. J., & Cook-Gumperz, J. (1982). Introduction: Language and the communication of social identity. In J. J. Gumperz (Ed.), *Language and social identity* (pp. 1–21). New York: Cambridge University Press.

Harré, R. (1977). The ethnogenic approach: Theory and pactice. In L. Berowitz (Ed.), *Advances in experimental social psychology* (Vol. 10, pp. 284–313). New York: Academic Press.

Heritage, J. (1986). Presentation at the International Communication Association Convention, Chicago.

Hymes, D. (1972). Models of the interaction of language and social life. In J. J. Gumperz & D. Hymes (Eds.), *Directions in Sociolinguistics: The ethnography of communication* (pp. 35–71). New York: Holt, Rinehardt & Winston.

Jackson, S. (1986). Building a case for claims about discoruse structure. In D. G. Ellis & W. A. Donahue (Eds.), *Contemporary issues in language and discourse structure* (pp. 129–148). Hillsdale, NJ: Erlbaum.

Jupp, T. C., Roberts, C., & Cook-Gumperz, J. (1982). Language and disadvantage: The hidden process. In J. J. Gumperz (Ed.), *Language and social identity* (pp. 232–256). New York: University of Cambridge Press.

Kochman, T. (1981). *Black and white styles in conflict.* Chicago, IL: University of Chicago Press.

Kress, G. & Fowler, R. (1979). Interviews. In R. Fowler, R. Hodge, G. Kress, & T. Trew (Eds.), *Language and social control* (pp. 63–80). Boston, MA: Routledge & Kegan Paul.

Mills, C. W. (1940). Situated actions and vocabularies of motives. *American Sociological Review, 5*, 904–913.

Mishler, E. G. (1984). *The discourse of medicine: Dialectics of medical interviews.* Norwood, NJ: Ablex Publishing Corp.

Morris, G. H. (1985). The remedial episode as a negotiation of rules. In R. L. Street & J. N. Cappella (Eds.), *Sequence and pattern in communicative behavior* (pp. 70–84). Baltimore, MD: Edward Arnold.

Owen, M. (1981). Conversational units and the use of 'well . . .' In P. Werth (Ed.), *Conversation and discourse: Structure and interpretation* (pp. 99–116). New York: St. Martin's Press.

Ragan, S. L. (1983). Alignment and conversational coherence. In R. T. Craig & K. Tracy (Eds.), *Conversational coherence: Form, structure, and strategy* (pp. 157–173). Beverley Hills, CA: Sage.

Rees, S. (1975). How misunderstanding occurs. In R. Bailey & M. Brake (Eds.), *Radical social work* (pp. 62–75). New York: Pantheon Books.

Sacks, H. (1972). On the analyzability of stories by children. In J. J. Gumperz & D. Hymes (Eds.), *Directions in sociolinguistics: The ethnography of communication* (pp. 325–345). New York: Holt, Rinehart & Winston.

Tompkins, P. K., & Cheney, G. (1983). Account analysis of organizations: Decision making and identification. In L. L. Putnam & M. E. Pacanowsky (Eds.), *Communication and organizations: An interpretive approach* (pp. 123–146). Beverley Hills, CA: Sage.

Weed, F. J. (1979). Bureaucratization as reform: The case of the public welfare movement. *The Social Science Journal, 16*, 79–89.

Wittgenstein, L. (1953). *Philosophical investigations* (3rd ed.). (Trans. by G.E.M. Anscombe). New York: Macmillan.

Zimmerman, D. H. (1970). The practicalities of rule use. In J. D. Douglas (Ed.), *Understanding everyday life* (pp. 221–238). Chicago, IL: Aldine.

Zimmerman, D. H. (1974). Fact as a practical accomplishment. In R. Turner (Ed.), *Ethnomethodology* (pp. 128–143). Baltimore, MD: Penguin.

PART II

SOCIOLINGUISTICS

7

Japanese Oral Narrative as an Interactional Event

LAURA MILLER

University of California, Los Angeles

In the past, researchers have tended to treat narratives as autonomous units that spring out of a teller's head as a linear sequence of sentences. In such a conception, narratives are viewed as preplanned wholes that can be analyzed as having internal structure and intent. In addition, some researchers have elicited the narratives they analyze from environments other than the natural, normal occasions of their telling.[1] These narratives are therefore analyzed as monologues performed apart from their naturally occurring context.

By abstracting stories and narratives from the settings in which they are told, the analyst is disregarding the fact that narratives are, first of all, social activities. Darnell (1974) criticizes folklorists for eliciting oral narratives in isolation from their natural social settings. In her analysis of Cree narratives, she notes that "the feedback between audience and performer may be crucial to the organization of a performance" (1974, p. 315). Darnell indicates that the appropriate behavior and responses of the audience in fact determines whether or not the narrative is even told. Tedlock (1983, p. 286) describes the audience response of *eeso* ("Yes indeed") which recipients of Zuni narratives are expected to produce. He finds that in an artificial setting, such as a recording session, recipients fail to provide these responses. Thus, the participation of an audience is an important feature of Zuni narrative that will not be evident unless one analyzes narratives in their social context.

Labov (1981) notes that personal narrative contain structured features such as orientation, evaluation, abstracts, and reportability. His analysis of the "parts" of a narrative is convincing, yet it underplays the role of the story's recipients in influencing the continuation, elaboration, or truncating of the story. Except for a "listener evaluation" at the *conclusion* of a narrative, listeners are not viewed as affecting the actual telling of a narrative. We are told that listener responses were present during the course of the telling for some narratives (1981, p. 227), but that they exist only as validation or questioning of

---

[1] Labov (1981) has made a good case for claiming that elicited data are nevertheless worthy of sociolinguistic analysis because they may still contain the grammatical, phonological, and other features found in natural speech.

the "reportability" of a narrative. Listener responses are not evaluated as having an important role in the ongoing production of a narrative.

Conversation analysts also have an interest in narratives and have taken care, in the past, to situate the telling of stories and jokes in their conversational context (Jefferson, 1978; Sacks, 1974). In addition, they have claimed that narratives or stories are sequentially organized. Sacks (1974) believes that stories are composed of three types of sequences which he terms *prefaces, the telling,* and *the response sequence.* A story is thought to be told from start to finish, after it has been "prefaced," without any talk or interruptions by the recipients. The actual telling of a story, in fact, is characterized as being "one turn at talk." For example, Jefferson describes storytelling as comprised of a preface, a next turn where recipient shows willingness to hear the story, and a "next turn in which teller produces the story" (Jefferson, 1978, p. 245). This is followed by a turn in which the recipient will give an assessment of the story. In this example, "M" does a preface in Line 1, and "S" in Line 3 gives consent to "M" to do the telling:

```
 1  M:  I wen' out one night with my friend Do:n?
 2      (0.2)
 3  S:  Yeah
 4  M:  A:nd uh (0.4) He wz almost arrested d'et a ba:r becuz he
 5      didn't have his eye dee:?
 6      (0.2)
 7  M:  There's a-friend of ours had it 'n his pocket? hhh then
 8      after that he gits inna car en 'e wz so furious that 'e
 9      smashed induhthe back of another car
10  (?) Tch
```

(SN-4:18, from Schegloff, 1984)

We notice that "M" proceeds to tell the story to the end without further comment from the recipient, thus supporting the conversational analysts' description of the structure of storytelling in conversation. Yet such an analysis of conversational and narrative structure, although intended to be universal and to hold for all human groups, is based only on English materials and may not be entirely relevant for other languages.

According to conversation analysts, recipients who do talk during the "telling" turn are interpreted as intruding on this turn. (The only exception is when a listener interrupts due to nonhearing or misunderstanding, to "initiate repair.") In fact, the function of the preface is supposed to be that of insuring that the recipient will not attempt to take the floor and will let the story proceed to its end.[2] A similar structure for English stories is also described by Polanyi

---

[2]Both Labov (1981) and the conversation analysts (Jefferson, 1978; Sacks, 1974; Schegloff, 1984) see the necessity for speakers to introduce or mark the beginning of narratives in order to get permission for an extended turn at talk or to warn the recipient that a story is about to unfold. For Labov, speakers do this by using an "abstract," and for the conversational analysts speakers use a "preface."

(1985). Japanese narrative, however, is not so amenable to clear-cut segmentation into preface, telling, and response. The "telling" is not one extended turn at talk, but is composed of an exchange of turns by both teller and recipient.

To determine what possible role the recipient of a narrative has on its structure and production, it is best to collect examples of narratives that are told in social interaction. The example below is transcribed from an audiotape of a radio program aired in Osaka, Japan. This program has a daily segment in which the listening audience is invited to call in with personal narratives recounting experiences reflecting a daily "theme" or topic. The topic selected for this particular program was: "It's raining today. Is there some incident connected to methods you used to compensate for not having an umbrella?" The participants are a female radio announcer (F), a male radio announcer (T), a male caller (A), and the radio station audience.[3]

1 F: Kyoo-kyoo wa kasa mo nakattemo mo nanika hoohoo jiken arimashita (As for today—do you have some incident where even though you didn't have an umbrella you somehow managed?)

2 A: hai
       (Yes)

3 T: donna koto
       (What sort of thing?)

4 A: Anoo ne
       (so, well . .)

5 T: un
       (Uh huh)

6 A: e-to kyoo chotto tomodachi to (doko ka//ikichatta)//Sannomiya ni =
       (Um I (went somewhere) in Sannomiya for a bit with my friend today)
                                          [   ]
7 T: //un un   // un
                                          (Uh huh, uh huh)

8 A: hondara ne//   // anoo::tomodachi anoo densha de kaeyotte
       (And so, this friend (and I) returned home um on the train)
                  [ ]
9 T: //um//
                  (uh huh)

10 T: densha de kaeyotte un un
        (returned home on the train uh huh)

11 A: um eki kara kaeyottara *ne* tomodachi wa saki kasa motte kaetteshimatta
        (An from the station my friend returned first (he) took
        the umbrella and went off home)

12 T: Iya kimi kasa nai yanka
        (Oh so you didn't have an umbrella)

13 A: soo yan ne
        (That's right)

---

[3]This conversation was in the Osaka dialect. Transcription is orthographic rather than phonetic, presented in a modified Hepburn romanization system. Overlapping speech is indicated with slashes and brackets, and speech that has a problematic hearing is enclosed in parentheses.

16 T: um
        (Uh huh)
14 A: harazutteru yo//(sore nanka //(na)=
        (I was brushing (water) off (right)
                    [   ]
15 T: // un //   = un
                    (Uh huh)   (uh huh)
16 A: hondara ne// a // n zutto matte itte
        (So then, I was waiting the whole time . .)
                    [ ]
17 T: //un//
                    (uh huh)
18 A: itsu kaette kuru ka=
        (wondering when to go home)
19 T: =un un un
        (Uh huh, uh huh)
20 A: Hondara ne anoo chuugaku no toki ni ne=
        (So then from my old Jr. High School days)
21 T: =un
        (Uh huh)
22 A: tomodachi na onnanoko ga kitte ne
        (a girl who was a friend came by . .)
23 T: ya:h (0.1) honde
24 A: honde ne
        (And then)
25   (0.2)
26 A: ne
        (you know)
27   (0.1)
28 T: kimi (kappa de atta mon na) un
        (You had a raincoat, right?))
29 A: de nain desu ne huh anoo ne// so//reno tomodachi ne irete morata kaeta
        (I didn't have one . . so, well this girl let me go inside
        (the umbrella) and we went home)
                                    [   ]
30 T: //un//
                                    (Uh huh)
31 T: Iya (0.1) kimi wa chuugaku no toki no onnanoko ni// i//rete motte kaeta
        (Wow-you were taken under by a girl from Jr. High School days!)
                                                    [   ]
32 A: //hai hai//
                                                    (yes yes)

It is evident that the hearer of "A" 's narrative is not a silent, passive recipient. In fact, the announcer "T" actively listend to "A" 's story by providing listener's response, called *aizuchi*.

Aizuchi is considered an aspect of appropriate conversational behavior, and those who are considered good company are those who are good at "giving *aizuchi.*" There is a tacit belief among Japanese that conversation is an interactional achievement by speakers and listeners. It has been noted that "Japanese feel uneasy when the listener remains silent without giving *aizuchi*" (Mizutani & Mizutani, 1977, p. 15). These feelings about the appropriate way to behave during a conversation extend to behavior during the delivery of a personal narrative. Just as a listener in conversation participates by providing *aizuchi*, a recipient of a narrative likewise is expected to give *aizuchi*.

In the example above, the listener occasionally repeats parts of the narrator's talk (Line 10, Line 31), or asks questions of the narrator during the course of the story (Line 12, Line 25). From the start of the narrative, the recipient contributes talk which is not interpreted by the teller as "overlapped" speech and resolved as such. Neither are "T" 's *aizùchi* simply serving as "continuer tokens" (Schegloff, 1981) because they do not always occur at possible turn transition relevance places in "A" 's narrative in the same way that English "uh huh" 's are said to. For example, "T" 's *aizuchi* in Line 9, Line 17, Line 5, and Line 30 are not at transition relevance places, because they follow expressions such as *hondara ne*, "so then. ." (Line 8, Line 16), and *ano ne*, "So, well . ." (Line 4, Line 29).

Research on *aizuchi* (Miller, 1983) suggests that there is a correlation between the presence of the sentence particle *ne* in a speaker's talk and a listener's giving *aizuchi*. Sentence particles are monosyllabic morphemes that follow a pause group or clause. Their use is dependent on factors such as sex, dialect, social status, and speech situation. They also function as "affect markers" that indicate emotive states. Previous studies claim that the sentence particle *ne* is often used to elicit listener's response (Jolly, 1971; Miller, 1983; Ueno, 1971). During the delivery of a personal narrative, speakers also use the sentence particles *ne* to elicit *aizuchi*. The importance of a recipient's giving proper *aizuchi* can be detected in the Japanese example above. In Line 24, "A" uses the sentence particle *ne*, and, when the expected *aizuchi* is not forthcoming (note the pause of 0.2), he repeats the *ne* again (Line 26). When "T" still offers no *aizuchi*, there is another pause rather than the continuation of the narrative (Line 27). In this manner we can observe that the production of "A" 's narrative is not an autonomous stream of uninterrupted preconceived talk, but is an interactional production dependent on recipient response. The narrative, in fact, is temporarily halted because the recipient does not give *aizuchi*.

In his analysis of Japanese narratives, Hinds (1976) contrasts certain aspects with English narratives. For example, he states that both Japanese and English narratives can have "acknowledgements" by recipients, but that these are not obligatory. He further states that Japanese speakers invite or solicit "acknowledgements" with pausing, nodding, rising intonation or the use of sentence particles. Most likely, what Hinds means by "acknowledgements" is *aizuchi*. His perceptive discussion of Japanese narrative closely attends to the structure of the narrator's talk. However, Hinds nevertheless treats discourse and narrative as autonomously structured units, and listener response and behavior as merely tokens of appreciation or understanding of the narrative rather than as themselves elements of the narrative's structure. Hinds has been criticized elsewhere (Inoue, 1978) for this conception of discourse as a linear sequence of discrete sentences, and it is not surprising, therefore, that he also thinks of narrative in this way.

The structure of Japanese narrative described here is somewhat different from that portrayed by other researchers for English. This perceived difference, however, may not be entirely due to a difference in listening styles between the two groups. There has been a general neglect of listener's response in the study of language and conversation. Transcripts regularly delete or overlook these listener's responses in an effort to describe "real" talk. For example, Walcott (1977) provides an analysis of English narrative yet does not bother to transcribe any listener response at all.

Until more attention is given to the role of the listener in both conversation and narrative, it is best not to characterize the Japanese pattern as unique. This chapter suggests that researchers need to account for social features, such as the obligations of listeners as a part of the structure of narratives. In Japanese, the speaker's use of the sentence particle ne indicates that listener's response is an important element in the unfolding of a narrative. This indicates that a narrative is not simply an object formed in the mind or imagination of a teller, but is an interactional product which has a dialogical structure just like other forms of talk.

REFERENCES

Darnell, R. (1974). Correlates of Cree narrative performance. In R. Bauman & J. Sherzer (Eds.), *Explorations in the ethnography of speaking* (pp. 315–336). Cambridge, England: Cambridge University Press.

Hinds, J. (1976). A taxonomy of Japanese discourse types. *Linguistics, 184*, 45–54.

Inoue, K. (1978). Review of *Aspects of Japanese discourse structure*, by John Hinds. *Journal of the Association of Teachers of Japanese, 14*, 226–232.

Jolly, Y. S. (1971). *A taxonomic study of Japanese sentence particles.* Ph.D. dissertation, University of Texas at Austin.

Jefferson, G. (1978). Sequential aspects of storytelling in conversation. In J. Schenkein (Ed.), *Studies in the organization of conversational interaction* (pp. 219–248). New York: Academic Press.

Labov, W. (1981). Speech actions and reactions in personal narratives. In D. Tannen (Ed.), *Analyzing discourse: Text and talk* (pp. 219–247). Washington DC: Georgetown University Press.

Miller, L. (1983). *Aizuchi: Japanese listening behavior.* M.A. thesis, University of California, Los Angeles.

Mizutani, N., & Mizutani, O. (1977). *Nihongo notes 1: Speaking and living in Japan.* Tokyo: The Japan Times, Ltd.

Polanyi, L. (1985). Conversational storytelling. In Van Dijk (Ed.), *Handbook of discourse analysis 3: Discourse and dialogue* (pp. 183–201). London: Academic Press.

Sacks, H. (1974). An analysis of the course of a joke's telling in conversation. In R. Bauman & J. Sherzer (Eds.), *Explorations in the ethnography of speaking* (pp. 337–353). Cambridge, England: Cambridge University Press.

Schegloff, E. (1981). Discourse as an interactional event: Some uses of "uh huh" and other things that come between sentences. In D. Tannen (Ed.), *Analyzing discourse: Text and talk* (pp. 71–93). Washington DC: Georgetown University Press.

Schegloff, E. (1984). Lecture Notes: Seminar on Conversational Structures. University of California, Los Angeles.

Tedlock, D. (1983). *The spoken word and the work of interpretation.* Philadelphia: University of Pennsylvania Press.

Ueno, T. Y. (1971). *A Study of Japanese modality: A performative analysis of sentence particles.* Ph.D. dissertation, University of Michigan, Ann Arbor.

Walcutt, J. (1977). The typology of narrative boundedness. In E.O. Keenan & T. Bennett (Eds.), *Discourse across time and space* (pp. 51–68). Southern California Occasional Papers 5. Los Angeles: University of Southern California.

8

Speaking as Reflected in Turkish Proverbs*

ASLI GÖKHAN
University of Pittsburgh

INTRODUCTION

A systematic ethnography of different genres of folklore can give a penetrating picture of a people's way of life. This chapter presents an analysis of how this communicative role is manifested in the Turkish culture, focusing on how speaking is reflected in proverbs.

In any culture, the study of proverbs involves the realization of a paradox. This form of speech is situational and specific in its use, yet it must be general, almost universal, in its applicability. Taylor (1982, p.3) refers to proverbs as "the wisdom of many and the wit of one."

Proverbs also require metaphoric thinking. Typically, proverbs cannot be interpreted literally. This artistic, traditional, and short form of metaphorical reasoning is used in an interactional context. Proverbs constitute the most complex genre in folklore since they are highly sensitive to social context. They are simple, yet subtle and complex. One must master more and more complex rules to be able to use and interpret proverbs (Seitel, 1981).

Seitel (1974) suggests that metaphors limited to speech can be analyzed because of similarities attributed to the common origins between language and other aspects of culture. Folklore, like language itself, is considered a mirror of culture, though there is disagreement on the extent to which it accurately reflects society (Bascom, 1965). Fischer and Yoshida (1981) point out that, for many societies, studying the traditional beliefs and values about speech codified in proverbs can make a considerable start on ethnography of speaking.

Seitel (1981, p.124) proposes an approach, applying directly to proverb study to "delineate the culturally-shared system which enables a person to use proverbs in socially acceptable manners" instead of "viewing proverbs as an instance of patterned speech to be fit into a system designed to handle a much broader range of data." With such an approach, cultural context is analyzed to explicate the meaning of proverbs. This distinguishes proverb analysis from a literal translation of proverbs. The meaning becomes clear only when the social

*The author gratefully acknowledges the advice of Donal Carbaugh and John M. Roberts on this project.

situation—the reason for its use, its significance in speech and its effect—is analyzed (Firth, 1926).

The proverbs about speaking examined here were gathered from four sources in Turkish. Their prominence was established through interviews with 16 native Turks. Twenty-two commonly used proverbs were selected from the interviews for analysis (see Appendix).

The proverbs can be categorized along a number of dimensions. One distinction is that of "quantity and quality." Proverbs of "quantity" relate *how much* should be said; proverbs of "quality" relate mostly to the *appropriateness* of a topic, particularly in terms of discretion issues.

Turkish proverbs can also be categorized with respect to the familiarity between proverb-bearer and receiver. A high level of familiarity would enable the use of certain proverbs that ordinarily would be inappropriate in the company of mere acquaintances. Similarly, social status plays an important role in invoking proverbs. Whether the proverb-receiver is a superior, equal, or subordinate will affect the proverb invoked. Rarely are proverbs directed toward superiors.

Proverbs can also be categorized in terms of whether they give advice or are gossip. Underlying "advice proverbs" are the morals or the ethics of the culture. As a result, they imply standards for appraising behavior in terms of the appropriate norms. Since they are "pugently, wittily and sententiously stated," they can be used to praise, criticize, and comment on the behavior of others (Bascom, 1965, p.295). By giving advice through proverbs, conformity to accepted patterns of behavior is ensured.

Especially in semiliterate societies (like Turkish), proverbs may assume many of the functions of formal education for children (Finnegan, 1981, pp.10–42). In Turkey's hierarchical society, where elders are greatly respected and the opinions of others are considered very important, this function becomes critical. This characteristic of the culture also affects the use of proverbs. Since a younger person is assumed to have less knowledge and experience, he or she is unlikely to give advice to an older person. Therefore, it is almost always the older person giving advice to a younger one or to an equal. When telling a child a proverb, an older person may also accompany the proverb with a story, or may explain the meaning of the proverb. Certain proverbs are deliberately not used with children.

In societies where public opinion is highly valued, gossip and criticism are used as social control. "A balance must be achieved between the permissibility of gossip as the safest outlet for aggressive impulses on the one hand, and the need for the responsibility in the use of gossip as a 'police' sanction on the other" (Fischer & Yoshida, 1984, p.34). Gossip proverbs also point out the broken social rules and identify acceptable norms. The importance of gossip in Turkish culture is best illustrated through a proverb: "What comes out of 32 teeth spreads through 32 neighborhoods." With the use of a proverb, a speaker may imply that he or she is not really gossiping, but stating what ancestors and elders have established as the wise and proper way of speaking.

ANALYSIS OF PROVERBS

Quantity
Most of the "quantity" proverbs seem to be used with children, usually serving as advice. However, when the proverbs relate to the "excessive use of words," they become gossip proverbs.

"Words are silver, silence is gold" is at the extreme end of the "quantity" scale, showing that speaking may be useful but keeping silent is more advantageous and valuable. This proverb offers a wide variety of situational uses, a characteristic not many proverbs have. When a child bothers others by talking too much, he or she is addressed by an elder with this proverb. Also, among equals, if one person has had trouble for saying something that should not have been said, the proverb may be invoked. It may also be used in reference to a third person who spike inappropriately. A person may criticize himself or herself in the same situation, adding the comment "I should have known better."

A proverb very similar in meaning and function is "talk little, listen much." At times, it may be used interchangeably with "words are silver, silence is gold." However, the latter can be used in a variety of contexts, whereas the former may be considered an insult if told to an equal. Even when this proverb is used as gossip, the speaker will start by saying: "What did our ancestors say? Talk little, listen much." In this way, the proverb is invoked without any embarrassment to the over-talkative one.

Another example illustrates the restricted use of proverbs: "Water is for children, the words are for the elders." To intrude upon an elder's speech or to express opinions contrary to that of the elders displays rudeness. Prior to exposure to Western culture, children were not even supposed to be present when the elders talked among themselves: at the dinner table a child was to be silent. The rules implied by this proverb are also true for all proverbs. Since they are the words of the fathers, they can only be used among adult equals or from adults to children. The reverse is a violation of social rules. Similarly, "an arrow that is sent cannot be called back" refers to the fact that words cannot be retracted once they are expressed. For emphasis, one may add "talk little, listen much."

A group of proverbs also state the consequences of talking too much. Proverbs that use metaphors are more likely to be gossip than advice. A person should hold his or her tongue because, just like "a nightingale (that) suffers from its tongue," he or she may get into trouble. However, as it is improper to tell a person directly to hold his or her tongue, this proverb would most likely be used in reference to a third person. Using it directly takes the form of advice. A similar proverb in both meaning and use is "one who speaks much is much mistaken." When addressed to a subordinate, this proverb takes the form of advice.

In "an empty barrel bangs louder," *louder* refers to both quantity and quality of talk. If this behavior leads to exaggeration, another proverb may be appropriately invoked: "abundance of property cannot be acquired but by illegal means, abundance of talk cannot be without lies." When a person's speech affects the people around him or her so much that they do not want to listen to that person anymore, this proverb would be appropriate. These two are strictly gossip proverbs. They would be very insulting if invoked directly to a speaker, saying, in effect, "you are stupid" or "you are lying."

Quality

The second category of proverbs distinguishes between good judgment and poor judgment in the selection of words, and sets the criteria for the quality of talk. How much is said is not as important as what is said. In this category, the primary function of proverbs is in gossip among adults.

The best judgment a person can use is to "first think, then speak." By frequently citing this proverb to a child, the adult is training the child in the use of discretion. Since it serves an educational function, this proverb is not used among equals. It is usually accompanied by an example of what would happen if one does not think before speaking. One has to think because words are very powerful particularly "sweet words" as in the proverb "sweet words bring a snake out of its hole." With children who cry and demand instead of asking, for example, a mother may say: "Instead of screaming, why don't you ask nicely; sweet words bring a snake out of its hole." Regarding a salesperson, one informant said, "I can't believe she was so rude. Doesn't she know that sweet words bring a snake out of its hole? She could have had me as a regular customer, but I won't go there anymore." In addition to being used for second or third persons, this proverb may be used in self-reference after accomplishing an important task by being polite.

If chosen properly, words can be used to one's advantage, and some proverbs point to the consequences when they are not: "some words take you to the mountain top, some words bring you down"; "some words close a deal, some words cost a life." While these two proverbs can be used interchangeably, the symbolism of death in the latter usually requires that it be used in more serious situations where damage results from inappropriate choice of words. Used among peers, both proverbs would refer to poor judgment of a third person. For example, one informant cited the second proverb in reference to a person injured in a fight started by personal insults. The use of the proverb here constituted sufficient comment; this made the gossip more discrete.

A similar proverb states that "the dog that doesn't know how to bark brings wolves to the flock," and yields two interpretations. First, a person may not

know "how to talk." In a classroom, a student who says something inappropriate may cause the whole class to take an unannounced test or have some kind of
punishment, a common situation in the strict Turkish educational system.
Peers would state the proverb in referring to the person who caused the
trouble. Second, a person may not know to speak up when appropriate; he or
she is like a dog that is supposed to bark when the wolves approach but causes
trouble instead by remaining silent. *This is the only Turkish proverb in the
sample that emphasizes the virtues of speaking.* However, one is required to
know the right time and place for it. It provides balance with proverbs praising
silence.

A number of proverbs deal with the speaker's lack of discretion regarding
what he or she says. These proverbs are classified according to the severity of
consequences resulting from this act. Worse consequences follow with "they
cut the head of the rooster that crows at the wrong time," and "they threw the
one who speaks without thinking into hell and he yelled 'more logs'." Since the
proverb makes reference to extremely poor judgment, it would similarly show
poor judgment to offer it directly to a person. The only context in which it can
be offered to a second person directly is when both parties clearly know it
constitutes joking or intimate friendship. Otherwise, it is used strictly as gossip.

In Turkish culture, it is believed that talk, alone, accomplishes nothing. A
talking fantasizer who never *does* would hear the following proverbs from a
peer: "if you can cook rice with words, I will give you butter as high as a
mountain"; "words alone won't fill your stomach"; or "you cannot make a ship
go with words." Like most proverbs regarding quality of talk, these can be used
as gossip, but they are also invoked as advice. However, "if one could do
everything he says, every man would be a king," serves to ridicule the person
who does nothing but talk. It can only be a gossip proverb, since it is improper
to ridicule a person directly.

Truth as a criterion for evaluating speech conduct varies from culture to
culture. In Turkey, "he who speaks truth must have one foot in the stirrup";
"he who speaks truth is kicked out of nine towns"; and "he who speaks truth
gets a hole in his head." These proverbs address the indiscriminate telling of
truth. Interestingly, the proverbs do not immediately offer an alternative to
truth telling. Yet, they should not be taken to imply that a person should lie.
Rather he or she should choose the words carefully, because "truth is bitter,"
and it can hurt. For example, when two friends met after being apart for some
time, one remarked that the other had gained weight (which was taken as an
insult). When the truth-bearer told another friend about this incident, he was
told that "he who speaks truth gets kicked out of nine towns." This proverb and
"he who speaks truth gets a hole in the head" may also be used in self-
reference. They would be offered in complaint, suggesting that others did not
appreciate an attempt to be honest.

Typically, these proverbs are accompanied by complaints about others, such as "I don't know what his problem is. I was only telling the truth, but *(the proverb)*." When they are used as gossip, they may be preceeded by a statement such as "poor *(name)*," showing sympathy, but at the same time implying that he or she did not choose the right words for the situation. On the other hand, "he who speaks truth must have one foot in the stirrup" can be told to a peer as advice, warning him or her of the consequences of telling the truth.

DISCUSSION

This analysis of Turkish proverbs suggests certain values in the culture regarding talk. These proverbs serve to control behavior in specific ways. They concentrate on what a speaker should not do. Working as either advice or gossip, the proverbs on speaking readily suggest the consequences a speaker will face if he or she violates them. The power that the words carry is recognized in the culture, and, therefore, one is advised to be careful on the amount of talk and choice of words.

It would be appropriate to conclude that silence is preferred over talk. However, one interesting finding is that, while six out of eight "quantity of talk" proverbs may be directed toward children, only two out of 14 "quality of talk" proverbs may be applied this way. Thus, it can be concluded that, while children are advised on the amount of talk they do, the quality of talk for children is not considered. Of the 16 gossip proverbs, only one is directed toward children, "he who speaks much is much mistaken." Yet, when this proverb is used with children, it serves as an advice proverb and would be inappropriate as gossip. Therefore, gossip proverbs and the proverbs regarding the quality of the spoken word are used primarily among adults. That Turkish elders have a subset of proverbs inapplicable to children may serve to insulate their position of authority in the society.

Whether speaking is, in fact, viewed in such a negative way in the Turkish culture requires further study. However, the analysis of commonly used proverbs suggest so.

REFERENCES

Bascom, W. (1965). Four functions of folklore. In A. Dundes (Ed.), *The study of folklore* (pp.274–298). Englewood Cliffs, NJ: Prentice-Hall.

Finnegan, R. (1976). *Folklore genres.* Austin, TX: University of Texas Press.

Firth, R. (1926). Proverbs in the native life with special reference to Maori. *Folklore, 27,* 134.

Fischer, J. L., & Yoshida, T. (1981). The nature of speech according to Japanese proverbs. *Journal of American Folklore, 81,* 34–39.

Seitel, P. (1974). Haya metaphors of speech. *Language in Society, 3,* 51–67.

Seitel, P. (1967). Proverbs: A Social Use of Metaphor. In A. Dundes & W. Mieder (Eds.), *The wisdom of many: Essays on the proverb* (pp.122–139). New York: Garland Publishing.

Taylor, A. (1967). The wisdom of many and the wit of one. In A. Dundes & W. Meider (Eds.), *The wisdom of many: Essays on the proverb* (pp. 3–9). New York: Garland Publishing.

APPENDIX

Quantity Proverbs

1. Words are silver silence is gold.
2. Talk little listen much.
3. Water is for children, words are for the elders.
4. An arrow that is sent cannot be called back.
5. The nightingale suffers from its tongue.
6. He who speaks much is much mistaken.
7. Empty barrel bangs louder.
8. Abundance of property cannot be acquired without illegal means, abundance of talk cannot be without lies.

Quality Proverbs

1. First think, then speak.
2. Sweet words bring a snake out of its hole.
3. Some words take you to the mountain top, some words take you down.
4. Some words close a deal, some words cost a life.
5. The dog that doesn't know how to bark brings wolves to the flock.
6. They cut the head of the rooster that crows at the wrong time.
7. They threw the one who speaks without thinking into hell, he yelled "more logs."
8. You cannot make a ship go with words.
9. Words alone won't fill your stomach.
10. If you can cook rice with words, I will give you butter as high as a mountain.
11. If one could do everything one says, every poor man would be a king.
12. He who speaks truth must have one foot in the stirrup.
13. He who speaks truth is kicked out of nine towns.
14. He who speaks truth gets a hole in his head.

			Speaker's Intent	
			Advice	Gossip
QUANTITY				
Restricted use of words	1.	Words are silver . . .	+	O
	2.	Talk little . . .	+	O
	3.	Water is for children . . .	+	O
	4.	An arrow that is sent . . .	+	O
	5.	The nightingale suffers . . .	+	+
	6.	He who speaks much . . .	+	+
	7.	Empty barrel . . .	O	+
Expressive use of words	8.	Abundance of property . . .		
		. . . abundance of talk . . .	O	+

			Speaker's Intent	
			Advice	Gossip
QUALITY				
Use of discretion/ good judgment	1.	First think . . .	+	O
	2.	Sweet words bring a snake . . .	+	O
	3.	Some words take you to the mountain top . . .	O	+
	4.	Some words close a deal . . .	O	+
	5.	The dog that doesn't know how to bark . . .	O	+
	6.	The cut the head of the rooster . . .	O	+
	7.	The threw the one who speaks without thinking into hell . . .	O	+
	8.	You can't make a ship go with words.	+	+
	9.	Words alone won't fill your stomach.	+	+
	10.	If you can cook rice with words . . .	+	+
	11.	If one could do everything . . .	O	+
	12.	He who speaks truth must have one foot in the		
Lack of		stirrup.	+	+
discretion/bad	13.	He who speaks truth is kicked out of nine		
judgment		towns.	O	+
	14.	He who speaks truth gets a hole in his head.	O	+

			Object	
			2nd person	3rd person
QUANTITY				
Restricted use of words	1.	Words are silver . . .	+	O
	2.	Talk little . . .	+	O
	3.	Water is for children . . .	+	O
	4.	An arrow that is sent . . .	+	O
	5.	The nightingale suffers . . .	+	+
	6.	He who speaks much . . .	+	+
	7.	Empty barrel . . .	+	+
Expressive use of words	8.	Abundance of property . . . . . . abundance of talk . . .	O	+
QUALITY				
Use of discretion/ good judgement	1.	First think . . .	+	O
	2.	Sweet words bring a snake . . .	+	+
	3.	Some words take you to the mountain top . . .	O	+
	4.	Some words close a deal . . .	O	+
	5.	The dog that doesn't know how to bark . . .	O	+
	6.	The cut the head of the rooster. . . .	O	+
	7.	The threw the one who speaks without thinking into hell . . .	O	+
	8.	You can't make a ship go with words.	+	+
	9.	Words alone won't fill your stomach.	+	+
	10.	If you can cook rice with words . . .	+	+
	11.	If one could do everything . . .	O	+

			Object	
			2nd person	3rd person
Lack of discretion/bad judgment	12.	He who speaks truth must have one foot in the stirrup.	+	+
	*13.	He who speaks truth is kicked out of nine towns.	O	+
	*14.	He who speaks truth gets a hole in his head.	O	+

*Also used for 1st person.

			Addressee	
			Subordinate	Peer
QUANTITY				
Restricted use of words	1.	Words are silver . . .	+	+
	2.	Talk little . . .	+	O
	3.	Water is for children . . .	+	O
	4.	An arrow that is sent . . .	+	+
	5.	The nightingale suffers . . .	O	+
	6.	He who speaks much . . .	+	+
	7.	Empty barrel . . .	O	+
Expressive use of words	8.	Abundance of property . . . . . . abundance of talk . . .	O	+
QUALITY				
Use of discretion/ good judgement	1.	First think . . .	+	O
	2.	Sweet words bring a snake . . .	+	+
	3.	Some words take you to the mountain top . . .	O	+
	4.	Some words close a deal . . .	O	+
	5.	The dog that doesn't know how to bark . . .	O	+
	6.	The cut the head of the rooster. . . .	O	+
	7.	The threw the one who speaks without thinking into hell . . .	O	+
	8.	You can't make a ship go with words.	O	+
	9.	Words alone won't fill your stomach.	O	+
	10.	If you can cook rice with words . . .	O	+
	11.	If one could do everything . . .	O	+
Lack of discretion/bad judgment	12.	He who speaks truth must have one foot in the stirrup.	O	+
	13.	He who speaks truth is kicked out of nine towns.	O	+
	14.	He who speaks truth gets a hole in his head.	O	+

9

Acculturation: Conversational Inference in the Interaction of Nonnative English Speakers

PATRICIA JOHNSON

U. of Wisconsin-Green Bay

The process of interpretation of verbal messages depends, not only on the interlocutors' knowledge of the language, but also on their knowledge of the sociocultural values associated with verbal components of a message. This study of the discourse of nonnative English speakers attempts to examine the process by which second-language learners interpret verbal utterances and make inferences for comprehension.

Gumperz (1976, 1977, 1981, 1982, 1984) systematically demonstrates how native English speakers' background knowledge is used in situational interpretations of verbal messages. "Contextualization cues" (1982, pp.130–152) are verbal and nonverbal means speakers use to signal how an utterance relates to what precedes or follows and how semantic content is to be interpreted. These contextualization cues are found in the speakers' verbal signals (i.e., choice of semantic items and formulaic expressions, co-reference, paraphrase, repetition, elaboration); nonverbal signals (i.e., gaze direction, proxemic distance and kinesic rhythm or timing of body motion and gestures); and paralinguistic signals (i.e., voice, pitch, and rhythm). Contextualization cues are covert, highly context bound, learned subconsciously through prolonged and intensive face-to-face contact under conditions allowing maximum feedback (e.g., in home and peer settings), and thus, reflect common sociocultural background. For example, Gumperz' (1982, pp.172–186) indicates differences in contextualization cues used by speakers of West Indian English, British English, and American English.

"Conversational inference" of meaning in verbal exchanges (Gumperz, 1982, pp.153–171) is the perception of contextualization cues, followed by a search for an interpretation that makes sense in terms of present and past experience. Thus, the ability to match message meaning with contextualization cues is learned from previous interactive verbal experience and forms part of a person's "instinctive" knowledge of the language.

In addition, an utternace is interpreted according to the listeners' comprehension of the situation or context during an interaction in terms of a schema or a familiar frame of sociocultural knowledge. Bartlett (1932) first defined the concept of *schema* as an organizing principle in interpreting events in oral stories. As new knowledge is added in discourse, relevant background knowledge or schema for comprehension change. Thus, as schemata are active and developing, interpretations of a verbal utterance reflect a dynamic process as interlocutors interact. According to Gumperz (1982, p.171), successful interpretations of an utterance depend on what happens in the interactive exchange itself, i.e., the extent to which context-bound inferences are shared, reinforced, modified, or rejected in the course of an exchange.

Successful or unsuccessful perception and use of contextualization cues depend on the communicative competence of the interlocutors. For Gumperz, communicative competence is "the knowledge of linguistic and related communicative conventions (contextualization cues) that speakers must have to initiate and sustain conversational involvement" (1981, p.324). This conversational involvement leads to comprehension and communication.

Retrospective interpretations of utterances can give hypotheses about the actual contextualization cues processed by the interlocutors and the range of alternative interpretations of an utterance. In Garfinkle's study of the interpretative processes which underlie communicative acts, the *meaning and intelligibility of discourse* is defined as "situated meaning," i.e., "meaning constructed in specific sociocultural contexts by actors who must actively interpret what they hear for it to make sense" (1972, p.302). Garfinkle asked subjects to fill out the sketchiness of what was said by writing what they understood they had been talking about. What was actually said was therefore treated as an incomplete version of what was meant. This method of retrospective interpretation of the written transcript of oral discourse by interlocutors seems to be one of the few ways to document with some degree of confidence the interlocutors' comprehension of discourse.

FOCUS OF STUDY

This analysis of discourse examines the inferential processes of second-language learners in verbal interaction in small group discussion. Specifically, the question of how these nonnative English speakers infer the meaning of a verbal utterance is addressed through an examination of their perception of contextualization cues. This perception is indicated in their own utterances and written interpretations of those utterances and in the utterances of others in the discourse. Thus, their retrospective interpretations of utterances are used as a means to make more explicit the unverbalized perceptions and presuppositions which underlie their understanding of verbal exchange.

SUBJECTS AND DATA COLLECTION

The classroom discourse examined in this study was taken from a teaching practicum class in English as a Second Language. The student teachers, nonnative speakers of English, had no classroom teaching experience. The students in this class were either university undergraduates who had at least 525 TOEFL scores or nonnative English speakers from the community with equivalent proficiency in English. These students took the class voluntarily to improve their oral communication skills. In the discourse examined in this study, various cultures were represented: the teacher was from Japan; the three female students from Chile, Venezuela, and Poland; and the male student from Saudi Arabia. Their average age was 20.

The class was divided into small groups of students, each with one student teacher as discussion leader. As the purpose of the course was to improve oral communication skills, discussion was impromptu. The topic depended on the teacher's choice of specific lines in a dialogue in an ESL textbook. Within 12 hours after the lesson, subjects were asked to read the transcript of the recorded verbal exchange and write what they had understood was being said by each speaker. If subjects interpreted what was said as a complete version of what was meant, they wrote nothing. None of the subjects read the interpretations of the discourse by the others. This method of interpretation of the written transcript of oral discourse through retrospection was adapted from Garfinkle's (1972) research.

TOPIC ANALYSIS OF DISCOURSE

One of the objectives of Bodman and Lanzano (1975) in their textbook (*No Hot Water Tonight*) is to present realistic aspects of situations in American society not usually included in ESL textbooks. The vocabulary is not carefully controlled, as the dialogues contain words considered necessary for coping with daily life in urban America. Therefore, students of other cultural backgrounds may have difficulty interpreting the language and the interpersonal relationships as portrayed in the Bodman and Lanzano textbook (Johnson, 1981, 1982).

The topic of discourse is based on specific lines of text dialogue judged to contain problematic linguistic elements crucial to comprehension. The following introduction to the dialogue proposes a schema representing a stereotyped situation for the native speaker of English.

> The next dialogue is a conversation between two young men in a bar. What do young men usually have conversations about? (About girls? About baseball? About what?) Read the following dialogue to see what these two men are talking about on this Friday night at the bar in Irene's. (Bodman & Lanzano, 1975, p.87)

Understanding this introduction may provoke one or more schemata of a bar. However, the title for the dialogue (Let's Find Some Girls) implies a bar where men and women can meet. Schema images are rendered more specific by a line drawing of Irene's bar which illustrates, from the perspective of the bartender, men and women talking at a bar and, in the background, a band with other people standing and talking or sitting at tables. Thus, relevant background knowledge is give to ESL readers who may have alternative schemata for culturally specific situations where men and women can meet.

The following dialogue lines were selected for discussion by the teacher, who believed that the sociocultural connotation of *chicks* would not be understood by the students and that comprehension of this linguistic item was essential to their understanding of the dialogue.

'*Man #1*   Hey! Look at those two beautiful girls at the bar.
Man #2   Wow! They're good-looking chicks.
Man #1   Let's go.

Readers must be able to integrate internal cohesive links within the text to understand these dialogue lines. They must understand that *they* and *chicks* in the second dialogue line refer grammatically and semantically to *girls* in the preceding line. In addition, readers must be able to relate the content of the text to their own knowledge of the world—that this may be appropriate language for two men looking for women in a bar. (Both strategies of the analysis of language for text cohesion and of concepts for text coherence exemplify theoretical models of text processing; see Rumelhart, 1977, for a model taking into account both strategies.)

TEXT ANALYSIS OF DISCOURSE

The discourse begins with the teacher's introduction of the topic and includes all subsequent, relevant exchanges. Much of the conversation consists of the teacher's attempt to explain the word *chicks*. Questioning to provoke conversation about the text was often used as a means to elicit conversation.

Each student (S) is identified by number. The symbol (Ss) refers to a simultaneous response by the students to the teacher (T) or to each other. The utterances are numbered consecutively and separated by a broken line from the interlocutors' verbatim written interpretations (grammar and spelling corrected) of the utterances and by a solid line from the next utterance in the discourse.

---

1.   T What . . . ok . . . What do . . . What does it mean by they're looking for chicks? What . . . What's chicks?

- - - - - -

T— I discussed meaning of *chicks* from the sentence first, helping students to know or realize what *chicks* are because I thought some students didn't know the literal meaning of *chicks*.

---

2.   S1 Chicks . . . chicks . . . chicks? I don't know.

- - - - - -

S1— T said: they were looking for *chicks* (line 1) not as the text said: they were good-looking *chicks*.

T— S1 might have know what *chicks* literally means, but maybe she just didn't know what it implied.

3.   T Ok. Chickens.

S1—   T answers the question of S1 (line 2) without a more detailed explanation. T thought that was enough and all the students would understand immediately the meaning of *chickens*. But textually T said that *chicks* means the animal *chicken*. Just that.

S2—   T was trying to tell the class about what is the meaning of *chick*.

4.   S1 The word chicks comes from chickens?

5.   S2 Girls.

T—   I think S2 knew what *chicks* meant already before T said what *chicken* means from the context (line 6).

6.   T Yeah. Girls.

7.   S2 Good looking girls.

S2—   What I say all the girls it refers to good looking girls.

T—   S2 doesn't interpret or understand the sarcastic implication toward girls behind this meaning of *chicks*.

S1—   S2 also answers the question of S1 but gives a further explanation of what *chicks* means.

8.   T So . . . you say that beautiful girls are called chicks?

T—   I suggest or lead students to the idea that *chicks* is not a respectful way to call girls.

S1—   So the T tries to clarify the answer of S2 by asking a new question.

9.   S2 No, the girls, all the girls.

S2—   All the girls including ugly-looking.

T—   S2 didn't still understand T's purpose (line 8).

10.   T All the girls chicks . . . Do they respect girls by saying they are chicks?

T—   I try to make S2 notice the way of looking at girls of guys in a bar was looking down on girls.

S2—   Yes because *chickens* are sweet and nice animals.

Examination of the utterances and their interpretations reveals that speakers assume that meaning is shared with listeners. Thus, they do not attempt alternative ways through contextualization cues (paraphrase and expansion of utterances) to clarify meaning.

The teacher's question (line 1) lacks co-referential cues for students to understand if she is asking for the literal or referential meaning of *chicks*.

However, her interpretation (line 1) indicates that she is asking for the literal meaning. Her paraphrase of the implicit meaning of the passage (line 1) leads to a misunderstanding of her question, as indicated by S1's interpretation (line 2). S2 responds to S1's comment (line 2) by giving the reference of *chicks* to *girls* (lines 5,7). S2's clarification of his reply to S1 (line 9), as indicated by his interpretation of this line, seems to result from the teacher's repetition of S2's answer in the form of a question (line 8). However, the teacher may actually be confirming S2's explanation of the reference of *chicks* to *girls* in the form of a question. Although S2 seems to understand that *chicks* is linked cohesively to *girls* in the text (line 5), his interpretation of the teacher's question (line 10) indicates that he does not infer the teacher's sociocultural meaning for *chicks* as posed in her questions (lines 8,10) and indicated by her interpretations (lines 7, 8, 10).

The teacher's paraphrase of the implicit meaning of the passage (line 1), repetition of S2's answer in the form of question (line 8), and indirect questioning (line 10) exemplify her signaling how the semantic content of *chicks*, is to be understood and interpreted by the students, as indicated by her interpretation of these lines. However, the students do not infer the meaning signalled by the teacher, as can be seen by their responses and interpretations of her utterances. They interpret these verbal contextualization cues (paraphrase, repetition, indirect questioning) in terms of what they know from past experience.

The teacher's use of questions to lead the students indirectly to the meaning of *chicks* seems to be based on the following assumptions. Students would use their knowledge of the language to infer the referential meaning of *chicks* as *girls* from the sentence context (T's interpretation of line 2). They would use their schema for a bar setting to infer the sociocultural meaning of *chicks* (T's interpretations of lines 8, 10).

The teacher's realization that students are not able to infer the meaning of *chicks* through analysis of reference to *girls* is exemplified by her interjections of *ok* and *yeah*, indicating agreement to give an explanation in answer to their questions (lines 3,6). However, her brief, one-word explanations lack contextualization cues for students to understand how *chicks* refers to *girls*. The teacher could have established conditions through explanation or questioning to lead students to understand how *chicks* refers grammatically and semantically to *girls* in the text dialogue.

In the following segment of the discourse, S3 ignores the teacher's question for an explanation of the sociocultural connotation of *chicks* (line 10) and requests another explanation of the reference of *chicks* to *girls* in the context of the sentence.

---

11.   S3 I don't know what they mean . . . they are good-looking chicks.

- -

S3— I really didn't know what the word *chicks* means. That is the resason I asked the teacher what it means.

T—   S3 didn't understand this expression at all. Of course, S3 didn't notice the implication of this *chicks*. She might not have known the word *chicks*, not knowing the relationship between words *chicken* and *chick*.

S1— The meaning of *chicks* is not clear for S3.

---

12.   T They are good-looking girls . . . chicks refer to girls.

---

13.   S3 Chicks comes from chickens?
      Ss (laughter)

T—   S3 still didn't know the relation between *chicks* and *chickens*.

---

14.   T Yes . . . how do you feel?

T—   I expected all students to understand the literal meaning and implication of *chicks*.

---

15.   S3 It's slang?

T—   S3 began to notice the disrespectful expression of *chicks* towards girls, because for S3 slang means something bad.

---

16.   T Um hm. Is it good slang? When you are called chick, how do you feel?

T—   I'm trying to make S3 understand the implication asking how she feels when she's called *chicks*, expecting she wouldn't feel good.

---

17.   S3 I don't like it if someone call me chick.
      Ss (laughter)

S3— But when you don't know an expression or what the expression means, you feel confused about it, and you don't like it because you don't know what a guy tries to say.

S1— S3 answers now, thinking that the meaning of *chicks* is *chickens* (animal), in reaction to T's question.

The teacher briefly answers S3's requests for another explanation of the reference of *chicks* (lines 12, 14), assuming that students are able to infer the meaning of *chicks* from the sentence context (line 14). At the same time, she persists on the point of the derogatory implication of *chicks* (lines 14, 16). The teacher's interpretations (lines 15, 16) indicate her inference, from S3's question if *chicks* is slang (line 15), that S3 understands the sociocultural meaning of *chicks*. However, S3 does not understand this connotation, as indicated by her interpretation of why she would not want to be called a *chick* (line 17). Unlike the teacher, S1, who is of the same general culture and language background as S3, seems to infer that S3 does not understand the referential or sociocultural meaning of *chicks* (line 17).

The teacher's strategy of not explicitly verbalizing results in a lack of contextualization cues (lines 14, 16) which would enable students to infer the sociocultural meaning of *chicks*. For example, if she had clarified why *chicks* has a derogatory connotation as a reference to women, the conditions for comprehension and acceptance of this interpretation could have been established.

In addition, the teacher implies that *chick* would be used in direct address (line 16); the teacher and students do not make a distinction between people using *chicks* among themselves in talking about a subject and in addressing a person directly.

In the following segment of the discourse, interpretations of silence resemble context-bound judgments based on the interlocutors' former experiences in communication, either in English or in their first languages.

---

18. T You don't like it . . . so . . . do you think these men respect girls?
     Ss (silence)

- - -

T— I expect now students to understand the meaning and implication of *chicks* and refer back to the men's attitude towards girls to make students understand the usage and implications of *chicks* in this context.

---

18. T No, they don't . . . You didn't like this expression . . . Right? . . . So you wouldn't like this.
     Ss (silence)

- - -

S1— T answers her own question where she says no, they don't. Then in the next sentence she answers for the students and confirms it. There is silence because the full meaning of the word is not understood yet.

---

18. T Don't you think they look down on girls by calling them chicks?

- - -

T— I'm expecting too much from students to understand why the men called them *chicks* as students didn't get chicks in this context.
S1— T reaffirms again that *chicks* is a bad word.

---

19. S1 No. In my country, we also have this expression but we don't mind.

- - -

S1— I explain that these words are not necessarily bad words.

The teacher infers from the students' silence that they do not understand the sociocultural meaning of *chicks*, and, thus, she has been unable to persuade them to accept her interpretation of *chicks*. The students' silence or failure to respond as she had expected them to do is interpreted by the teacher in attitudinal terms as expecting too much from students (line 18). After one last question, the teacher makes no more attempts to question students about this meaning of *chicks*. S1 interprets the silence as a signal that students do not comprehend the teacher's sociocultural meaning for *chicks*. In addition, S1 understands but does not accept this derogatory meaning of *chicks* (line 19).

In the following discourse segment, the teacher changes strategies for teaching the sociocultural connotation of *chicks* and asks students to give equivalent expressions for *chicks* in their first languages.

---

20.   T Could you tell me about that?

T—   I expect student to explain the literal meaning and implication of the word.
S1—   T wants to know the word itself.

---

21.   S1 No. It's in Spanish.

T—   S1 thinks that teacher can't understand because it's Spanish and because it's their own usage so that outside people can't understand.

---

22.   T What does it mean?

T—   I expect students to tell me what it literally means, restating line 18.
S1—   What does the expression mean? Are they bad words?

---

23.   S1 They also have expressions. Young boys to call girls or girls to call boys. And we don't mind. We are used to it.

S1—   These are just expressions, young boys' talk.

---

24.   T Um hm. Yeah. What are they? How do . . . how do boys call girls?

T—   Restatement of question in line 20.
S1—   T wants to know the word, no matter if it is in Spanish or any language. Just the word.

---

25.   S1 It's the same thing like you say.

S1—   I think that T wants to know only the meaning of the word, even though S1 has not yet clarified the meaning of the word in Spanish.

---

26.   T So . . . they call them animals?

T—   I got what it means, but wanted to know the literal meaning, not only the implication and the usage.
S1—   T assumes that definitely *chickens* means only *animals*, or all the words that usually the boys or girls call each other are animal names.

---

27.   S1 Yeah, mostly.

---

28.   T What animal?

T—   I expect some kind of animal because *chickens*, *turkeys*, and those animal names are not respectful words to call girls in most cultures.

29.   S1 Turkey.
       Ss (laughter)

T—   In S1's culture, men constantly call girls *turkey* and maybe it implied disrespect
       for girls originally. But girls get too used to be called *turkey*. So for S1 it
       didn't mean anything bad for guys to call girls *turkey*. So for her it was hard to
       understand *chicks* meant something bad towards girls.

Students infer that the teacher wants to know an equivalent expression for
chicks in Spanish, while the teacher is actually asking for the meaning of this
Spanish expression in English. This miscommunication could be caused by a
lack of co-referential contextualization cues such as reference or elaborations
(lines 20, 22, 24). S1 seems to infer that the teacher is asking if the meaning of
such expressions is derogatory (line 22) and delays in answering the teacher's
questions. She finally gives an example from her experience of a similar word in
reference to a woman in Spanish, *turkey* (line 29).

In the last segment of this discourse, interlocutors seem to have found a
common base of experience on which to build interaction.

---

30.   T Turkey! So you don't feel bad if someone calls you a turkey?

T—   I make sure that S1 and S3 don't feel bad about being called *turkey*.
S3—   When the teacher explained to me, I compared it with an expression in Spanish
       which has almost the same meaning. This word is *turkey* (in Spanish: pava).
       Now I know both words and their meaning; I know these words are not an
       insult. It's just a popular way to say this is a nice girl or a pretty girl.
S4—   I think that T tries to show us that we have some feelings connected with words in
       our native language. But we don't have yet the same connections in English.
       Some words in English, precisely their meanings are strange for us. So first
       we should not only learn new words, but also we should find their emotional
       meaning and feeling connected with them.

---

31.   S3 You know . . . not in Spanish. Maybe in English if someone calls you a turkey.

S3—   Now if someone calls me *turkey* in Spanish, I don't care about it because I know
       that this person don't try to insult me. I don't feel bad. Probably in English if
       someone call you a *turkey* is because he/she try to fool you or try to insult
       you. I don't know exactly so I feel bad because this person try to insult me.
       After this discussion, I like to ask this person what he/she means when call
       me *turkey*.

T—   In Spanish for her the meaning of the usage of turkey is changing to good as a
       general meaning for girls, because language is always changing.
S1—   Here the meaning of the word *chicks* is fully understood by S3, in reaction to T.
S4—   If someone call you a *turkey* (in Spanish) it means that he/she likes you, loves you.
       You can compare this expression with English *darling* or *my sweetheart*, etc.

You use this expression not for labeling girls, but to make your sentences more nice, sweet.

---

32. S4 in Spanish, it's very sweet.
     Ss (laughter)

- -

S1— S4 also understood completely the meaning of words like *chicks* or *turkey* and explains that in Spanish it is not a bad word.

---

33. T Do you have any kind of expression like this in your country? . . . No? How about you . . . You don't know?

---

34. S4 How about you?

---

35. T Um. I don't know. We don't have that kind of expression. How about you?

---

36. S4 We have pussy cat.

- -

S4— In Poland we have a similar expression. When we would like to be nice, to say something nice for people we like (for instance—a husband to a wife, a boyfriend to a girlfriend), we use this—expression—*pussy cat.*

---

37. T Pussy cat, that's sweet.

- -

T— For me *pussy cat* sounds cute personally, because I have a good image about pussy cat.

S4— I think that the teacher likes this expression because it compares people with an animal that we like, that is very nice, sweet, little, warm, cute.

---

38. S4 Or rabbit.

- -

S4— There is another expression in Poland: *rabbit.* This expression may have the same meaning as English *chicks.* But it doesn't mean that boys don't respect girls. It is simply synonymous for girls in slang. Sometimes boys call their girl-friends *rabbits.* In this case it has a nice meaning (as *baby* in English). But it is impossible for a husband to call his wife *rabbit* (because a husband should show respect for his wife and this expression shows only feeling among young people without respect).

---

39. T Wow, that's cute.

- -

T— I only personally like *rabbit* ignoring the implication of the word *rabbit.* Actually my cat's home is *Rabit.*

The smoothly moving exchanges seem to indicate the achievement and maintenance of mutual comprehension and agreement in the discourse. However, there are alternative interpretations of utterances. For example, in response to the teacher's question if she would feel bad if someone called her a *turkey* (line 30), S3 states: "You know . . . not in Spanish. Maybe in English if someone calls you a *turkey*" (line 31). Examination of the interpretations of this utterance illustrates the interlocutors' varying interpretations as they infer meaning from the discourse preceding this utterance to fill in what is not said by S3. The teacher infers that the meaning of *turkey* has changed to a favorable connotation of a woman in Spanish. S1 infers that S3 now fully understands the meaning of the word *chick* that the teacher has taught, and S4 infers that the usage of *turkey* for a woman in Spanish is an expression of love.

An examination of the interpretations of utterances reveals that the students have understood but failed to accept the sociocultural connotation of *chicks* as presented by the teacher. S1 and S3 seem to equate this word with a similar expression and its implication in their own cultural context (lines 19, 23, 30, 31). S2's interpretation of the teacher's utterance (line 10) and subsequent silence for the rest of the discourse and S4's interpretation of the discourse utterances (lines 31, 36, 37, 38) also seem to indicate comprehension but nonacceptance of the teacher's sociocultural meaning for *chicks*. As the teacher does not provide relevant background information, conditions that would have made her desired interpretation acceptable to the students are not established through contextualization cues in the interaction. Thus, the students' interpretations of the teacher's utterances have been matched with what is known from past experience.

Although her questions had been prepared before class, she was very hesitant in introducing the topic (line 1). Moreover, a superficial understanding of the connotation of chicks which she was trying to teach is indicated by her explanation of why such expressions as *chick* no longer have a derogatory meaning (lines 29, 31), her expression of concern for the feelings of women when called *turkey* (line 30), her statement that there are no such expressions for women in her native language, Japanese (line 35), and her positive reaction to similar terms for women in Polish (lines 37, 39). Although the teacher pointed out later that her interpretation of chicks had been given her by an American female friend, she seemed not to realize that this word may not be considered disrespectful to women by all native-English speakers.

DISCUSSION

The findings of this study on the interaction of nonnative English speakers generally concur with those of Gumperz for native English speakers. Communicative experience in the language and sociocultural situations provide background knowledge which is used in conversational inference by native and nonnative English speakers. Thus, individual differences in background knowledge might cause instances of miscommunication to occur naturally in passages of apparently successful verbal interaction.

Using communicative strategies successfully is a result of the amount of intensive verbal interactive experience in the language with native or proficient nonnative speakers. However, nonnative English speakers' difficulties in using communicative strategies may prevent them from entering into verbal contact with native English speakers and eliciting the type of feedback necessary to understand and use contextualization cues. A similar discourse analysis of a native English-speaking teacher able to use contextualization cues effectively in interaction with nonnative English speakers might reveal how contextualization cues are actually acquired by ESL learners for discourse comprehension.

In addition, nonnative English speakers' misuse or lack of knowledge of contextualization cues in the language may make it difficult for them to initiate and sustain conversational involvement. The teacher in this study seems to be aware of difficulties in explaining the meaning of a word and persuading the students to accept this interpretation. However, she may be unaware that such difficulties in communication have a linguistic basis: how to respond to a student's utterance, how to introduce a topic, how to elaborate on a point, or how to present information in order to make clear to the class what she is trying to point out about text material. Her lack of communicative competence in the English language may make it difficult for her to find alternative ways of encoding and to recognize the need for re-encoding the meaning that she wishes to convey. The teacher's inability to use contextualization cues (e.g., coreference, elaboration) in her language to aid students to make inferences for comprehension may have been caused by her own lack of much previous intensive interactive experience in the language with native speakers of English. In addition, her difficulties in communication with her students may have been caused by classroom inexperience.

There are weaknesses in using the interpretation of utterances through written retrospection of the interlocutors. Phonetic and stylistic contextualization cues that interlocutors also rely on in face-to-face conversation were not examined, because of their transitory nature. Moreover, interlocutors might have remembered imperfectly what they actually understood at the time that the discourse took place. They also might not have stated their complete comprehension of an utterance in writing. An oral interview questioning technique might have given more data on the range of interpretation of utterances and the actual cues processed. However, this technique might have unintentionally led interlocutors to different interpretations than those they actually had. Interpretation of utterances through retrospection does allow for investigation of aspects of verbal interaction which external observation cannot assess.

This pilot study seems to indicate that the ability to match verbal contextualization cues with message meaning is necessary for the communicative competence of nonnative English speakers who would like to participate meaningfully in verbal encounters. However, more data-based studies of verbal interaction in more varied situations could reveal more about the inferential processes of second-language learners.

REFERENCES

Bartlett, F. C. (1932). *Remembering*. London: Cambridge University Press.

Bodman, J., & Lanzano, M. (1975). *No hot water tonight*. New York: Collier MacMillian.

Garfinkle, H. (1972). Remarks on ethnomethodology. In J.J. Gumperz & D. Hymes (Eds.), *Directions in sociolinguistics*. New York: Holt, Rinehart and Winston.

Gumperz, J. J. (1976). The conversational analysis of interethnic communication. In E.L. Ross (Ed.), In *Interethnic communication* (Southern Anthropological Society Proceedings, No. 12). Athens, GA: University of Georgia Press.

Gumperz, J. J. (1977). Sociocultural knowledge of conversational inference. In M. Saville-Troike (Ed.), *Linguistics and anthropology*. Washington, DC: Georgetown University Press.

Gumperz, J. J. (1981). The linguistic basis of communicative competence. In D. Tannen (Ed.), *Analyzing discourse: Text and talk*. Washington, DC: Georgetown University Press.

Gumperz, J. J. (1982). *Discourse strategies*. London: Cambridge University Press.

Gumperz, J. J. (1984). Communicative competence revisited. In D. Schiffrin (Ed.), *Meaning, form, and use in context: Linguistic applications*. Washington, DC: Georgetown University Press.

Johnson, P. (1981). Effects on reading comprehension of language complexity and cultural background of a text. *TESOL Quarterly, 15* (2), 169–181.

Johnson, P. (1982). Effects on reading comprehension of building background knowledge. *TESOL Quarterly, 16* (4), 503–516.

Rumelhart, D. E. (1977). Toward an interactive model of reading. In S. Dornic (Ed.), *Attention and performance VI*. Hillsdale, NJ: Erlbaum.

PART III

PERFORMANCE
AS CULTURAL REFLECTION

10

Popular Art as Rhetorical Artifact: The Case of Reggae Music

BECKY MICHELE MULVANEY
Florida Atlantic University

This case study of reggae music first requires description of Jamaican culture, including its oppositional subculture of Rastafari. Jamaica is a product of imperialism (Yawney, 1983, p. 121). Current economic and political tensions reflect traces of institutions and cultural traditions codified during Jamaica's history as a slave-labored sugar producer for the British empire. The island's continued struggle for racial, cultural, and national identity amidst contemporary and interrelated problems of class, race, and poverty has found no voice louder than that of the Rastas and their reggae music.

Rastas, via their reinterpretation of biblical passages which focus on the glorification of traditional African cultures and social philosophies, work in direct confrontation to the legitimized political and social systems of Jamaica.[1] This analysis of reggae music primarily addresses reading constructions by the dominant audience, an audience composed of various sympathizers and members of Rastafari, ranging from the revolutionary efforts of political and religious radicals to the reformist efforts of those favoring legitimized political strategies.

The following analysis of the Youth Consciousness Festival, Part I, held at the National Stadium in Kingston on December 25, 1982, identifies typical codic interrelationships in reggae music and interprets those interrelationships in light of a roughly symmetrical correspondence between moments of encoding and decoding (Hall, 1980, p. 136). The assumption of relative symmetry in meaning constructions is explained first by contextualizing the festival in terms of promotional strategies, time, place, and audience expectations. Preceded by a brief description of the festival itself, the analysis concentrates on an examination of the various semiotic codes employed in the finale song, "No Woman, No Cry" (Marley, 1974).

Following the concert, international reggae critics labeled it the "concert of the decade," "one of the great reggae events of all time" (Steffens, 1984, pp. 66–74). Yet, on the whole, information available prior to the concert suggests

---

[1] See Barrett (1977) for a description of the history and primary concepts of Rastafari, Owens (1976) for an ethnographic explication of Rasta theology, and Nettleford (1970, pp. 109–111) for his discussion on how Rastafari has impinged upon Jamaican politics.

that the event was meant for the Jamaican people and was organized primarily as a benefit, a strategy common to many local dances and concerts held in conjunction with Rasta oriented organizations and causes. Inexpensive ticket prices and location of ticket sales in neighborhood record stores further affirms this conclusion, as does the festival's location in the nontourist, South Coast city of Kingston.

Local expectations concerning the concert were high. The line-up of performers was impressive. The list included popular Jamaican artists such as Gregory Isaacs and international stars such as Jimmy Cliff, but, most important, the majority of the musicians included individuals who had been part of the original Bob Marley and the Wailers. Any Wailer, by association, is a reminder of Bob Marley and the near-divine status granted him by many Jamaicans. A mere year and a half after Marley's death, a reunion of Wailers at Youth Consciousness promised much. Most anticipation focused particularly on the promise of a performance by Bunny Wailer.

Slated to begin at 6:00 p.m. on Christmas night, the festival started 3 hours later due both to intermittent showers and the sense of timing for which Jamaicans are famous. Roughly 12 hours long, the festival developed its own sense of dramatic rhythm due to scheduling, weather, and the changing mood of the audience.

LYRICAL ANALYSIS OF "NO WOMAN"

For this song, each singer on stage took part in developing harmonies. Bunny Wailer, Jimmy Cliff, and Peter Tosh served as lead vocalists on the different verses. What follows is a transcription I have rendered of the vocals as sung at Youth Consciousness.

Bunny Wailer (lead vocals):

Yeah, yeah, now now, yes
No woman, no cry
No woman, no cry cry cry
Little darlin'
Don't shed no tears
No woman, no cry

I remember when we
used to play
Ina government yard
In Trench Town
Yeah, yeah, yeah, yeah
Observing all
The little children
Mingling with the
Good people we meet
Idrens we've met

Good friends we've lost
Along the way
In this great future
You can't forget
Your past
So dry your tears I say
Now little woman

No woman, no cry (chorus)
No woman, no cry cry cry
Little darlin'
Don't shed no tears
No woman, no cry

Now I remember when
We used to sit
Ina government yard
In the ghetto, yeah
Then brother Georgie
Would make
That firelight
Which was log wood
Burnin' through
The night
Then we would cook
Cornmeal porridge
Of which I'll share
With you
As for my feet
It's my only
Transportation
Outta here
And that's why I've
Got to push on through
And while I'm gone
(everyone sing along)
Everything's gonna
Be all right (eight times)

Chorus

Jimmy Cliff (lead vocals)   Bunny Wailer (background)

'Cause I remember
When we used to sit
In the government yard
In Trench Town
I remember brother Hicks
He would make
That firelight
It was log wood burnin'

Through the night

We would cook fish tea
Of which I'll share
With you

My feet are, are
My only carriage
I gotta push
On through

Everything's gonna
Be all right (eight times)

Chorus

Peter Tosh (lead vocals)

'Cause even me too
Do remember the days
[audience applause]
When we used to cook
That fish tea
In Trench Town
and my good
Little brother
Would make
Some firelight
And we burn some
Bush in the night
To drive away
mosquitos
Those were the times
Everything sounds wrong
And we'd get lost
Running away
From the police
But I know they can't
Keep us down
'Cause when we check
It was the least
But this time I can say
Everything
Everything
This time, no
Now don't

No, no, no—umm,
No woman, no cry
No woman, no cry (in unison)

It was burnin' burnin' burnin'
burnin' burnin'
Ital fish tea, ya'll

I 'n' I's gonna drink it
All up, ya'll

But while I'm gone, but
while I'm gone

Bunny Wailer (background)
'Cause I 'n' I knows

Oh yes

Oh I remember

No woman

Oh yeah

But I love ya, but I love ya,
But I love ya

No woman, no cry

No woman, no cry
Little darlin'
One more time I'd like
To say it

In this personal narrative, the singer reminds the woman of their past together. Whether the audience will hear clearly, let alone understand, the lyrical phrases depends entirely on its level of knowledge in the general street culture of Jamaica and specifically the subculture of Rastafari. The relatively standard use of English as printed is scarcely representative of the way in which these words are voiced in Jamaican patois. Without much exposure to Jamaican talk and lyrical style, the listener may catch little of the verbal construction (Cassidy, 1961, pp. 1–9). For the Jamaican audience, however, the verses hold a rich narrative tapestry reflecting their daily lives.

The introductory chorus requires little analysis. The speaker consoles the woman and initially cues the personal and emotional character of the song. "In a government yard in Trench Town" situates the narrative. The reference is known universally to Jamaicans. Trench Town is one of Kingston's ghettos.

The qualifier "government yard" more clearly focuses the scene. The government-furnished yards, fenced in by tall cement walls, hold two-story apartment units. White's somewhat exaggerated description suggests that each small concrete one-room apartment serves as many as eight people, yet the horseshoe-shaped yard, communal outhouse, and standpipe represent one step up from the cardboard scrap tin squatter shacks and open pit latrines which service much of Trench Town, pressing in upon the yards' illusion of order and cleanliness (White, 1983, pp. 119–120).

The allusion to many people milling about, for the dominant audience, is redundant of the previous lines. The yard in Trench Town already signifies the sights, sounds, and smells of people of all ages sharing a small living space just as it indexes the range of connotations for "friends lost." While the reference might suggest the inevitability of friends drifting apart, within this subculture the location in Trench Town evokes a different set of signifieds: illness, death, and incarceration due to poverty, ghetto violence, as well as a corrupt and sometimes overzealous police department.[2]

The seemingly vague claim, "in this great future, you can't forget your past," refers to Rasta philosophy. Bunny's choice of the noun *Idrens* calls up both the theology and lexicon of Jamaica's influential subculture. While *Idren* parallels the Old Testament's term *brethren*, the use of *I* at the beginning of words evokes an intimate relationship between God and humanity. The *I* at the end of Rastafari and the *I* that Rastas call themselves serve as verbal representations of the theological premise that all human agents are part of God.

Furthermore, the "great future" alludes to the Rasta interpretation of Revelation, the inevitable "turning of the tables" spoken of in so many reggae lyrics. The fall of the racist Western world will give rise to "Jah Kingdom," say the Rastas, and present international hostilities along with the current spread of reggae and Rastafari are evidence of this turning tide.

"You can't forget your past" represents an historical consciousness on the part of Rastas. Rastas understand that ellipsis and distortion repressed and

---

[2]Illness due to malnutrition and poor medical care, violent death due to the politically motivated importation of American guns into Jamaica's ghettos, and the daily practice of "running-in" street people for vagrance, gambling, or petty drug charges are all common topics of conversation concerning "struggle" among Jamaica's poor.

disfigured the history of the African peoples, and they are committed to retrieving their lost cultural traditions.

The chorus further constrains the listeners' interpretation of the prior narrative description. The literal meaning of "play" as something delightful is juxtaposed with the ghetto location, thereby rendering an ironic meaning. "Play" in the ghetto is more painful than pleasurable, as is signified by the plea to "dry your tears."

The second verse finds the singer still in the yard scene, yet now darkness has fallen. Description of night-time activities further emphasizes the Trench Town situation. An evening meal of cornmeal porridge and fish tea instantly signifies poverty. Similarly, the "log wood burnin' " has its own ghetto-related functions. Tosh explains one of these in the final verse of "No Woman." Those with no windows or screens burn dried grasses or "bush" to drive away persistent mosquitos. Even more tenacious, however, is the stench from Trench Town's open latrines. Bonfires fed with all manner of trash are lit at dusk to mask the ever-present odors (White, 1983, p. 120).

The textual reference to leaving on foot does not focus necessarily on the financial necessity of transportation by foot, nor on the self-centeredness of an individual who would abandon family if given an opportunity for exodus from the ghetto. One implication, developed in Tosh's verse, is that the singer must temporarily take on ghetto invisibility to avoid a run-in with officials. Elusiveness is a necessary survival skill in the ghetto, especially for male Rastas constantly harassed by police.

It is interesting to note that the performers, notably Tosh, change, in small ways, the song's original (as recorded by Marley) lyrics. These changes (e.g., Tosh's line, "Cause even me too do remember") introduce individual testimony. Informed audience members can interpret these moments, recalling, in this case, Tosh's earlier trouble with both the band and (for political causes) the police. Thus, these changes compound the meaning of the lyrics by laminating the references to Jamaican poverty and struggle with more personal experiences.

INSTRUMENTAL ANALYSIS OF "NO WOMAN"

Analysis of reggae also requires an examination of its instrumental code. The following analysis of "No Woman" is taken from both the live Youth Consciousness version and Marley's Island pressing. In both versions, the instrumental structure most common to reggae remains intact; thus, the typicality of instrumentation affords a rich body of information.

Like most other popular music, reggae maintains a simple ¼ time (four main beats to a bar) (Ehrlich, 1982, p. 52). Yet the downbeats in reggae are stressed differently than in most other contemporary popular music. The stressed or emphasized downbeats in reggae are beats two and four, while most Western popular music stresses beats one and two or one and three (Ehrlich, 1982, p. 52). The skeletal framework indicative of the rhythm is produced by the snare drum on beats two and four, complemented by the chordal instruments (rhythm guitar and/or keyboards) on the upbeat.

There is an emphasis on percussiveness in reggae, not merely with traditional percussive instruments (drums), but also in the way typically melodic instruments (keyboards and guitar) are utilized. The role of most of the instruments in the reggae ensemble is one of a "syncopated drum part" (Ehrlich, 1982, p. 53). This represents one of the many aspects in which reggae draws from its mother culture of Africa (Johnson & Pines, 1982, pp. 1–64).

African influences on reggae are also manifested in both the primacy and character of the rhythmic structure employed. The rhythmic statement, in reggae, takes priority over melodic/harmonic considerations. In fact, the bass guitar part, which functions as a drum "that plays a definite rhythm, but may or may not play a distinct melody line" is called a *riddim* in Jamaica (Ehrlich, 1982, p. 53). These riddims, along with the percussive staccato rhythm guitar "clip," are given dominance in the engineer's mix. It is the low "loping" rhythm of the bass guitar and the staccato "chink chink" sound of the rhythm guitar which form the skeleton of the rhythmic structure.

The philosophy here is one of sparseness. The rhythmic structure possesses "room"—ample space within each bar of music—with which to accommodate the addition of an array of complementary rhythmic parts. The sparseness in the basic instrumental framework allows for polyrhythmic elaboration. In "No Woman," for instance, the bass drum and woodblock develop rhythmic variations by entering in relationship to the basic ⅓ beat established by the bass guitar riddim.

The constant swing in each bar from the low bass tones to the light, staccato treble sounds creates an effect which some have described as an oscillation between consonance and dissonance (Boot & Thomas, 1976, p. 34; Barrett, 1977, p. 167). This suggestion calls attention to elements of the code which parallel the lyrical signification.

Reggae lyrics, which describe the present poverty-ridden situation of its dominant audience and attempt to provide relief through allusion to better times coming, are mirrored by the "dissonance-consonance" metaphor often used to describe the rhythmic structure. The rhythmic strategy used in reggae, then, tends to re-present in sound the creation and release of tension found in the lyrics.

It is fair to say that many reggae lyrics concentrate on an historical representation of the Jamaican situation. Hence, the bulk of the verbal discourse is devoted to unpleasant descriptions and stories. The instrumental structure, in its typical dance style, however, focuses on release from tension. If the instrumental code is looked at as a whole, the dissonance, which is but one part of the rhythmic structure, is overridden by the generally buoyant, fluid sound of reggae songs. By examining the two codes in relationship to each other, a new tension is revealed: the generally serious tone of the lyrics is accompanied by a rather lighthearted dance rhythm.

PHYSICAL MOVEMENT AND "NO WOMAN"

By juxtaposing but two of the codes used in reggae, lyrics and instrumentation, the analysis simply renders a dialectical opposition. How, then, does the listener build a coherent construction of the semiotic phenomenon when two of the codes employed seem to conflict?

The cultural history of the Jamaican people is one source of information here, just as it was in understanding the rhythmic idiom used in reggae. African musicologists recently have been turning to Jamaica to retrieve extant pieces of their own cultures. Both the isolationist culture of the free Maroons of Jamaica and the striking "absence of a sense of Christian mission among the slave masters" allowed the black Jamaican population to keep whole pieces of their original African traditions intact (Johnson & Pines, 1982, pp. 1–64). One of those pieces serves as an example which helps explain the analytical issue at hand.

Bennett traces the "tension" in reggae back to the concept behind an African-derived ritual called dinkie-minnie. The death rate among Jamaican slaves was quite high, and, as Bennett explains, the ritual functioned to

> banish sorrow and to prevent the family from grieving, when I say grieving, you are aware of the tragedy but you don't let it overpower you. There is no inward grieving, you dance it off, you move it off. The dinkie-minnie is full of movement. (Johnson & Pines 1982, pp. 42–43)

This historical situation lends a sense of purpose to the tension between verbal and instrumental codes. It also guides the analysis to the code which brings closure to the "composite message" (Meijer, 1982, p. 235).

Just as reggae lyrics draw from the historical experience of African diaspora, and as the instrumental code takes its rhythmic structure from African poly-rhythm, so does reggae keep intact the traditional African inseparability of music and dance (Chernoff, 1979, p. 23). Dance is seen as the expression of percussive concepts in African traditions and functions to develop a "conversation" between motion and music (Thompson, 1966, pp. 89, 94). Dance serves as a physical reflection of the rhythmic code, enabling the critic to see empirically the way in which audience members receive and respond to the interaction between lyrics and rhythm.

This physical re-presentation serves as more than just a mirror effect. In mastering the rhythmic concepts through dance, the participants also project an attitude advocated by the music. Bob Marley described this attitude in a 1975 interview with writer Fikisha Cumbo:

> Reggae music is one of the greatest musics, you know . . . Me know that, 'cause you can dance the whole night and it keep you in a mood . . . You love yourself

when you dance reggae music. You proud of yourself. . . . When you get up in the morning, you have to be proud. . . . You have to be a sufferer who say to yourself, "Feeling all right." (Whitney & Hussey, 1984, p. 92–93).

The reggae dance, or *skank*, requires an understanding of the instrumental structure that goes beyond simple recognition of the downbeat. The beats clearly emphasized by the treble instruments of rhythm guitar and keyboard occur on the upbeat. Yet the most astute reggae dancers emphasize the moments at which the "beat drops."[3] The upbeats are performed in the treble signature, delivering high frequency sounds which function to pull the dancer out of the downward movement, bringing the foot off the ground and raising the opposite arm in front of the dancer in preparation for the next "drop."

The Jamaican dancer does not perform these steps in the light, airy, skipping style common to North Americans, who often concentrate on the staccato "clip" in the upbeat. Instead, the movements appear more serious minded, the dancer focusing on the dipping motion which brings the foot in contact with the ground. The dance looks like a slow, confident walking stride. Indeed, the experienced dancer brings to these simple repetitive steps nuances which magnify a sense of determination. The dance creates the image of an immovable force.

The tension between the verbal and instrumental construct, indicative of the struggles of the Jamaican populace, is transmuted into something wholly positive in the dance code. The determined style of the dance replicates the tension points, but does not translate them as such. Instead, struggle becomes strength. The tension which directs the footwork is redefined by the dance.

Kenneth Burke's rhetorical concept of the ultimate ordering of terms is illustrative here. Typically, the lyrical code in reggae works to create a *positive term*, defined by Burke (1969, p. 183) as that which "names things having a visible, tangible existence." Reggae lyrics, which essentially "name" the historically situated position of the Jamaican people, provide the positive term, a material situation which can be represented by the word *oppression*. The instrumental code in reggae works to complicate the situation described by the positive term in that it introduces an antithesis to oppression, what Burke calls the *dialectical term*, or competing *voice*: the upbeat dance music (Burke, 1969, pp. 185–87). In parallel terms, the playful mood of the instrumentals can be situated directly opposite to oppression by the use of the word *freedom* (one must feel free to play). If lyrics and instrumentals set up the terms of a dialectical opposition, then the dance code functions as an *ultimate term*, defined by Burke (1969, p. 187) as a unitary principle which arises out of successive moments in a single process. The transformation of this thesis/

---

[3]Where the *beat drops* is a musical term more easily heard than explained. Reggae instrumentation works extensively to manipulate silence, setting up, then "dropping" the bass in and out of the mix seemingly at random to frustrate the audience's expectations momentarily. Emphasis is often placed on the re-entrance of the bass line, specifically in dub (instrumental) music.

antithesis illustrated in dance produces an ultimate term represented most clearly by the word *resistance*. Within the conversation between motion and music, the last word is rhetorical.

Rastas cope with their daily struggles by focusing on the power and strength they gain from them. Because of these struggles, both historical and contemporary, Rastas see themselves as a strong people capable of moving forward toward economic, social, and political freedom. Positive, constructive movement, or *resistance*, represents the dialectical synthesis which grows out of the tensions inherent in struggle. This attitude is not only found in reggae dance, but is common in the Rasta idiom and reflected in the imagery of reggae lyrics: "just get up and move," "keep on moving," "pave the way," "trodding through creation," "trod until Babylon falls," "forward onto Zion," "we forward in this generation," "stepping out of Babylon," "got to move," "get on up," and "stand up for your rights."[4]

Reggae music re-presents the situation of poverty and oppression, while physical movement, as guided by the rhythmic structure, subverts the situation, transforming it into a positive attitude through "forward" movement.

REFERENCES

Abyssinians, The. (1982). *Forward.* Alligator, A-18305.

Barrett, L. E. (1977). *The Rastafarians: Sounds of culture dissonance.* Boston, MA: Beacon.

Boot, A., & Thomas, M. (1976). *Jamaica: Babylon on a thin wire.* London: Thames and Hudson.

Burke, K. (1969). *A rhetoric of motives.* Berkeley, CA: University of California Press.

Cassidy, F. G. (1961). *Jamaica talk: Three hundred years of the English language in Jamaica.* London: Macmillan.

Chernoff, J. M. (1979). *African rhythm and African sensibility: Aesthetics and social action in African musical idioms.* Chicago, IL: University of Chicago Press.

Ehrlich, L. (1982). The Reggae arrangement. In S. Davis & P. Simon (Eds.), *Reggae international* (pp. 52–55). Munich, Germany: Rogner and Bernhard.

Hall, S. (1980). Encoding/decoding. In S. Hall, D. Hobson, A. Lowe, & P. Willis (Eds.), *Culture, media, language* (pp. 128–138). London: Hutchinson.

Johnson, H., & Pines, J. (1982). *Reggae: Deep roots music.* London: Proteus.

Marley, B., and the Wailers (1983). *Confrontation.* Island, 90085-1.

Marley, B., and the Wailers (1974). *Natty Dread.* Island, ILPS-9281.

Marley, B., and the Wailers (1980). *Uprising.* Island, ILPS-9596.

Meijer, J. (1982). Concerning clustering of codes, mainly in art and culture. In W. B. Hess-Luttich (Ed.), In *Multimedial Communication* (Vol. I, pp. 230–43). Tubingen, Germany: Gunter Narr Verlag.

Moses, P. (1981). *Pave the Way.* Mango, MLPS-9633.

Nettleford, R. (1970). *Mirror, mirror: Identity, race, and protest in Jamaica.* Kingston: Sangsters.

Owens, J. (1976). *Dread: The Rastafarians of Jamaica.* Kingston: Sangsters.

---

[4]These lyrics are taken from the following sources: B. Wailer (n.d.), *Protest*, Solomonic; P. Moses (1981), *Pave the Way*, Mango, MLPS-9633; B. Marley and the Wailers (1983), *Confrontation*, Island, 90085-1; The Abyssinians (1982), *Forward*, Alligator, A-18305; B. Marley and the Wailers (1980), *Uprising*, Island, ILPS-9596; The Wailers (1973) *Burnin'*, Island, ILPS-9256; B. Wailer (1978), *Struggle*, Solomonic; and B. Youth (1981), *Some Great Big Youth*, Negusa Negast, 39453.

Steffens, R. (1984). Reggae 1984: Fragments of a fallen star. *Musician, 64*, 66–74.

Thompson, R. F. (1966). An aesthetic of Cool: West African dance. *African Forum, 1*, 85–102.

Wailer, B. (n.d.). *Protest*. Solomonic.

Wailer, B. (1978). *Struggle*. Solomonic.

Wailers, The. (1973). *Burnin'*. Island, ILPS-9256.

White, T. (1983). *Catch a fire: The life of Bob Marley*. New York: Holt, Rinehart, and Winston.

Whitney, M., & Hussey, D. (1984). *Bob Marley: Reggae king of the world*. New York: E.P. Dutton.

Yawney, C. (1983). To grow a daughter: Cultural liberation and the dynamics of oppression in Jamaica. In A. Miles & G. Finn (Eds.), *Feminism in Canada* (pp. 119–144). Montreal: Black Rose Books.

Youth, B. (1981). *Some Great Big Youth*. Negusa Negast, 39453.

11

The Latent Meaning of a Dance: The Cebuano Sinulog as a Model of Cultural Performance

SALLY ANN NESS

University of Washington

In the symbolic patterning of dance movement, individual performers can, under certain conditions, represent the operating social systems of their cultures. More specifically, performers can embody essential social themes and values in their dance. By studying these patterns of social action that are communicated by individuals dancing, we can learn about social processes and the distinctive features of a given society's style of social action. The objective of this chapter is to give a specific example of how this kind of meaning can be grasped with regard to a particular Philippine dance form.

FOCUS: THE SINULOG OF CEBU CITY PHILIPPINES

The specific form of dancing under consideration is called the *sinulog*, a dance that is performed in Cebu City, which is the second largest city in the Philippines. It is a religious dance, done for the patron saint of Cebu City, the Santo Nino.[1] The *sinulog* has traditionally been regarded as a form of petition or thanksgiving for favors that have been or may be granted by the Santo Nino to the Santo Nino's devotees.

In former times, the *sinulog* was performed by devotees of the Santo Nino themselves. However, since the end of the Second World War, and particularly since the 1960s, the *sinulog* is no longer performed as a ritual by the community at large. Today, the main performers of the ritual *sinulog* are women, called *tinderas*, who sell candles around the church housing the Santo Nino, the Basilica Minore del Santo Nino, and those who are members of the lowest economic class. The *sinulog* is danced by these women (who are mainly between the ages of 45 and 80) as part of their candle-selling business. The practice of lighting a candle for a saint is a tradition of the Roman Catholic religion. Devotees of the Santo Nino who wish to make such an offering have the *tinderas* dance a *sinulog* as a sort of blessing for the candle before it is lit.

---

[1] The *sinulog* is performed for a variety of patron saints in different towns in the Central Philippines (the Visayan Islands). In Cebu City as well, it is performed for other saints besides the Santo Nino, but it is most commonly associated with the Santo Nino in this city.

The dancing is believed to increase the candle's ability to persuade the Santo Nino to show mercy on the customer, or on the person in whose name the customer is lighting the candle.[2]

The *sinulog* dance is considered to be an improvisational form. That is, every *tindera* develops her own style of *sinulog*. The dancing is described by the *tinderas* as a "natural" form of movement, and movement patterns may occur differently in every performance. Improvisation is preferred because it is believed to show genuine intentions of devotion, which, in turn, is thought to have the greatest influence over the Santo Nino. Spontaneity and improvisation are thus closely associated with concepts of genuineness and sincerity. To be "natural" is to be unplanned, unpremeditated, and, as such, to be honestly sincere. "Artificialness," on the other hand, is associated with practiced or rehearsed movement, and this kind of performance is avoided because it is believed to anger the Santo Nino.

Because of the preference for spontaneity, no set list of gestures, no "vocabulary" of action, is associated with *sinulog* dancing. As a result, a great deal of variation occurs in performance style; however, there is more commonality of performance style than might be expected. In fact, several characteristics typical of all performances of *sinulog* dancing are observable, and these characteristics form a pattern that is generally representative of the *tindera sinulog* style and is also symbolic of a typical form of social performance in Cebuano culture.

THE TINDERA SINULOG PATTERN: A SUMMARY DESCRIPTION

The *tindera sinulog* usually lasts no longer than 2 minutes. It requires the active use of only three body parts: the eyes, one or both hands (holding candles), and the central core or column of the torso.

Most essential in the performance is the restrained gesturing of the hand, which uses what is called peripheral spatial tension in performing gestures.[3] That is, the way the candles are manipulated in the dancing makes apparent a distance between the center of the *tindera's* body, which is maintained in a fairly rigid posture, and an edge, where the candle is moved in a relatively free-

---

[2]In 1980, two forms of the *sinulog* dance (one of them being the *tindera sinulog* discussed here) were selected as the center for a new fiesta celebration, which was sponsored initially by the Augustinian Community in connection with the Philippine Ministry of Youth and Sports Development, and, after 1981, by the Mayor's Office of Cebu City and the Sinulog Foundation. Dances were designed for this promotional event, that represented the traditional ritual *sinulog* dances and have been called *sinulogs*. These *sinulogs* are different in both form and function from the traditional *sinulog* dances and should not be confused with the *tindera sinulog* dance ritual that is the subject of this article.

[3]This analysis of the *sinulog* dance movement is made using some of the terms of Laban Movement Analysis. The Laban Movement Analysis system analyzes human body movement in terms of its dynamic statement—its energy quality—its spatial design, and its bodily organization (cf. Bartenieff, 1980; Dell, 1970).

flowing style. Even though the hand gestures may be performed at different reach lengths—some occur close to the torso, while others occur at full arm's reach away from it—a distance between the gesturing end of the body and the center of the upper torso, the region around the heart, is always made visible in *tindera sinulog* performances. The visual effect is very different from one in which a spatial path is made visible that radiates out of or into the body's center—the kind of spatial form typically revealed in more friendly versions of the American's handshake, for example. The gesture of offering in *sinulog* dancing is thus not one that reveals an intention to offer which develops outward from the heart. Instead, it is one in which the object offered, as well as the process of offering, is made to appear at a distance from the central core of the body.

In addition, *sinulog* gesturing is performed in such a way that the candle appears to initiate and inspire its own movement. That is, the gesture is not governed or initiated by the mid-limb or the proximal joint of the body, by the elbow or shoulder joint. Neither is the gesture performed in a controlled or sculpting manner, a manner in which the hand or arm would heighten an awareness of the fact that the candle is indeed being held captive. Instead, the movement at the edge, which is distally initiated by the wrist and seemingly by the candle, flows freely, such that the performer would have difficulty if she were to find it necessary to halt the gesture abruptly. Meanwhile, the torso of the dancer remains contained, presenting a restrained contrast to the relatively unrestricted movements of the distal end—the candle.

To summarize, the pattern here identified as characteristic of the *tindera sinulog* form is a spatial constellation that reveals a self-motivated object moving freely on an edge, which operates at a distance from a more tensely held central area of the body.

INTERPRETATION OF LATENT MEANING

When *tinderas* are asked about the meaning of *sinulog* dance movement, they say that it has none—that the gestures have no conventional symbolic associations. The dancing doesn't bring to mind ideas or images otherwise absent from the performance. The differences in movement style that are apparent in *tindera* dancing are differences that make no difference, because the movement has no designated references. Moreover, the dance movement is not symbolic of the *tinderas'* sincerity—it *is* their sincerity. It is the manifestation of deep devotion, which the *tinderas* describe in words as the tightening of their insides, or the binding of their hearts. Being sincere, according to the *tinderas*, is feeling deep tenseness in the region of the heart. The posture of the torso, then, indicates the presence of sincerity in *sinulog* dancing, but is not recognized as having a symbolic function.

The only recognized symbolism in the performance of *sinulog* dancing is the symbolism of the candle, which is used to stand for the soul that receives the mercy of the Santo Nino. This soul, which may be the customer or someone of the customer's choosing, is not involved in the dance performance. So the candle is symbolic, while the movement doesn't appear to have a representational function.

While the dynamic constellation of hand, heart, and distance is not recognized as symbolic, it nevertheless has a "latent" symbolism. This latent symbolism goes unrecognized by those involved in the performance, but yet communicates the guiding principles of a traditional Cebuano social performance.

To understand this latent symbolism, it must be understood that, when the *tindera* takes a candle into a performance, she is taking up an object she has just sold to a stranger, an object that has become essentially foreign to her. In other words, the *tindera* is taking upon herself an object that symbolizes an "other." The *tinderas* do not typically perform for friends or family when they dance. They do have regular customers, but by and large the people they deal with are strangers, people who are not "their own kind." So, when they dance, they play hostess to a symbolic visitor, to an *unfamiliar* other. The latent symbolism of the *sinulog* dance movement, then, is this: The treatment extended to the candle by the *tindera's* body represents the treatment that visitors or guests are traditionally accorded in Cebuano society.

THE CEBUANO TRADITION OF GUEST/HOST INTERACTION

The Cebuano traditional treatment of guests is best revealed in the way Cebuanos celebrate their community fiestas (cf. Balane, 1954; Briones, 1983, pp. 78–80; Tenazas, 1965). The fiesta revolves around visiting and receiving visitors, and, thus, the process of dealing with nonlocals is the main activity of the fiesta. In most cases, guests are not entirely unfamiliar visitors. Most visitors are friends and family from distant locations. However, an ideal of hospitality prevails during fiestas that allows for welcoming total strangers into the hosting network. Cebuanos recount with enthusiasm stories of travellers who happen upon a town fiesta and are taken in at house after house, encouraged to share in the festivities of all. The perfect stranger, during fiesta time, is the ideal guest.

A key attitude in this process is that guests should be refused nothing. Hosts typically go to great expense to accommodate their guests. Guests are expected to act without inhibition, and they are exempted from rules that would prevent nonguests from acting in a like manner. Ideally, guests are allowed to do or have whatever might bring them pleasure and contentment—just as the candle appears to do as it pleases in *sinulog* dancing, where it appears to move freely in gestural paths that are not controlled by the body, but are instead accomodated by the body. In short, the visitor for Cebuanos is ideally an individual who behaves as the candle in the *sinulog* dance behaves. A guest is a free spirit who must be accomodated, treated with generous delicacy, and indulged in whatever way possible.

The organization of hosting networks, however, is characterized in very different terms in Cebuano society. Being a part of the local structure, being on the "inside" of a group, is generally spoken of in terms of restriction and obligation. This is typical, not only of Cebuano interpersonal relationships, but of Filipino interpersonal relationships in general. The idea of "the debt" (*utang* in Cebuano and Tagalog) has long been recognized as a widespread dynamic of Filipino social structure (cf. Hollensteiner, 1973).

This form of bonding is reported in the oldest descriptions of Cebuano social life (cf. Leitz, 1962, p.71). Whenever a person enters into the heart of a social system, he or she becomes indebted to someone and is owed favors by someone else. Students and teachers, teachers and administrators, employees and employers, parents and children, all kinds of individuals on familiar terms with one another use the models of the debtor and the debtee or the master and the servant—which are viewed as the equivalent of the Older and the Younger—to organize their interaction. This relationship of debt binds the inner workings of Cebuano society.

The hosting operations of Cebuano society exhibit the same quality of "be*holde*n-ness"—of being a mass of tensions—that is exhibited in the core of the dancing *tindera* . Likewise, the behavior of the ideal visitor in social interaction resembles the behavior of the candle. Finally, the spatial constellation—that of isolated edge and center—identified earlier in *sinulog* dancing is also present in the Cebuano guest/host relationship as well. That is, guests are set apart, physically, in terms of where they are housed or how they are placed in social gatherings. For example, guests are typically given the better chairs, or the only chairs available, at social gatherings.

Guests are indulged, but they are also distanced from the heartfelt relationships existing within the hosting group. A "warm" welcome is thus very different in Cebuano society from what it is conceived to be in American society. Cebuano society is "designed to exclude" (S. Silliman, personal communication, November, 1984). Although friendliness and goodwill are obvious in the treatment one is accorded, isolation is nevertheless typically an accompaniment to this accomodating treatment.

CONCLUSION

As the above comparison of dance style and traditional social action illustrates, a relationship of resemblance exists between the design of *sinulog* dancing and the social performances connected with receiving visitors in Cebuano society. Hosting networks, characterized in terms of tension and binding, interact with nonlocals/strangers in a spirit of indulgence and accomodation, while reenforcing a distance that keeps the visitor's activity on the society's surface, and at its edge.

In this regard, the movement of the *sinulog* dance form, like the movement of dance forms in general, can be described as "polysemic" (cf. Turner, 1967, p.50). That is, the dancing speaks simultaneously about immediate circumstances, in this case about emotions of sincerity and devotion manifest in an act of ritual supplication, and it speaks as well, in a voice unheard, about general conditions, in this case about the social tradition connected with the reception of and conduct toward visiting strangers. The polysemy or multivocality of *sinulog* dancing lends its movement a particular kind of communicative complexity which allows it to address personal and collective concerns at once. That is, the dancing gives voice to the soul of the performer herself, while at the same time revealing the way in which that individual's body can embody a pattern of the Cebuano culture.

It is no accident that the latent symbolism of the *sinulog* dance form reveals a general pattern of social action. Traditional dance forms may well be riddled with this kind of latent meaning, because the kinesthetics embodied in them are those of the culture that generated them. Further research is necessary, however, to determine the extent to which dance forms may represent the social dynamics of their respective cultures. The analysis of *sinulog* dancing nevertheless illustrates that the movement patterns displayed in dance forms, inasmuch as they can be understood to serve as models of the social life of various cultures, can be considered as important sources of communication about the distinctive principles of cultural and social performance.

REFERENCES

Balane, J. I. (1954). *The fiestas of the coastal towns of Southern Bohol: An evaluation of their socioeducational significance.* Unpublished Master's Thesis, University of San Carlos, Cebu City, Philippines.

Bartenieff, I., with Lewis, D. (1980). *Body movement: Coping with the environment.* New York: Gordon and Breach, Science Publishers.

Briones, C. G. (1983). *Life in Old Parian.* Cebu City, Philippines: Cebuano Studies Center, University of San Carlos.

Dell, C. (1970). *A primer for movement description: Using effort/shape and supplementary concepts.* New York: Dance Notation Bureau.

Hollensteiner, M. R. (1973). Reciprocity in the Lowland Philippines. In *Four readings on Philippine values* (IPC Papers #2, pp.69–91). Manila, Philippines: Ateneo de Manila University.

Leitz, P. S. (1962). *Preliminary translation of the Munoz Text of Alcina's History of the Bisayan Islands* (Vol. 4). Chicago, IL: Philippine Studies Program, University of Chicago Anthropology Department.

Tenazas, R. C. (1965). *The Santo Nino of Cebu* (Series A, no.4). Cebu City, Philippines: San Carlos Publications.

Turner, V. (1967). *The forest of symbols: Aspects of Ndembu ritual.* Ithaca, NY: Cornell University Press.

12

Br'er Anansi: Individual and Cultural Expressions in Antigua, West Indies

INGA TREITLER

University of Illinois, at Urbana-Champaign

This chapter attempts to reconstruct a cultural theme inferred from performances like folklore and calypso, and from a 100-year-old key informant, Mr. Mack. Mr. Mack also talks at length about several episodes in his life which are crucial to one of his constructions of self and he seems to relate them to analagous episodes in the "Anansi" tales of the region. It is by reference to the characteristics of Anansi the spider, the popular West Indian trickster of Ashanti (West African) origin, that the cultural theme becomes apparent.

Br'er Anansi has a special significance in Antigua, as well as in the other parts of the Caribbean, with cultural features of West African syncretic origin. He is a focal symbol in Turner's sense (1974, p.88), representing as he does a coincidence of opposites and embodying qualities of liminality (Pelton, 1980). For example, he is sometimes a man, and sometimes a spider; sometimes a family man and sometimes a bachelor; sometimes an aggressor and sometimes a victim. It is this kind of ambiguity in his identity and behavior that makes him a threatening figure who challenges assumptions about what to expect in every day life from kin and friends, and these challenges are played out with variations in every folk tale.

Anansi has been written about by West Indian commentators and scholars for many years. And in addition to the wide popular appeal as folklore, Anansi is recognized as a useful metaphor. He appears in many political and social analyses (Bennett, 1966; Jekyll [1907], 1966; Nettleford, 1966; Omard, 1984; Salkey, 1964, 1973; Sherlock, 1966).

The story summary presented here is from a collection of West Indian folktales for children (Sherlock, 1966), but is also documented in the oral tradition of Antigua. The story is called "Br'er Anansi and the Plantains."

It takes place on market day, when all Anansi's friends and neighbors are taking the produce from their gardens to sell at market. Anansi hasn't been working his field, so he has nothing to sell, and no money to buy anything. He's thinking about his predicament, and is especially concerned about how to find food for himself, when his wife, Crooky, appears and tells him to get out and find something to eat because the kids are hungry. He tells her not to worry, that he's going out to *work* for some food . . . and he heads on down the road. At noon he's still empty-handed, but the sun is hot and he takes a nap. When he sets off again, he runs into his friend Rat, burdened down with a bunch of plantains so big and heavy, that he has to bend down almost to the earth to carry it. Anansi greets Rat like a long-lost friend, asks about the family . . . and looks hungry. Rat returns Anansi's concern, asking after the family, and Anansi gives a full report of his hardship. He tells his tale in four different ways before Rat finally gives him some plantains. Now, Anansi has a family of five, and Rat gives him four plantains. Anansi goes home to his wife and she cooks the plantains. He comes and distributes the plantains among his family members, taking none for himself. He sits down looking despondent and hungry. He explains, first to his wife then to his children, that his needs must be met last. With this, the three children and his wife each give him half of their plantain, so he gets two plantains, while each of them gets only a half.

The key elements of this story are (a) Anansi hasn't worked; (b) He is worried about feeding himself; (c) His wife wants food for the children; (d) He goes out to get food and meets Rat; (e) He gets Rat to give him food; (f) Rat only gives him enough for the family; (g) Anansi gets some for himself anyway; (h) His family is deprived as a result of his guile.

There should be no manifest difficulty in understanding this story; however, by examining the level of interpropositional relations (to reconstruct some of the unarticulated cultural themes that underlie the text), the textual understanding is thickened. Two of these themes are outlined here, although they would neither be apparent to the uninitiated reader/listener nor articulated by most Antiguans telling the story.

It is assumed within Antiguan society that, when resources are scarce, and they often are, one shares with those who are less fortunate, especially family and friends. This prescription is strongly enforced in Christian churches and is reinforced by belief in the undesirability of being what is called "bad-minded" (i.e., being "small," "covetous," etc.). In this story, Anansi twice plays on this prescription: once with Rat and once with his family. If, in either case, they had turned him down, they would have been accused of being bad-minded.

Another background theme, "tiefing," is complementary to the bad-mind theme and metonymically evoked by bad-mindedness. *Tiefing* is what Anansi does by taking what's not his and profiting from the bad-mind notion which lurks in the background. With these two background themes outlined, the story gains a special significance—a thickness of meaning that it lacks for the uninitiated reader or listener.

What has so far been referred to as a cultural theme can be called a schema, because it evokes the literature in cognitive anthropology from which the theoretical framework here has been developed. A *schema* is a formal unit of knowledge to which the speaker refers in organizing an utterance or recounting an experience. Schemata imply knowledge structures which make it possible for the speaker–actor to leave large units unarticulated, taking this information to be a fact of the way the world works and assuming that others will share the relevant schemata. Those interactions that build on schemata that are idiosyncratic or more restricted can leave the participants with feelings of disorientation . . . an experience shared at some point by most ethnographers.

The analysis for schemata in a text develops around three key assumptions:

1. Through minute examination of the text, unspoken information, taken for granted by the author, can be elicited.
2. With access to this unspoken information, the analyst can reconstruct the schema by reference to which the author has organized the text. Thus, the argument is made that, by looking closely at a text, one can learn something about the author's cognitive processing of the world.
3. Schemata are used by individuals to interpret experience and make decisions for future action.

The analyst can expect to find indices to a given schema across texts, in the form of key terms, subject matter, metaphors, or a range of other possible clues.

These points, and the methodology followed in the analysis, are based on a series of collaborative efforts by Michael Agar and Jerry Hobbs (1982, 1983, 1985). They apply techniques from artificial intelligence to informant-controlled interviews and reconstruct schemata underlying the construction of the text.

To analyze a text for its underlying schema, it is partitioned into its natural parts in units of decreasing inclusiveness. Following Agar and Hobbs (1985), the crucial first step toward revealing underlying schemata is to articulate the linkages between propositions. These linkages are often taken for granted and remain unstated in natural texts. Some of these linkages are *background*, *cause*, *enable*, *then*, *contrast*, *explain*, and *specify*. From every linkage, certain inferences can be made. If, for example, A *causes* B then we infer some unequal power relation between the referents in the two propositions.

The segment of the Anansi story that is selected for minute analysis lies at the beginning of the story, when Anansi tells his wife that he's going out to work for food. In Figure 1, the segment is notated according to proposition, the smallest unit of analysis. The relations between the propositions are diagrammed in Figure 2. The complementary forces discussed earlier as cultural themes are the schemata that were reconstructed from this analysis. For example, between the pair of propositions 10 and 11: "I am going out to work for food, do not worry," and the pair 12a and b: "Every day you have seen me go out with nothing and come home with something," a tension is created, because, whereas one would expect a relation of *enable*, the relation is in fact *contrast* because of Anansi's record of not working (see propositions 1b, 3a, 3b in Figure 1). To arrive at this analysis, one has to play with the various possible relations before discovering the one that makes sense, given the rest of the story and otherwise elicited background knowledge.

Working for food will not *enable* him to get food. It never has, as we know from the first few propositions. *Contrast* is the reverse: that is, it points to an untruth in Anansi's words. It is here that the tiefing schema first enters, although the uninitiated listener might not recognize the allusion until he or she has acquired the schema. This schema can be diagrammed for this story as in Figure 3, with hardship as the key to the schema, and the lower nodes as alternative means of solving the problem. Every node is, however, necessarily implied by the tiefing schema. Furthermore for this diagram to work one has to assume that the speaker has knowledge of the bad-mind schema.

I have suggested that a given schema may be used in all cases involving a common problem. Here the problem is hardship. The stories that Mr. Mack tells about his own life reveal many episodes around the theme of hardship. The segment analyzed is part of a story about his father's aspirations that he become a minister. In this segment, Mack accounts for why he does not become a minister.

Among the necessary points of background information are the following:

1. Ministers gain respect. The work is desirable for this reason, and for the reason that it is a more secure livelihood than that of a share cropper (Mr. Mack's ultimate work).
2. Mr. Mack's father shows favoritism among his sons, because he expects the rest of the family to support Mr. Mack while he trains to be a minister.
3. There is a rule of primogeniture in Antigua, and the son referred to in the segment is the oldest son.
4. In the story of Cain and Abel, about the first two sons of Adam and Eve, Cain is the eldest and thought of as treacherous and ill-willed, whereas Abel is upstanding and honest. Abel is favored by God, and, out of

Figure 1. Anansi

Local Coherence: propositions, Segment I—Block A

1a It was market day
 b. but Anansi had no money.
2a He sat at the door of his cottage
 b. and watched Tiger and Kisander the cat, Dog, Goat and a host of others
 c. hurrying to market
 d. to buy and sell.
3a He had nothing to sell
 b. for he had not done any work in the field.
4. How was he to find food for Crooky and the children?
5. Above all, how was he to find food for himself?
6. Crooky came to the door and spoke to him.
7. You must go out and find something to eat.
8. We have nothing for lunch, nothing for dinner, and tomorrow is Sunday.
9. What are we going to do without a scrap of food in the house?
10. I am going out to work for food.
11. Do not worry.
12a Every day you have seen me go out with nothing
 b. and come home with something.

Figure 2   Anansi: Block A, interpropositional relations. Local Coherence—Block A: "Anansi"

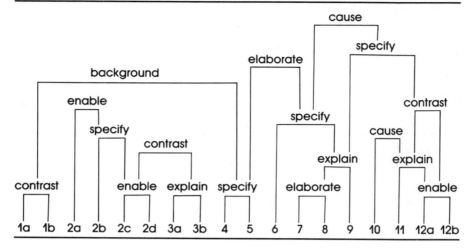

jealousy, Cain slays Abel. Good Christians are exhorted to be like Abel not like Cain.

Block A of Figure 4 represents an idea of how the schema emerges. Mr. Mack says that his bother's ill-will (his badness: see proposition 2, Figure 4) caused Mr. Mack to have to go to work to feed himself (4a-b). So propositions 1-3 *cause* 4a and b (Figure 5). In this way, Mr. Mack accounts for his current hardship by reference to his brother's unwillingness to share his good fortune. In other words, his brother's bad-mindednes *causes* Mr. Mack's hardship.

In other portions of the interview, Mr. Mack paints his relationships with

Figure 3.   The *tiefing* schema. Definition: taking what belongs to someone else, without violating cultural rules . . . presupposes knowledge of "bad-mind" schema.

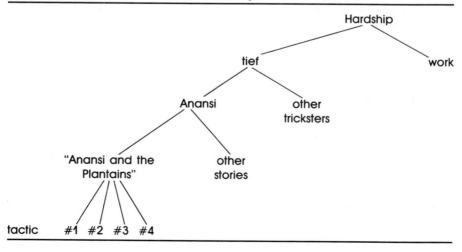

Figure 4. Mr. Mack

Local coherence: propositions

Block A	1.	No [I didn't become a minister].
	2.	Bad brother.
	3.	My brother stopped me.
	4a.	I had to work
	b.	to feed myself
	c.	because of him.
Block B	5.	You know about Cain and Abel in the Bible?
	6a.	He didn't love me,
	b.	he only pretended he loved me.
	7a.	He left my father and went away first
	b.	and my father did not give the others the trust of his key.
	8.	He gave it to me.
	9.	With the money.
Block C	10a.	Well [my brother] felt hardship on his soil
	b.	so he came back down
	c.	and wanted to get back what he had before he left.
	11.	But I didn't give it back to him.
	12.	Nor did my father.

other members of his family in similar ways. In this way he is constructing himself as an individual who has been victimized by family members who tief him. Among these is his mother's brother, who sold land that his father inherited after Mack's mother died, causing the family to have to move from place to place. The children of this well-off uncle were not any more generous: they were too small to help. In another story, Mr. Mack wills his sister's son all the savings he has. When this nephew finds out about the will, he draws out all the money, leaving Mr. Mack with nothing.

In both of these stories, Mack reveals his construction of self as a man who has had a hard life, made harder because others in his family either tief him or bad-mind him. This construction helps him account for why he is suffering such hardship despite his intelligence and his upwardly mobile striving. Some of the

Figure 5. Mr. Mack: Block A—interpropositional relations

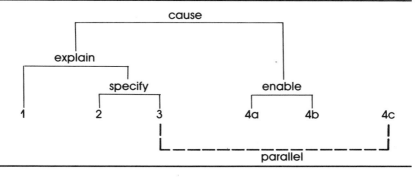

symbols for this last construction are his membership in the Anglican church and dream of becoming a minister, his pride in the achieved position of deputy manager on the estates, his work in Panama, and his father's desire that he get out of the cycle of contract labor.

Construction of self is an individual performance whose emergence is dialogical, that is, dependent upon a defining other, like the second voice in a dialogue. The number of selves can be infinite, or as infinite as the number of defining others. In the various constructions of self, the individual calls on familiar schemata. This is what happens in Mr. Mack's interview.

As indicated, the interrelated schemata of bad-mind and tiefing have cultural as well as individual expressions. They emerge in most Anansi tales, and in many calypsos (Prince, 1984) and have been recognized as having generality across the Anglophone Caribbean (Austin, 1983). In Antigua they are discussed by politicians and social commentators. The schemata described here could *not* have been constructed without reference to this broader cultural context.

This chapter points to the importance of undertaking an analysis of texts at the level of individual utterances to complement and buttress the global-level analysis of the interpretive mode. This calls for taking the perspective of the individual in cultural and individual performances, as well as looking at cultural performances from the group perspective.

REFERENCES

Agar, M., & Hobbs, J. (1982). Interpreting discourse: Coherence and the analysis of ethnographic interviews. *Discourse Process, 5,* 1–32.

Agar, M., & Hobbs, J. (1983, Spring/Summer). Natural Plans: Using AI planning in the analysis of ethnographic interviews. *Ethos, 11* (½).

Agar, M., & Hobbs, J. (1985). Building schemata out of interviews. In J. W. D. Dougherty (Ed.), *Directions in Cognitive Anthropology.* Urbana, IL: University of Illinois Press.

Austin, D. J. (1983). Culture and ideology in the English speaking Caribbean: A view from Jamaica. *American Ethnologist,* 223–240.

Bennet, L. (1966). Introduction to *Jamaican Song and Story,* Walter Jekyll. New York: Dover Publishers.

Jekyll, W. ([1907] 1966). *Jamaican song and story.* New York: Dover Publishers.

Nettleford, R. (1966). Introduction to *Jamaican Song and Story,* Walter Jekyll. New York: Dover Publishers.

Omard, D. (1984). Socio-cultural development in the Caribbean since 1834. Unpublished paper presented at the celebration of 150 years freedom from slavery, held in St. Johns, Antigua.

Pelton, R. (1980). *The trickster in West Africa: A study of mythic irony and sacred delight.* Berkeley, CA: University of California Press.

Prince, A. V. (1984, Winter). Anansi folk culture; an expression of Caribbean life. *Caribbean Review, XIII*(1).

Salkey, A. (1964). Political spider. In *Black Orpheus, an anthology of African and Afro-American prose.* Nigeria: Longman's.

Salkey, A. (1973). *Anansi's score.* London: Bogle-L'Ouverture Publications.

Sherlock, P. (1964). Introduction to *Jamaican song and Story,* Walter Jekyll. New York: Dover Publishers.

Sherlock, P. (1966). *Anansi the Spider Man.* London: MacMillan.

Turner, V. (1974). *Dramas, fields, and metaphors.* Ithaca: Cornell University Press.

PART IV

SALES, PROMOTION, AND ORGANIZATION

13

Organizational Cultures: An Examination of the Role of Communication

University of Alabama

The recognition, study, and understanding of organizational cultures has become increasingly important. With the decline in productivity, Americans began looking at the Japanese organizations which were increasingly successful, and discovered the operating cultures were a major part of the reason (Pascale & Anthos, 1981, pp. 21–33). In their study of excellent American companies, Peters and Waterman (1982) presented profiles of strong, cohesive, and productive organizational cultures with outstanding financial success. Numerous other studies have followed in an attempt to understand the interrelationship between the behavior, values, norms, and communication processes. This study will outline communication behavior used to establish, develop, and maintain organizational cultures. Included is an examination of the impact of the environment on the culture. From this study's point of view, the issue is not whether culture is an important variable, but which culture is operating, what information is available because of the norms, and how it affects the individuals in the organization.

ORGANIZATIONAL CULTURES

Every organization has a culture which is its shared beliefs and values—its distinct identity. The factors which constitute the culture include the various procedures, activities, and behavior which members regularly or occasionally perform (Baker, 1980, p. 9). Inherent in this definition is a recognition that all actions taken by the organizations, ranging from strategic planning to the process of performance appraisals to the type of lunch room, function as determinants of the organizational culture. The beliefs, values, and identities of the group, office, or organization are created by the interrelations between individuals.

One of the problems with the study of cultures from a communication perspective has been the attempt to draw a distinction between classical theory, human relations, social systems, information theory of organizing, and cultural approaches (Kreps, 1986). A more useful approach is to accept the culture as the overriding influence in the organization. For example, the scientific management approach, or classical theory, is based on top-down control features with management being the ultimate power in the organization. Although the individuals implementing this approach probably are not too concerned with its cultural impact, the members of the organization certainly pick up, respond, adapt, and understand the cultural manifestations. The same is true for each of the other approaches. Implicitly or explicitly, each approach depends on cultural cues and behavior to explain the relationship between the theory and the communication factors in an organization. By broadening the approach to make culture all-encompassing, individuals interested in studying organizational communication have a much more useful tool. More than any other term, *culture* accurately describes the communication practices and behaviors which comprise an organization.

ENVIRONMENT

The two overriding factors in the culture are the environment and the structure. The environment in which the organization operates provides the framework for the entire culture. A very useful way to divide the business environment is to look at the degree of risk in any decision and the speed of feedback on the decision's success. Deal and Kennedy (1982) use these interacting variables to explain their four classifications of corporate cultures. In the "macho/tough guy" culture, there is a high risk with great expenses, and the feedback regarding the decision is quick. Their examples for this operating environment include construction, cosmetics, management consulting, venture capital, advertising, television, movies, publishing, sports, and entertainment organizations. The obvious uncertainty of the entertainment field, with the extremely costly outlays for a movie or television program and the speed with which the critics, box office, or Neilson ratings decide success, make this category clear.

When the degree of risk is small and the feedback is immediate based on sales, the corporate culture is labeled "work hard/play hard." Included in this group would be real estate, computer companies, automotive distributors, door-to-door or neighbor-to-neighbor programs, mass-consumer companies such as catalog promotions or T.V. sales, office equipment companies, and retail stores. Within this type of culture, the specific risk is minimized by the inconsequential outlay by the organization for the actual product. Whether a new Levi jean or a specific computer program sells is not determined over a broad time frame, and the cost to the specific store is minimal if it fails and success in sales is very quick. Producing the Cabbage Patch doll was much more risky to one organization that the risk taken by a particular consumer outlet store.

"Bet your company" is an appropriate title for high risks in research and development and the slow process of feedback which will eventually determine the success of the product. As can be seen by the list of company types, the decisions are incredily ponderous and the impact massive. Capital goods companies, mining and smelting, large-system businesses, oil companies, investment banks, architectural firms, computer design companies, and the actuarial end of insurance companies provide examples of these types of cultures. Choosing to finance a housing development or design a shopping center provides operating examples of this group.

Finally, when the process is slow and the feedback practically nonexistent, the culture is labeled "process." Many matured organizations become oriented to this type of behavior, since their actual day-to-day operations have little apparent impact on much of anything. Examples include banks, insurance companies, financial service organizations, large chunks of government, utilities, and heavily regulated industries such as pharmaceuticals. For most individuals connected with universities or hospitals, or any other organization where the planning time frame is extremely long range, this type of culture is all too apparent. If one is thinking about a 5-year plan, the everyday behavior of a given unit simply does not seem to matter, and demands for action are rarely well received.

These four types of corporate cultures—macho/tough guy, work hard/play hard, bet your company, and process—offer four useful means for discriminating the culture's major characteristics. Since organizations exist within a larger environmental framework, looking to the degree of risk and the type of feedback regarding the decision's success provides an excellent means for determing culture types.

STRUCTURE

How the organization responds to the environment constitutes its structure. Three basic schemes can be used to determine the type of structure operating.

The first is represented by the classic breakdown of authoritarian/ bureaucratic, compromise/supportive, and performance/innovative. The authoritarian/bureaucratic culture is often seen as the archetype of traditional management. Decisions originate at the upper levels of the organization, are enforced through rules, rewards and punishments, and compliance is the most important behavior. Cultural success requires careful acceptance of the established order. The compromise/supportive culture is group based with an interest in consensus and interpersonal and group commitments. When it works well, the concept of participatory management represents the characteristics of this culture. Finally, the performance/innovative culture tries to get individuals to produce for their own satisfaction. Entrepreneurs (as epitimized by Hewlett-Packard, where every individual seems to find personal gratification in the organization's phenomenal yearly growth rate of 25%) provide a useful example of this type of atmosphere. Even more specific would be a sales force where each person does what must be done for personal success.

These are useful means for dividing the culture's structure, since some predictions can be made regarding the success in developing innovations or changing the structure. For example, attempts at participatory management will be likely to fail in all but the compromise/supportive culture.

A corporate culture grid can also be constructed based on the amount of participation and the tendency toward reactive or proactive behavior (Ernest, 1985). This provides four cultures. The *interactive* culture is high on individual participation but slow to react (e.g., McDonalds and Sears). Apple Computer and IBM are *integrated* cultures where there is high participation and very proactive behavior. A *systematized* culture is reactive and uses little individual participation, which has historically been the case with Ford Motor Company. An *entrepreneurial* culture is proactive but not highly participative in the decision making. A company like Merrill Lynch, for example, might be bullish on America but bearish on seeking out individuals for their input. Ernest contends the grid allows management to understand what changes must be made in the structure before trying to introduce an innovation or change.

The last structural analysis is also the most complete. Peters and Waterman (1982) outlined those factors which have lead to excellence for over 20 years for 49 American companies. They conclude that "without exception, the dominance and coherence of culture proved to be an essential quality of the excellent companies" (p. 75). Specifically what constitutes the excellent cultures can be summarized by eight characacteristics.

A *bias for action* means the excellent companies avoid bureaucratic entanglements and needless paperwork. Being *close to the customer* means that the customer actually becomes part of the organization's information structure and acts as a human resource for the company. In the best high-technology companies, for example, this attribute is practically an obesssion. This style can be contrasted with the traditional view of customers as something to be manipulated.

Productivity through people is characteristized by language which indicates the importance of each individual, the informality of the chain of command, extensive training and socializing, and a tendency to see the organization as an extended family. In this way, employees do not experience traditional feelings of being easily replaced, laid off, transferred, or terminated whenever the business changes.

Autonomy and entrepreneurship are both encouraged in the excellent companies through communication, norms, and incentive systems designed to protect and reward the innovators. Failure is seen as an attempt at success, and being wrong is much less of a prohibited behavior than not taking a chance. *Hands-on, value driven* means these companies know what they stand for. The values are rarely transmitted in writing or put down formally, but, instead, take the form of stories, myths, legends, and metaphors. So, "Frito-Lay tells service stories, Johnson & Johnson tells quality stories, and 3M tells innovation stories" (Peters & Waterman, 1982, p. 282). Too often, organizations become driven by remote control where structure is the only force in operation.

When you are good at something, you *stick to the knitting*. In other words, Proctor & Gamble stays out of the computer business and IBM does not try to sell toothpaste. For some organizations, more is simply better, with the hope that apples and oranges will lead to synergy and growth.

Finally, *simultaneous loose/tight properties* provides a summary of the reasons why the excellent companies have maintained their predominance. There is a combination of central control with substantial decentralization, autonomy, and entrepreneurship.

Any of these three structural schemes will allow a better understanding of how things are done in a particular organization. The traditional divisions provide an accurate test of the potential success for various changes. The Culture Grid divides cultures on two important interacting variables. The last one provides a useful contrast between what has been done traditionally and what has been done successfully.

VALUES

Organizational cultures provide basic values for the individual regardless of the quality of the organization. The common beliefs and values of the employees provide the unwritten guidelines to be followed. When there is a clear congruence between personal and organizational values, the impact on the organization's success is significant (Posner, Kouzes, & Schmidt, 1985, p. 308). Essentially, by articulating the values and making sure they are consistent with underlying assumptions, a philosophy for operating as an organization occurs (Schein, 1985, p. 17). These values are the bedrock of the culture and "they define 'success' in concrete terms—'if you do this, you too will be a success'— and establish standards of achievement within the organization" (Deal & Kennedy, 1982, p. 14). At 3M, for example, employees are told "never kill an idea." The value of innovation is therefore clearly translated to managers, engineers, and office staff.

The four types of cultures identified earlier also foster different values. For the macho/tough guy culture, a fast-paced youth orientation a results in an "all or nothing" attitude. The expectation is for early rewards for effort expended and the belief is that individuals prove themselves with a great productive concept. The work hard/play hard culture emphasizes fun and action. In fact, activity is the key to success. Deliberateness is the behavior most valued in the bet your company culture where long term, careful decision making is the norm. In the process culture, *how* things are done is most important since *what* is done cannot be managed. So, being technically perfect is the most prized value.

These four culture types indicate that, regardless of the particular attributes of an organization, the cultural underpinnings lie in the values. If the values are shared between employees and the organization, then there can be a common purpose. When there are divided loyalties, such as a union-management conflict, individuals find they cannot easily apply cultural norms since the values are unclear. If it is clear that management values profit over employees or innovation, the "bottom-line" cost-control measures will dominate, since employees will assume that rewards will come from following the prevailing value. If there is an abundance of memos responding to memos, the shared value is probably one of survival in the future rather than an orientation to problem solving in the present. In any case, the values represent the translation of the culture into individual and group behavior.

RITES AND RITUALS

Every organization has ceremonies which celebrate and reinforce the interpretations of the organization's values. These ceremonies are also used to reinforce heroic behavior. The rites and rituals can range from the annual company picnic or the predictable Christmas bonus check to graduation ceremonies to a more ongoing, continuous behavior pattern.

Once again, Deal and Kennedy (1982) offer an interesting look at the different types of rites and rituals depending on the cultural expectations. In the macho/tough guy culture, rituals are used extensively to reinforce willingness to make big decisions and take big chances. Since the driving force includes intense pressure and a fast pace, the rituals often involve superstitious behavior and bonding meetings which serve to indicate some extra special "force" might be operating. The advertising industry, for example, often reinforces rather bizarre behavior to support the value of creativity.

Since the work hard/play hard culture values activity, there are a large number of contests and morale-boosting conventions. The language is infiltrated with words such as "I've got a live one" or "let's rope this one" or "let's pull this one in." The cross between the sports world and the sales world is obvious, and retired sports figures such as Fran Tarkenton are in high demand as convention speakers and providers of numerous motivational tapes, videos, books, and training courses. Through video, Herbalife, among others, extends their sales conventions to the entire sales force. In such cases, the content of a meeting is not as important as the morale-boosting impact.

The bet your company culture relies greatly on meeting format, including who attends and the titles given to the attendees. In fact, titles are almost a preoccupation, and receiving a new one is considered a major ritualistic reward. These rituals serve to reinforce the structure and formality of the organization. Being well prepared for the meetings is interpreted as a personal belief in the values of the organization.

Most individuals have experienced the difference between productive and nonproductive meetings. The process culture tends toward the latter, with drawn-out meetings going nowhere. Although the meetings do act as a reinforcement of the group, the value underlined is internal fortitude rather than a sense of accomplishment. Probably nothing epitomizes this type of culture more than the extensive use of memos and reports that seem to disappear. Individuals must still write the memos to perpetuate the process, but energy is spent on making sure one's life is safe rather than courageous. In the process culture, meetings and memos become ends in and of themselves.

Every culture provides distinct means for reinforcing the behavior through encouraging certain activities. The excellent companies go to a great deal of trouble to provide celebrations which make people feel good about themselves. Catch phrases like KISS—Keep it Simple, Stupid—are continually reinforced so the process does not take away from the activity. Proctor & Gamble forces all memos to be one page in length so others can act on the information quickly. Texas Instuments clearly states that more than two goals equals no goals at all. In other words, the structure is kept simple and the rituals are made very direct. The rites are used to let employees know just how well they are doing in maintaining the culture's values.

HEROES, LEADERS, SURVIVORS, AND ROLE MODELS

When Peters and Waterman started their study of the excellent companies, they did not expect to find leaders playing a particularly positive part in the success of the organizations. In fact, they "found associated with almost every (one) of the excellent companies, a strong leader or two who seemed to have a lot to do with making the company excellent in the first place" (Peters & Waterman, 1982, p. 26). The importance of Lee Iaccoca of Chrysler, Mary Kay Ash of Mary Kay Cosmetics, and other well-known celebrities is apparent. However, the less flamboyant founders of the IBMs, Bechtels, Maytags, and many other organizations are still leading forces in how the culture is interpreted. "The culture of an organization is influenced by the words, attitudes, values, and style of the chief executive officers" (Donnelly, 1984, p. 9). When Tom Watson of IBM acts out his belief in "respect for the individual," or Ray Kroc of McDonalds honestly "sees beauty in a hamburger bun," the employees have a strong statement of values by the leader and hero.

These heroes carefully fulfill their commitment to their organization. J. Willard Marriott, Jr., CEO of Marriott Corporation, logs 200,000 miles a year visiting more than 100 of the Marriott hotels and resorts (*Wall Street Journal*, February 22, 1985, p. 29). Sam Walton, founder of Wal-Mart Corporation, visits each one of his 750 stores at least once a year. Peters and Austin (1985, p. 5) discuss successful leadership, which usually involves M.B.W.A.—Management By Wandering Around. The object of M.B.W.A. is to reinforce values, not to catch job-shirking individuals. By listening and being available to workers, the abstract is made very real.

The four classifications of cultures can also be used to predict the type of behavior expected from heroes, role models, and survivors. For the macho/tough guy culture, those who are internally competitive are regarded as those who make a difference. These individuals survive the "war of ratings" or the perils of publishing. The super salesperson who "never says die" is the hero of the work hard/play hard culture. This individual will meet a client at any time, overcome any objection, and rebound from rejection. When the culture is betting its company, heroes are those people who persist with the correct decision and accurately analyze the risks. Anyone who violates these traits will not survive. Finally, the process culture values individuals who protect the system. Careful attention to when and where to send memos, which channels to use, etc., is highly valued.

If an organization is operating effectively, individuals supporting the cultural goals will be rewarded. Under the macho/tough guy culture, individual winners will be celebrated at the various rites and immortalized in the myths of the organization. The work hard/play hard culture makes over employees who fill customer needs. When the organization is designing buildings, as in the bet your company culture, being right and careful is glorified. As might be expected, in the process culture being conservative and trivial is rewarded.

> No one company fits perfectly into any of these molds, and different parts of the same organization will exhibit each of the four types of cultures. Still, most companies have overall tendencies toward one of the cultures because they are responding to the needs of the market place. (Deal & Kennedy, 1982, p. 125)

CULTURAL NETWORK

All these types of behavior are bound together by a cultural network which functions as the primary, although informal, carrier of corporate values and heroic mythology. Storytellers, spies, priests, cabals, and whisperers from a hidden hierarchy of power within the company. "Working the network effectively is the only way to get things done or to understand what is really going on" (Deal & Kennedy, 1982, pp. 14–15).

Each company has a large number

> of unwritten rules of communication (let's call them "howdy" rituals) which occupy an amazing amount of company time. But take them away and no one will know how to behave. They let people know where they stand, reinforce an individual's identity within the company, and set the tone for the way in which people relate to each other. (Deal & Kennedy, 1982, p. 64)

The excellent companies use a large number of "atta boy" comments. One study of successful general managers found they depended on a great deal of informal communication and joking, rather than formal chains of command (Kotter, 1982, p. 127).

Finally, there is a strong dependency on the use of small groups which are the basic building blocks of a culture (Peters & Waterman, 1982, p. 126). How the group is used shows the influence of effective or ineffective cultural patterns.

Two very different examples demonstrate the point. When faced with the first Tylenol poisoning case, Johnson & Johnson was strongly advised to abandon the brand name and the familiar red box and retreat to a different label. The management group in charge of Tylenol strongly objected, since they felt Johnson & Johnson was not to blame and should not therefore change their product. The J & J group was so confident in the ability of their team to reach a good decision, they invited *60 Minutes* to tape the deliberations for a public showing. The team decided to keep the brand name, and Tylenol, after several months of severe losses, regained the number one ranking among pain-relief products. The power of a group to carefully examine a particular action was clearly demonstrated by J & J.

At the opposite end of the scale is the information-management process used by NASA which culminated in the Challenger tragedy. What happened to lead to the fatal launch "was as much a failure of decision-making as technology" (Kruglanski, 1986, p. 48). As became well known after the disaster, engineers at Morton Thiokol, the company that manufactured the solid rocket booster, were opposed to the launch. The group was not used effectively and the result was a damaged organization. In many ways, the impact of the type of culture demonstrated in the second example leads to a lack of creativity on the part of organizational participants.

> Managers are not stupid people. They quickly learn which kinds of behaviors produce reward and which produce punishment. All the managers in my study (of courageous decisions) whose ideas were accepted said they would likely act courageously in the future. Three-quarters of those whose ideas were rejected said, "No, never again." (Hornstein, 1986, p. 60)

The culture provides the means by which people know what to do and not to do.

IMPLICATIONS

Organizational cultures are so important it may be necessary to alter the prevailing culture to guarantee productivity, employee satisfaction, and, perhaps, survival. However, the success or failure of corporate reform hinges on management's ability to change the firm's driving culture (Allaire & Firsitotu, 1985). Organizational cultures tend to go through three distinct stages of birth, midlife, and maturity. At the point of maturity, the organization must be willing to change and adapt the culture. Processes like employee participation and the creation of new leadership styles are required (Schein, 1985, pp. 314–327). But change is difficult, since the culture has already set the operating standards for the organization. U.S. Steel, for example, has a "corporate culture (that) is old-fashioned and extremely out of date, and (it) may take a decade or more to change" (Symonds, Miles, Ivey, & Prokesch, 1985, p. 52). Naisbitt and Auburdene, in *Reinventing the Corporation*, are concerned with the reaction of leaders to the need for a change. Faced with the challenge, "the attraction of the authoritarian style is irrestible, and wrong" (1985, p. 35). So, new cultures require new leadership techniques which emphasize participative values and procedures.

Fortunately, there are many examples of successful cultural changes. The most dramatic type of example would be the General Motors' Saturn Plant, which simply created an entirely new structure and cultural attributes. On a smaller scale, GM also conducted what they labeled the Black Lakes Experiment, where they were able to get labor and management to reach joint goals for success (Solberg, 1985). An even more complete explanation of cultural transformation is outlined in *Tranforming the Workplace* (Nora, Rogers, & Stramy, 1986). The General Motors Linovia Engine Plant successfully redesigned the entire operating procedures, plant culture, and labor-management relations in order to guarantee survival and success.

In the health field, which is fundamentally different from the production of automobiles, cultures have been altered. Blue Cross of California was able to step back, look at its prevailing culture, and develop a new one which adapted to the many changes in the health industry (Ulrich, Clack, & Dillon, 1985). J & J is in the process of entering the medical technology field, and the company has accepted new ways of operating in order to fit in the environment (*Business Week*, May 14, 1984, pp. 130–133, 137).

Each of these examples underscore the relationship between culture and the environment. Since the glue holding the structure together is communication, it is obvious that behavior must be altered to make the culture more successful.

One of the major differences between organizational cultures and cultures in general is the matter of time frame; in most cases, organizations have fewer than 50 years of cultural history. Acculturation occurs rapidly in the working place, and the excellent companies go to a great deal of effort to teach their culture to the uniniated (Pascale, 1984). The choice would seem to be between allowing the individual to pick up the cultural cues and rules or to teach these cultural expectations. To obtain cultural change, organizations find the participative process the most likely vehicle, since it provides immediate feedback to the individual and, when done well, success to the group.

Somewhere in between the reports of the failures and successes of organizational cultures are examples of attempts at cultural shifts that have both failed and succeeded. From my own experience as a organizational consultant, three examples may help explain this middle ground.

Almost all financial services organizations have seen the need to shift their prevailing cultures toward sales. Given the precarious nature of the industry, this is a wise strategic choice. With a large bankcorp, we designed a set of extensive training seminars to help shift the bank and its employees away from a process culture to a sales-oriented or work hard/play hard one. Traditionally, bankers have been very concerned with how things are done and not too interested in going out and selling bank services. We used intense role plays and case studies and were able to shift the approaches used by the seminar's participants toward highly successful sales techinques.

The bank's culture did not change as quickly. In fact, there was virtually no feedback to individuals who attempted to make sales or venture into new sales territory. Instead, the people who had been with the bank for the greatest period of time still made the established, "big ticket" calls, since the culture still placed a great deal of importance on titles and length of service. Quarterly reports, and the subsequent recognition, were based on total dollar amounts instead of the number of calls, number of new accounts, or additional creative ways of increasing business. Ironically, this created or maintained heroes who protected the system and frustrated those trying to implement the needed change. Gradually, changes have occured and the culture has shifted, but the needed changes have been minimized by inattention to the prevailing culture.

Value Analysis, an engineering-oriented, problem-solving technique, was adopted by a large utility to meet criticism by the state regulatory agency'that the utility was not being innovative enough. This technique requires 40 hours of training. We trained five groups of 15 participants. Each group had three subgroups which solved a major problem or procedural issue at the utility. During the sessions, our belief in the method was reinforced as we consistently saw innovative, well-designed, extensively documented solutions to the problems. To determine the actual success of the program, we distributed a questionnaire to each participant about the program. Almost every individual indicated a lack of response by upper-level management to any of the proposed changes. Because utilies are accustomed to operating in a process culture, every one of the proposals has to be reviewed by two committees and then reviewed by upper management. With 15 well-documented proposals, this system bogged down. So, the proposals, and therefore the participants' enthusiasm, have languished. The utility is in the awkward position of having supported a major cultural change without building in any feedback or reinforcement mechanism to support the change.

The third example reflects a successful change in culture because of a shift in leadership and in operating methods. A profitable plastics company had been suffering under an autocratic leader for many years. An international conglomerate purchased the firm and turned it over to an individual with a vision for a new culture. He created a motto which reads "Our Commitment to Each Other" and emphasized four terms: "fairly, honestly, justly, with dignity." He implemented a major training and development program and open-door management. Suggestions were rewarded regardless of their financial worth, as an indication that each person was a valuable asset for making the effort. Hourly workers were guaranteed part of the company's profits through a profit-sharing program.

Although the changes were extensive, many of the employees were already schooled in the autocratic culture and were slow to change. The new leader simply maintained a consistency of vision and proved his sincerity. After 5 years, changes in the culture have occured, albeit slowly. The training and development seminars have evolved from disinterested, mandatory attendence to active and willing participation.

These three examples are intended to show the pervasive impact of an organization's culture. Changes not acceptable to the culture will be rejected. Assimilation of new techniques and operating procedures will occur with the proper system support.

CONCLUSION

Looking at organizations from a cultural perspective provides some useful insights. The various types of communication behavior operating in specific cultures are, initially, a consequence of the environment and the structure. Once established, rites and rituals and prevailing values perpetuate the culture. The hero and leader show other individuals in the organization the importance of specific behavior. The cultural network pulls it all together.

Observing the need to alter an organization's culture and actually being able to do so are very different issues. For most organizations, changes must occur as the standard operating procedures becomes outdated. By developing a full understanding of the interrelationship of all the variables of a culture, changes can successfully occur.

REFERENCES

Allaire, Y., & Firsitotu, M. (1985). How to implement radical strategies in large organizations. *Sloan Management Review, 26,* 19–34.

Baker, E. L. (1980). Managing organizational cultures. *Management Review, 69,* 8–13.

Deal, T. E., & Kennedy, A. A. (1982). *Corporate cultures.* Reading, PA: Addison-Wesley.

Donnelly, R. M. (1984). The interrelationship of planning with corporate culture in the creation of shared values. *Managerial Planning, 32,* 8–12.

Ernest, R. C. (1985). Corporate cultures and effective planning. *Personnel Administrator, 30,* 49–50, 52–56.

Hornstein, H. A. (1986). When corporate courage counts. *Psychology Today, 20,* 56–60.

Kotter, J. P. (1982). *The general managers.* New York: The Free Press.

Kreps, G. L. (1986). *Organizational communication: Theory and practice.* New York: Longman.

Kruglanski, A. W. (1986). Freezethink and the Challenger. *Psychology Today, 20,* 48–9.

Naisbitt, J., & Aburdene, P. (1985). *Re-inventing the corporation.* New York: Warner Books.

Nora, J. J., Rogers, C. R., & Stramy, R. J. (1986). *Transforming the workplace.* Princeton, NJ: Princeton Research Press.

Pascale, R. T. (1984). Fitting new employees into the company culture. *Fortune, 109,* 28–30, 34.

Pascale, R. T., & Anthos, A. G. (1981). *The art of Japanese management.* New York: Warner Books.

Peters, T., & Austin, N. (1985). *A passion for excellence.* New York: Random House.

Peters, T. J., & Waterman, R. H. (1982). *In search of excellence.* New York: Harper and Row.

Posner, B. Z., Kauzes, J. M., & Schmidt, W. H. (1985). Shared values make a difference: An empirical test of corporate culture. *Human Resources Management, 24,* 293–309.

Schein, E. H. (1985). *Organizational culture and leadership*. San Francisco, CA: Jossey-Bass.

Solberg, S. L. (1985). Human resource management in action—Changing culture through ceremony: An example from G. M. *Human Resource Management, 24*, 329–340.

Symonds, W. C., Miles, G. L., Ivey, M., & Prokesch, S. (1985, February 25). The toughest job in business. *Business Week*, 50–54, 56.

Ulrich, D. O., Clack, B. A., & Dillon, L. Human resources in a changing world. *Human Resource Management, 24*, 69–80.

14

Loaded Images: An Analysis
of the Music-Video Industry

AUDREY KORELSTEIN

The Graduate School of the City University of New York

NEAL WEINSTOCK

META-COMMODITIES AND PROPERTIES

Music videos add pictures to records; they illustrate, too, the interworkings of art and commerce in the music industry. Videos clarify the murky transmutations of media properties—and they parallel similar transformations in the companies that produce them. They also serve as motors for social reproduction. In this chapter we elaborate on these processes by proposing that music videos be viewed as *meta-commodities*. That is, they are commodities that grease the tracks on which other commodities move.

Additionally, music videos create particular sets of contradictions and mediations in both production and consumption. While music videos serve to mediate certain dilemmas of their teenage audiences, their production creates contradictions in the lives of the people who make them. The latter part of this paper develops these ideas.

Obviously, music videos are products that sell other products. This observation has become conventional wisdom with regard to record albums, feature films, clothing and the like—that is, as pertains to consumer products. That ho-hum observation, however, glosses over the ways music videos also sell, promote, or add value to, various interindustry products, services, and careers. These other products include: stars' concert appearances; the talents of the production company that made the video for little other compensation; the popularization of nightclubs; and a certain cohesion of corporate togetherness within conglomerates with interests in the various consumer product areas that videos promote. Because, thus far, videos only sell themselves on a limited basis, in theatrical music features and on home videocassette, their producers have been encouraged to realize their worth through a combination of all these means. In fact, their interindustry uses make videos an exotic new form of capital.

The industry term *property* was originally used in theater and film, and is now used throughout the communications industries (or the self-called "marketing media") to denote an entertainment that belongs to a certain producer. It is always in a producer's interests to find the most possible markets for a property, and also to prevent imitative products from competing; it is always in other producers' interests to imitate successful properties and capture their markets. These economic forces have honed an industry-wide recognition that the term property defines the group of all possible permutations based on an entertainment.

Such transformations are an essential part of the marketing of properties. Music and books are commonly presold to filmmakers before they are even written. Licenses to produce toys, magazines, comic books, games, clothing, various memorabilia, books and movies about the production process, songs, television and radio programs, theatrical plays, and other transmutations of a property are routinely sold by licensing divisions of each major communications company. More important, though, to the economic success of all concerned, the licensing campaign is orchestrated to coincide with advertising; ad "impressions" and product introductions are timed so that each meets its market at a "window" appropriate to maximize the profits of those who own the property.

What Levi-Strauss said about permutations of Amerindian myths (1963, p. 223) probably applies more so to record and movie properties:

> By systematically using this kind of structural analysis it becomes possible to organize all the known variants of a myth into a set forming a kind of permutation group.

All marketable properties demonstrate these transformations. Fictional properties go through the same multiple transformations as myths, but ostensibly, in the worlds of commercial song, cinema, and television, for a commercial reason: a previously successful property is a proven audience grabber; investors think it can perform its magic again in other media—or over again in the same medium, as movie remakes and song covers demonstrate. This diachronic tendency has a synchronic corollary, which James Monaco, in discussing movies, refers to as a doctrine of "just like/completely different"(1984, p. 14). In peddling a project, it must be demonstrated to investors or distributors (typically one and the same) that said project is just like some current hit. But direct copies of hits not only are of questionable legality, they also tend to bore audiences with base lack of originality. So a project must also be completely different from the recent hit it is just like. How to reconcile these two opposites? Similar mythic essence is called into service, with enough incidental differences thrown in for the project to qualify as a different property.

Monaco's "just like/completely different" calls to mind Levi-Strauss's statement (1963, p. 203) that myth is, both the same thing as language, and also something different from it. Here, too, the past experiences of linguists may help us. For language itself may be analyzed into things which are at the same time similar and yet different. That is precisely what is expressed in Saussure's distinction between *langue* and *parole*, one being the structural side of language, the other being the statistical aspect.

We have no desire to claim universality for certain myths or mythemes, in our opinion a serious weakness in Levi-Strauss's work. We see merely that his work and the work of other structural analysts of fairy tales and myths, especially Vladimir Propp (1968), is quite relevant to the structures of fiction motion pictures, popular music, and music videos, which wed the two.

Filmmakers of the New Hollywood are very often quite conscious of their own use of myth, though they may not understand their actions within a general structural framework. Most of our current generation of filmmakers studied the subject in school, and the results can be seen in iconographic quotes, homages, and outright cribbing from past masters. Stanley Kubrick and Shelley Duvall study Bruno Bettelheim on fairy tales before making the former's *The Shining* or Duvall's *Faerie Tale Theatre* television series. George Miller, director of *The Road Warrior*, calls Joseph Campbell a formative influence, and Campbell corresponds with George Lucas after seeing *Star Wars*, a remake of a retelling of a Japanese myth (*The Hidden Fortress*, directed by Akira Kurosawa) using images from John Ford westerns reset in outer space. There are other examples, all of which would surprise few participants in an industry whose product is storytelling. Myth in the form of old movies or far older poetry is equivalently and commonly thought of, in the industry, as a repository of popular, and therefore profitable raw material. Exploitation of myth is a conscious economic activity in the motion picture business, and, by extension, in the making of music videos—because most workers in production companies making videos see themselves as at an early stage in a filmmaking career that will someday culminate in producing or directing feature films.

Such conscious exploitation of myth has been much less the case in the music business; music videos are effecting changes that are making this into a conscious activity there. In the last few years, each album project must be thought of as a *high concept* (a film industry phrase for a quickly communicated, mythic theme). The image of the artist is now far more important then ever.

MYTHIC ECONOMICS

Just as music videos make clear a continuum of content between various popular media, they make clear an economic continuum. Indeed, a common term used throughout the communications industries to denote what they do is *marketing media*. Advertising, film, television, pop music are bought, sold, and produced by companies with fingers in each pot, ready to exploit the "synergies" of properties.

Usually, a motion picture is the transmutation of a property that is most important to its owner; it is the riskiest and possibly the most profitable. Producing a feature film represents a tremendous investment—thus tremendous risk. In 1985 all films lost, on average, $16 million each. Pop records are risky, too; they take as long to produce and cost up to $1 or $2 million to produce. Film and record-label cosubsidiaries of the same conglomerates like to share risk and costs by using each to sell the other. Music videos perform the transformation at an average investment of only $50,000.

Transmutations of star identity are more at the heart of the record business than they are at center stage of the film business. Here, the "artist" is the property, and only the performer is the "artist." Concerts, licensed products, singles, albums, appearances in films and on television, and, of course, music videos, are all transformations of the artist's identity. The recording artist is a product, but the record made by the artist is a product, too; one may be created by the other, but they are certainly not the same product. There is a commercial tension between them, as economic interests in each product sometimes clash.

The difference between a star in motion pictures and an artist in pop music is worthy of note, since music videos are blurring the two. In films and TV, a star is only one of a "package" of "elements," all of which are marketable components of a property—even as they may also be properties in their own rights. The package is what gets marketed by a film's producer so as to get investors and a distributor. The ideal investor in any film is its distributor, because the distributor realizes the bulk of a film's profits. The old Hollywood studios have metamorphosed into a combination of these two functions—and of practically nothing else—while also having become part of larger entertainment conglomerates. Record labels perform the same two functions, and are also parts of the same conglomerates. Stars are only part of a package in motion pictures (albeit the most important part), while, in the record business, they have usually been the entirety of the package. The added complexities video brings to the music art form are welcomed (in private) by record industry executives, who hope they will help make the artist only a part of a package of elements, and thus more easily dominated. The package of elements in a property can be seen as a smaller-scale metaphor for the combination of entertainment industries into the marketing media, and also into a few large conglomerates.

Even if video making submerges the artist in a medium that dilutes his or her economic power versus the label, and even if the recording artist would prefer to remain merely a musician, not a multimedia star, video has become an economic necessity to any artist's recording career. Even those who prefer to be known only for their music, and who already have sufficient fame to sell records, have found that their public forgets quickly without a video to market their product. Thus there are now no pop stars so recalcitrant as not to have made a few music videos.

Such choice is totally unavailable to beginning artists. For them, the traditional "demo tape" now must be produced on video as well as audio. The expense of doing so is far more than twice as high and necessitates involving whole other areas of expertise and equipment. Industry insiders generally believe that the need for video restricts entry into pop music stardom by, first, raising the necessary investment, and, second, demanding incorporation of more various talents into a product. This will be seen as but one aspect of capital concentration in the marketing media, with related causes.

The filmmaking dictum that all the money in a project should be "seen on the screen" is especially germain to music videos, which are reknowned for their low budgets. In other words, each element in the financial entity of the package should be seen in the video; the goods used as locations, props, special effects, etc. (all these are typical "elements"), should add visible value to the entertainment. The video thus becomes a metaphor for the diversified marketing media corporation.

JUXTAPOSED ELEMENTS

Of course, the plot of a music video production must call for the performers to utilize some products (besides themselves). The performer must wear clothing, and that clothing must be fashionable. The function of a music video is to make the commodities within it appear fashionable, at least partially by association with other fashionable commodities.

Michael Jackson is fashionable: therefore, the soft drink he drinks is fashionable. Or, the single white glove he wore was fashionable. Was this single white glove any more or less fashionable than Bruce Springsteen's tee shirt and jeans of the same period? Bruce Springsteen and Michael Jackson each identify target markets (which overlap to some extent), and sell their associated fashions to each of those markets. The music video form needs to create glamour by association. The star, or would-be star, shows association with the items he or she uses in order to take on some of their magnetism. Likewise, these items take on value from their association with the star. Stereos, soft drinks, cars, and clothes are sold at the same time as the commodity that is the star, or that is the video.

Bruce Springsteen has been singled out for his reputation as a pop star with a relatively noncommercial image. But Bruce Springsteen as entertainment is not merely Bruce Springsteen. He is himself plus the added value of his association with working-class clothing, acoustic and electric instruments, old-fashioned microphone, smoky halo of light, etc. All of this goes well into a pure concert video, with no added dream imagery, visual storytelling, or other techniques to sell the commodity that is Bruce Springsteen. Even as a minimalist commodity, there has been a great deal of iconic value added to the artist/musician who is Bruce Springsteen.

When Madonna performs in concert, she benefits from different but equivalent added values. When imagery and musical sounds are added to her videos which are not possible to add to her concert performance, the product that is Madonna benefits at the same time as the entertainment that is Madonna benefits. The product that is Madonna may indeed have little entertainment value (thus little commodity value) without the added value of all the other commodities with which she associates. Conversely, the product that is Springsteen might just shrink in value if combined with the "production values" (as the motion picture industry historically refers to the added value under discussion) that are used to raise the value of the product that is Madonna. Springsteen in dinner jacket would be a very different Springsteen than the one the buyers of the Springsteen product have come to like. The added value of products used in music video is not constant; they vary in their juxtapositioning. In Saussure's terms, they are signs that take meaning as they associate and contrast with each other.

HARDWARE/SOFTWARE

The recording artist is a product, but the record made by the artist is a product, too; one may be created by the other, but they are certainly not the same product. There is a commercial tension between them, as economic interests in each product often clash.

Records are merchandised, in typical consumer capitalist fashion, as tangible, ownable goods. Large-scale distributors who think of themselves as labels sell their goods to smaller distributors who call themselves distributors but are called "rack jobbers" by much of the industry. Their existence is justified by the service they provide retailers: they perform all inventory functions, decide which products are selling well and which aren't, and stock only those that sell well. Retailers often simply provide floor space and order-takers. As in most U.S. distribution chains, the middle-man, who in this case is the rack jobber, is often blamed by the consumer for the putative high cost of goods. In fact, both the label and the public have reason to resent the rack jobber, not for raising product costs, but for the way in which the rack jobbers lower individual product costs.

Essentially, a rack jobber performs an extensive market research service by continually inventorying how well each record sells at various retail locations. The rack jobber then limits the stock of products to those that "sell through." This is the service the retailer is most interested in; it allows a maximization of investment in display space, and it allows the retailer to employ unskilled, cheap labor to watch that space. Precisely the same pattern may be observed in record shops as in supermarkets (which, incidentally, sell some 25% of records in the U.S.), auto parts stores, fast food restaurants, electronics retailers, jewelry shops—in fact, all the basic businesses one might find operating in a typical suburban mall.

These last two categories of commodities (jewelry and electronics, the latter including audio and video hardware) are now increasingly found in the same

shops, a very interesting juxtaposition in light of the historic failure of continued attempts to profitably sell both records and record-playing machinery in
the same stores. (Though relatively uncommon, it is not difficult to find a very
few examples of stores selling both in most major cities. However, where stores
do carry both records and record-players, it is always only one that is specialized in, and the other that is used as part of the "sales environment," as
retailers say, to help sell what the store is more interested in selling.) Jewelry
and electronics are both examples of "hardware"; records are "software."
Hardware/software has come to be a most important opposition to modern
consumers. Mystified views of a hardware/software dichotomy (there is little
basis in engineering fact for polarizing the twain) are equally held by consumers
and by producers on all levels of the social pyramid; in an information age this
opposition is an ever greater support for the organization of that pyramid.

Records have always persuasively demonstrated the hardware/software opposition. For most of the technology's existence, they have demonstrated it
better than anything else; but for most of that existence, records were the only
example most consumers were familiar with, and thus the opposition was of far
less note. Now computers, motion pictures, photography, indeed any medium
of intellectual endeavor (including the older media of writing and plastic art
which were never seen in this light) are seen as software which runs on
hardware. Any browse through popular literature will support a view that the
English-speaking world is popularly seen as a great producer of software and a
bad producer of hardware. The Japanese are equally thought of as wonderful
producers of hardware. Software, popularly, is imaginative, artistic, intellectual. Hardware is machinery, something better made by other machines, or by
people of a different "race."

The reality behind this popular view is partly produced by the view itself,
partly coincidental to it. American corporations have tended to produce software in this country because less labor is involved, and profit margins are
higher; hardware production shifted to low-wage countries, and eventually
ownership of the production process shifted to Japanese, Korean, and Tai-
wanese companies. At the same time, producers of software know American
consumers would never accept foreign faces and accents (much less languages)
in their programming, even if other countries routinely accept American faces,
voices, etc., in their entertainment.

Realistically, hardware contains software and software is made of hardware.
There is such a vast grey area of mixed technology and "intellectual property"
(as a current euphemism for software goes) that it is impossible to demarcate
what each is—except in a relative sense. X may be harder or softer than Y, but
when fixing absolutes of what is fully hardware or software, a problem emerges.
For example, a live improvisational performance is probably the ultimate in
"soft." It isn't even soft*ware* until it is recorded—a process that makes intrinsic
use of hardware. When a consumer needs no hardware to decode the
software—as in the case of a photograph—this may be considered the penulti-

mate in software. Next might come a theatrically shown motion picture. Hardware is needed to decode the software, but the consumer isn't aware of its use. In music industry practice, an analogous but more enlightening situation exists in a club; an audience tends to stand at attention to watch "live" bands perform, then will dance to "canned" but indistinguishable music. The same programming on radio or television (hardware) is very soft, but, as a record or tape, it has physical dimensionality to the consumer, and is thus a little hard. Software such as a videogame which is intrinsically built into its console—as in an arcade—seems wholly hardware to the consumer. Videogames in interchangeable cartridge form are software to be plugged into hardware devices. Software and hardware are terms in the eye of the beholder.

But software and hardware are distinctly unhelpful terms to describe the real process of designing or producing either. In designing an electronic integrated circuit (hardware) or a computer program (software), the procedure is remarkably similar: the designer writes code at a computer terminal, tests the code against design parameters, writes more code, strikes off a copy, tests this in other predetermined environments, and so forth. Mass producing either involves factory processes that are more or less complex to a degree not predictable by whether the product is hardware or software. Vinyl phonograph records may be far easier to produce than hi-fi equipment, but then videodiscs are far more difficult to produce than videodisc players. And if songs themselves imply a different, more artistic sort of production from the design of discs they are encoded on, the cultural perception of this difference has been continually narrowing, at least since the Museum of Modern Art began exhibiting industrial design as art.

To go back to the most soft example, a live performance, it is interesting to note that almost all performers use microphones and other amplification equipment, even for wholly acoustic (nonelectronic) performances in rooms which are so small as to make amplification unnecessary. Even more interesting, amplification systems in small nightclubs are often so bad as to make the performer sound very distorted—to an impartial ear. Yet performers, clubs, and audiences tend to prefer the distorted sound of a bad amplification system to natural, unamplified sound. Amplification renders the performance into something more "professional," something more like hardware, more of a valued commodity. Performers and clubs buy into this way of thinking to considerable cost.

Before music videos, there was no reason at all for any interconnecting network among nightclubs. Now, nightclubs tend to subscribe to video distribution services to program software for their extensive standing investment in video display hardware. Thus music videos can be seen as intensifying the same sort of changeover that occurred in the 1960s, when most night clubs switched from live music to recorded music, and which grew through the 1970s with ever more realistic sound equipment, all complementary to the slow growth of nightclub chains in suburbia. Just as music video represents an added investment on the part of pop performers and their record labels, so the equipment to reproduce music videos in nightclubs represents added capital investment. The numbers are not insignificant: theatrical-size video projectors sell for $60,000, (small ones sell for $3,500) and a bank of video cassette recorders, time base correctors, switcher/special effects generator, and video amplifiers can cost $20,000. Popular music is, on all levels, ever more capital-intensive and centralized.

The hardware/software dichotomy is the rationale for increasing capital intensiveness and capital concentration in the music club business. Club owners believe, and believe that their customers also believe, that the more worthwhile nightclub experience is one surrounded by more hardware gadgetry. Since competition for the most technologically advanced nightclub has progressed in the last decade from the need to have impressive audio technology through video and now various robotics, it is therefore to be expected that satellite delivery of videos to chains of nightclubs is on the not-very-distant horizon, as is the purchase of complex production-type special effects devices by independent clubs.

In the eye of the average beholding customer, software is easy to buy. Some sort of reputation about the product has been communicated; the consumer may or may not be satisfied with how well the software lives up to that reputation but does not blame the seller if it does not. The seller is not expected to teach a consumer how to consume the product, and neither expects to haggle over price. Just the opposite is true of hardware; it is hard to buy, and often intimidating. Often, hardware is manufactured to be purposefully intimidating, as in hi-fi systems with many knobs and switches that are best left unused. Here the expected "impressive-technology look" decides the form, but it is common knowledge among hi-fi marketing executives that most consumers who use equalizers, dynamic expanders, video-effects devices, or other gadgetry degrade sonic and visual quality by doing so. Many engineers who design products see themselves as reluctantly responding to uniformed demand. Most salespeople are little more aware of electronic technology than consumers, and are also "sold by the sizzle, not the steak." Such equipment, then, appeals to the same consumptive itch that jewelry and fancy cameras scratch. However nonsensical it might seem to expect electronic expertise from jewelers or camera salespeople, these items are frequently sold in the same stores.

There may seem to be no direct link between consumer hardware and music or film software, but consumer hardware is of direct interest to producers of software as something that their own consumers are interested in buying. Also, software producers are concerned with hardware as it affects the physical form of the soft product. Finally, artists and producers are also consumers; they make their products as a commentary on the tools used in production. Producers are aware that, without the right hardware in place, there would be no music-video industry. They have an interest (though likely a subliminal one) in perpetuating it in place, in order to perpetuate their own positions.

THE FLOATING CRAP GAME

The record label, more than most corporations, is a conglomeration of shifting alliances among quickly changing employees and contractual obligations. Artists are all free agents; production companies are formed by ad-agency employees moving toward more creative work, and generally have only a few full-time employees. Many job categories are entirely filled by free-lance employees. Industry job tenure, whether free lance or standard employment, is relatively short. Most of the corporations in the field have been run by most of the same people, at one time or another. The profit-making goals of a corporation as a whole balance against the goals (not all related to income) of the people who fill its roles. Decision making thus implies large and quick profits on individual projects.

The business of making music videos is as glamourous to would-be workers as music videos can be to their viewers. This glamour continually keeps the industry's labor pool extremely large. While unemployment in America generally tends to swing between extremes of 5% to 10%, music, motion picture, and music video unemployment is generally estimated at over 50%. There always exists a large labor pool willing to work for next to nothing—in exchange for nonfinancial rewards such as artistic concerns or association with a glamour industry. Even directors of music videos make very little money for their efforts, especially as compared to the television commercials most also make (and which subsidize their forays into music video).

The quick and huge profits of the few rest on the wishful artistic servitude of the many; the music video production industry thus exemplifies a most volatile laissez-faire capitalism. Its labor market has more in common with the America of the 19th century than the rest of the late 20th century U.S.

Certainly, this structure could not exist if it were not subsidized by the rest of corporate America. Music-video workers can afford to do such work by working at other, more dependable jobs whenever necessary. The position of record and motion picture production companies within large scale corporate ownership can be similarly understood. A record company that can produce a "Thriller" is a prized subsidiary; in the years when that record company has no such hits, it is subsidized by the steadier income from more prosaic fellow corporate divisions.

The corporate giants, after unprofitable learning experiences, tend to give free rein to the executives in charge of their entertainment subsidiaries. It is important to note that, while the same few corporations may have record, film, television, and other relevant divisions, different transmutations of a property frequently are sold to the film division of one corporation, the record division of another, the television division of a third, etc. Within the large corporate structures, personal contacts create their own shifting structures.

The record labels have given similarly free rein to the content of music videos. This may seem surprising in light of the similarity of the form to advertising, which is rigidly programmed, but is only to be expected when the medium is placed within the pop music world; labels only rarely have been known to dictate content to recording stars. Conspiracy theorists will be disappointed to discover that the homogeneity of commercial popular music is but an extreme example of conformism: if any product finds great success, countless other products will copy it.

Makers of both commercials and music videos often feel that, if content were to be dictated in music videos as in commercials, record labels would have to pay more for the privilege. However, instead of this money going to directors to assuage artistic egos, it would most likely go toward employing scriptwriters, analogous to the copywriters and creative directors who devise commercials. As the income that music videos produce begins to seem more sure, budgets continue to rise, and continue to justify ever-larger hierarchies of creative decision making. Eventually, this should result in a more corporate style of decision making regarding content—as has happened in the previous growth curves of older media. It will also be in the interests of label managers, in their struggle for power with their own stars.

A long-standing bit of industry jargon refers to the ever-changing but some-how seldom-changing number of major Hollywood studios (traditionally seven, with various temporary majors filling in for the dismembered M-G-M), as the "floating crap game." Two of the current line-up (Universal and Warner Bros.) have corporate ties to the major record labels (MCA and Warner/Elektra/Asylum). The other two major labels, CBS and RCA, have recently been sold to foreign owners—new players from other industries—Sony (hardware) and Bertelsmann (print).

CONSUMERS/PRODUCERS

The logic of using videos to sell products rests on the key notion that teenagers identify with the performers whose records they buy. Music videos must give expression to teenage feelings as a first step to succeeding in their purpose; once the viewer's sympathy is gained, the second step is to sell the product. While most videos overtly glorify individual accumulation—and target audiences respond by buying—for one large subset of rock and roll, rebellion and alienation from the adult world are overarching battle cries. Music videos associated with this subset assume a particularly interesting dynamic. Because videos also must act as commercials for products, the expression of rebellion and alienation serves as what advertising people call "the programming environment" for the sales message. If the overt theme of a video is rebellion, the commercial purpose of that video must subvert that theme. In such music videos, there exists a constant tension between these recurring overt and underlying themes, mirroring the tensions of those adolescents ambivalent to the consumer culture in which they must take part. Their combination in music videos seems to make the contradictory themes compatible, and thus helps viewers do as they must do to join society: channel rebellion into consumption.

In these cases and where overt and underlying themes are less contradictory, music videos are successful tools for social reproduction; eventually, "buying into" identification with the performers leads to buying the $6.99 record purchase (but how much better it seems to sound on a $12.99 Compact Disc), and also the clothes, the cars, the endless "I consume therefore I am."

Arguably, by demonstrating lip-service sympathy for the impressionable teenager, music videos trick the viewer into becoming a good consumer capitalist. To restate this relationship in a less cynical way, commercial music videos do for teenagers what many believe fairy tales do for young children: mediate the dilemmas of socialization.

Similarly, the last points we wish to make concern the contradictions embodied by those on the production side of music video. Producers buy into a romantic view of themselves as artists—even the businessmen atop corporate structures think of their risk taking and deal making as a high art. To elaborate the analogy, if some artists are driven to produce art no matter what other returns they get in life, many people can only comprehend that motivation as compared to the greater number of society's members who are driven to make money, no matter what else is sacrificed. Pop music, movie, and video industry participants typically demonstrate this equivalence quite neatly: they chase the golden fleece in both the forms of art and dollars, and consider the production or attainment of either an art form.

Finally, one last contradiction. In our experience, industry participants are most often convinced they are engaged in vaguely subversive lives, or careers outside the gray corporate system; the glamour of the videos they make, and their self-view as artists, conveniently block realization that their product exists largely to reproduce that system. In this light, note the recent crop of music benefits, such as Live Aid, Band Aid, and Farm Aid: These activities communicate a certain level of altruism and political consciousness compatible with an emic view of that workforce's sensibilities. Industry participants signal these interests as identity markers. This current fashion inflects the self-congratulatory tones always permeating industry-award nights and other public group-solidarity functions. The ideology demands a signalling for themselves as concerned artists rather than as agents of consumer capitalism. Only privately do record company executives confide that such concerns are good for business too.

The art of music video can be seen as a motor for social reproduction; through its seductive allure, it ensures a constant source of labor, and in the process defines and constructs elitism and nonelitism. It channels rebellion into consumption just as it channels different commodities into permutating with each other.

REFERENCES

Barthes, R. (1967). *Elements of semiology*. New York: Hill and Wang.
Barthes, R. (1977). *Images, music, text*. New York: Hill and Wang.

Goldman, W. (1983). *Adventures in the screen trade*. New York: Warner Books, Inc.

Hawkes, T. (1977). *Structuralism and semiotics*. Berkeley, CA: University of California Press.

Levi-Strauss, C. (1963). *Structural anthropology*. New York: Basic Books.

Levi-Strauss, C. (1975). *The raw and the cooked*. New York: Harper & Row.

McLuhan, M. (1964). *Understanding media: The extensions of man*. New York: Signet Books.

Monaco, J. (1984). *American film now*. New York: Zoetrope.

Panofsky, E. (1955). *Meaning in the visual arts*. New York: Doubleday.

Propp, V. (1968). *Morphology of the folktale*. Austin, TX: University of Texas Press.

Wollen, P. (1972). *Signs and meaning in the cinema*. Bloomington, IN: Indiana University Press.

Wollen, P. (1982). *Readings and writings: Semiotic counter strategies*. London: Verso Editions.

15

Cultural Norms and Foretalk in Direct Sales Interactions

MARK SANFORD

Montaigne, Inc.

Everyone is familiar with approaching a stranger to make a request for a service, for information, for an action, or for an opinion. This approach to a stranger, often uninvited, is a key feature of *direct sales*. This work may be defined as crossing the social gulf to consort with a stranger for the purpose of requesting his or her business and gaining compliance with that request.

Requesting a light from a stranger; asking for directions from someone in the street; making an approach for service at a bank, restaurant, or convenience store; requesting permission to pass in a patrolled area—these are all *crossings*, bridgings of the social gulf that exists between each of us and those unknown to us. They are comparatively easy crossings, because not much is requested, no further relationship is intended, and the investment of time and energy is limited; thus the crossing is limited in scope and jurisdiction. Rejection is unlikely or, if it occurs, not significant for deeply held values or a significant identity.

A crossing made for the purpose of requesting business from a stranger, however, is fraught with difficulty. This is because the approach may be unwelcome, and failure or rejection is likely to occur. And, perhaps most importantly, this process is likely to generate various negative emotions such as fear, humiliation, shame, frustration, doubt, and dismay.

The salesperson's chief task is to manage these negative emotions so that he or she may negotiate the crossing necessary to succeed in sales. In fact, it is the management of these emotions—and the emotions of the prospect as well—that constitutes the "work" in this kind of labor.

For the past 5 years I have been engaged in real estate, home improvement, and encyclopedia sales. The observations offered here have grown out of my personal experience of the sales process and out of interviews with colleagues in the field.

It is commonly assumed in the social sciences that all actions are goal oriented. Therefore, activity may be viewed as attempts to restructure the environment to satisfy some desire. Social behavior, then, becomes a matter of managing, inducing, and controlling other people to help the actor achieve his or her goals.

Thus, passages across the social gulf are usually motivated by desires and consist of interacting with people to get them to help achieve one's goals. People, in this view, become resources, tools, means, opportunities, impediments, obstacles, and challenges.

People do try to get desired behavior from others. These are compliance-gaining behaviors. They are "ways of getting results in interactions" (Parsons, 1963, pp. 37–62). And it is also true that people vary in the ways they go about doing this.

Among the strategies for getting results are those pertaining to the warm-up—or foretalk—to get the prospect in the proper frame of mind to receive a request for compliance. Foretalk in sales may be defined as that bit of talk that comes before a sales presentation. It may embrace a great variety of topics that often pertains to activities or objects in the immediate setting or to an event common to both agent and prospect. It usually is of short duration—anywhere from a minute or so to 10 or 15 minutes, depending upon the congeniality of the subjects. However, longer warm-up sessions are possible, and it is thought by some that the longer the foretalk, the shorter "the close," i.e., the final, successful gaining of compliance. Tales—probably apocryphal—are told of sales folk still patting the family dog a half-hour into the interview, but this is uncommon. While business talk comes later, the foretalk is meant to prepare the way.

Foretalk may follow the cultural norm of making complimentary remarks about the others' appearance, demeanor, or domestic space, thereby acknowledging the other as a valued person. It is also done to convey positive sentiments to the other so that the other feels closer to him or her and more relaxed.

Foretalk is a form of wooing in the commercial arena. It is a way of generating fascination and attraction to fortify one against later dangers, particularly rejections and failure.

Foretalk serves several functions. First, it paves the way to securing the trust of the prospect. Trust is conveyed verbally by reference to past sales, by providing a list of previous clients, by a vocabulary that represents some minimal level of education and understanding, and by a sincerity of tone that shows that the matter at hand is serious and worthy of credible attention. Trust is conveyed nonverbally by dress—much emphasis in direct sales is placed on good appearance. Corollary possessions like a late model car, or personal accessories like an expensive diamond ring or gold watch, are used to convey credibility.

Second, foretalk helps gain the positive regard of the prospect for the agent. A pleasing manner helps ease the way. The salesperson is taught several stratagems for obtaining a positive evaluation by the prospect. The main ones are to ask questions, show interest in the prospect, and find something in the immediate environment to compliment. One can usually find something in the garden, or kitchen, or living areas, some feature of interior decoration or artifact, that stands out as especially attractive or unusual and thereby warrants favorable comment.

A certain amount of self-disclosure is usually recommended by sales managers. They caution, however, that too much tends to violate the rule that, by getting the prospect to talk about himself or herself during the warm-up, one stands a better chance of gaining their friendship.

A final function of foretalk is to gain information and insight about the prospect's interests, proclivities, or urgent desires that can later be used to shape the presentation to appeal to these features.

Foretalk, then, is an opportunity to sound out the prospect about personal interests and domestic conditions with an eye to how this information can later be used to strengthen the attractiveness of the offering.

What one is trying to convey during foretalk is an experience that, once the prospect has undergone it, will lead to compliance with a request to purchase goods or services. Thus, lobbyists, fund raisers, solicitors, canvassers, negotiators, and salespeople all must face this challenge to render the experience so attractive, appealing, and inviting that it leads to their common objective— compliance with their requests. Foretalk, in this perspective, is the first step, and it is a crucial one, for it establishes the groundwork from which all else must follow.

The various functions of foretalk mentioned all are subsumed under a larger purpose, which is to induce the prospect to buy, to attract his or her positive compliance to one's request, to lure him or her to a positive decision.

Foretalk should be seen as one among other strategies of compliance-gaining behavior.

In Parsons's (1963) view, these strategies may be divided between those that seek to change the prospect's definition of the situation and those that seek to change the situation itself. Foretalk obviously belongs to the former category. It may be seen as part of an active manipulation of the prospect's environment in a positive way, termed *rewarding activity* as distinguished from coercion, negative reinforcement, altruism, debt, or moral persuasion (Marwell & Schmidt, 1967, pp. 350–364).

Skinner (1953) mentions "emotion" as a positive reinforcer which involves manipulation of the target prior to a request for compliance. Here the actor tries to establish "emotional predispositions" towards himself or herself or the desired action, so the prospect is more likely to comply. This is identical to our analysis of foretalk. Skinner also mentions drugs and alcohol as serving the same function. In this regard, I was taught in sales always to refuse alcoholic beverages if offered by a prospect, although any other drink was acceptable since it allowed the opportunity to show one's exhaustion from serving so many willing buyers before arriving at that prospect's doorstep.

Foretalk in the sense used here is a form of ingratiation analyzed by Goffman (1959). In a later work Goffman (1983) speaks of "small talk" that may initiate a transaction, as a mini-version of the "preplay" that brackets larger social affairs, and as evidence of a change of alignment in natural talk which he labels a "footing." He also reminds us that preplay is followed later by "postplay," or what in sales is known as the "button-up." In this maneuver, if the prospect has just purchased a set of encyclopedias, for example, he or she will be showered with small gifts to prevent "buyer's remorse" later on.

If foretalk can be viewed as a legitimate and recognized strategy that sales folk use to gain compliance from their prospects, how important a strategy is it in terms of frequency of use? Marwell and Schmidt (1967, pp. 350–364) developed a list of 16 compliance-gaining behaviors derived from the literature on persuasion, social power, and stimulus response theory. Then they administered a test to a sample of 600 college students, asking for the frequency with which each respondent believed he or she would use a given strategy in four different compliance situations including one involving a sales presentation. Of 16 strategies, three were found to be the most frequent and to be interrelated. These three were: the *promise* strategy, where the actor offers a reward in exchange for compliance; the *pregiving* strategy, where the actor rewards the prospect before requesting compliance; and the *liking* strategy, where the actor is friendly and helpful so that the prospect will get in a good frame of mind before a request for compliance is made. This latter strategy is clearly subsumed under foretalk.

All three involve active manipulation of the prospect's environment in a positive way. And—to rephrase the findings of Marwell and Schmidt—all three were found to be the most socially acceptable, the compliance-gaining styles that people will most readily use. The authors argue that individual compliance-gaining styles may primarily reflect the extent of each power resource possessed by the individual and his or her willingness to tap the source. Thus, many people may eschew all techniques of a given strategy, either because they don't possess the requisite type of power or because they find its use distasteful, risky, or costly.

In this regard, it is important to emphasize the fundamental difference between foretalk and offering rewards, for, although they are functionally equivalent in terms of their usefulness for persuasion, their emotional impact is quite different.

As Hochschild (1983) has noted, the chief problem facing those in people-interacting jobs is one of managing feelings in reaction to what people do to us as well as managing others' feelings. The management issue in foretalk is how to avoid being too obvious in making compliments, not showing too much interest or charm, for then the prospect may suspect manipulation. If this occurs, the prospect may take offense at being treated like a pawn or puppet and subsequently resist appeals for a sale. It is important, then, that the agent manage by *inhibiting* more obvious displays of deference, attention, and appreciation.

Since all agents are not equally adept at foretalk, and since foretalk is not necessarily effective, it is not surprising to lean that many direct-sales organizations provide a back-up lure—the bribe. Sometimes known as the "freebie," or give-away, or door-opener, these gifts, offered before the sales presentation, are also meant to facilitate compliance. There is a switch here from an appeal by charm to an appeal to avarice—from sweet talk and compliments to a hard-nosed offer of an economic advantage, disguised as a "free" gift. It is not really free at all, of course, because, as the prospect receives the offering, he or she also incurs the obligation to reciprocate by listening to the pitch.

The salesperson's dilemma here is how to manage possible ethical qualms in the face of an opportunity to increase the likelihood of a sale. Some agents are unwilling to become bribers, since they do not like exploiting people's greed in this manner. They avoid this conflict by simply refusing to offer free gifts even when pressed by management to do so. Others justify their use by arguing that they need all the help they can get in the face of recalcitrant buyers and an insufficient number of qualified prospects.

In fairness, the salesperson does serve an important and useful function in society inasmuch as he or she informs the consumer about features and benefits of products and services. In a capitalistic system, salespeople are in the front lines; it is on the persuasion of the consumer to buy that the whole system rests.

It can be said that there are different emotion-management problems associated with different kinds of compliance-gaining behaviors. The strategies of *inhibition, avoidance,* and *rationalization* were identified as ways direct sales agents control feelings that tend to arise in the sales process. The argument has been put forward that, for an agent to make a successful passage across the social gulf to consort with a prospect, these strategies may be used. And, further, it has been shown that these strategies are likely to be associated with compliance-gaining behavior of foretalk and award-giving.

More attention needs to be given to the social-psychological cost of this kind of work. As Hochschild (1983) has noted, a worker may become estranged from an aspect of self used in the labor, i.e., feelings. Or he or she may become estranged from the experience that induces these feelings. The large number of people employed in sales work, and the high turnover rate, suggests that these costs are considerable.

REFERENCES

Goffman, E. (1959). *Presentation of self in everyday life.* Garden City, NY: Doubleday Anchor.
Goffman, E. (1983). *Forms of talk.* Philadelphia, PA: University of Pennsylvania Press.
Hochschild, A. R. (1983). *The managed heart.* Berkeley, CA: University of California Press.
Marwell, G., & Schmidt, D. (1967). Dimensions of compliance-gaining behavior: An empirical analysis. *Sociometry, 30,* 350–364.
Parsons, (1963). On the concept of influence. *The Public Opinion Quarterly, 27,* 37–62.
Skinner, B. F. (1953). *Science and human behavior.* New York: MacMillan.

16

Convenience Stores and the Consumer:
Interaction Patterns and Influence

FRANK DANIEL NEVIUS

INTRODUCTION

The Southland Corporation currently has 8,100 convenience stores in the 7-11 chain. These stores cover virtually every American city and are also present in Canada, Mexico, Europe, and Japan. The U.S. market has reached a development point where the 7-11 chain is approaching the designed saturation point of one store for every 12,500 consumers (Liles, 1977).

With yearly service to over one billion consumers, the convenience store chain has become a part of the daily living and social interaction experience of the consumer. Its effect on consumer behavior, product orientation, or acculturation has not been systematically examined. It is necessary to understand the consumer/convenience store interaction to begin to determine the larger social implications of convenience-store operations.

This paper develops an outline of research areas concerning the convenience store and suggests some effects of this store/consumer interaction which have already developed.

STANDARDIZATION

The 7-11 store is operated from corporate headquarters in Dallas, Texas via a sophisticated data network. Each store sends daily accounting data to regional data centers which then transmit this information via satellite to company headquarters. (*Computerworld*, June 3, 1985, p. 4) This is only part of the standardization of the 7-11 stores. They are set up according to company location specifications, stocked according to national sales data, and managed by personnel trained according to company manuals. Any 7-11 store in the United States can be visited and will be found to have little or no variation from any other 7-11 stores (Liles, 1977). Regional or individual variation has been excluded from store operations.

These stores, then, have virtually no local cultural referent. DeFleur and Ball-Rokeach (1982) state that a key element in effective communication for the individual is regular and positive information about the groups and categories to which the individuals belong. Those who rely on the convenience stores for any significant part of cultural information thereby can experience changes in the level of social alienation when their local cultural groupings are not distinctly recognized.

Even if overt change is not apparent due to standardized store operations, subtle influences are almost inevitable. The convenience stores carry national brand products and nationally popular magazines, and have limited clerk/consumer interaction due to average shopping times of 3.5 minutes (Liles, 1977).

INFORMATION ACCESS

The information gained from convenience stores is especially important due to their status in the local consumer area. Since the 7-11 chain built its stores specifically in suburban areas during the growth periods of the 1950s–1970s, it is often the single local information source or part of a limited grouping. With the extended hours and close locations, convenience stores have become a repeat shopping experience for virtually all neighborhood residents (Liles, 1977). A study into the communication environment of the poor (Dervin & Greenberg, 1972) shows that the reliance on local sources for information is greater than with more affluent and more mobile consumers. Therefore, those groups least likely to be acculturated into the larger society are presented with only the majority viewpoints of the convenience stores in their areas, increasing social alienation, and decreasing creative thinking. (Nemeth & Kwan, 1986).

This information limitation is significant even in terms of more affluent middle-class consumers, Recently, the Southland Corporation removed the magazines *Playboy, Penthouse,* and *Forum* from its selection. (*Wall Street Journal,* April 14, 1986, p. 31) These magazines provided liberal articles to consumers of the convenience stores and helped to increase exposure to diverse viewpoints. With the removal of these sources, many convenience-store shoppers will not go to the effort to acquire these magazines elsewhere and so will be exposed to more limited and less diverse viewpoints.

AFFECTING CONSUMER BEHAVIOR

Store Effect on Consumer Patterns

The convenience store has helped to shape consumer patterns in numerous ways. Frequent interaction between the store and consumer, regular patterns of exposure and some degree of acceptance of the operation are major elements in consumer change (Greenberg, 1975), leading to acceptance of practices accompanying store operations.

Times of shopping, consideration of items for consumption, degrees to which a consumer is willing to prepare food, and the actual process of shopping and social interaction during the process have all changed significantly since the start of convenience-store growth in the 1940s. Prior to the advent of convenience stores, most shopping was done at small single-owner stores. These stores stocked merchandise based on owner preference, were open primarily during daylight hours and varied significantly from store to store (Liles, 1977).

The convenience stores by comparison stocked fewer items, specialized in impulse items such as cigarettes, beer/wine and soft drinks, emphasized longer hours, and fast service. Their design was open or glass fronts and store location on the back of property lots to encourage drive-in shopping.

The current profile of a convenience store customer is a middle-class male between the ages of 25 and 35, shopping mostly from 3 p.m. to 11 p.m., spending 3.5 minutes in the store and spending an average of $6.16. Most of the customers are under 30 years of age, buy single items in the categories of beer/wine, cigarettes, or soft drinks, and live within one mile of the store. The average customer shops at the convenience store six times per month, with younger customers visiting the stores much more frequently (Liles, 1977).

Expectations

Product limitations.   The convenience consumer has fewer product choices than he/she does in larger supermarkets. The product lines are fewer, and depth within those lines is narrower. Exotic or less popular items are excluded from shelves for profit reasons. Convenience foods have a particularly high emphasis: prepared foods, "junk" foods, and other products which emphasize ready use are common.

Impulse shopping.   With unlimited hours and close-to-home locations, consumer are encouraged to shop on impulse. Convenience stores are furthering this trend by providing coffee and breakfast foods. Fast "hot-to-go" foods are intended to replace lunch and snack items which the consumer might otherwise prepare. Originally, these stores carried full lines of fruits and vegetables, but, generally, such items have been reduced to a few items in the dairy cases.

Standardization.   The standardization within the 7-11 chain of store operation, product selection, and employee training presents consumers with a more impersonal organization with which to interact. National standardization has eliminated regional variations to any significant degree. Employee/customer interaction is standardized and limited by training programs and the limited purchases of consumers. Less mobile local consumers and repeat consumers are then led into an expectation of shopping as an impersonal experience. This experience, especially for repeat customers in younger or less-mobile categories, limits local acculturation and directs the consumer to other information sources, which have been shown to usually represent majority values as well (*Wall Street Journal*, April 14, 1986, p. 31).

IDEOLOGICAL INSTITUTIONS

Influence

The effect which convenience stores have on individual consumption patterns, and the prominence of these stores in daily life escalates their influence level to that of an ideological institution. These stores are directing consumer disposition towards action and thought. Items, such as junk food and fast food items, have gained legitimacy by their exposure in a major convenience chain which specializes in a clean, respectable image. The consumer which enters the 7-11 store enters a cultural landscape designed according to company expectations and becomes subject, to some degree, to respecting the product decisions.

Majority Culture
This cultural landscape which the store projects is one which is based on mainstream elements of contemporary U.S. society. To maximize the consumer base and maintain the greatest possible profits, the convenience store seeks to attract the average consumer, and so generalizes its operation and product selection and rejects interests which don't reach for the highest percentages.

Exposure
Continued consumer exposure to store operation leads to acceptance of this operation and an eventual generalization of this acceptance to other areas (Greenberg, 1975). The purchases in convenience stores consist of prepared food and limited selections. The consumer accepts this and has worked it into his or her lifestyle—using prepared foods instead of preparing his or her own and planning purchases around limited selections rather than seeking out alternative items. The purchases are expected to be made in a rapid manner, with little or no interaction between the clerk and customer. The entire consuming experience is expected to be fast, impersonal, and based on what is available.

The most influenced consumers are those which make up the majority of convenience store customers; individuals under 30 years of age. Their assessments are more strongly formed by the store decisions, and their increased use of the convenience store more strongly supports their belief in the legitimacy of store operations and, thereby, in product and information availability (Greenberg, 1975).

The consumer's passive retention of this information increases the likelihood of its effect. Information sources such as magazines are legitimized simply by their presence in an accepted cultural institution, the convenience store. Consumers influenced by convenient access and purchase will be less likely to seek out alternative information sources if they are not available at the convenience store. The withdrawal of information sources or products from convenience stores can then be viewed as a withdrawal of their legitimacy. Store operations may have a much greater effect on social reality than may be realized.

Socializing Function
Convenience stores do have a socializing function within the local community. Their customers are generally repeat customers, and, often, local teenagers will spend more time in the stores than adults (Dervin & Greenberg, 1972; Liles,

1977). One such function relates to the stores' implicit denial of cultural diversity. The Southland Corporation has worked to standardize their 8100 stores in looks, operation, product mix, and employee orientation. This homogenization of culture across the U.S. aids in the reduction of cultural diversity and individual community orientation and socialization.

Operating procedures and employee training follow this standardization, insuring that any customer will be treated the same in any store. Unique customer/store interaction is limited or nonexistent.

The convenience store, particularly a nationwide, pervasive chain like the 7-11 stores, then impresses its image of social acceptability on the consumer by its marketing and operating decisions. The fact of its nationwide orientation reduces the level of local or regional identification and adds to the consumer image of larger social reality while reducing the legitimacy of distinct regional variation.

CONCLUSION

Convenience stores have grown from their inception in 1927 as neighborhood additions to groceries to their current status as an intrinsic element of daily consumer lifestyle. Their growth has paralleled the growth of suburban-living patterns and the increase in personal transportation. The growth of convenience stores started in accordance with consumer demands. These stores saw a profit opportunity in serving the needs of local consumers and based their product selections and operations on these local needs. Continued growth has made these operations national and also changed the consumer/store interactions.

Starting in the 1960s and 1970s, a major shift in convenience-store consumer action was taking place. The stores shifted from simply meeting consumer needs to leading consumer demand. Their abilities to influence consumer action and decisions, increased by their part in consumer lifestyles, gave increased dimensions to their product selections and operations.

Some of the effects which have been seen are consumer shopping patterns, which now include a wider range of shopping hours, the lessening of consumer planning in food preparation, the increased consumption of impulse items and "junk" food, and the expectation of rapid, impersonal service. With product decisions being made at corporate levels, product inventory increasingly excludes regional variation. Consumers are considered less likely to seek out local information or products not available in convenience stores, due to the consumption expectations which have been developed by their interaction with these stores.

The future plans of convenience stores are to continue expansion to a greater nationwide concentration and to expand past national borders. Their expected shift in product selection and customer orientation is towards a more affluent clientele and away from working-class consumers (*Wall Street Journal*, March

16, 1986, Sec. 2, pp. 1, 8). This shift will further reduce information access for the poor consumer dependent on local stores, and the young consumer with limited income resources. This abandonment of local consumers with limited resources for the more established, richer consumer will further limit convenience-store orientation towards individual customer needs and reduce catering to regional needs.

Research into the effects of convenience stores on consumers has not been done in a systematic manner. Useful directions of inquiry would include content analysis of magazine selection, the effect of standardized customer/store interaction on social orientation of consumers, and the changes in food product development and consumption as related to convenience store growth. Considering convenience stores as large, pervasive organizations, their collective operation as ideological apparatus demands closer scrutiny.

REFERENCES

Defleur, M. L., & Ball-Rokeach, S. (1982). *Theories of mass communication*. New York: Longman.

Dervin, B., & Greenberg, B. S. (1972) The communication environment of the urban poor. In F. G. Kline & P. J. Tichenor (Eds.), *Current perspectives in mass communication research* (pp. 195–223). Beverly Hills, CA: Sage.

Greenberg, B. S. (1975). Mass communication and social behavior. In G. J. Hanneman & W. J. McEwen (Eds.), *Communication and behavior*. Menlo Park, CA: Addison-Wesley.

Hall, S. (1977). Culture, the media and the ideological effect. In J. Curran, M. Gurevitch, & J. Woollacott (Eds.), *Mass communication and society*. Beverly Hills, CA: Sage.

Liles, A. (1977). 'Oh thank heaven!' The story of the Southland Corporation. Dallas, TX: The Southland Corp.

Nemeth, C. J., & Kwan, J. L. (1986) Originality of word associations as a function of majority vs. minority influences. *Social Psychology Quarterly, 48*, 277–282.

17

Are There Bolsheviks in Your Breakfast Cereal?

STEPHEN PRINCE

The University of Pennsylvania

This chapter concerns what might be called an irony of history in which one set of formal codes of cinematic representation was transposed from the quite specific historical and cultural situation in which it developed and was applied in another, quite disparate setting. More specifically, certain editing codes of the revolutionary Soviet cinema of the 1920s are now being used by modern corporate advertising. The cinematic discoveries of Marxist filmmakers are today used to sell toothpaste and mouthwash. Editing rhythms designed by Russian filmmakers to stir revolutionary passion are now supposed to ignite the ecstasy of consumption.

To see how this transition occurred, some attention should be focused on the cinematic discoveries made in the aftermath of the Russian revolution. Aesthetic theory in the immediate postrevolutionary years was shaped from a remarkable convergence of art and science. The Formalist attempt to specify with precision the structure of the literary work, the Constructivist valorization of the artist as engineer, the use by Meyerhold of a system of biomechanics to guide theatrical performance—all attempted to reconcile art with the age of industrial production. This was no less true in film. Russian filmmakers had the work of American director D. W. Griffith as the example of the most sophisticated filmmaking then in existence. A print of Griffith's *Intolerance* was smuggled through the economic blockade imposed on Russia by the Western powers, and Russian directors were deeply impressed by Griffith's accomplishments with parallel editing, or the representation, by means of alternating images, of events occurring simultaneously in time but separated in place.

Griffith discovered that, by presenting two events in this manner, temporal and spatial relationships could be established between them. But the Soviet directors went further than such simple, straightforward representation.

The Soviets set out to specify more precisely the nature of cinematic meaning. One of their fundamental discoveries was the demonstration that meaning in cinema is not a function of the photographed reality. The meaning of a shot is not the same as the content of the image that has been captured by the camera. In his workshop, Lev Kuleshov conducted a series of experiments in what he called "creative anatomy," or the construction in the viewer's mind of a composite, whole human figure out of separate close-ups of isolated body features.

The close-up of a woman's hand, the close-up of another woman's leg, the close-up of a third woman's eyes, and so on—all these shots were edited together so that viewers were convinced they were seeing the representation of a single woman. Viewers had the impression of a reality which, in fact, existed nowhere except on the screen. In other experiments, Kuleshov discovered that the ordering of shots is crucial to the meaning conveyed. To viewers, a close-up of a man smiling, followed by a close-up of a gun, followed by a close-up of the man looking frightened signified cowardice, but when the shots of the man were reversed, the sequence was interpreted by viewers as signifying bravery.

Thus, cinematic meaning is not a function of the reality which is photographed, but of the reality which is constructed through the ordering or editing of images. This was a seminal discovery, which today, perhaps, we take for granted. But it was of decisive importance for the character of Russian cinema, because it made something else possible.

Russian filmmakers attempted something of grand proportions, which was, simply stated, the attempt to translate the Marxian dialectic into film "language." In the hands of a director like Sergei Eisenstein, film, as a global art, would become a kind of world-mind by approximating the epistemological structure of all reality, which Eisenstein (1949) believed to be a dialectical one, as described in Marxist philosophy. Lenin proclaimed, "The identity of opposites . . . is the recognition (discovery) of the contradictory, mutually exclusive, opposite tendencies in all phenomena and process of nature. . . . Development is the 'struggle' of opposites" (Selsam & Martel, 1977, pp. 130–131). It is this view of the struggle of opposites, of course, which allows Marxist philosophy its revolutionary optimism. But, more importantly, the discovery that cinematic meaning was a function of shot order fed quite well into a view of reality which stressed process and conflict. Since meaning did not depend on any single shot, but on the linkage of shots, cinematic meaning could be dialectical if those shots were linked dialectically, that is, in a way that emphasized conflict and shock. This, in fact, was the cornerstone of Eisenstein's filmmaking. His voluminous writings document in great detail the myriad of ways that conflict can be generated between cinematic images. Eisenstein called these conflicts *montage*, borrowing a term from industry, which referred to the assembly of pipes and fittings. Montage—conflict between and within shots—would become his scientific unit of measurement.

All of this is made concrete in the celebrated sequence from *Potemkin* in which Czarist troops fire upon unarmed citizens on the steps of Odessa. A mutinous battleship comes to the defense of the citizens, firing its guns so that the sleeping lions of revolution awaken. Eisenstein stresses an extreme fragmentation of detail through the abundance of shots, the brevity of their length, and the way that the whole exists, dialectically, only through the relations of its parts. At the end of the sequence, Eisenstein edits separate shots of three stone lion statutes so that they become a single, living stone lion rising up in revolutionary wrath. Shot A, plus shot B, plus shot C do not equal merely Shots

A + B + C but a new concept, D. Three shots of three separate stone lions form a new idea, the methaphor of an outraged, mobilized populace.

Eisenstein's (1949, p. 62) intention was, as he wrote, to "encourage and direct the whole thought process" of the viewer. "Montage thinking is insepar-able from the general content of thinking as a whole" (p. 234). And of D.W. Griffith, he wrote, "The structure that is reflected in the concept of Griffith montage is the structure of bourgeois society. . . . And this society, perceived only as a contrast between the haves and the have-nots, is reflected in the consciousness of Griffith no deeper than the image of an intricate race between parallel lines" (p. 234). Therefore, Eisenstein was advocating not merely paral-lel montage, but a revolutionary, dialectical montage for a new, revolutionary society.

Despite the ambitious nature of Eisenstein's theory and the frequently powerful example of his filmmaking, his work had little immediate impact upon the cinema, except in the realm of theory and criticism, where it was very influential. However, a few filmmakers after Eisenstein practiced his methods of editing, and, in Hollywood, montage deteriorated to the point where it came to signify sequences indicating the passage of time through dissolves of calendar pages or tumbling leaves. In Hollywood, montage became an interlude in a film narrative rather than the underlying structural principle of filmmaking. There were exceptions, of course. The films of Sam Peckinpah owe a lot to Eisenstein. But it wasn't until the advent of filmed advertisements that the legacy of Eisenstein and Russian montage truly reappeared.

To understand why this is so, it is important to glimpse the ideological links between revolutionary Soviety society and the industrial culture of the West-ern world. To the impoverished, peasant society that was Russia during and immediately following the revolution, the mechanized, efficient, industrialized societies in the West were powerful sources of inspiration. Inspired by their example, postrevolutionary Russia attempted to emulate their record of eco-nomic productivity and material development through a harnessing of science and the machine. This attempt so permeated the new culture that its rever-berations are felt in the aesthetic theories of the Formalists, of the Constructi-vists, and of Eisenstein. The irony is that from the revolution was born as powerful an obsession with production and productivity as ever characterized Western bourgeois culture. Both Lenin and Frederick Taylor were heroes of the new age. The tools of an analytic, scientific approach to reality not only became the means, for designing the industrial infrastructure but also provided the method for understanding the arts and the human mind. Constructivism, Formalism, dialectical montage—all have their structures rooted in measurable units of the material world. In part, the socialist realism backlash, which came later, was a reaction against what can, with some justification, be called a "revolutionary positivism."

Such an outlook, applied to the human realm, had yielded in the United States the fields of human engineering or industrial psychology. This field represented the use by psychology of the labor studies of Frederick Taylor and was founded upon the notion that mental variables might be specified and then manipulated in the interest of economic productivity. Advertisers, who saw their own field develop into an industry in the 1920s, shared the interest of the industrial psychologists in isolating and manipulating units of human thought and feeling. The ways in which advertisers carried out this task, beginning in the 1920s, are too complex to cover here, but the important point to note is that the responsibility of advertisers was (and still is) to create public desire for the commodities produced by the industrial system. Like the industrial psychologists, advertisers, in their work, are motivated by the belief that sufficient analysis of mental variables will in turn generate the ability to manipulate those variables.

It is here that we may find the cross-over of Soviet editing codes into modern advertising. For one of the ways in which desire is created for cars or toothpaste or Presidential candidates in filmed advertisements is through dialectical editing, in which one thing (the car, the candidate) is cross-referenced with other, unrelated things (a beautiful landscape; smiling, happy faces), so that the car or the candidate being sold takes on the positive associations of those other things, to which, in reality, it is unrelated. I am not suggesting that modern advertising necessarily incorporates Einsenstein's methods of generating visual conflict, but I am suggesting that it does use the Soviet montage principle of deliberately joining unrelated images to generate new concepts and feelings that are not expressed through the representations of any of those images taken separately. Let us look at a few examples of how this occurs.

SCREEN ADVERTISEMENTS

Just as, in Eisenstein's work, unit of meaning "A" and unit of meaning "B" are unrelated, but they are metonymically conjoined. In this case, it is the Peugeot and the well-dressed, handsome, self-confident couple. From this, new concept, new feeling "C" is created: the Peugeot Turbo as a poised, sleek, sexy machine. In the other ad, montage principles have been extended to include the soundtrack as well as the picture. Abstract, but emotionally resonant, qualities of "pride," "patriotism," and "optimism" are attached to Reagan America through the metonymic fastening of the images to the President's spoken words.

Film is an industry, an art that is historically constrained to a profound degree and toward which it seems meaningless to apply a search for timeless, eternal forms, such as that conducted by Wolfflin (1950). However, we have just seen what is apparently a confirmation of Wolfflin's approach: the example of a visual form—dialectical editing—crossing cultures, nations, ideological epochs. However, the apparent confirmation is deceiving, because a common epistemological configuration and cultural practice underlies both revolutionary Russia and the corporatized West. And it is this paradigm, forming a substrate of both societies, which is responsible for generating the visual form that we have studied today: the use of montage to shape and manipulate variables of human thought and feeling. In this sense, there are Bolsheviks in our breakfast cereal, just as there are Jordache jeans on the legs of young Russians.

REFERENCES

Eisenstein, S. (1949). *Film form.* New York: Harcourt, Brace and World.

Selsam, H., & Martel, H. (Eds.). (1977). *Reader in Marxist philosophy.* New York: International Publishers.

Wolfflin, H. (1950). *Principles of art history.* New York: Dover Publications.

PART V

TECHNOLOGY IN ITS SOCIAL CONTEXT

18

Initial Reactions to the Introduction of Television, 1938–1953

GWENYTH JACKAWAY
University of Pennsylvania

INTRODUCTION

Television in this culture has a strange double identity. While not *owning* a TV is tantamount to cultural isolationism, not *watching* it is a badge of cultural elitism. Owned by all and scorned by many, television is the medium we love to hate. Over 98% of American households have at least one TV, and the average set is on for 7 hours a day, yet the prevailing image of television is that it is an hypnotic time waster, a threat to "aesthetic sensibilities," and disruptive to family and social life. Are these qualities, as some have suggested, intrinsic aspects of the *medium's* message? If this is the case, what was the response when television was first introduced? Did early TV audiences react differently to the arrival of *this* new medium? Did they notice these so-called "inherent" qualities of television that we are so quick to blame on the technology?

This investigation of the initial reactions to the introduction of television revealed that the conflicting attitudes about TV so familiar to us today were indeed voiced by the first audiences. In addition, and more importantly, the sentiments expressed in these articles provide evidence that early TV viewers had concerns which were remarkable similar to those voiced by the early recipients of telephone, cinema, and radio. From the public reactions to the telegraph, to those provoked by the introduction of television, a common theme can be traced: consisting of two polar extremes—celebratory and castigating, the response to the arrival of new media has been consistently ambivalent. Despite the differences in the *kind* of communication the various new channels made possible—interpersonal or mass—underlying the response to them all is the same fundamental question: how is the new channel (be it telephone or TV) going to alter the patterns and norms of social interaction, and will the change be therapeutic or disruptive for the community?

Examined here are the hopes and fears of various segments of the population as expressed in a variety of popular magazines during TV's early years, from 1938 through 1953. In this short span of 15 years, the medium went from being a science-fiction fantasy to a household item. In 1938, just before television was officially presented to the public at the World's Fair the following year, virtually no one knew what TV was, would be, would do, or would be used for. By 1952, as the FCC lifted its temporary freeze on new station licenses, penetration of TV was nationwide, with sets in over 16,000,000 households (*Business Week*, April 19, 1952). Not since the arrival of the automobile had a new technology been so rapidly adopted, and, as many observed at the time, is was one invention that would rival the car in the extent of its impact on American lifestyles.

Those having contact with television in its initial decades discussed the new communication technology in a variety of forums and contexts. Different groups of people focused upon different aspects of the medium, each employing their own thematic tone, style, and language to cover the issue. From the discussions in the *New Yorker* about TV's tremendous potential to bring opera to the masses, to guidelines in *Parent's* magazine on how to keep television from dominating family relations, popular periodicals of the late 1930s through the early 1950s reflect this wide range of social discourse. The primary sources for analysis were chosen on the basis of their high circulation figures, to gain access to those forums of public discussion most pervasive in the US. A diverse range of publication genres was sought in making selections for this sample, (drawing, for example, from both *Reader's Digest* and *Business Week*) in an attempt to incorporate the diversity of voices that made up the social dialogue then taking place about the new medium.

The publications studied were categorized both in terms of content and "class"-orientation (i.e., "mass" (m) *versus* "elite" (e) magazines): News: *Newsweek* (e); Business: *Business Week* (e); American Culture: *The New Yorker* (e), *Saturday Review* (e), *Life* (m), *Saturday Evening Post* (m), *Reader's Digest* (m); Home Services: *Better Homes and Gardens* (m), *House and Garden* (m), *House Beautiful* (m), *Parent's Magazine* (m); Science: *Popular Science Monthly* (m).[1]

Among the major themes in the popular periodicals explored in this study are: (a) the anxieties of the elites about the capacities of the new medium to disrupt established class and power boundaries; and the carefully constructed agenda for the "proper" uses of television, which they prescribed as the means to prevent the feared social disruptions; (b) the presumption on the part of this social elite that it was their prerogative to use television as an "electronic missionary" to deliver their values—both aesthetic and political—to the viewers at large, and the attendant assumption that the general audience was a passive "blank slate," cooperatively willing and ready to be "written upon"; (c) the concerns of the masses that established patterns of interaction and division of labor in the home would be disrupted by the arrival of television into the living

---

1. While these categories do not describe particular demographic groupings of magazine readers, the content, writing style, and tone of each publication is aimed at a unique audience. Thus, while *Better Homes and Gardens* and *The New Yorker* are in different categories because of the differences between the nature and content of articles in these two publications, it can be fairly safely assumed that a corresponding set of differences separate their respective readerships.

room, bringing fundamental changes to the structure of the family; (d) the fears, expressed in the mass publications, that the new living room toy offered temptations that threatened traditional norms of productivity and morality.

In addition, it will be argued that the conflicting sentiments about television presented in these articles are *not* a response that is unique to this particular medium. Rather, they reflect what seem to be fairly consistent concerns about how new communication technologies alter social interaction patterns in a community, and, ultimately, how such changes are potentially threatening to the structure and order of social relations.

DISCUSSION

Television, like other new communication technologies, was recognized from the start as being a potential change agent. As such, it had the power to facilitate transformations in social interaction patterns that could either be helpful or debilitating to one's self-interest. Not surprisingly, therefore, responses to the introduction of television were characterized by the expression of emotions of two extremes—either highly optimistic or terribly pessimistic.

The hopeful reactions are often idealistic, anticipating not only reinforcement or strengthening of the values already held dear, but an actual achievement of dream-like version of a particular ideal. This can be seen, for example, in the idealistic model of the Community predicted by the elites, or the rose-tinted picture of the Family longed for by the masses. Here we read of hopes that utopian visions will be realized upon delivery of the new medium, solving social problems through technological solutions. On the other extreme are the expressions of resistance to the introduction of television. These pessimistic reactions predict the new medium will bring about deteriorations in the status quo or cherished values. This perspective, like the optimistic viewpoint, attributes to new communication technology the power to alter fundamentally the very scaffolding of social reality.

Sentiments of the Elites

While the articles on the introduction of television in the elite magazines address a range of topics, the various subjects covered are all linked by a central theme. This group of periodicals presents the agenda that the social elites had for the uses of television and society and reveals the shared assumptions of its readers about the nature of the mass audience. Evident throughout these publications is the goal of employing the tools of tomorrow to recapture the clear-cut class divisions and power structures of yesterday. This is manifested in the many proposals to use television to promote high culture and political elitism. These ambitions are coupled with fears that TV threatened the same structures it promised to restore, for anything with the power to bring back yesterday also had the power to destroy it.

The solution to these fears, and the route to the goals of preserving the status quo in which they occupied the role of social elites, was to use the new medium to disseminate their worldview to the population at large. In proposing a form of cultural propaganda, they set out an agenda to employ television as an electronic missionary. Just as one could use Bibles to turn heathens into Christians, so too, it was assumed, the transmission of opera on television could transform the mass population into a cultured audience.

Underlying this solution are several assumptions about mass media and the general audience. Based on a one-way model of communication, this is a proposal for the injection method of spreading culture and democracy. Members of the mass public are perceived as passive, receptive, and devoid of their own opinions. Finally, this ethnocentric view of the general audience presumed that they would welcome the messages sent by their self-appointed tutors—in both the realms of culture and politics—and also that the message would be understood with no need for translation.

Art and culture: TV and the "high culture" agenda: Typical examples of this agenda for television discuss, in hopeful tones, the "blue-sky" possibilities of bringing opera, drama, and other cultural products to the population at large. The *Saturday Review of Literature*, for instance, observed: "Here is the great mass market for many events which have heretofore been regarded as 'class.' TV opens this chance—from mass to class—not only in the arts, but in education as well" (Benton, 1951). The bulk of the early prime-time fare, however, did not fullfill these hopes of bringing high culture to the masses. Then, as now, TV programming was disparaged by the self-appointed arbiters of taste.

Throughout the articles on television in the elite publications, one message is clear: certain channels of communication and uses thereof are superior to others. The significance of such sentiments about a ranking of media is their reflection of the belief in a hierarchy with far more serious implications: namely, that those who use the better media—and the higher cultural fare associated with literature and live theatre, for example—are themselves superior (see Fowles, 1982, for his discussion of media snobbery).

The view that voracious reading is of far greater value than voracious televiewing is integrally linked with assumptions about which kinds of people engage in which forms of media consumption. Far more than the traditional resistance to novelty and change, this adoration of the printed word reflects a longing for the clear class boundaries of earlier times, when only the privileged had access to information through reading. Judging by the amount of space devoted to thematic variations of this issue, media snobbery can be seen as one of the shared assumptions of the interpretive community which comprised the audience of these elite publications.

The conflict between the hopes of using the medium for artistic and cultural purposes, and the economic structure of programming, was very problematic for those who had high hopes for TV. Because market interests clearly lay in programming for the largest audience, the cultural agenda of the elites was incompatible with the economics of advertising-supported mass media. The dilemma facing these tastemakers was that the programming which they considered to be the most cultural was also in fact the least profitable.

The solution to this problem proposed in the elite magazines was the ghettoization of cultural programming onto a private channel for those who could pay, thereby freeing TV from the economic necessity of programming to the "least common denominator." As one *Saturday Review* article observed, the solution to this problem lay in devising a method for collecting fees from the viewers for those programs in which they were interested. "If this were possible," the writer continues, "then the thousands of people who want to see the opera or a play could do so, which . . . would finally solve the problem of how to collect for those many *desirable* uses that could be made of television but which cannot be profitably sponsored by advertisers" (Faught, 1950; emphasis added). The limited definition of what constituted desirable uses of television reveals that the rhetoric praising the broad reach of the mass medium as democratic was just that: rhetoric. In the face of evidence that the mass audience did not have the good taste to appreciate quality entertainment, the social elite would retreat to the familiarity of charging high admission for high culture. The nondemocratic nature of such media stratification was easily justified by the refusal of the general public to recognize fine art when they saw it.

Politics and persuasion.   Like other new media, TV was celebrated as offering new possibilities in participatory democracy. Not only could the whole nation *listen* to democracy in action, now they could *watch* it. Heralded as making the town meeting possible once again, now on a coast-to-coast basis, television was praised as being:

> the most magnificent of all forms of communication . . . the supreme triumph of invention, the dream of the ages . . . the magic eye that could bring the wonders of entertainment, information and education into the living room . . . a tool for the making of a more *enlightened* democracy than the world has ever seen. (Cousins, 1949; emphasis added)

The anticipated payoff for television's provision of the politician with access to the living rooms of America was the elicitation of more citizen participation in national issues, and ultimately, the delivery of more votes.

Censorship and regulation: For the social elite and their political representatives, the way to keep the power of television working in their favor was to find some means of influencing the control and regulation of its use. This can be seen in the considerable amount of space the elite publications devote to the discussion of the regulation of programming. At issue in the debates on this matter are fundamental questions of who is to control whom, in what ways, and under what circumstances.

In his article, Senator William Benton proposed the formation of a Citizen's Advisory Board, to be composed of "outstanding private citizens, drawn from the fields of education and communications and from among leaders in the civic, cultural and religious life of the nation" (Benton, 1951, p. 32). This board, he explained, would submit annual reports to the Federal Communications Commission, Congress, and the American public, reviewing how well radio and television were serving the public interest. Benton closed with an impassioned plea for citizen action and input on this issue, urging the enlightened readers of the *Saturday Review* that the future of democracy could depend upon *their* participation. Indeed, he emplored, the public opinion must come "from those who are articulate—and that includes you, my reader. I urge you to make yourself articulate to your congressmen and senators" (Benton, 1951, p. 32). Here again, while the ideal of preserving democracy is envoked, it is only the influence of the enlightened and articulate readers of a *literary* magazine that is being solicited. For those wishing to see television used for the promotion of high culture and the preservation of familiar social structures, it was clearly beneficial to lend their political and financial support to those representative of their interests such as Senator Benton.

In response to increasing pressure to regulate the new medium, the National Association of Broadcasters met in the fall of 1952 to set a new set of programming standards. Among those things outlawed from the video screen, in the stringent guidelines they agreed upon, were the following:

> profanity, obscenity, smut and vulgarity; attacks on religion and creeds; casual treatments of divorce; exhibitions of fortune telling or astrology; camera angles that emphasize anatomical details indecently. Officers of the law would have to be portrayed with dignity and respect; the use of liquor in American life, except for plot or proper characterization could not be shown. (*Business Week*, Nov. 24, 1951)

In short, the overriding guidelines by which the networks were to abide stressed that "due care . . . be exercised in developing programs 'to foster and promote the *commonly accepted* moral, social and ethical values of American life' " (*Business Week*, Nov. 24, 1951; emphasis added). This emphasis upon the preservation of traditional moral standards and support for figures of authority in the name of "fostering the values of American life" makes plain the influence of conservative values on those setting these regulations. Furthermore, the narrow definition of acceptable behavior and values reveals yet another instance of closed-minded denial of cultural differences among national subpopulations, and, once again, an assumption that the audience is a passive, willing and highly impressionable recipient of whatever is depicted on the video screen.

Sentiments of the Masses

Despite the fact that the hopes and fears of the readership of *Better Homes and Gardens* appear, at the outset, to be quite different from those of the *New Yorker's* subscribers, the issues underlying their respective concerns are quite similar. While the elite magazines discussed its effect on society as a whole, the popular culture publications focused upon TV's impact on the immediate viewing environment: the home and family.

The Work Ethic and Morality

To accomodate the new time demands of daily viewing, the scheduling of daily events in many household had to be reconsidered. Throughout the articles addressing this issue, the pervading question seems to be: how can we make room for TV in the schedule of the day? Why such concern over the issue of time use in the family? One of the main reasons is its integral connection with the preservation or disruption of traditional patterns of labor division among household members. The disruption of such roles had potentially dire consequences for the stability of the family. The concern with this issue is clear, for example, in the numerous articles which worriedly predict that television would greatly disrupt the productivity of the nation's housewives (see, for example, Johnston, 1946; "Salute to Television," Dec. 5, 1948; "Small Town Television," 1949). It was feared that, while the homemaker could . . . "listen to radio while she does her work," she would be unable to "keep her eyes on a television set and perform household tasks at the same time" (Johnston, 1946, p. 26).

Some articles offer solutions for women trying to cope with the hypnotizing draw of the screen, advising, for example, that the housewife rearrange and carefully plan her day, starting earlier in the morning and doing additional chores in the evening, to make room for TV viewing during the daytime. Another option, depicted in *Life*, shows a clever homemaker who has propped a mirror in the corner of the living room so that she can see the reflection of the TV from the kitchen while doing her ironing. This photo is accompanied by a caption which reads: "Geneva cook irons by feel with her eyes *glued* to TV program reflected in mirror" ("Small Town Television," 1949). The ultimate danger here, of course, is not the uncooked dinner of the burnt shirt, but the threat to the strength of marriages and families which depended upon everyone playing their part.

The mother of the family was not the only one faced with the dilemma of whether to watch or to work. The impact of TV on the work habits of children is also addressed here. *Parents* magazine, for example, observed that television had become the "new invader of children's time" (Witty, 1952), and a major concern that was expressed about this nation of child viewers was that spending so much time in front of the set would result in poor work habits later in life. As one article worriedly asked: "Will constant attention to TV produce a generation of adults more passive with less initiative than past generations of Americans?" (Witty, 1952).

TV and morality: sex and violence.   While discipline and self-control are prescribed as the means to limiting television's disruption of standard patterns of time use in the family, this approach is not invoked nearly so often in discussions of TV and morality. In this, more sensitive, area, the tendency is to look *outside* the viewer for both the cause and the solution to the problem. Here we read of the inclination to place the blame on the technology, and to ask that rules and controls be imposed by higher powers.

New communication technologies facilitate social contact between groups of people previously inaccessible to one another. In the late 19th century, it was feared that the telephone would be used to bypass traditional norms channeling proper interactions, and would thus make possible illicit liasons and relations between persons in different social stations (Marvin, 1988). Similarly the mass publication articles portray television as being a conduit through which low necklines, foul language, inappropriate subject matter, and violent programming will infiltrate the sanctity of the home. Typical was a comment like this, in *Life* magazine, which observed with concern that: "The American chorus girl, who used to be considered a fit companion only for playboys, is now . . . being invited on TV music shows, into everybody's living room where she sashays before the entire family" ("TV Chorus Girls," 1951, p. 146). Like the telephone, the television had made it possible for one group of people to have access (either interpersonal interaction or visual observation) to people and places outside of their daily experience. Regardless of the fact that *this* medium provided only one-way contact, the threat to the moral sanctity of the family was still perceived to be quite serious.

While they complained about explicit and violent programming, viewers across the country tuned in loyally each week to their favorite thrillers, making these very lucrative genres for the industry: "Crime shows," TV officials explain, "are surefire with the public. They cost little to produce and therefore sponsors like them" ("Murders Most Foul," 1952, p. 95). Simultaneously drawn to and repelled by the sex and violence, the viewers sent mixed signals to those making the programming decisions: high ratings and loud complaints.

The paradoxical problem here was many family members seem to greatly enjoy these "bad" programs, thus posing a serious dilemma: should regulations be extablished to control the *programming* or the *viewers*? In an article entitled "Congress Vs. the Plunging Neckline," *The Saturday Evening Post* explains that the biggest question haunting the representatives of the industry was why people couldn't simply *turn off* the set if they found certain programs offensive. This very advice, in fact, *was* given to a mother who wrote to the FCC complaining that her son was being polluted by horror shows. At first she sent back a grateful note reporting that this solution was working fine. However, in a few weeks a second protest from her arrived in Washington: "Grandma has discovered that *she* likes that particular program and turns it on every time! What shall I do now?" (Pringle, 1952, p. 25). The public, it seems, wanted the government to take on the role of "super ego" for the national audience, for here, and in many related articles, it is not self-control, but government regulation, that is sought.

The temptations offered by television created a difficult problem for the viewers: namely, the challenge of chosing between upholding proper norms and values on the one hand and indulging in the pleasures of forbidden programming on the other. Faced with this dilemma, the ultimate solution, apparently, was to lay the blame on the *technology* itself—thus absolving the audience, the programmers, and the regulators. The language employed in these articles to describe the dangers of television often draws from drug-related terminology. Parents were urged to limit and monitor their children's viewing habits in order to "lesson the likelihood of *chain viewing*" (Smith, 1951, p. 96), and viewers were cautioned that nervousness and other physical, psychological and behavioral symptoms could be signs of TV "overdose" ("Who Looks Like," 1950, p. 120).

If media effects can be blamed on the medium and not the social context in which it is situated, then human agents are not to be held responsible, and the fault can lie with the machine and not those who use it. By labeling the tube as hypnotic and attributing it with the power to hook the viewers into an uncontrollable addiction of viewing, those who were unable to resist turning in to their favorite shows could then be forgiven.

SUMMARY AND CONCLUSION

These early public debates about television address issues and concerns which echo those voiced by the first users of radio and telephone. That such reactions were *not* unique to TV alone strongly suggests that the harmful powers so often associated with this medium *cannot* be attributed to some quality inherent in the technology. Rather, they reflect what seem to be fairly consistent concerns about how technology changes communication in a community, and, ultimately, how such changes are potentially threatening to the structure and order of social relations. In the case of television, since it is a one-way medium, the discussions about its proper use could be focused on the nature of the programming content, rather than on concerns about interpersonal interaction that were raised by the arrival of the telegraph and telephone.

The hopes and fears about the impact of television can be seen as being merely different sides of the same overarching issue. Whether positive or negative in tone, and whether appearing in the publications ready by the elites or the magazines of the masses, the two extremes are attempts at answering the same fundamental question: How will the introduction of this new medium change our lives? The two polar responses consistently evoked by this question have much to reveal about the expectations we have for the way that mediated communication differs from other forms of communication.

Rather than operating independently on people's lives, new media are received into a preexisting setting of cultural attitudes about technology, communications and community. Our relationship with new communications technology is profoundly influenced by the fundamental belief that the very survival of the community is dependent upon successful communication. With a conflicting agenda of utopian hopes and Luddite-like fears, we look to new media to provide the technological solutions to our social communication problems while simultaneously blaming the same machines for robbing us of our idealized community of yesteryear.

The consistency in the sentiments expressed whenever a new communication technology is introduced strongly suggests that each new medium does *not* have its own unique message. It is the *social* determinants, rather than the technological ones, which are of greatest importance in shaping the impact of the various media upon our lives. Whether we are experiencing the arrival of the first telephones or the first VCRs, we bring a set of themes and issues reflecting *social* concerns, to the machine. Thus our new media are employed in the ongoing negotiation for social control and the continually evolving exploration of new definitions for patterns of family and community control.

REFERENCES

Barry, J. (1952, January). The expanding world of your living room. *House Beautiful*, p. 39.

Benton, W. (1951, August 25). Television with a conscience. *Saturday Review of Literature*, pp. 30, 32.

Brooks, T., & Marsh, E. (1981). *The complete directory to prime time network TV shows, 1946-present*. New York: Ballantine Books.

Censorship—private brand. (1951, November 24). *Business Week*, p. 130.

Codel, E. A. (1948, December). Television has changed our lives. *Parents' Magazine*, pp. 42, 64, 66.

Cousins, N. (1949, December 24). The Time Trap. *Saturday Review of Literature*, p. 20.

Douglas, M., & Isherwood, B. (1979). *The world of goods: Towards and anthropology of consumption*. New York: W. W. Norton.

Faught, M. (1950, August 26). TV: an interim summing-up. *Saturday Review*.

Fowles, J. (1982). *TV viewers versus media snobs: What TV does for people*. New York: Stein and Day.

Hamburger, P. (1951, March 3). Television: Joint sessions of Senate Foreign Relations and Armed Services. *New Yorker*, p. 21.

How to enjoy television. (1950, August). *House Beautiful*, p. 83.

Johnston, A. (1946, June). Television: Boom or bubble? *Reader's Digest*, p. 26.

Marvin, C. (1988). *When old technologies were new: Thinking about electric communication in the late nineteenth century*. New York: Oxford University Press.

McFadden, D. (1949, January). Television comes to our children. *Parent's Magazine*, p. 73.

Medill School of Journalism. (1974). *Magazine profiles: Studies of a dozen contemporary magazine groupings*. Evanston, IL: Author.

Murders most foul. (1952, April 28). *Life Magazine*, p. 95.

New age a-comming? (1950, February 20). *Saturday Review of Literature*, p. 36.

Pringle, K. (1952, December 27). Congress vs. the plunging neckline. *Saturday Evening Post*, p. 25.

Radway, J. (1984). *Reading the romance*. Philadelphia, PA: University of Pennsylvania Press.

Salute to television: It lacks radio's polish but it is a lot of fun. (1948, December 5). *Saturday Evening Post*, p. 50.

Second round for TV boom. (1952, April 19). *Business Week*, p. 27.

Shayon, R. L. (1950, October 28). Television in review. *Saturday Review of Literature*, p. 47.

Shayon, R. L. (1951, April). An open letter to the television industry. *Saturday Review of Literature*, p. 32.

Shayon, R. L. (1951, April 21). TV's streamlined bowdlerizer. *Saturday Review of Literature*.

Smith, H. K. (1951, September). Seven rules for TV. *Parents' Magazine*, p. 96.

Small town television. (1949, May 2). *Life Magazine*, p. 104.

The television and radio in the pace-setter house. (1949, November). *House Beautiful*, p. 270.

TV chorus girls. (1951, September 17). *Life Magazine*, p. 146.

Television has become a member of the family. (1951, April). *House Beautiful*, p. 118.

Who looks like Howdy-Doody? (1950, May 1). *Life Magazine*, p. 120.

Witty, p. (1952, December). Your child and TV. *Parents' Magazine*, pp. 36, 37.

19

Lentil Soup*

A. D. COLEMAN

The Western world was deeply involved with lens-derived information and imagery for several centuries before the invention of photography. This fact goes largely undiscussed in visual communication discourse. This chapter attempts to fill a small part of that gap.

By examining the evolution of the lens, its impact on our culture, and its effect on abstract thought, it is possible to establish a context in which the emergence of photography can be understood as a logical stage in human visual communication.

During the 16th and 17th centuries, the lens became what Bolter calls a *defining technology*:

> A defining technology develops links, metaphorical or otherwise, with a culture's science, philosophy, or literature; it is always available to serve as a metaphor, example, model, or symbol. A defining technology resembles a magnifying glass, which collects and focuses seemingly disparate ideas in a culture into one bright, sometimes piercing ray. Technology does not call forth major cultural changes by itself, but it does bring ideas into a new focus by explaining or exemplifying them in new ways to larger audiences. (Bolter, 1984, p. 11)

With respect to the lens as a defining technology, one need not adopt a position of technological determinism. Rather, as White (1962, p. 28) states:

> a new device merely opens a door; it does not compel one to enter. The acceptance or rejection of an invention, or the extent to which its implications are realized if it is accepted, depends quite as much upon the condition of a society, and upon the imagination of its leaders, as upon the nature of the technological item itself.

* * * *

Most communication technologies are invisible, in the sense that we as communicators are prone to paying attention to the *content* of our messages

---

* The research on which this chapter is based was undertaken during the course of a seminar in Media Ecology conducted by Christine L. Nystrom and Neil Postman in the Department of Communication Arts and Sciences at New York University.

rather than to the media transmitting them. As an instrument of visual communication, the lens is unique in that, for all practical purposes, it is literally as
well as metaphorically invisible. Made (most commonly) of glass, or some other
transparent substance, it is not in itself *seen* during the process of image
encoding, transmission, and decoding; rather, it is *seen through*.

Most people who use cameras, telescopes, binoculars, and other lens instruments usually give no active thought to the lenses; when looking at lens-
derived imagery—film, video, and still photography—again, we generally do
not consider the lenses involved in producing it. Yet the Western world is,
arguably, the most visually sophisticated culture in recorded history. Most of
that sophistication is comparatively recent, specifically attributable to
photography—both directly, through what camera vision and photographs have
taught us about the appearance of things, optics, and the phenomenon of visual
perception; and indirectly, through the proliferation and repetition of imagery
that photography makes possible. Though the theoretical grounding for most
members of this culture is skimpy at best, the direct experience with lens
systems and lens imagery is extensive.

The perceptual revolution engendered by the lens and consolidated by
photography has been profound, and so pervasive that it tends to be taken for
granted. We do seem to be aware that, over the past century and a half, we in
the West have become a *photographic culture*, aware too that a photographic
culture is radically different in quality and in kind from a nonphotographic
culture (Ivins, 1969, p. 116). We do not seem to understand that photography
was not thrust sui generis upon Western culture (as it has been, subsequently,
on so many societies that were in no way prepared for it). Photography took
root in already fertile and well-tilled soil: a *pre*photographic culture deeply
involved with lens instruments, lens-derived information, optics, vision, and
representation. Europe developed into a photographic culture as a consequence of being a *lens culture*—that is, a culture in which the lens was well-
established as a defining technology. Optical principles and concepts, as well as
attitudes and theories related to broader issues of information gathering, observation, and verification, had been introduced to that culture via the lens, had
become entrenched in the scientific method, and had come to form the groundwork for a new epistemology, well before the invention of photography.

Historians date that invention somewhere between 1826 and 1839, the
period in which the processes for fixing, or making permanent, a specific lens
image were discovered. Yet the imagination of the general public in Western
culture had been fired by the lens and its consequences for the previous two
centuries, via the cameras obscura/lucida, the telescope, and the microscope. It
seems logical to propose, then, that the invention of photography in (for
convenience's sake) 1839 was only one event, though a predictable one, in the
morphology of the lens as a cultural tool for information management.

An actual lens culture developed in the years 1550–1553. We became
formally committed to that new status some 60 years later—on the night of

January 7, 1610. A few reference points are necessary to support this argument.

The eye extends the reach of the hand, enabling us not only to flee and survive, but to perceive, to imagine grasping, and to plan to grasp that which is beyond our immediate physical reach. Similarly, the artificial lens as a tool extends the reach of the eye. Thus we could say that the evolution of the lens as a tool is implicit in the human eye itself, embedded as a potential even back in the dim recesses of biological evolution.

But that's not what made us a lens culture. Nor was it the fascination with the phenomenon of vision, though interest in the sense of sight goes back to such early theorists as Democritus and Euclid; evoked theoretical investigations from Ptolemy, followed centuries later by those luminaries of the Arabian age of optics, Alkindi and his successor, Alhazen; and continues as a primary concern of philosophy and theology through the work of St. Augustine, Roger Bacon, Descartes, and many other central figures in the cultural history of the West. As Bolter (1984) has suggested, what makes a tool into a defining aspect of the culture is not merely its presence, but its integration into the conceptual assumptions of the culture and the derivation from it of understandings that become fundamental to the culture's world view.

More than 2,000 years ago, an early form of lens had been developed: a spherical bottle filled with water, used as a fire-starting device, known as a *burning glass*. By the 10th century A.D., simple magnifiers had been produced; and, circa 1285, eyeglasses—or spectacles, as they were then known—had been introduced in Italy. Though all of these had an impact on culture (eyeglasses, in particular, added decades to the useful life of people), they did not transform our understanding of the *world* in any essential way.

By the year 1500, visual images in multiples—produced by the woodblock printing technique—were circulating throughout Europe. It is not coincidental that this was the historic moment of the rise of mercantile capitalism, whose lifeblood is *information*. With the surge of manufacture and trading that followed the recession of the Black Death in 1398, the resolution of the Hundred Years' War in 1453, and the consolidation of alliances around the Hanseatic League through the various Wars on the Herring during the early 16th century, M. Richard Kirstel (personal communication, January 15, 1984) proposes that an information-based culture was established for the first time in history. And visual information was becoming as invaluable as verbal or written information: books on such subjects as engineering, architecture, archaeology, astronomy, machinery and techniques of labor and production, anatomy, biology and zoology, books illustrated with printed images, would flood Europe during the 16th century.

At this juncture, the system of representation known as Renaissance perspective had already been devised and was in use; this is an essentially arbitrary method for what William Ivins (1975) called "the rationalization of sight"—a means for ordering the depiction of objects and their relations in space. (By arbitrary I mean to indicate that other cultures have developed other systems;

for example, in some, the relative size of objects in pictorial descriptions is determined by their significance rather than by either their actual size or their proximity to the picture plane.)

Thus, by the time Durer's treatise on perspective was published in 1523, the fundamental understanding of the relation between seeing and picturing had been transformed and standardized, while the means for reproducing and disseminating pictures had been introduced.

Between the years 1550 and 1553, several concepts and components came together to create the framework on which lens culture has been constructed. In 1550, Girolamo Cardano was the first to mount a lens in the light-admitting aperture of the camera obscura. This lens was made of crown or plate glass; it was of biconvex form (Habell, p. 836).

Three years later, in a treatise called the *Diaphana* (1553), Franciscus Maurolycus, an Italian professor of mathematics, became (in the words of one historian) "the first optician who thought of employing the theory of glass lenses to explain the action of the crystalline lens [of the eye]" (Disney, Hill, & Baker, 1928, p. 34), a hypothetical correlation later verified by Kepler.

At roughly the same time (circa 1550) the compound lens was invented, possibly by the British mathematicians Leonard and Thomas Digges, though there is endless dispute over its actual originator (Nicolson, 1935a, pp. 241– 242).

I would propose that it is within this 4-year period, from 1550 to 1553, that Europe became a lens culture. Though Cardano, Maurolycus, and (for convenience's sake) Digges were working independently of each other, their separate ideas combine, when viewed in retrospect, to form the necessary infrastructure of a lens culture.

Cardano's lensing of the camera obscura allowed one for the first time to study the *lens image* without one's own eye being, in Gage's (1947, p. 554) terms, "an integral part of the optical train"—as it is, for example, in its relation to eyeglasses, magnifying glasses, and telescopes. This crucial displacement permits us to see the imaging process itself—to contemplate that process, abstract ideas from it, and metacommunicate about it. As a device, Cardano's tool is the prototype of the contemporary photographic camera. Indeed, it can be argued that the photograph (i.e., the permanent version of that lens image) is implicit in Cardano's invention, an inevitable consequence of it, since the reproduction and dissemination of visual images was already a century and a half old.

Maurolycus's analogizing of the eye to the lens provided, for the first time, a working model of the process of visual perception itself. Thus the culture could begin to study the act of visual perception through the use of that model— thereby beginning to understand the principles of perception, to think abstractly about the process, and to metacommunicate about it.

The compound lens—which is, in essence, a system of two or more lenses in a (usually adjustable) fixed relation to each other—transcended by far the mere supplementation of human vision that spectacles represent. The compound lens embodied a radically different, far more aggressive relation to the cosmos, the microcosmos, and the process of the acquisition of knowledge through perceptual inquiry; it was the first optical tool that had as its sole function the *generation* of information. Implicit within the compound lens was the assumption that the reach of the eye is potentially infinite.

In short, in that 4-year span, using materials and ideas already in hand, Western culture created an interlocking set of instruments and paradigms that permits the endless reframing of humankind as perceiver, the world as perceived, and the lens image as both vehicle and repository for that transaction.

This made Europe (and its colonies in North America) a lens culture, though a prephotographic one still lacking the means for permanent encoding of lens images, the invention of which would take almost 3 full centuries more. Now it should not be difficult to explain why our status as a lens culture was confirmed on a particular evening early in 1610, which is considered a turning point in intellectual history (Nicolson, 1935a, p. 235).

On that date, it was Galileo's looking up into the night sky through a compound lens (and, more to the point, the meaning he ascribed to the information he acquired in that fashion) that transformed the worldview of Western society, demolished Ptolemy's geocentric model of the solar system, and made of Galileo the patron saint (though hardly the father) of telescopy.

When Galileo saw what he saw—which included four "new" planets—he was confronted with a choice that symbolizes the differences between lens culture and pre-lens culture. He could believe his theology, which was based on a shaky interpretation of the evidence provided by the unaided eye; or he could believe the information which the lens had provided. Galileo took the latter path, embracing and amending the Copernican version of the universe. Understandings of fixed-point perspective surely affected Galileo's interpretations of the lens-derived information he had acquired through these observations. Those rules governing the relations of objects in space had already revolutionized pictorial depiction and mathematics; they had been studied and absorbed by Galileo (Edgerton, 1984a, 1984b).

This was the first time that our culture's fundamental beliefs were permanently reshaped on the basis of lens-derived understandings. Galileo's act reverberated for a century and more: the trauma and upheaval that followed gave the measure of the gulf between lens culture and pre-lens culture. Yet, though many, especially in the corridors of power in the institutions of church and state, could not accept the news that Galileo brought, there were others who were quick to see where it led and rejoiced at the doors it opened for the mind.

For example, within a few months of Galileo's publication of his findings under the title *Siderius Nuncius* (*The Starry Messenger*), the philosopher Tommaso Campanella realized fully the implications of this discovery. Campanella, then in jail for his unorthodox opinions, wrote to Galileo on January 13, 1611. In his letter, which praises the *Siderius*, Campanella "raises for the first time the question which was to tear the seventeenth century asunder: the question of a plurality of worlds and of the possible inhabitants of these [four] new planets" (Nicolson, 1935a, pp. 252–256).

Campanella was not alone in realizing the expansiveness of Galileo's revelation. Other theorists followed suit. In 1630, Christophorus Scheiner noted in his *Rosa Ursina sive Sol* the conceptual relativity that the microscope encouraged, speaking of it as an instrument "by which a fly was made as large as an elephant and a flea to the size of a camel" (Gage, 1947, pp. 561–562). By 1663, philosopher Henry Power prophesied that, as a result of the telescope and microscope, men would come to consider themselves "but middle proportionals (as it were), 'twixt the greatest and smallest Bodies in Nature, which two Extremes lye equally beyond the reach of human sensation" (Nicolson, 1935b, p. 10).

The impact of the lens and its implications did not only affect scholars, scientists, and philosophers. It spread to artist and writers and, through all of these, to the population at large. Nicolson (1935a, p. 234) points out that "the seventeenth century, as it becomes conscious of indefinite space, became aware also that in the little world a new microcosm reflected the new macrocosm." She suggests that there was, in this, a degree of comfort and reassurance:

> Before the telescopic vision of the cosmos, even a brave man might shrink back, appalled at immensity, lonely before infinity. But the material of the microscopists was at once intelligible and flattering to man's sense of superiority. (Nicolson, 1935b, p. 90)

References to the microscope and telescope began to enter literature at this point; the lens and its effects were becoming cultural reference points. There is mention of these instruments in the writings of Samuel Pepys, Andrew Marvell, Samuel Butler, and many other writers. The microscope, for the reasons suggested above, was the first lens instrument to enjoy an actual vogue; it was a fad in England from the mid-17th century all the way through the 18th. "The microscope becomes the toy of ladies," writes Nicolson (1935b, p. 3), "and the familiar theme of the 'learned lady' enlarges to include the 'scientific girl.'" Thus the compound-lens instruments—particularly the microscope—were perhaps the first entry points into science and natural philosophy for women.

Though he certainly was not the inventor of the microscope, Anthony von Leeuwenhoek (1632–1723) did discover bacteria, in 1676. In a telling passage, Nicolson argues for the tremendous shaping effect of this lens-derived understanding, along with Galileo's, on literature:

> As Milton in *Paradise Lost* [1668] produced a new kind of cosmic poetry, a drama of interstellar space, which could not have been written before the telescope opened to a generation of men a new vision of the universe, so *Gulliver's Travels* [1776] could not have been written before the period of microscopic observation, nor by a man who had not felt at once the fascination and repulsion of the Nature which that instrument displayed. (Nicolson, 1935b, p. 50)

Once again, as in Henry Power's metaphor of humans as "middle proportionals," a relativistic view of the human position in the natural order had been extrapolated from lens understandings, this time by Jonathan Swift.

At the end of the 17th century, heated debate arose in the sciences between those followers of the classical scientists, or *ancients*, and the *moderns*. The latter were Baconians, anti-hypothetical in their attitude, insistent on the primacy of observation, experiment, and verification. "The telescope and the microscope came to be the most powerful weapons of the 'moderns,' and the arguments drawn from them proved more embarrassing to the supporters of the 'ancients' than any others which they were forced to answer" (Nicolson, 1935b, p. 61).

These debates were actively followed by the educated sector of the public—a sector which, it should be remembered, had access for much of that century to compound-lens instruments as well as to the concepts derived therefrom. Swift's *Battle of the Books* (1697), for example, was in part a refutation of the "modern" attitude as reflected in William Wotton's *Reflections upon Ancient and Modern Learning*, the second edition of which was published also in 1697. According to Wotton, "the most important contribution of the new instruments is the coherence and intelligibility which they have shown to exist in the universe" (Nicolson, 1935b, p. 61). The telescope diminished humankind; the microscope revealed humankind's similarity to many other forms of life.

* * * *

If the lens is a central human invention, equivalent in importance to the bow and arrow, then some recording process for lens imagery was virtually inevitable once a full-fledged lens culture had emerged.

The preconditions for the invention of photography were two-fold. One was the availability of the necessary materials, tools, and processes. With Johann Heinrich Schulze's discovery of 1727, that the tarnishing of silver could be employed as an image-making technique, these were all in place. The second precondition was the imperative within a lens culture to develop the essential instrument that would make culture-wide metacommunication about lens imagery possible. That instrument was some permanent, reproducible form of lens-image encoding. The impulse toward such an instrument came from two sources: art and science.

It has been argued by some that photography was a direct consequence of the Industrial Age, unimaginable without it. For instance, Schwarz (1931, p. 3) reasons that "the discovery depended upon a changed social order, upon an aesthetic attitude of man to his environment which was new and based on scientific assumptions."

The sociocultural context in which photography finally emerged has already been indicated to some extent. Among its salient features were: a mercantile-manufacturing economic system that placed a premium upon information, a growing and increasingly educated middle class accustomed to ideas derived from lens-based understandings, centuries of cultural experience with images reproduced in large multiples, and widespread contact with lenses and lens images.

If this is the agar-agar in which photography grew, then the needs of artists and scientists were the spores. The issue is not whether the lens influenced art, but rather the extent to which it did so. For example, Spengler (1939) must have suspected the pervasive cultural impact of the lens when he wrote that "between the space-perspective of Western oil-painting and the conquest of space by railroad . . . are deep uniformities" (p. 7). Fixed-point perspective, and the symbolic compression of space via the telescope, together constitute the link between the two.

Yet there is a more specific reason for the imperative of photography in the context of Western art during the late 18th and early 19th centuries. The ability to observe the world through the lens has come to fascinate the public, and microscopic observation, in particular, had profoundly affected the public attitude toward and respect for art. In a culture that placed progressively less emphasis on imagination and more on reason, the extraordinary complexity and delicacy of the world seen under the microscope led to a denigration of visual art as such. God was reconceived as the Divine Artist; compared to His handiwork, in even something so small as the shell of a snail, humanly produced works of art seemed necessarily cruder, less detailed, incomplete. The thrust of art, then, began to turn toward that which was culturally approved: realism, description, the documentary attitude. God and/or Nature having been defined as the epitome of creativity (Nicolson, 1935b, pp. 62–66), the only proper function of art could be the observation and recording of that cosmic oeuvre. The cameras obscura and lucida were in common use by artists for exactly that reason. The urge to arrest their images would have been widespread, the frustration at the tedious manual method thereof endemic.

In science, a parallel need was being felt. With the discarding of the "reasoned" science of the ancients, the Baconian ideal of directly observed and verified fact became the watchword of modern science, with the lens as its primary tool. Yet the problem there (especially given the erratic quality of available lenses) was in the *verification* of observation, i.e., independent corroboration of perception. Though not restricted to microscopy and the sciences built around it, this problem manifested itself there most emphatically. "Without photographic emulsions a great part of modern science could not exist" (Turner, 1980, p. 20).

Thus we might say that when Joseph Nicephore Niepce (1765–1833) produced the first permanently encoded lens image in 1826 he himself was the instrument of a cultural urge that had been building steam for some three centuries. And when, in 1839, the daguerreotype process and the calotype (positive-negative process) were announced, lens culture had at last completed its first cycle. The capacity for rendering a lens image in static two-dimensional form in large multiples permitted the widespread cultural dissemination of such images, thus making them available for study and introducing them as a form of cultural currency, as reference points. Lens culture thereby had the means for time-binding its visual perceptions and understandings, making possible their transmission through time as well as across space.

* * * *

It is important to understand that photography as we know it is one extension of lens-image consciousness. But it is no less important to realize that the spaceship is another. On November 16, 1974, the United States broadcast a message to the cosmos via the Arecibo radio telescope—the world's largest radio telescope, located in Puerto Rico. Transmitted in binary code, the message, when reconstituted, forms a series of images, the first of which is an image of the telescope itself. The reasoning? "Advanced civilizations may use radio telescopes to talk to one another" (Sagan, 1978, p. 119). "Thus," he adds, "we described the state of advancement of our technology" (Sagan, 1979, p. 63)—first by depicting ourselves as a lens culture, then by portraying and demonstrating our most highly evolved version of lens instrumentation. Perhaps we have been a lens culture long enough that we have become *lentocentric*—unable to conceive of a scientific, advanced culture that lacks the lens. Only the future can confirm or disabuse us of this conviction, but there's no denying that, consciously or not, we now all share it.

Thus, to bring this argument full circle, it would seem vital to our advancement as a culture that we come to understand the extent to which lenses shape, filter, and otherwise alter the data that passes through them—the extreme degree to which the lens itself *informs* our information. This influence, though radical in many cases, often manifests itself subtly. Yet even the most blatant distortions tend to be taken for granted as a result of the enduring cultural confidence in the essential trustworthiness and impartiality of what is in fact a technology resonant with cultural bias and highly susceptible to manipulation. The very derivation of its name—from the Latin *lentil*, due to the resemblance of the double convex lens to the lentil seed—suggests the humble and the bland. The lens is neither, though many things may be said to have sprouted from it. Western society's daily diet now includes a hefty serving of "lentil soup"—that stock of lens imagery, perpetually simmering, that is also lens culture's primary export to the rest of the world.

REFERENCES

Bolter, J. D. (1984). *Turing's man: Western culture in the computer age.* Chapel Hill, NC: University of North Carolina Press.
Disney, A. N., Hill, C. F., & Baker, W. E. W. (Eds.). (1928). *Origin and development of the microscope.* London: Royal Microscopical Society.
Edgerton, S. Y., Jr. (1984a). The relations between representations in art and science: Galileo's observations of the moon—a case study. In Callebaut et al. (Eds.), *George Sarton centennial* (pp. 55–56). Ghent, Belgium: Communications & Cognition.
Edgerton, S. Y., Jr. (1984b, Fall). Galileo, florentine 'disegno,' and the 'strange spottednesse' of the moon. *Art journal,* 225–232.

Gage, S. H. (1947). *The microscope* (17th edition, revised). Ithaca, NY: Comstock.

Habell, K. J. (1971). Lens history. *The focal encyclopedia of photography*. New York: McGraw-Hill.

Ivins, W. M., Jr. (1969). *Prints and visual communication*. New York: Da Capo Press.

Ivins, W. M., Jr. (1975). *On the rationalization of sight*. New York: Da Capo Press.

Nicolson, M. (1935a). The telescope and imagination. *Modern Philology, 32*, 233–260.

Nicolson, M. (1935b). The microscope and English imagination. *Smith college studies in modern languages, 16*(4), 1–92.

Sagan, C. (1978). *Murmurs of earth: The voyager interstellar record*. New York: Random House.

Schwarz, H. (1931). *David octavius hill*. New York: Viking Press.

Spengler, O. (1939). *The decline of the west*. New York: A. Knopf.

Turner, G. L'E. (1980). The history of optical instruments. *Essays on the history of the microscope*. Oxford, England: Senecio.

White, L., Jr. (1962). *Medieval technology and social change*. London: Oxford University Press.

20

Recent Research on McLuhan's Theory of Content

JEFFREY KITTAY
Department of French and Italian
New York University

This chapter focuses on the shape writing must take as practices of communication *change* and examines that point in time (if it is historical) and that line in space (if it is ethnological) where writing is called upon to embrace that which is not written. These moments are paradigmatic, not only of writing, but of anything that newly holds and manipulates and processes kinds of communication. In other words, it applies to what is called *media*.

McLuhan (1964) states that a new technology or medium has as its content the preceding medium.

> When machine production was new, it gradually created an environment whose content was the old environment of agrarian life and the arts and crafts. This older environment was elevated to an art form by the new mechanical environment. The machine turned Nature into an art form. . . . Each new technology creates an environment that is itself regarded as corrupt and degrading. Yet the new one turns its predecessor into an art form. [p. ix]

A broad dictum. Let us neither accept nor reject it at its face. Rather, let us reflect upon it. Restated, the claim is that one can see the stages of development of a culture as a process of progressive envelopment of existing media by novel ones, which enter the ecology of communicative practices not by explicit dethronement or toppling of the preceding medium, not by taking the limelight, but *from the back* as it were, functioning as a ground rather than a figure, and as such the new medium is meant to be abstracted from, not attended to. It is environmental in the diffuse sense: meant to bring to the foreground not itself, but the preceding environment, which is thereby detached from the background where it had reigned and is exposed as medium.

Since a medium is a container, one would think that a switch from one medium to another would retain the same content. Just as biologists can drop a fungus into a nourishing medium in a petri dish, they can at a later point lift out just the content and deposit it in another medium. McLuhan is saying that what the new *communications* medium embraces as content is the previous medium. Implied by him but unpursued is the fact that one result is a heightened complexity of communicational means: the second petri dish now has two media in it. This moment of face-off between technological environments is pivotal.

One may consider aesthetics-oriented issues, for example, a show of many years ago at the Museum of Modern Art on The Machine. The galleries were filled with both fantastic and real machines. To have those machines there, as objects of disinterested contemplation, certainly shows them to have become uprooted and unproductive. Similarly, a piece of driftwood on the beach is part of a natural environment, but, once spotted, picked up, carried home, and put on the mantelpiece, it is made to stand for nature. A kind of promotion, a putting-on-a-pedestal, but also a sterilizing, the removal of the driftwood from participation in cycles of degradation and generation. Like noted scholars (for example, the historian of philosophy Gregory Vlastos) who reject the proposal of an *hommage* or *festschrift* in their honor: such a work would guarantee them a rise in authority, if anything, but for them it means a removal from where the action is. The action is elsewhere. The process is best exemplified by the rise in the value of a painting or sculpture upon the death of the artist. Some artists are just not ready to make that kind of sacrifice for their careers.

So a later medium brings to consciousness, elevates, and limits the preceding medium. It is provocative, then, when "the media" characterize McLuhan's book as the equivalent of a much-earlier medium, an *oracle*. *Life* Magazine called it "the oracle of the electronic age," and *Newsweek* "The oracle of the New Communications." The oracle speaks (the word comes from *orare*, to speak), and the book should have taken its distance from such activity. Books have put oracles in their place; they may have heightened them in value, but they have also put them at the *mercy* of the book, we might say. But a book may actually seek to attain the oracular, in spite of its sophisticated, silent and linear, rational and configurational, grain. Most of McLuhan's readers have no acquaintance with oracles except through other media (epic verse, adventure movies, etc.). So the progression of media is not a simple procedure in which the new medium retains but reprocesses the old. It is full of ricochet and paradox, like those special mirrors which split laser beams by both allowing the beam to go through and making it bounce to the side. Of course, McLuhan is aware of the counterintuitive and paradoxical nature of the phenomena he treats (which is what makes him so insightful), but he does not discursively unfold the paradoxes, he just does it allusively and gnomically, which is what is so infuriating about him, and also, by the way, what makes him resemble an oracle.

Critics have long pointed out paradox in the fact that he uses a book to depose the Gutenberg Galaxy, the world of the book. With the unmasking and unmaking is a remasking and remaking, and even a worshipping of relics if need be. The process is one of enveloping but also of involution, enfolding, entangling. We know that, in the *Phaedrus*, the god Thoth claims that his invention of writing will extend man's memory, but King Thalmus rejects it on the grounds that it will make men forgetful. This attack upon writing is, in Plato, written, so we have the paradox, but it is given, in writing, as a speech, as a story told by Socrates to Phaedrus. The dialogue is a writing holding speech; it is made up of two media, the younger of which (writing) certainly denatures the older, to a certain extent, and also elevates it to something of an art form (but we don't know what it was like before, we do not know what silent rules it followed). And certainly, in Plato's words at least, writing is placed in a degraded position. But it is meant to be read as spoken; it is meant to defy its medium. It is not a face-off between media but precisely a way in which a single medium can and must exploit existing media, not just as content but as very means of expression. There is much that writing cannot do unless it relies upon representing some of its utterances as speech. There is much that McLuhan would not have been able to write if there were no such things as oracles and prophets. A new medium is not only a new technological possibility but a new way in which previous media and perceptions and senses and discourses can intersect and interact once within it. It establishes new rules of combination, which forge new links between communicative practices that could up to that time find no connection, and that also create new voids and implicitness, intolerable earlier. The containing medium cedes momentum almost immediately to the discursive operations of one of its contained media, and then moves to another. It is, certainly in its initial stages, more orchestrative than innovative. In this way one can look to a writing as merely representing, and orchestrating, a speaking (as much as that may go against the grain of writing's possibilities). One could have a writing that seeks to preserve a preliterate stance vis-à-vis its own discourses. Many anthropologists find a dilemma precisely in the fact that, while they must inevitably use writing for their own, professional brand of communication, that writing must be read and interpreted in such a way as to preserve the preliterateness of the culture which it represents.

Members of the Lollardian movement in the 14th- and 15th-century England wanted all individuals to have access to and read the Bible themselves. This would allow a more individual interpretation, rather than that which had been elaborated through an abstract exegetical tradition, which, in their eyes, only distanced the sacred Word from the Faithful. The scholastic tradition did not want such widespread individual reading, as it could produce interpretations which might circumvent current Church thinking and authorized interpretive apparatus (Pattison, 1982). So it would seem that the Lollards, in saying "give us the Bible to read," were advocating a literate lay public, and that the scholastics, in keeping the Book from the laity in favor of reading it to them, were advocating a mediated form of communication between the written word and the congregation. But it was in many ways the reverse. The Lollards wanted the faithful to read the Bible as the *resonating* word, as if in front of a charismatic preacher. The utterance through their kind of reading should have the kind of presence and immediacy which immediately touches. They looked to reading for certain of its aspects (privacy and ease of dissemination) to preserve what was a quality of *oral* communication—immediacy—which was thwarted by the Church fathers and exegetes who wanted to discourage individual reading precisely because of its immediacy. The scholastics kept interpretation distant and authoritarian, monitored and controlled. Though they discouraged such individual reading, however, the kind of interpretation they themselves did could not have been done upon a text received only as spoken. It called for methods of scrutiny and comparison which were only possible for a sacred Word *in writing*. They were actually proponents of the literate world, but not for the laity. For them the laity should receive the truth orally, although it is a truth as product of a literate process. (Those who teach adult literacy have in many cases been surprised by the fact that many if not most of those who enroll in their courses do so not with the aim of reading expository prose or even to ease their everyday interactions with the world of the written—such as how to fill out an application or read a timetable—but so as to be able to read and recite the Bible.)

Here the content of the new medium of writing is the previous medium of speech almost in defiance of much of what writing could do. When a new medium embraces already existing media, it is difficult to predict what happens to those media. What will be subordinated, what superordinated? What kind of hierarchies are we talking about? Writing down the spoken word can memorialize and consecrate it, as if in stone, even make it even oracular, or it can cheapen and degrade and corrupt it, make it almost discardable everyday currency, which is what King Thalmus in the *Phaedrus*, and many anthropologists today, are so worried about.

The recent research mentioned in the title of this chapter refers to work regarding how prose began (Godzich & Kittay, 1987). Literatures usually start in verse. Prose is a subsequent development, and there are many cultures which have writing but do not yet have prose. The procedure is quite traceable in medieval France, where all writing in French was in verse until a certain point when, rather abruptly, verse was discredited as lying and nonverse discourse was posited and used as if a truer conveyor of historical fact. Prose, not verse and the epic song from which it derived, became the medium of authority. Prose could, however, and indeed had to, include verse within itself, but it was now a verse used only in particular situations. Prose replaced song and its verse as the medial ground, and it was a different kind of ground, cognitively and conceptually, than verse had been. The paradoxes spoken of earlier are relevant here, in particular the liar paradox: the prologues to prose works, stating that the work which follows is in prose because verse lies, were often themselves in verse. This is what I meant earlier about a more complex environment of communicational means.

Prose begins in a way similar to that in which McLuhan says new media begin: prose does create an environment that is itself regarded, not really as "corrupt and degrading" (in McLuhan's words), but certainly as devalued, unworthy of note. Prose is considered to be unremarkable—a natural output of language activity. This attitude remains even in the face of the fact that it is not universal in all cultures, even in all literate ones. It is a subsequent development, a new way language is conveyed. And it is also true that prose turns its predecessor, verse, into an art form (if we use the term *art* pretheoretically). What happens is that prose, by coming from the back, as it were, and containing verse along with other kinds of utterances, relegates verse to certain kinds of functions, to those utterances seen to make momentousness. It does not so much turn verse into art as much as use it as the discourse of certain framed public acts, while the rest of the work, the surrounding prose, concerns itself more with representing less locatable, less free-standing, and less resonating utterances, not speech or not what speech had come to be in an environment of verse and song. Writers wrote prose to produce an utterance that has its source on a more foundational ground than verse, or song, or even speech.

And this earth-shaking switch from verse to prose all happens, strictly speaking, within one single medium, writing. It is *within* writing that there is fashioned a divide between a writing that was interpreted as the verbal string of an oral event (verse for song, dialogue for speech) and a kind of writing that emerges as if it were an underwriting, a proto-writing, and that is not to be interpreted as speech but can *open quotes*, going into what we as readers are to interpret as if it were heard in one's presence, and then *close quotes*, and yet keep on uttering, keep on being written. Prose comes on in a quiet and self-effacing fashion, and holds and quotes verse, relegates it to a shrinking role in the ecology of communicative practice which it contains, and eventually pretty much does without it. Verse loses its monopoly as the way in which history is conveyed, it becomes revalued, a special thing, with sometimes a sensuous dimension. It becomes fetishized, like a Model T Ford today, which *says* too much to be regarded only as another means of transportation. Verse is prized, but it is now prose that holds the ground.

Verse has been put down, but also elevated, in the kind of movement caught very well in the phrase used to describe what happened to General William Westmoreland as the Vietnam War worsened so palpably: he couldn't be fired, as that would have been too embarrassing to all concerned, so, alternatively, he was promoted, and the phrase which captures it so well is: he was *kicked upstairs*. In medieval France, verse is kicked upstairs. *This procedure is hardly media-specific.* It is one way status shifts through the hierarchies that govern all kinds of entities. What is most valuable in McLuhan's statement is the assertion that, for media, the hierarchy is bottom-up, not top-down. The struggle for dominance is for the medial *ground*. This is certainly the bid that prose makes in medieval Europe. Insofar as it is ground, it is powerful, but also, insofar as it is ground, it is not attended to, which makes it all the more powerful.

A successful medium makes us feel we stand within it, that it is an environment. It appears to be everywhere, filling up that part of what we sense as nothing. We posit it as that against which or upon which all salient phenomena operate, like the TV, to which we immediately have recourse after having witnessed a crime in person, to assure ourselves that it had to have taken place on the screen as well, it had to have been contained there. This is what a dominant medium is: that which we do not locate but which we allow to locate us, the environment whose horizon we identify as our own. Seeing the grounding medium is difficult, like seeing prose, but is analogous to taking any world as pervaded or permeated, as fully extended, like Descartes's conception of the world as a *plenum*, as inhabited even when one senses nothing. It is to see the grounding medium as having properties similar to those ascribed in the 18th and 19th century to the aether, that in which we cannot avoid operating.[1]

But upon that medial ground are the already-existing media which, though emptied of certain aspects of their former power, can be recycled, refilled, even perhaps reinvigorated. A new medium can empty previous media or discourses, and then fill them anew. (Using ecological models, we can suggest that a certain medium that would usually die out under competition with others can remain vital and powerful if embraced by another medium, acting as a parasite upon its new host.) Maybe to visit the real Delphi today would seem fake to us; maybe we can only reach toward it and hear its sacred voice in a book.

We change the ground on which we stand, the aether through which we pass, the screen or backdrop against which we act and are represented as acting. And we change the media in which we preserve things, in which we locate our difference from some other collectivity, and through which we pass ourselves on to future generations. A medium becomes interesting when it is not just replacing a previous one, or embracing it (in McLuhan's formulation), but engaging it like a collage containing a newspaper clipping which purposefully draws the spectator in and out of the focus of the painting as such. *This diversity of means* of decoding and interpreting, as in that kind of painting

---

[1] Has the meaning of the word *medium* been sufficiently probed? It is used to mean either a container (like a solution in the petri dish) or a conveyor. The idea of an aether came to be of use to science not because we needed to understand what was all around, but because science needed to account in mechanical terms for the *transmission* of certain phenomena, such as, in Newton's case, heat through a vacuum, and later light as wave, which must be seen to go through what was called a *propagating* medium, as water and sound are conveyed through waves. The aether might be seen as an archaic form of media consciousness, since it was understood not only to fill up the space between things, but also, according to some 19th-century scientists, to suffuse solid objects as well through their porous structure.

which calls upon you to read as well as contemplate, is the hemisphere of media change which McLuhan does not treat. What McLuhan does correctly see is that change of media has a basically *vicarious* complexion.

REFERENCES

Godzich, W., & Kittay, J. (1987). *The emergence of prose.* Minneapolis: Minnesota University Press.

McLuhan, M. (1964). *Understanding media.* New York: Signet.

Pattison, R. (1982). *On literacy.* Oxford, England: Oxford University Press.

21

Natural Language and Computer Conferencing

RICHARD D. HEYMAN
The University of Calgary

INTRODUCTION

For the conversation analyst, an underlying concern in research on talk is how members organize their interaction so that the meaning of the talk is made clear to all, and any problems of meaning, or problems of participation in the ordering and structuring of the interaction, are solved for all practical purposes. Conversation analysts have been engaged in research on talk in diverse situations, including face-to-face talk, telephone talk, radio and television talk, classroom talk, medical talk, legal talk, service encounters, cockpit talk, criminal talk, and many aspects of written discourse as well.

The findings of this research have taught us a great deal about how members communicate: that is to say, how they organize their talk so that the talk and the setting work reflexively to create the meaning and the context of the interaction. As Garfinkel suggests, "members' accounts of every sort, in all their logical modes, with all of their uses, and for every method of their assembly are constituent features of the settings, they make observable" (1967, p. 8). For all practical purposes, then, the relationship between the meaning and the context of talk is observable as the talk unfolds sequentially in real time where members take their turns at talk and by so doing show both attention to and understanding of the talk that has gone before and that which is to come. It is in the talk's sequence that the warrant of its meaning and/or structure is found. A member's judgment as to an appropriate next utterance must be in terms of both the contextual features of the talk and the member's common-sense understanding of the meaning and appropriateness of the utterance in the sequence of utterances. As Schegloff (1978, p. 88) has argued, "co-participants in conversation operate under the constraint that their utterances be so constructed and so placed as to show attention to, and understanding of, their placement."

For example, conversation analysts argue that categories of speech acts such as greetings, promises, commands, etc. should not be understood as technical categories of action, but as common-sense categories created and understood as members cooperatively orient their talk to practical, instructional ends and understandings, such as asking and answering questions, making and hearing promises, giving and taking commands. The work done by Sacks, Schegloff, and Jefferson (1974) describes the ways in which conversationalists sequence their utterances in connection with a number of variables.

In general, we can say that conversationalists locally manage and control turn size and turn order using a principle which is called *recipient design*. Recipient design refers "to a multitude of respects in which the talk by a party in a conversation is constructed or designed in ways which display an orientation and sensitivity to the particular other(s) who are co-participants" (Sacks, Schegloff, & Jefferson, 1974, p. 727)

A second related analytic feature of conversation is the notion of the *adjacency pair*. An adjacency pair consists of a two-utterance sequence with adjacent positioning of the component utterances and different speakers for each utterance. Most importantly, "given the recognizable production of a first pair part, on its first possible completion its speaker should stop and a next speaker should start and produce a second pair part from the pair type the first is recognizably a member of" (Schegloff & Sacks, 1973). Adjacency pairs are an obvious organizational structure of talk in that a first pair part may be formed by a speaker to implicate a particular form of next utterance, as in a question/answer adjacency pair. This form of linked utterances is clearly evident in conversation, not only in question/answer sequences but in greetings, commands, goodbyes, complaints, and so on.

However, it is important to point out that a reflexive relationship exists between the two parts of the adjacency pair. Each pair part takes its meaning interactionally from the other. Interactionally, an utterance becomes a question because it is an utterance which elicits an answer, rather than because it syntactically and/or intonationally resembles the ideal form of a question in English grammar. This issue, of course, is more complex than stated here, but the essence of the relationship between pair parts is nevertheless reflexive. Members' talk illustrates the practical use of this understanding in utterances such as questions and in the *repair of utterances* which were intended to be heard as questions but which were not, in that they were not answered.

COMPUTER CONVERSATION

Having briefly outlined the focus of some important research concerns in conversation analysis as a frame of reference, this chapter attends to some questions regarding how people talk to one another using the computer as the medium of communication, as in computer conferencing.

Communication through this medium seems, on the surface at least, to be a new mode of people talking to one another: it is not face-to-face, like normal interaction in real time, yet it is interactive; it is not verbal, like talking on the telephone; it is not radio communication, neither verbal nor code; and it is not mail correspondence, though it is written. It is, however, a mode in which people talk through the use of a computer keyboard and monitor. It has multiple participants who may speak to one another in real time or over extended periods of time, making comments, asking and answering questions, expressing opinions, disseminating news, and doing, it would appear, most of the kinds of communication we do in every day face-to-face interaction. The work of this paper is to use the tools of the conversation analyst to describe the methods that people use in talking to each other in this way, and compare them to ordinary face-to-face interaction, i.e., how members of a computer conference orient their utterances to each other so that their construction and placement show both attention to and understanding of the talk thus far and the talk to come, as the talk unfolds sequentially in the conference, and how the structures of turn-taking, adjacency pairs, and utterance repair work in the computer conference context.

The raw data for the following discussion are from a 1983 computer-based conference of the COSY Conference System developed at the University of Guelph in Canada. This system allows use by both novice and expert. The command structure is hierarchical, and the system allows for three classes of conferences: open, closed, and confidential. All users have a nickname for logging on which also indexes a resume file of all users containing their full name, address, and any other information entered there by their owner. Any user may look at any other user's resume file (Mayer, 1985).

In addition:

A "conference" in COSY is a specific data structure, comprising information common to the whole conference (title, moderator, and member list) and one more "topics" and their associated information (title and message text). Messages are stored in chronological order within a topic. Each message has header information associated with it, including a timestamp, the nickname of the author, and pointers showing which (if any) message it is a comment on, and which (if any) messages are comments on it. Thus, the messages within a conference can be viewed either as a simple, linear sequence, or as a tree structure based on whether a message is a new thought or a comment to a previous one. (Mayer, 1985, p. 26)

The specific conference analyzed here (from hardcopy) involved 75 turns at talk extending over 26 months (1983 through 1986). The length of utterances ranges from 28 characters (#39) to 1,989 characters (#23). The title of this conference was Telidon, and it was an open (general) conference. It involved 19 different users over the 26-month period.

Social psychologists and sociologists have long been interested in the effects and limitations on communication found in human interaction mediated by machines of one sort or another. Kiesler (1986) has recently reminded us that communication using the computer as intermediary seriously limits the information members get about social context in all its aspects. For example, we are faced with problems involving the absence of visual and verbal cues. Both areas can affect members' sense of social and sexual identity, status, class, occupation, personality, style, intention, motivation, physical size and demeanor, race, and other features which may be important contextual information used to interpret the meaning of talk in normal face to face interaction.

Conversation analysts recognize that the meaning of an utterance cannot be decided unless a context is made up of "who the speaker is (his/her biography), the relevant aspects of that biography, his/her current purpose and intent, the setting in which the remarks are made, or the actual or potential relationship between speaker and hearer" (Leiter, 1980, p. 107).

However, even when context is supplied, it has been shown (Garfinkel, 1967) that members still work at organizing their talk in such a way that context is never a given, but always a construction by members, so that context and the meaning or sense of talk are mutually constitutive; that is to say, context is open-ended; anything can be used as a contextual particular, so, therefore, context and meaning illuminate or inform each other.

Therefore, in the mediated talk of computer conferencing, members must work to organize their talk so as to exhibit some sense of appropriate context and, therefore, appropriate talk.

RECIPIENT DESIGN IN COMPUTER CONFERENCING

The command structure of COSY allows the speaker to identify the prior messages which his or her message comments on. Cumulatively, the COSY program works retrospectively by noting at the beginning of each message whether or not there are subsequent messages which are comments on that message. For example, message #2 says at the beginning, "This is a comment to message 1. There is/are comment(s) on this message." When we look for the comments on message #2 in the transcript, we do not find the first one appearing until message #59. This comment is 57 messages removed from message #2 in space, and almost 14 months removed from it in time.

It is clear that messages which are to be heard as comments on prior messages must explicitly formulate that relationship, given the facility of computer conferencing to retain in memory or on hard copy the entire sequence of conference messages. We are of course able to comment retrospectively on prior utterances in ordinary conversation, but we also must formulate the relevance of our utterance by saying something of the order of "I wanted to comment on what you said a moment ago," or "last week," or "last month," etc. Also, in ordinary conversation the speaker so addressed may say, "Oh, but that's not what I said." In computer conferencing there can be no question as to what was said!

The problem of receipt design in conversational turn taking is to some degree mitigated in computer conferencing by this retentive feature of the program. The construction of messages can always be specifically attuned to the members' prior messages, because they are all continuously available. Members may still disagree on the sense or meaning of the message, but they cannot disagree on the words.

TURN TAKING

The structuring of turn taking in computer conferencing using the COSY system is an interesting study in the affects of non-face-to-face interaction on conversation. Firstly, we can observe that a number of turn-taking structures found in ordinary conversation do not appear to differ on computer conferencing. Those features which remain constant are the following: (a) occurrence of speaker change, (b) variable time order, (c) variable turn size, (d) variable conversation length, (e) unscripted talk, (f) variable distribution of turns, (g) variable number of conversationalists, (h) continuous or discontinuous talk, and (i) various turn-constructional units such as turns of one word or turns of sequential length.

Those features that appear to be different are the following: (a) one party talks at a time; (b) coincidental speakers common but of brief duration; (c) speaker transitions with little or no overlap; (d) the use of turn allocation techniques such as current speaker selects next speaker, or self-selection; and (e) repair mechanisms for turn-taking errors and violations, as when two speakers talk at the same time, one will stop prematurely.

I would now like to comment briefly on each of these differences.

(a) In face to face interaction, speakers must themselves manage the organization of turns at talk to ensure that only one speaker speaks at a time. In the COSY conference system, turn organization is managed by the program such that it is electronically impossible for more than one party to talk at a time. The turns are arranged sequentially, according to the time one's message goes into the conference system, and messages appear in that order on the video display terminal and on hard copy.

(b) However, although messages are not displayed simultaneously, it is possible for two or more participants to be composing comments on prior messages at the same time. This allows any participant to comment immediately without "waiting one's turn." Coincidental turn construction is then mediated by the program to prevent coincidental display. It is of course possible, in split screen systems, to have simultaneous display. However, this would create the same problem which arises when two people are talking at the same time, because of the obvious differences between listening and reading as sensory modes of understanding language.

(c) Speaker transition in the COSY conference system is effected by the speaker insofar as the participant indicates the end of a message using a specific command through the keyboard. The system also structures the transition by electronically preventing overlapping utterances from interfering with each other and allowing a new speaker to enter a message at any time. The message becomes the next comment automatically as the time of its entrance warrants.

(d) Turn allocation in computer conferencing, because it is mediated by the program, is structured differently from informal conversation. The current speaker may select the next speaker through the use of the first part of an adjacency pair, such as addressing a question to a specific conference member; however, because of the programmatic control of sequential messages, the next message to appear is determined by time of its entry, not by the structuring of turns and speakers through the use of adjacency pairs. In computer conferencing it is theoretically and practically possible for the next speaker to be controlled by appropriate programming, such as giving that control to a moderator, or linking the right to be next speaker to some feature of a prior utterance, such as the naming of next speaker by the current speaker. But because computer conferencing does not necessarily take the form of continuous talk as normal conversation does, such programming might adversely affect conference participation, since the right to speak might not be taken by the next speaker chosen, yet that speaker may also not specifically relinquish that right. In that case, no messages might be entered on the conference until the problem of the right to speak is somehow remedied.

(e) In the COSY system there appears to be no possibility of overlapping or simultaneous turns because of the electronic control of turn taking. Therefore, no repair mechanisms are necessary. There is, of course, always the chance of the electronics going wrong, but the repair of such a breakdown in communication is obviously not conversational.

Initially, COSY contained a mode of communication called CHAT. CHAT permitted "the user to send a message directly (and in real time) to another COSY user" (Mason, 1985, p. 38). Such a mode required safeguards which are germane to our analysis of possible problems in speaker turn taking. These included the following: that one member should not be able to use CHAT to interrupt another member who is either engaged in sending a long message from his microcomputer, or is engaged in chatting with someone else. In both circumstances the control of interruptions was put into the system and taken out of the hands of the members, thus imposing limitations on the interactive potential of the system while reducing the possibility of problems on the social organization of turns by participants.

This trade off between real time interactive capability of a conference system and greater user control of turn was expressed by one of the developers of the COSY system in the following way:

> the real time of CHAT disrupts the users' conceptualization of the conferencing system as something with which he may comfortably interact, intermittently, under his own control. (Mason, 1985, p. 41)

In most conference systems the moderator or editor has the power to edit or delete all messages, giving him or her virtually complete control over turns in terms of both structure and content. This person has direct control over the corpus of talk in the system and, with this control, is in a position to manage the scene of the talk with regard to speaker and topic. In face-to-face interaction the chair or moderator has normative control over the speaker and, through choice of the next speaker, some control over the topic, but not to the extent imaginable in computer conferencing, where such control could be relatively complete.

CONCLUSION

This chapter has briefly compared the turn-taking structures in natural language, face-to-face interaction with those in computer conferencing. There are significant features of communication found in these differences.

First, it is evident that members use the resources of the computer hard and software to produce recognizably coherent talk. Even though many contextual, nonverbal cues are absent, members appear to be able to talk to each other and to make sense of each other's comments in a way that, for all practical purposes, shows a masked absence of trouble. I would attribute this to a number of features on the system which serve to make explicit what in normal face-to-face talk is often only implicit, and which serve to increase the chances of intelligent talk being produced. These features under the general heading of turn-taking and recipient design include participation rights, topic formation, topical coherence, and member biography.

Briefly, the following argument can be made regarding the importance of each of these features to understanding:

(1) *Participation rights.* The turn allocation system allows virtually unlimited participation by all members of the conference. Any member who has something to contribute can do so at any time, be it a comment, new information, a question, a request, a clarification, and so on. Unlike face-to-face talk, one does not have to wait one's turn; no member who has some potentially important contribution is excluded from making it. Turns cannot be interrupted, shouted down, or refused.

(2) *Topic formulation.* The explicit identification of topical talk at the beginning of conference messages provides a framework for interpreting the meaning and relevance of the talk in a way that is often absent in face-to-face conversation. In everyday interaction members will occasionally formulate the topic or relevance of the talk in so many words, but there is no formal structure or protocol ensuring such formulation.

(3) *Topical coherence.* It is a feature of computer conference systems that, regardless of when one becomes a member, the entire corpus of messages in the conference is always available. This allows members to know all that has been said up to the present time and to design their message accordingly. This knowledge of the talk thus far should decrease the possibility of nontopical talk, because the full corpus of talk or any individual message may always be used immediately as a reference for the design of one's own message.

(4) *Member biography.* In the COSY system, members' biographies are available as a resource. Members are able to call up and consult this information at any time to assist them in designing their message. Personal information may be incomplete or limited, but in any form it is more systematically and easily available than in face-to-face encounters, particularly with strangers.

In this examination of the relationship between face-to-face talk and computer-mediated talk, it is impressive to note the features of the latter which seem to *ncrease* the chances for successful and meaningful talk.

REFERENCES

Garfinkel, H. (1967). *Studies in ethnomethodology.* Englewood Cliffs, NJ: Prentice Hall.

Kiesler, S. (1986, January–February). Thinking ahead: The hidden messages in computer networks. *Harvard Business Review,* 46–60.

Leiter, K. (1980). *A primer on ethnomethodology.* New York: Oxford University Press.

Mason, R. (1985, January 22–23). On what the user expects. In *Computer conferencing and electronic messaging: Conference Proceedings* (pp. 35–44). University of Guelph, Ontario, Canada.

Mayer, A. (1985, January 22–23). User friendliness at 300 baud (the COSY approach to the human interface). In *Computer Conferencing and Electronic Messaging: Conference Proceedings* (pp. 23–34). University of Guelph, Ontario, Canada.

Sacks, H., Schegloff, E., & Jefferson, G. (1974). A simplest systematics for the organization of turn-taking for conversation. *Language, 50* (4), 696–735.

Schegloff, E. (1978). On some questions and ambiguities in conversation. In W. Dressler (Ed.), *Current trends in textlinguistics* (pp. 81–102). Berlin: Gruyter.

Schegloff, E., & Sacks, H. (1973). Opening up closings. *Semiotica, 8,* 289–327.

PART **VI**

MASS MEDIA AND SOCIALIZATION

22

Inside Stories: Gossip and Television Audiences*

SUE BROWER

University of Texas at Austin

Cultural studies scholars of mass communication have described the relationship between audience and televisual text as active, using various models to suggest the nature of the viewers' participation in a narrative program.[1] Newcomb and Hirsch's (1983, pp. 45–55) cultural forum model, based on Carey's ritual view of communication, emphasizes "the collective, cultural view of the social construction and negotiation of reality." For Newcomb and Hirsch, "the rhetoric of television drama is the rhetoric of discussion"—a rhetoric based on multiple levels of meaning in the text and a range of readings among viewers, or by the same viewer.

Liebes applies the cultural forum model to her focus-interview study of foreign viewers of *Dallas*. The basis of this study is talk:

> Talk about shared viewing experiences takes place naturally in society and is a key to the process by means of which program content seeps, if it does, into personalities and cultures. That people discuss *Dallas* in everyday situations and view it together are facts that we can certify from background data as well as from allusions in the discussion groups themselves. (Liebes, 1984, p. 47)

This suggests that viewers' reading, appreciation, and enjoyment of television drama are processes much more gradual and more social than is often assumed.

This chapter describes a specific mode of audience/textual interaction which is by nature collective and extended over time. Gossip, a traditional speech genre, has combined with mass media to produce what some call *personality journalism* and others *gossip*. Despite the negative connotations of the term, gossip as a social practice has special meaning particularly for devoted fans of night-time soap operas. Supplemented by mass-mediated texts, especially

---

* Written in 1986, this chapter was developed without the benefit of John Fiske's *Television Culture* (London: Methuen, 1987), which further elaborates the theory that gossip is a mode of significant interaction between audiences and texts.

[1] See, for example, S. Hall, "Encoding/decoding" (Hall, Hobson, Lowe, & Willis, 1980, pp. 128–138), Morley, "Texts, readers, subjects" (S. Hall, et al., 1980, pp. 163–173), Newcomb and Hirsch (1983, pp. 45–55), and Newcomb, (1984, 34–50).

those in nationally marketed tabloids, gossip creates opportunities for richer readings of the prime-time serial by extending the scope of the program both paradigmatically (to include actors and production personnel as well as the program's characters) and syntagmatically (between weekly episodes and during the summer production hiatus).

Gossip in the press may encourage intimate audience discussion about and participation in a program. By reading the tabloids, fans may construct parallel narratives about characters and stars as well as metanarratives about the television industry. Indeed, gossip as a mode of audience/text interaction may be seen as a synthesis and serialization of related texts. Studies in anthropology and literature suggest the role this speech genre may play in the social interpretation and circulation of television texts.

PUBLIC AND PRIVATE

Gossip has become so lucrative and controversial a feature in the media that *Harper's* devoted its January 1986 cover story to it. A forum that included writers, an editor, a publisher, two academics, and two members of the press specializing in personality journalism considered the rise of such phenomena as *People* magazine, *Entertainment Tonight*, and *Lifestyles of the Rich and Famous*. Not surprisingly, real gossip came off badly. *Public* gossip, that which deals with the public lives of celebrities, was claimed by columnist Liz Smith and *Entertainment Tonight* correspondent Barbara Howar as fair game and good copy. But *private* gossip—news about the personal lives of celebrities—most participants in the forum agreed should not find its way to print. Even the *Harper's* forum, however, quickly became mired in the distinction: If a public official's personal life would seem in the editor's eyes to jeopardize service for the public, then perhaps the item is no longer shabby gossip, but hard news.

While the mixture of public and private may damage the image of some celebrities, it is sought by others. Dyer (1982) argues that the marketing of a movie star requires the construction of an image in the press, including glamor and candid photos, stories of the star's "real life," and rumors of upcoming roles. In the case of television stars and their programs, the public image fuses with what we might consider the semipublic (the press agent's version of personal or behind-the-scenes events), and occasionally even the private. These moments of fusion may offer the opportunity for fans to elaborate the star's image and the fictional text in which he or she appears.

The prime-time soap operas have an aura of glamor and wealth that make for "good" gossip—equivalent in some ways to film-star gossip. Unlike traditional celebrity news about film stars, however,[2] personality journalism about TV stars creates an image, not only of the star, but of the production milieu in which he or she works. Gossip columns, fanzines, entertainment periodicals, and, most

---

[2]Based on a review of fanzines from the classic Hollywood era, Dyer argues that the film star's image traditionally is based on a projected lifestyle of consumption, leisure, and success.

prominently, the national tabloids offer a nearly ideal illustration of Meyrowitz's thesis that the distinctions between "backstage" and "onstage" regions have become blurred (1985). Following Goffman's dramaturgical model of social behavior, Meyrowitz argues that the electronic media have affected social contexts that were once discrete but now are permeable.

The applications of this perspective to network television fictions and their stars are obvious, but also limited. On the one hand, Meyrowitz's argument may be applied to the rise of the national tabloids,[3] which combine old-fashioned sensationalism about ordinary people with "inside stories" about stars and their programs.[4] Gossip is one means by which a fictional text proliferates into many related texts that the audience member can manipulate and share with others. In the context of the tabloids, TV stars, like the film stars analyzed by Dyer, are portrayed as both special (attractive, wealthy, interesting-because-they're-actors) and ordinary (news of their lives shares space with stories of women on diets and favorite pet pictures). Moreover, Meyrowitz's thesis begins to explain the current popularity of reflexive texts in every aspect of popular culture—creators who no longer enjoy a backstage space for the perfection of their work are transforming rehearsal—that is, the production process—into performance. (Hence also the trend in performance art.)

On the other hand, the television industry's backstage is not so easily penetrated, as Carol Burnett's highly publicized libel suit against the *National Enquirer* illustrates: the truth about stars' personal lives remains as elusive as ever. Instead, the industry, the tabloids, and the fans themselves increasingly are constructing parallel narratives about the industry, its productions, its stars, and their professional but backstage lives. Gossip is initiated by the industry for marketing purposes; the national tabloids are the ideal vehicle for reaching a target audience to generate speculation and discussion about programs and stars. But rather than being duped by the two media's intertwined marketing strategies, the audience may engage in this gossip as yet another fiction, knowing that another real backstage continues to exist.

THE SOCIAL USES OF GOSSIP

Gossip through the mass media is significantly different from its interpersonal form. Typically interpersonal gossip connotes intimacy and mutual exchange (Spacks, 1985) and is community bound, whereas mass-mediated gossip is removed from the audience by social and geographic factors. Despite these differences, however, public and private gossip share a process that anthropologists call *collaborative narrative.*

Employing studies of both tribal and postindustrial societies, Gluckman interprets a group's use of gossip as an affirmation of social status and group unity as well as an articulation of moral standards. The right to gossip, in fact, is

---

[3]The surge in the number of tabloids and their circulation has been reported in *U.S. News and World Report* (Sanoff, 1982), and *Business Week* (November 7, 1983).

[4]For an analysis of themes and content in tabloids, see Bird, (n.d.).

seen by some groups as a sign of group membership (Gluckman, 1963, p. 311). From this perspective, gossip promotes a feeling of intimacy, not only among those who share the secrets, but *with those of whom they speak*.[5]

Abrahams's study of the Vincentians of the West Indies supports Gluckman's perspective. While gossip among the Vincentians is considered "talking nonsense," it is nonetheless a route to intimacy. Abrahams notes that the gossiping person will risk disapproval to solidify a relationship with a trusted friend. In this culture where verbal art is highly valued, gossip appears to be in a special category, being judged not on the stylization of words, but "on the validity of [the gossipers'] claims to knowledge of [others'] personal doings" (1985, p. 87).

Although neither of these studies emphasizes the storytelling nature of gossip, Weigle argues that disparaged speech genres such as gossip and old wives' tales are actually forms of collaborative storytelling. These speech genres, unlike the traditionally male genres associated with talk in public spaces, are usually performed in domestic arenas—back yards, front porches, kitchens—and are performed collectively, with one person assuming the role of *facilitator* rather than solo performer. The shape of the genre may seem merely conversational, but, Weigle argues, "Narration, narrative and narrator's sensibility are also very much a part of gossip and gossiping, forms of a verbal art too often associated solely with women and thus casually dismissed" (1978, pp. 1–9).

Carefully avoiding the term *gossip*, Kalcik links the sharing of personal news with storytelling in her study of a women's group in the 1970s. The group engaged in what Kalcik calls "collaborative narrative," developing and structuring one member's "kernel story," linking other stories with the first and occasionally serializing a narrative that was particularly lengthy or involved. Members of the group would ask for updates on a situation, and together the group would construct the next installment (Kalcik, 1978, pp. 3–11). This tendency toward seriality will be discussed later.

While neither the intimacy and skill connected with traditional gossip, nor the commercial impetus of mass-mediated gossip, should be dismissed, it nevertheless appears that gossip surrounding television stars and their programs, like traditional gossip, promotes moral consensus, generates group esteem for the one imparting guarded information, and places the object of gossip in the dual position of ordinariness (identified with the group because they are discussing him or her) and specialness (possessing unique characteristics worth discussing). Gossip is one way people can make sense of what is at best dubious and is more often a fictional representation of reality.

It may also be one way audience members make meaning from fiction as part of a *social process*. In reference to literary fiction, Spacks (1985) argues the

---

[5]Similarly, discussing fan behavior, Chaney and Chaney note that fans strive to share appearance and values with the stars they idolize in order to share the celebrities' "social reality" (1979, pp. 129–144).

relationship between reader and narrator, characterized by the gossipy elements of intimacy, complicity, and moral judgment, contributes to the reader's pleasure. Radway's (1984) observations suggest a tendency among readers of romance novels to collectively reconstruct, critique, and evaluate favorite stories when readers meet, thus merging private with interpersonal experience of the narrative. Similarly, the *Dallas* viewers in Liebes's (1984) study wove together the program's stories with their own and collectively negotiated their evaluations of both televised and interpersonally shared *on-going* narratives.

GOSSIP AND SERIALITY

In her study of British soap opera, Brunsdon (1983) theorizes a "social reader's" interactive mode of viewing. The enigma posed by the serial, she argues, raises not only the question of what will happen, but what *should* happen—hence "the site of the construction of moral consensus" (pp. 76–83), implying both discussion and judgment. As Allen (1985) has observed, the open, interrupted soap opera narrative offers opportunities for individual *or group* speculation and exchange (p. 81).

Even a casual eavesdropper on conversations about television can confirm that viewers' discussions of events in a serial are interpersonal as well as intrapersonal. But is such discussion the same as gossip?

Geraghty's (1981, pp. 9–26) definition of the serial argues that the exchange of opinions both within the narrative and among viewers *can* be labeled gossip. She sees gossip playing an important role within the serial, helping to "create the feeling of day-to- dayness" (because characters have the time for "aimless speculation"); further, gossip constitutes a comment on the action; it provides new or additional information on the action; it binds together various plots and various characters; and it heightens the question, "What will happen next?" thus encouraging the audience to pursue the enigma (pp. 22–24).

Geraghty's interpretation of gossip's role among viewers of the serial is, for my purposes, even more significant. She argues that the serial poses questions that are taken up for speculation and discussion among viewers, offering "a place, a metaphoric elbow on the bar, as commentator on the events as they unfold" (p. 25). Not only does Geraghty's metaphor underscore the communal, neighborly feel to the practice of gossip, but she identifies the imaginative position the viewer assumes. Commentary is performed not in a state of delusion (viewers know they aren't discussing reality), but in a way that acknowledges the fiction while engaging in the questions it poses:

> Indeed, the pleasure of such discussions comes from [audience members'] performing the delicate balancing act of discussing the characters as if they were real people with histories, motivations and futures while at the same time recognizing the formal conventions of the serial in which they appear. (p. 25).

This "as if" state suggests one way viewers interact with the text, becoming deeply involved in the lives of television characters to the point of elaborating well beyond the televisual text.

Further, Geraghty notes, the discussion can be extended to an analytical and narrative level if, for example, a press item reports that two characters will be written out of the program. Viewers "can use this knowledge, for example to speculate on how this will be done" (p. 25).

Geraghty stops short, however, of exploring the next level of gossip—gossip about a program's stars, about the motivations of the production company, about the motivations of the network. Not only are ratings and production budgets routinely covered by publications such as *TV Guide*, daily newspapers, and *Star* magazine, but press stories about actors' contracts routinely cover salary disputes and conflicts over character development, offering fans the opportunity to consider, for example, whether an actor/character is worth the money, as well as how a star's requested change in his or her character might affect the show. If, as Dyer (1982, pp. 110–111) argues, film stars who move from one film project to the next have a serial quality, perhaps television stars remaining with the same program over several years can take on a similar quality when the shifting elements behind the scenes are revealed (or seem to be).

As will be discussed in the following section, an important element in the promotion of Patrick Duffy's return to *Dallas* was the revelation or creation of conflicts that center on Duffy, his return to the set of *Dallas*, and the impact on other members of the cast and crew. Indeed, coming out in weekly installments like the programs they cover, the tabloids construct a serial that parallels or complements developments in the broadcast serial.

BOBBY COMES BACK—THE INSIDE STORY

Bennett (1982, pp. 9–10) has argued that a singular *text* no longer exists in fiction. Instead, there is a proliferation of related *texts*. In the case of James Bond, the films, interviews with actor Sean Connery, 007 products, and other items that refer to the figure of Bond constitute *incrustations* around the original novels which cannot be read without some interaction with the other texts of Bond. These incrustations, Bennett argues, *activate* our reading of the novels, enriching the literary text with film images and with fantasies connected with 007 products.

The prime time soap operas—especially *Dallas* and *Dynasty*—have developed similar incrustations that now activate viewers' reading of the programs. *Dynasty* texts include a line of men's and women's colognes named after two of the characters; a *Dynasty* collection of designer wear has been released. In the case of *Dallas*, Larry Hagman's J. R. has appeared in slightly modified form in Schlitz and B. V. D. commercials; a series of *Dallas* novels recounting past plots is now being marketed. Most recently the return of Patrick Duffy to the show has generated a wealth of texts that incrust the program itself.

Ang concedes that the texts surrounding *Dallas* may have some effect on viewers' involvement with the program, but she restricts this effect only to attracting potential viewers.

> The popular press can perhaps fasten the attention of (potential) viewers on the existence of a programme or arouse curiosity for it, but it is improbable that it can have a straightforward and direct influence on the way in which *viewing* is experienced. . . . Relatively independent of the competing discourses revolving around *Dallas*—in the popular press, in advertising, but also by television critics, journalists and other intellectuals—the programme has made its way into the experiential worlds of millions of viewers. (1985, p. 16)

Nevertheless, the letters from *Dallas* fans upon which she bases her study *do* make reference to fan paraphernalia and to gossip magazines. Although, as Ang says, it may be impossible to measure the degree to which everything from tee shirts to fanzines is incorporated in viewers' program interaction, it remains that viewers' experience of serials cannot be separated from their experience with the surrounding texts. As Lorimar publicist remarked, the tabloids' stories about *Dallas* are "part of the show's mystique."

For all of the prime-time soap operas, but particularly *Dallas* and *Dynasty*, the national tabloids provide a wealth of supplementary and conflicting texts via continuous coverage of the programs, the stars, and the production milieu. Three of the four nationally-marketed tabloids sold in supermarkets and drug stores regularly cover entertainment and celebrity news, along with such topics as new diet plans, AIDS, and self-made millionaires (with some exceptions, the fourth tabloid, *Sun*, does not feature celebrity news). Unlike most magazines, the tabloids—*Star, Globe, The National Enquirer* and *Sun*[6]—are supported primarily by subscriptions and sales rather than advertising. The trade journal for the magazine industry, *Folio*, reported in 1982 that, together, the four tabloids had the greatest growth for that year, rising from a total of 9.9 million copies per week to 11.4 million—a 15% increase (*Business Week*, November 7, 1983). The "pass-along" rate is not incorporated in these figures: each copy of *Star* magazine, for example, is shared by 3.3 readers (Brooks, 1986)—a significant practice that parallels an oral exchange of news.

The sources of advertising, however, are most interesting: *Star*'s major advertisers are R. J. Reynolds Industries, Inc., Brown & Williamson Tobacco Corp., and Lorimar (*Business Week*, 1983; Caridi, 1986). Although the tabloids—especially *Star*—occasionally carry ads for programs, none of the issues examined for this paper include ads for Lorimar programs or films. There

---

[6]Representatives of *Star* maintain that their publication is not a tabloid because it is staple bound and uses a better grade of paper (Brooks, 1986). Because of its position in the market, however—the point of purchase, the price, and the content—I classify it as a tabloid for this study.

is, however, plenty of copy on Lorimar productions. We might conclude that Lorimar has developed an arrangement with *Star* that allows the production company to place stories in the magazine—stories which frequently conflict—to generate speculation and intensify audience interest in both the program and the stars.

Even without such arrangements, the celebrity tabloids have carved out a unique territory. Although, like other tabloids, such as the *Sun*, they continue to offer some unorthodox items, these publications tend to favor "happy news" over stories of the freakish or bizarre. Content analysis is not the method or goal of this paper, but it is important to note that, invariably, these particular publications devote their covers and the majority of their stories to television stars and other celebrities—not only those associated with one production company. Celebrity news offers ample opportunity for both happy news and the sensational: Princess Grace's death not only introduced speculation about her daughter's role in the accident, but eventually led to stories centering on the ghost of the Princess of Monaco (*Business Week*, 1983).

Generally, but especially during the summer, stories about the night-time serials figure prominently in all three of the celebrity tabloids. Usually at least one of the prime-time serials will have one or more photos on the cover, and the cover stories often pit two programs against one another, emphasizing ratings battles and plot developments to be aired in the future—hence predictions of characters' fates in a TV season. Stories that center on a star's career will frequently merge with stories of his or her personal life: "Larry Hagman gets more like J. R. every day" and "Linda Gray has found a real life J. R."

The tabloids' chronicle of Patrick Duffy's return to *Dallas* exemplifies all of these treatments of celebrity and television news, most importantly the industrial perspective. Lorimar's problem of re-introducing a "dead" actor became the topic of considerable speculation even before the cliffhanger episode of May 23, and Duffy's enigmatic appearance in Pam's shower fueled the debate, making the cliffhanger a question not only about the outcome of the story (both Sue Ellen Ewing and Jamie Barnes did seem to die in explosions), but a question of narrative development:

> Not since the world agonized over Who Shot JR? has there been such cliffhanging fever. This time, the big gut-wrencher will focus on Bobby Ewing, and the puzzlers are: How was he brought back to life—and is this really the old Bobby everybody loves?
>
> Whatever the answers eventually turn out to be, one thing is clear: *Dallas* has done it again.
>
> Actor Patrick Duffy, who played Bobby Ewing, will return to the small screen in millions of homes this Friday, and JR can bet the last drop of Ewing oil that the episode will be a ratings blockbuster. (*Star*, May 20, 1986, p. 20)

The story, then, is not only the story of *Dallas*, but the story of the *creation* of *Dallas*. Coming out in weekly installments, this story draws on the combined image of actor and character and provides the service of updating or reminding readers of developments within the program, while making frequent reference—in general terms—to the activities of writers and producers behind the scenes: The story of Patrick Duffy/Bobby Ewing's return to *Dallas* becomes a serialized *and conflicted* account of producers' "risking their shirts" to satisfy fans' wishes to see Bobby back.

Tying together the soap opera plots, the industrial perspective, and the stars' personal stories are the backstage stories that discuss the potential impact of plot developments on the actors. In the case of Bobby's return, the careers of Victoria Principal, Priscilla Presley, and John Beck were most immediately affected, and not coincidentally these actors received special attention in articles about their personal lives during the summer of 1986. Readers who may not have cared for the actors' character were given a chance to care about the fate of the actor him- or herself.

As Geraghty (1981) has asserted, unresolved plot lines invite viewer speculation on future plot lines, and the tabloids generate possible plots for fans to consider. If Bobby comes back, will there be room for his rival for Pam's affections, Mark Graison? Out of this question comes speculation on plot lines that would eliminate Mark—Bobby as murderer was proposed—*and* speculation on what the death of Mark Graison will mean to actor John Beck, photographed in front of his (modest by Hollywood standards) home and with his family: bills to pay, mouths to feed (*Globe*, July 8. 1986).

And if Bobby remarries Pam, forcing Jenna to move out of Southfork, what does this mean for Priscilla Presley? *The Globe's* July 22 lead story, "BOBBY'S BACK—AND HE'S TAKING CHARGE AT SOUTHFORK" is not about Bobby Ewing, but Patrick Duffy and his first day of location shooting in Dallas. Here, contrary to the standard *Dallas* mythology of Larry Hagman's power on the set and Duffy's wimp image, the reader is given a new, tough, professional Patrick Duffy, photographed with cameras in the background, shunning air conditioned comfort to talk with members of the crew.

By late August, the central question of Bobby's return seemed largely resolved, or at least played out for the time being, but other related onstage and backstage *Dallas* stories were spun off the Bobby cliffhanger to keep the story going—and the readers buying.

THE POETICS OF MARKETING

Serialization as a marketing tool is by no means a new journalistic or fictional strategy; nor, as Dyer's work attests, is the serialization of stars' images new with the coming of television. What *is* new about the relationship of the tabloids to the night-time serials, falls into three categories: (a) the use of tabloids by production companies to sustain audience interaction with the program during the summer; (b) the frequent portrayal of actors at work rather than the traditional star image as wealthy, eccentric people-at-play; and (c) the generation—by publicists, tabloid journalists, or both—of real, serialized narratives involving conflict between actors, between actors and producers, and among networks, producers, and the audience.

Together, the tabloids and prime-time soap operas offer a text for viewers that is far more complex than the night-time time serial alone. Allen (1985) has applied reader-response theory to suggest that the open narrative in daytime soap opera imposes a hiatus (along with the minor gaps created by commercials) in the viewer's reading of the text, and that this hiatus allows the viewer to reflect on recent developments and to speculate on future plots—a process which seems to heighten the pleasure for many viewers.

Unlike the daytime serials, which offer new installments 5 days per week without summer break, *Dallas* and the other prime-time serials seem increasingly to rely on the tabloids and other elements of the popular press to sustain viewer involvement in the program's stories, characters, and stars between seasons. During the TV season, viewers may use the tabs to enrich *and supplement* the programs. Future plot developments are clearly intimated by previews for the next week's episode, so real cliffhangers appear only at the end of a season: suspense is relocated in the larger sweep of the season (not "Will Sue Ellen betray J. R. next week? but "Will Sue Ellen overcome her drinking problem this year?") and in the program's backstage stories, as reported by the tabloids (e.g., Will conflict on the set force the termination of *Dallas*?). During the 4-month summer hiatus, the tabloids generate an array of possible resolutions to the cliffhanger, inviting viewer speculation—generating new *talk* about the show, when the show isn't on. Through the exchange of tabloids and opinions, readers may use the opportunity to enjoy some of the sense of community, moral consensus, and group membership that is associated with traditional gossip.

Because the prime-time soap operas rely on stars much more than do the daytime serials (see Newcomb, 1974, p. 176), the actors are treated as the characters they portray (Linda Gray as Sue Ellen), as powerful components of the program's creation and development (Larry Hagman as a major influence in the production and direction of *Dallas*), and as independent agents (John Beck as an out-of-work actor). Tabloids can use the well-known figures of these actors to open up the backstage region of television, tapping into a world of contracts, scriptwriters, and producers that give viewers a sense of knowledge about and closeness to the creators of their favorite program.

Regardless of the marketing value of this strategy, viewers gain a rich source of material that can enhance their experience of the program. Even as the serial provides a text that is richer than episodic programs because of history and multiple plot lines (Newcomb, 1974; Allen, 1985), tabloid serialization offers further intertextual readings, more storylines with more enforced gaps, greater potential for narrative pleasure, and opportunities for collaborative narrative among fans. Like the gossip about the serials themselves, the gossip among a community of viewers and readers about stars and the industry is spoken from the same delicate "as if" perspective—a participation in fiction that is safer than real gossip, but which permits viewers to share, articulate, and affirm social values.

REFERENCES

Abrahams, R. D. (1985). *The man of words in the West Indies: Performance and the emergence of Creole culture.* Baltimore, MD: Johns Hopkins University Press.

Allen, R. (1985). *Speaking of soap operas.* Chapel Hill, NC: University of North Carolina Press.

Ang, I. (1985). *Watching Dallas.* London: Methuen.

Bennett, T. (1982). Text and social process: The case of James Bond. *Screen Education, 41,* 3–14.

Bird, D. A. (n.d.). *The national weekly tabloid phenomenon: An analysis of themes, values and world view.* Unpublished paper, Long Island University.

Brooks, L. (1986). Telephone interview, October 3, *Star* magazine advertising office, New York, NY.

Brunsdon, C. (1983). Crossroads: Notes on soap opera. In E. A. Kaplan (Ed.), *Regarding Television.* Frederick, MD; American Film Institute.

Caridi, K. (1986). Telephone interview, July 30, *Star* magazine office, Tarrytown, NY.

Chaney, D. C., & Chaney, J. H. (1979). The Audience for Mass Leisure. In H. D. Fischer & S. R. Melnick (Eds.), *Entertainment: A crosscultural examination* (pp. 129–144). New York: Hastings House.

Dyer, R. (1982). *Stars.* London: British Film Institute.

Geraghty, C. (1981). The continuous serial—a definition. In R. Dyer, C. Geraghty, M. Jordan, T. Lovell, R. Paterson, & J. Stewart (Eds.), *Television monograph: 'Coronation Street'* (pp. 9–26). London: British Film Institute.

Gluckman, M. (1963). Gossip and scandal. *Current Anthropology, 4*(3), 307–316.

Hall, S., Hobson, D., Lowe, A., & Willis, P. (Eds.). (1980). *Culture media language.* London: Hutchinson.

Kalcik, S. (1978). ". . . Like Ann's gynecologist or the time I was almost raped": Personal narratives in women's rap groups. *Frontiers, 3*(3), 3–11.

Liebes, T. (1984). Ethnocriticism: Israelis of Moroccan ethnicity negotiate the meaning of *Dallas. Studies in Visual Communication, 10*(3), 46–72.

Meyrowitz, J. (1985). *No sense of place: The impact of electronic media on social behavior.* New York: Oxford.

Newcomb, H. M. (1974). *TV: The most popular art.* Garden City, NY: Anchor.

Newcomb, H. M. (1984). Dialogic aspects of mass communication. *Critical Studies in Mass Communication, 1,* 34–50.

Newcomb, H. M., & Hirsch, P. M. (1983). Television as a cultural forum: Implications for research. *Quarterly Review of Film Studies,* Summer, 45–55.

Now the story can be told! How tabloids survived the recession. (1983, November 7). *Business Week,* pp. 145, 148.

Radway, J. A. (1984). *Reading the romance: Women, patriarchy and popular culture.* Chapel Hill, NC: The University of North Carolina Press.

Sanoff, A. F. (1982, January 18). Celebrity Journalism: It Sells, But . . . *U.S. News and World Report,* pp. 55–56.

Spacks, P. M. (1985). *Gossip.* New York: Knopf.

Weigle, M. (1978). Women as verbal artists: Reclaiming the daughters of Enheduanna. *Frontiers, 3*(3), 1–9.

23

Interpreting Viewing:
Creating an Acceptable Context

ALISON ALEXANDER
University of Massachusetts

VIRGINIA H. FRY
University of Connecticut

This paper adopts an interactionist perspective to explore the interpretative processes through which viewers of daytime serials construct and reconstruct the meaning of their viewing activity. This investigation is based on two assumptions which make possible an interactionist approach to the study of text and audience. First, the interaction between text and audience occurs, not merely at the moment when a viewer is engaged by a text (the primary context), but also at numerous ongoing moments diffused across diverse communicative contexts (secondary contexts). Any time a communicative situation requires a viewer to explain and/or justify to others his or her viewing activity, the viewer must interact meaningfully with the text. Second, constructing the meaning of one's engagement with a text is simultaneously a process of creating, defining, and presenting one's self to others. Each time a viewer is asked to provide reasons for viewing behavior, the viewer must construct an expression of self as well.

This is of particular importance in a study of daytime serial viewing. Given a cultural context in which television viewing in general, and soap-opera viewing in particular, is devalued, viewers find that they engage in an activity which stigmatizes them. In secondary contexts, viewers must correlate their explanations of the meaning of their viewing with the impression which they wish to make on others. Presenting one's self as the kind of person who does or does not view soap operas is a complex interactional process in which viewers create and recreate constantly the place of serial viewing in their lives.

This study describes how viewers interpret their involvement with program content in light of common cultural values that negatively connote content and, by implication, viewers themselves. Focusing on the everyday secondary contexts in which viewers are confronted directly with cultural depredation of the worth of their activity should provide information regarding the strategies viewers use to construct and reconstruct the acceptability of their viewing.

This study departs from other work in at least two ways. First, it reconceptualizes audience. Though we all share a commitment to the view that mass communication is a complex *process* involving producers, texts, and audiences, researchers typically focus on one part of this process. Concerned with the manufacture and reification of a culture's dominant ideology through its production of mediated texts and artifacts, critics of mass culture investigate primarily the production moment of the process. Some researchers are involved in textual criticism which produces close "readings" of mediated texts. While cultural critics imply that the meaning(s) of the process can be understood through an analysis of the ideology of the producer class, textual critics generally assume that the meaning(s) reside within the structure of the text. Though both are interested in audience, audience usually appears only obliquely as an undifferentiated mass to whom some communication is directed. By contrast, audience-centered researchers, typically operating form a sociobehavioral perspective, assume producers and texts while they make problematic both the uses and gratifications audience members glean from media use, as well as the effects of media exposure and use. Audience-centered research usually assumes that meaning(s) reside in the attributions audience members make regarding media programming, attributions which can be studied by delineating not only the uses to which audiences put mediated programming but also the effects of program viewing on audience behavior.

The interactionist stance of this study assumes that the meaning(s) viewers have for mediated texts can be studied only by examining a combination of textual and extratextual factors (Fry & Fry, 1985). This perspective leads to the second way in which this study deviates from the work of others. Existing research on soap operas has been concerned primarily with texts (the content analyses of Cassata & Skill, 1983), with producers of the texts (Cantor & Pingree, 1983), with viewer motivations (Herzog, 1944; Rubin, 1985; Compesi, 1980), or with the effects on audience members of prolonged viewing (cultivation studies of Buerkel-Rothfuss & Mayes, 1981; Carveth & Alexander, 1985). By contrast, this study adopts a perspective which derives from the following assumption: while viewers are clearly engaged *by* the texts, these same texts exist within a larger cultural context which places values on them and on their consumption. Viewers may have difficulty constructing the meaning(s) of a soap opera text in isolation from the meaning(s) those texts have within the society within which they are produced and consumed. Meaning, then, cannot be constructed in isolation from the meaning those same texts have in secondary as well as primary contexts. It is less crucial to understand *what* a specific text or genre of texts mean to individual audience members or why a viewer choose specific texts than it is to explore *how* selected texts come to acquire various meanings as viewers interact with the texts during both primary and secondary encounters with given texts.

Studying that interaction process requires delineating the ways in which viewers talk about their viewing activity, and, by extension, about themselves.

This is particularly important in secondary contexts, when viewers are confronted by value statements which indicate the stigma of their viewing behavior. Goffman's (1963) work provides a point of departure for this study. His concern is with communicative contexts in which "stigmatized" and "normal" persons are co-present to one another either in conversation or in an unfocused gathering (p. 12). According to Goffman, an individual can become stigmatized in three different ways: as a result of a physical deformity, illness, or condition; by virtue of some individual shortcoming or flaw inherent to the person's character; or, by extension, because of family lineage, nationality, race, or religion (these are called tribal stigmas). Goffman (1963) notes that the normal and the stigmatized are not different kinds of persons, but, rather, are roles or perspectives individuals assume in actual interactions (p. 138). Because the notions of self as normal or blemished arise and exist through repeated interactions, both normal and deviant are, communicatively speaking, part of each other.

For the purposes of this study, we draw specifically from Goffman's (1963) distinction between the *discredited* and the *discreditable* (p. 4, p. 138). An individual who, by virtue of one of the three reasons cited above, is blemished, is potentially discreditable. One would expect such persons to strive to manage information about themselves in ways which would reduce and/or mask their stigma in order to reduce the likelihood that they would become actually discredited at any point during an interaction. Once one is found out, the function of the interaction shifts from the management of information to the control of interactive tension produced by the discovery or acknowledgement of the stigma. At this point, the discredited may attempt to offer satisfactory explanations or reasons for the stigma.

The degree and manner in which the discreditable may manage information depends, in part, on his or her perception of *other*, of the person or persons who are co-present. Goffman notes that two groups of persons, *one's own* (those who share one's stigma) and *the wise* (those who are normal, but for some reason are highly sympathetic to one's plight), present the discreditable with interactive situations in which the management of information to hide or minimize one's stigma is less important. With others, however, the presentation of self requires extensive information management in order to avoid becoming actually discredited.

In terms of this particular study, the interest is in the way in which soap opera viewers talk about their viewing activity, and, consequently, about themselves, when presented with secondary communicative contexts in which their viewing makes them potentially discreditable persons. The goal is to identify the strategies viewers employ to manage information about themselves and their viewing, as well as the strategies employed to reduce tension when they are discredited. The patterned ways in which viewers' experience of a primary context become redefined and reconstituted within a secondary context is a process quite similar to one Goffman (1974) has termed as *keying*. A key, for Goffman, "is a set of conventions by which a given activity, one already meaningful in terms of some primary framework, is transformed into something patterned on this activity but seen by the participants to be something quite else. The process of transcription [or transformation] can be called keying" (pp. 43–44). These conventions take the form of "lines" which individuals create in order to prevent themselves from becoming discredited and/or to minimize interactive tension when they are actually discredited. This paper examines the conversational work which takes place when stigmatized and normal are co-present in secondary communicative contexts.

METHOD

Data for this study were derived from focused telephone interviews, question-naires, and unobtrusive observations of naturally occurring conversations over a 7-month period. Observations concentrated on the social management of soap-opera viewing in conversation. These observations were used to refine interview and questionnaire items.

Telephone interviews were conducted with 48 adult serial viewers from urban and suburban areas of Massachusetts. Respondents were asked their serial preferences, time spent viewing, and the perceived strengths and weak-nesses of the serial format. Viewers were asked to discuss interactions with others in which they were questioned about their serial viewing. Respondents indicated the bases upon which individuals had challenged their serial viewing habit, and their responses. These responses were elicited in an open-ended form and were organized into a category scheme by the researchers. Additional data of the same type but in written form were gathered from students in a communication fundamentals course. Of 60 students, only 11 indicated they were serial viewers. These data were used in conjunction with the adult viewer data in this analysis.

RESULTS

At the outset we noted the importance of understanding the ways in which viewers talk to others about their viewing. Soap-opera viewers are often placed in communicative contexts in which viewing is considered unacceptable. In this research, 49 of the 59 individuals interviewed were able to provide examples of being kidded, questioned, or attacked for their serial viewing. It seems clear that soap-opera viewers are aware of the low value placed on the soap opera form, and, by implication, on their viewing activity.

Of interest in this study was identifying the strategies, conversational con-ventions or keys, viewers employed in secondary contexts to present their primary viewing activity to others who devalued it. Several strategic conven-tions emerged. First, when confronted with a communicative context in which viewing was clearly unacceptable, viewers tended either to deny legitimacy to the secondary context and to those who did not value their viewing, or they accepted the challenge as legitimate and denied the legitimacy of their viewing (the primary context) by offering a socially acceptable explanation of their viewing.

When a viewer assumed the legitimacy of the challenge to his or her viewing, we found two general classes of responses that allowed the viewer to deny the legitimacy of the primary context by offering a socially acceptable account of viewing: those in which the viewer detached the self from the primary serial viewing context, and those in which the viewer attached the self to the context.

Detaching the self from the soap-opera viewing experience took several forms. We suspect that one form is denial of viewing or silence in the face of potential opportunities to discredit self by identifying self as a viewer. This inference derives from observations made by ourselves and others (Lemish, 1985) in which individuals denied watching soap operas but in subsequent conversations revealed considerable knowledge about the characters and plots of various serials.

Another method whereby individuals detached the self from viewing appeared when individuals claimed they watched soap operas as comedy. This strategy not only placed the viewer in a superior position to the text but also described the self as a critic amused by the absurdities of the genre. This strategy placed the viewers who adopted it in a superior position vis-à-vis other consumers of the genre.

However, detaching self from the primary viewing context can also be accomplished indirectly. Twenty-eight individuals described their viewing as simply entertaining. One added that everything didn't have to be intellectually stimulating. One noted that soaps were better than prime-time because they were less violent, and another viewer stated that her boyfriend watched cartoons and that soaps were "no worse than cartoons." In such responses viewers seem simultaneously to assert their right to pleasure—i.e., entertainment—while at the same time deny any further importance to the activity. By invoking the value of entertainment, and by defending their own choice of entertainment, viewing becomes defined as a ritualized use of the medium dependent upon function rather than content. One viewer made this distancing even more explicit with the comment "I am not an addict." This strategy established the self as somehow different from and superior to those for whom viewing might be out of control.

A second class of responses which accepted the legitimacy of the challenge did so by attaching the self to primary serial viewing. In this strategy, viewers accepted the legitimacy of the challenge but attempted to counter criticism by showing that they used the texts in some socially valued way. Thus, serial viewing was legitimized by linking it with wider social values. One such value was "activity" vs. "passivity." A number of viewers (16) noted that serials made their lives appear less complicated in comparison. These responses identified a mentally active approach to the genre in which the individual actively compared self to text rather than depicted self as a passive consumer of the genre. Acknowledging implicitly that watching soap operas is considered a waste of valuable time, one viewer attempted to redeem self-image by adding, "I do other things so it's not a waste of time." Though in a somewhat different way than viewers who actively used the programs in their lives, this viewer appealed to the same cultural value of productive use of time.

Another method whereby viewers attached self to the primary viewing context involved a depiction of the text as powerful and intrinsically attractive. Viewers, sometimes ruefully, asserted that they were engaged by the plot, structure, and/or performers in their favorite serial programs. While denying that serials were important in their lives, they nonetheless noted an ongoing desire to see what happened. Comments such as "I like them; there's so much going on" typify the appeal of the genre. The self, then, was engaged by the intrinsic textual properties which constituted the interest value of the genre. Other studies have indicated that such textual properties have clear use values as well (Carveth & Alexander, 1985).

Finally, some viewers denied the legitimacy of the challenger, thus asserting that others had no right to criticize. Viewers preferring this strategy refused to acknowledge a negative definition of self (that is, they refused outright to accept that they were discreditable) because of their serial viewing. Twelve people reported that they typically responded in such a manner. Five indicated that they advised challengers to begin watching soaps themselves; six noted that they didn't care what others thought; two reported on specific ongoing debates with family members, with one indicating that a typical response was "Mom, leave me alone." Another had whittled down the response to the straightforward rebuttal "You're a fool."

DISCUSSION

Goffman (1963) suggests that when something socially unacceptable is revealed about an individual, that person has been discredited. When a stigma is revealed, considerable conversational work must be done in order to recreate an acceptable context for continuing interaction. Part of that work requires the discredited individual to adopt a strategy capable of indicting to others how the individual sees self and how the individual expects others to respond to their apparent stigma. This research identified three conventions by which this conversational work was accomplished when viewers were treated negatively by others: detaching self from the primary viewing context, attaching self to the primary viewing context, and denying the legitimacy of the challenge.

The first two conventions function, in fact, to assume the right of the challenger and to accept the inference that viewing is an unworthy activity. In those two strategies, viewers admit that they are potentially discreditable while adopting strategies which assert that they as individuals actually are not as discredited as the challenger assumes. Whether or not viewers attach or detach self from their primary viewing activity, their interactive strategies implicitly reinforce the cultural and social debasement of the form.

Those viewers who negate the legitimacy of the secondary rather than primary context, however, actually deny that they are discredible because of their viewing. This class of strategic conventions calls into question, then, the cultural and social "wisdom" which devalues the soap opera form.

It seems clear, as Goffman (1963) noted in his study of various types of stigmas, that stigmatized and normal are roles assumed by communicators in specific types of interactive contexts. As such, both are part of one another as well as of the larger social and cultural context in which the interaction takes place. This is apparent in this study in at least two ways. First, regardless of the strategies employed by stigmatized and normal in the secondary contexts which were the concern of this study, all participants positioned themselves in some particular way in terms of the cultural and social devaluation of the soap opera genre. In other words, microinteractive contexts took place within the larger cultural context which established the script for discourse on soap opera viewing. Second, the specific reasons provided by some viewers indicated their implicit knowledge of cultural values likely to be shared by challengers as well as regular viewers. That some viewers appealed to what might be termed a naive and popular psychology of television viewing which elevates choice and individual difference as the means by which television effects are mediated calls forth the claim "television affects everyone else but me." The mythology of the individual who is free and capable of making intentional and reasoned choices permeates the conventions viewers use in secondary contexts. Additionally, many viewers indicated their knowledge of the cultural value placed on the productive use of time and on being active rather than passive. Thus, when the opportunity arose, these viewers appealed to the cultural values they were likely to share with the challenger as a strategy for reducing interactive tension and for asserting that they, in fact, were not as discredited as the challenger had assumed.

It is possible to suggest that the different conventions we have identified suggest fundamental differences in the ways in which individuals cognitively respond to the soap-opera genre. For example, those viewers who were caught up in the text—either as an object to be ridiculed, to provide them with shear entertainment, or because of the plots, performers, or some other distinguishing property of the genre—respond primarily to the denotative characteristics of the texts in this genre. Other viewers, for example those who assert that they take the text and *do something with it* in their own lives, intentionally and self-consciously extend the textual signs inherent in the genre by making a series of connotations which may have little to do with the text itself. The significance of denotative and connotative processes as they relate to viewers engagement with specific genre is a fruitful area for research (Fry & Fry, 1985, 1987).

The connection between the text and the audiences' engagement with it in the primary context could be explored also by considering the degree to which the denotative content of the genre centers around the presentation of the three types of stigmas discussed by Goffman (1963). It is possible that one of the intrinsic appeals of the genre is its unique treatment of various types of stigmas.

Finally, this study could contribute in a programmatic way to the development of a series of interconnected research projects which attempted to compare the strategies employed by those who are discreditable and/or discredited for numerous different reasons. Extending this notion to soap opera viewers is only one way in which such projects could evolve.

REFERENCES

Buerkel-Rothfuss, N. L., & Mayes, S. (1981). Soap opera viewing: The cultivation effect. *Journal of Communication, 31*, (3), 108–115.

Cantor, M., & Pingree, S. (1983). *The soap opera.* Beverly Hills, CA: Sage.

Carveth, R., & Alexander, A. (1985). Soap opera viewing motivations and the cultivation process. *Journal of Broadcasting & Electronic Media, 29*, 259–273.

Cassata, M. B., & Skill, T. (1983). *Life on daytime television: Tuning-in American serial drama.* Norwood, NJ: Ablex Publishing Corp.

Compesi, R. J. (1980). Gratifications of daytime TV serial viewers. *Journalism Quarterly, 57*, 155–158.

Fry, D., & Fry, V. (1985). A semiotic model for the study of mass communication. In M. McLaughlin (Ed.), *Communication yearbook 9* (pp. 443–462). Beverly Hills, CA: Sage.

Fry, D., & Fry, V. (1987). Some structural characteristics of music television videos. *Southern Speech Communication Journal, 52*, 151–164.

Goffman, E. (1963). *Stigma: Notes on the management of spoiled identity.* New York: Simon and Schuster. (First Touchstone Edition, 1986.)

Goffman, E. (1974). *Frame analysis: An essay on the organization of experience.* New York: Harper and Row.

Herzog, H. (1944). What do we really know about daytime serial listeners? In P. F. Lazarsfeld & F. N. Stanton (Eds.), *Radio Research 1942–1943* (pp.3–33). New York: Duell, Sloan and Pearce.

Lemish, D. (1985). Soap opera viewing in college: A naturalistic inquiry. *Journal of Broadcasting & Electronic Media, 29*, 275–93.

Rubin, A. (1985). Uses of daytime television soap operas by college students. *Journal of Broadcasting & Electronic Media, 29*, 241–58.

24

Ethnic Diversity and Mass-Mediated Experience

PAUL J. TRAUDT
Duquesne University

INTRODUCTION

The flight from economic or ideological persecution has long motivated the arrival of individuals to this country—a land first developed and then constitutionally founded upon the promise of new beginnings and communicative freedoms. Over time, the promise has grown to mythic proportions and stands as a sign for the very perceptual foundation of what this country represents to many around the globe.

As essential constituents in this mythology, the mass media interpret this theme to their own ends. Through their role as news gatherers, we are exposed to the current struggles of individuals intent on reaching our borders—individuals fleeing various contemporary forms of economic or ideological persecution. A host of special features embedded within nightly newscasts as well as hour-long specials are devoted to such struggles.

Such programming makes viewers confront their position within this aggregate of individuals—individuals who came, or whose ancestors came, from somewhere else. And, perhaps contrary to original intent, the mediated coverage of American mythology does more to reaffirm the fact that we are something less than a homogenized group.

This chapter explores the characteristics of this social texture with an eye toward isolating the contribution that the mass media, and notably television, play in this process. Implicit in this observation is the assumption that different groups in this country, characterized by hard and fast differences with regard to ethnicity, have the potential for experiencing the popular mass media quite differently. This paper begins with the assumption that contemporary social experience in everyday life is, with certain variance, a mediated experience based on one's utilization of the popular mass media and television in particular. Further, it seems that there is potential within this form of mediated experience to both reaffirm as well as confuse traditional ethnic divisions among individuals.

DEFINING ETHNICITY: DIVERSITY OF APPROACH IN THE SOCIAL SCIENCES

The concept of ethnicity is fundamental in social-science scholarship. Various fields of social inquiry have theoretically and operationally utilized the concept differently. For example, in mainstream sociology, *ethnicity* has been operationally defined to fit the antecedent–consequent conditions, conforming to the prediction and control models, anchored in the principles of logical positivism. The result has been sociology's commitment to discovering the larger strata of life in terms of measured characteristics built around aggregates. Ethnicity, often defined in terms of race, has been used extensively as a marker for such aggregates, as has sex, age, income level, education level, and so on. Within this approach, ethnicity has been often studied for its associative characteristics with other markers, such as poverty level and social class. Whether used alone or in some combination with other variables, the dominant practice within sociology has been characterized by the assumption that persons who fit within these broadly defined, aggregate categories share a good deal in common—in terms of their socialization, their environment, and their worldview.

The historical antecedents of logical positivism also inform much of the work we do within the field of mass communication. Ethnicity measures have long been used as an organizing schema for the categorization and analysis of mass-media messages. Ethnicity-type variables have also been examined for their power in predicting an isolated audience segment's exposure patterns to various mediated messages. The general understanding up to this time has been that ethnicity acts as one of a host of primary perceptual filters seen to influence how mass-media messages are received by the ethnic group's collective persona.

This body of literature has gone a long way in characterizing the simplified and stereotypic depictions of ethnicity as they are presented in the mass media—notably those content-analytic studies of entertainment genres found in commercially based television. This literature has also seen some success in predicting the degree of exposure and content preferences of various ethnic groups when it comes to televisual fare—ethnic groups distinguished largely by skin color.

However, this traditional mass-communication literature is subject to critical scrutiny on both theoretical and empirical levels regarding ethnicity in its relevance to the televiewing experience. How such audiences, characterized by ethnic diversity, engage the permeating flow of such televisual contents, and how these contents get incorporated into the fixtures of daily life, becomes the natural focus of inquiry. This is not to say that more traditional studies do not provide essential baseline information. Indeed, they do, and most of this research does not claim to establish the parameters for explaining how it is that ethnicity contributes to the perceptions of and social actions derived from mass-mediated content.

Though sociology as we know it tends toward the explanation of larger aggregates of social strata, it is not without its pre-Positivistic leanings. The social-interaction schools of sociology will ultimately inform the techniques incorporated here for depicting how it is that individuals, characterized by their ethnic differences, confront day-to-day experiences. The exigencies of day-to-day experience as they conform to ethnic differences within and between cultures have been the domain of anthropology. It is to anthropology that we turn for the defining and understanding of ethnicity. Anthropology has long recognized that ethnicity does more than provide the social researcher with a set of broad topologies for consequent analysis and classification. For anthropology, the term is more complex in its concern with how individuals in society see themselves and their relationships to others in that society. Anthropology typically goes beyond mere classifications based on race, and probes into both the history and living practices of individuals. As De Vos indicates:

> An ethnic group is a self-perceived group of people who hold in common a set of traditions not shared by others with whom they are in contact. Such traditions typically include "folk" religious beliefs and practices, language, a sense of historical continuity, and common ancestry or place of origin. The group's actual history often trails off into legend or mythology, which includes some concept of an unbroken biologic-genetic generational continuity . . . members of an ethnic group cling to a sense of having been an independent people, in origin at least, whatever the special role they have collectively come to play in a pluralistic society. (De Vos, 1982, p. 9)

Royce amplifies the distinctions between ethnic group, feelings of ethnicity, and requirements for an operationalization of ethnicity as a key variable in consequent research:

> An "ethnic group" is a reference group invoked by people who share a common historical style (which may be only assumed), based on overt features and values, and who, through the process of interaction with others, identify themselves as sharing that style. "Ethnic identity" is the sum total of feelings on the part of group members about those values. . . . "Ethnicity" is simply ethnic-based action. (Royce, 1982, p. 18)

A composite definition of ethnicity may be developed from the complementary work of these two anthropologists. Ethnicity, for our purposes here, is the living practice of social actions on the part of individuals who share a common historical origin, who maintain through social interaction a dynamic system of beliefs founded in formal and informal rituals that may include the use of special languages. *Ethnic identity* is the degree to which an individual maintains the place such membership has for him or her in daily life.

We can see from this operationalization of ethnicity, how traditional mass communication inquiry has sacrificed a valid construct of ethnicity for the sake of empirical expediency. This trend is evident within the existing body of mass communication research intent on classifying mediated representations of ethnicity, as well as in those audience-centered assessments of the effect of exposure to such representations.

The problem is compounded when we examine how the fields of mainstream sociology and mass communication have organized ethnicity into analytic schemes. For example, when race has been used as a predictor variable, the implicit assumption is that all members of that race share a good deal in common in terms of socialization, social status, or even media consumption and exposure patterns. The assumption is that race as an ethnic measure informs us of the individual's understanding of the larger world. However, as informed by anthropology, the day-to-day practices of ethnic-based behavior go far beyond those predicted simply on the basis of skin color. After even cursory examination of available literature, one is struck with the variety of ethnic-type labels used in designating even one segment of the population. *Hispanics, Chicanos, Spanish-speaking, Spanish-American,* and so on have all been used to describe that portion of the population whose families originate from Spanish-speaking countries. Within the right social context, these labels *are* meaningful, and reflect observable subculture characteristics within the larger ethnic population. Concurrently, these labels, including the most contemporized form, *Latino,* have been used interchangeably to refer to individuals who comprise very large and diverse groups.

Media research has often treated all Hispanic peoples as one in the same, as has related inquiry into both mediated representations and media-exposure patterns for Blacks, Orientals, and Native Americans. Even more recent research has examined a broad pool of Hispanics residing in both southwest and Pacific regions of the United States who are classified by virtue of their common Mexican origin as a homogeneous group (Greenberg, Burgoon, Burgoon, & Korzenny, 1983).

Given an increased sensitivity evident in anthropological definitions of ethnicity, the diversity found within these broader classifications forces us to rethink how we study such groups. Moreover, such recognition demands our attention to the fundamental social dynamics of both *intraethnic* and *interethnic* considerations in future mass communication research.

ETHNICITY AND THE STUDY OF EVERYDAY EXPERIENCE

Paramount with this new understanding is the examination of how individuals, noted for their common ethnic membership, utilize the mass media to make sense of their everyday worlds within and outside their immediate ethnic culture. The goal is problematic, because it forces inquiry to become cognizant of the processes most of us take for granted. For Hall,

> The rules governing what one perceives and is blind to in the course of living are not simple; at least five sets of disparate categories of events must be taken into account. These are the subject or activity, the situation, one's status in a social

system, past experience, and culture. The patterns governing juggling these five dimensions are learned early in life and are mostly taken for granted. (Hall, 1977, p. 87)

We can view Hall's categories as a form of obligatory agenda when studying culture or subcultures. The agenda is, clearly, overwhelming in terms of what it requires us to do in social research intent on unveiling the dynamic relationship among ethnicity, mass media, and human communication. Yet, there is a certain elegance of fit when we examine the parameters of ethnic-media inquiry and those parameters drawn by Hall. The *subject* or *activity* components are clearly those that beg the larger question of the relationship between ethnicity, mass media, and human communication. The *situation*, as well, is defined by the parameters of a social life influenced by mass mediation. Situated contexts are those communicative contexts at the point of mass-media message reception as well as those interpersonal-communication contexts where meanings derived all or in part from the mass media are displayed as they contribute to the negotiation of meaning. Ethnicity contributes to one's position or status within a particular group as well as in the larger culture. What constitutes the subject matter for such inquiry? For Hall, and for this effort, the focus lies at the point where ethnicity gets practiced and maintained communicatively— where culture systems are displayed in the ongoing, normative actions of people within exquisitely defined groups:

> The cultural unconscious, those out-of-awareness cultural systems that have as yet to be made explicit, probably outnumber the explicit systems by a factor of one thousand or more. . . . These rules [governing features of a system] apply to the formative and active aspects of communications . . . and the action chains by which humans achieve their varied life goals. . . . The investigation of out-of-awareness culture can be accomplished only by actual observation and real events in normal settings and contexts. (Hall, 1977, p. 166)

Some scholars have gone so far as to argue that ethnicity should become the focal point for any productive theory of mass communication processes—that traditional models of mass communication have characterized the audience as heterogeneous:

> In this perspective the primary relationships for analysis are those between linguistic and cultural codes and patterns of class . . . race . . . and sex. . . . We are therefore proposing a model of the audience, not as an atomized mass of individuals, but as composed of a number of subcultural formations or groupings whose numbers will share a cultural orientation towards decoding messages in particular ways. (Morley, 1983, p. 108)

All that remains, then is some method of inquiry which transcends the taken-for-granted nature of the mundane social world and illuminates the social process of culture systems (read as ethnic systems) as they are evident in daily life. For purposes defined here, the technique must examine the process by which individuals display meanings as they are displayed communicatively in the process of experiencing the world. Further, the technique must be able to identify those instances when ethnicity is seen to operate as a filter on this meaning system, particularly as that filter engages, perceives, and incorporates mass-media messages to personal ends.

A PHENOMENOLOGY OF ETHNICITY AND THE MASS MEDIA EXPERIENCE

There are multiple interpretations of the goals of phenomenological inquiry. These include the contemporary derivations of symbolic interactionism, dramaturgy, and ethnomethodology. The current interpretation takes its direction from Husserl's phenomenological philosophy, with amplification provided by the work of Schutz (1967), Kockelmans (1967), and others. At base, these interpretations all incorporate some systematic method to account for the activities of conscious experience as it contributes to what we know of the world and ourselves in relationship to that world.

According to Husserl, the conscious practice of experiencing is fueled by the cognitive functions of intentionality and reflexivity, as they are practiced in everyday life. The intentionality function is that which directs attention to the surrounding world. As Kockelmans would have it:

> The object of any act is an inseparable aspect of the meaning phenomenon itself. In Husserl's philosophy, the object appears as essentially determined by the structure of thinking itself; this thinking itself first gives meaning to the object and then continues to orient itself to the pole of identity which itself has created. (Kockelmans, 1967, p. 34)

Conversely, the cognitive functions of reflexivity are produced out of our directed, intentional involvement with the world of experience. Reflexivity is the related method by which we understand the knowledge claims derived from intentional involvement to be part of the very world being experienced. We understand this knowledge only in relation to the meanings created from our cognitive confrontations between directed experience and the signifying frame in which we find ourselves.

The functions of intentionality and reflexivity best serve the current problem when applied to the study of selected communication contexts. In interpersonal experiences, for example, intentionality and reflexivity interact to construct meaning. But what of those day-to-day experiences when technology comes between reciprocating senders and receivers? Ihde (1982) examined the hermeneutic role performed by telephone technology and identified certain invariant features of the mediated-communication experience. The invariant features of telephone technology included both "amplificatory" and "reductive" dimensions (1982, p. 63). These features represent those "governing features" of a communications system drawn earlier by Hall. These are conditions having real *and* essential influence on the communication setting, but are those generally "blind" to participants within that setting:

The artifact (telephone) is taken into intentionality and occupies a mediating position. . . . I am able to recognize your voice as yours, and although your presence to me is reduced perceptually to a mere voice, the presence is one in "real space-time." . . . I call this advantage the amplificatory dimension of the media. . . . But the advantage is gained at a price. Your presence to me through the telephone is—compared to global perception—a reduced presence and lacking in the perceptual richness of the face to face situation. I call this the reductive dimension of a medium. (Ihde, 1982, p. 63)

Others (Traudt, Meyer, & Anderson, 1985), have performed phenomenological analyses of television. Drawing from descriptive ethnographies of television-mediated social settings, the authors demonstrated how television can play at least two essential roles in the individual's day-to-day meaning constructions. First, they confirmed how members of a group use televiewing to acquire information, to confirm inferences about the surrounding world, and to express those inferences to other members of the group. Second, they documented how members of these groups take the meanings derived from mass-media contents into the social realm of nonmedia exposure events and use these derived meanings as a constitutive of ongoing interactions. They also discovered television's potential for providing amplificatory and reductive features to this process of meaning construction:

When taken into intentionality, television extends the individual's experience to worlds otherwise unattainable, providing an experientially compressed record of past, current and imagined future events that, reflexively, are interpreted into the shape of lived experience. . . . Concurrent to the expansion feature of the television experience is its reductive feature. As with all media, television is a component of the technological embodiment in which we all live. . . . We ponder the evolution of a lived experience, of social reality construction, increasingly dependent on the decoder's interpretation of messages inherent within the dominant mass media. (Traudt et al., 1985, pp. 25–26)

ETHNICITY AND MASS-MEDIATED EXPERIENCE

To review, ethnicity is the living practice of social action by individuals who share a common historical origin and who practice formal and informal rituals as they are displayed communicatively, often through the utilization of special languages. When viewed phenomenologically, ethnicity can be seen as an essential component this world of experience. For example, Berry and Mitchell-Kernan argue that "It is our view that ethnicity may be a significant viewer characteristic and may channel the way in which messages transmitted by the media are perceived, conceptualized and evaluated" (1982, p. 7). With specific focus on children, they argue how the ethnic experience can be seen as a major determinant, a primary filter by which the young person comes to know his or her world:

It is not that ethnic identity strictly determines the learning experiences of children, but rather that ethnic identity is associated with patterns of experience that exhibit significant common denominators from the perspective of socialization. These shape the manner in which the socialization potential of television is realized. (Berry & Mitchell-Kernan, 1982, p. 8)

Though it is unlikely that Berry and Mitchell-Kernan were entertaining the fundamental tenets of phenomenology at the time, their idea that ethnicity provides shape to the social experience is very much in harmony with the concepts of intentionality and reflexivity.

Ethnicity can be seen to fuel intentionality as, cyclically, the shaping of ethnic identity can itself be seen as a function of indexicality. Ethnicity, modulates directed experience in the larger world. When taken into intentionality, television provides the amplificatory function of extending our world of experience beyond the interpersonal realm—the realm most often associated with the ongoing maintenance of group-ethnic identity. There is a fair amount of available mass-communication literature which, at least implicitly, examines television's amplificatory features for their contribution to the erosion of ethnic identity. These authors claim to demonstrate television's potential for cultural homogenizing (cf. Eastman & List, 1980; Morgan, 1986) as a function of above-average media consumption. One interesting contribution to this argument is advanced by Meyrowitz (1985), who provides an amalgam of Goffman's social theory of dramaturgy and McCluhan's views on the embedded pattern of media, culture, and social reality. Meyrowitz argues for the potential for the mass media to "blur" traditional culture distinctions:

The greater the number of distinct social-information systems, the greater the number of distinct "groups"; the smaller the number of distinct information-systems, the smaller the number of distinct group identities. The merging of many formerly distinct situations through electronic media, therefore, should have a homogenizing effect on group identities. . . . Formerly distinct groups not only share very similar information about society in general, they also share more information about each other—information that once distinguished "insiders" from "outsiders." As a consequence, traditional bonds are weakened and traditional distinctions among groups become partially blurred. (Meyrowitz, 1985, p. 131)

As counterargument, there is a corresponding body of literature whose evidence, when taken collectively, suggests that ethnicity is maintained and even strengthened by virtue of selective reinforcement from mass-media content (cf. Glenn & Simmons, 1967; Dunn, 1975).

Both sides of the argument point to television's potential for providing a hermeneutic role in the shaping of directed experience. This previous work points to television's tremendous potential for helping to shape the meanings derived from daily life. Television's window on the world is not without its own unique set of filters. When we take television into intentionality, we both amplify and reduce our world of experience. We amplify our experience by gaining access to information unavailable within the confines of interpersonal-communication contexts. We learn more about the world and, reflexively, compare that new learning to those existing concepts that constitute our ethnicity.

Concurrently, by taking these electronic images into intentionality, we reduce our world of experience. First, it is plausible that we reduce the influence of other communications contexts when we engage in mass-media behavior. By spending time with television we can only, at best, share the context provided by others party to the televiewing setting. We also reduce the world of experience by virtue of that content we generally encounter in the mass media. The field of mass communication is replete with ethnic-based studies which document the limited variety of representations available from the majority of televisual content. Much of this literature warns that members of traditionally defined ethnic groups encounter limited representations of their own kind in the mass media.

AGENDA FOR THE STUDY OF ETHNICITY AND MASS-MEDIATED EXPERIENCE

The controversy surrounding the relationship between ethnicity and the mass media continues. The phenomenological analysis provided in this paper provides plausible characteristics for this ethnicity–mass media relationship. Still missing is regular and systematic investigation of how individuals in society, isolated by their evidentiary practices of ethnicity, experience the mass media. We must now come to understand, for example, how meaning taken from preferred and widely available programming genres gets used by individuals of different culture groups.

There is very limited precedent available to inform the acquisition of such goals. The most promising methodological models might be those provided in the work of scholars intent on examining the effect of transnational flows of mass communication. Theories motivating this body of work are often different from the ethnic-media theories providing focus to the current effort, but both share an interest in documenting how meanings get formed as a function of exposure to mass-media content. Much of this literature examines the role the mass media play in the acculturation of a country's various ethnic groups:

> The fact is that the majority of Latin American countries have large urban populations which are being incorporated into a new mass society through the mass media and television most especially. It is also true that most audiences seem eager to watch the programs and the advertising that come from national and transnational sources, often in contradiction to what their "true interests" seem to be to intellectuals and other critics. The theoretical effort, then, is to focus on the process of incorporation of popular classes into the structures of urban, capitalist society in such a way that it detects both the incorporation as well as resistance to hegemonic structures of their situations. (McAnany, 1986, p. 15)

The most illuminating work of this kind, in terms of informing appropriate methodologies, is provided by Christol (1984) in her examination of television as an acculturation source for groups distinguished by social class in Mexico. In contrast to more conventional survey methods, Christol argues for ethnography as the method of choice when the research is intent on examining the process of meaning constructions derived, at least in part, by mass-communication contents:

> To date, virtually all research studies investigating acculturation via the media have shared a common research method, the survey questionnaire. This has allowed researchers to study large samples. . . . However, it has not permitted an examination of the nature of the acculturation process, or analysis of contextual forces at work during an individual's reception and construction of meaning from messages received. . . . This study uses an ethnographic methodology to investigate the process by which acculturation, particularly along the dimension of consumption patterns, is taking place via television exposure. (Christol, 1984, pp. 188–189)

Though the study of ethnic-media relationships in natural settings is without precedent, there is a growing body of literature that documents how individuals incorporate television into their everyday experience (Lull, 1980a, 1980b; Pacanowsky & Anderson, 1982; Wolf, Meyer, & White, 1982; Traudt & Lont, 1986). These ethnographic methods, conducted largely within U.S. borders and diverse in their interpretation of mainstream phenomenology, have demonstrated that the shape of daily experience is unquestionably modified by our accommodation of the mass media and their contents.

REFERENCES

Berry, G., & Mitchell-Kernan, C. (1982). *Television and the socialization of the minority child.* New York: Academic Press.

Christol, S. (1984). Television as an acculturation resource in the third world: Mexico—a case study. In S. Thomas (Ed.), *Studies in mass communication & technology: selected proceedings from the Fourth International Conference on Culture and Communication.* Norwood, NJ: Ablex Publishing Corp.

De Vos, G. (1982). Ethnic pluralism: Conflict and accommodation. In G. De Vos & L. Romanucci-Ross (Eds.), *Ethnic identity: Cultural continuities and change.* Chicago, IL: University of Chicago Press.

Dunn, E. (1975). Mexican-American media behavior: A factor Analysis. *Journal of Broadcasting, 19*, 3–9.

Eastman, H., & List, M. (1980). TV preferences of children from four parts of the U.S. *Journalism Quarterly, 57*, 488–491.

Glenn, N., & Simmons, J. (1967). Are regional cultural differences diminishing? *Public Opinion Quarterly, 31*, 176–193.

Greenberg, B., Burgoon, M., Burgoon, J., & Korzenny, F. (1983). *Mexican American and the mass media.* Norwood, NJ: Ablex Publishing Corp.

Hall, E. (1977). *Beyond culture.* Garden City, NY: Anchor.

Ihde, D. (1982). The technological embodiment of media. In M. Hyde (Ed.), *Communication philosophy and the technological age.* University, AL: University of Alabama Press.

Kockelmans, J. (1967). What is phenomenology? In J. Kockelmans (Ed.), *Phenomenology: The philosophy of Edmund Husserl and its interpretation.* Garden City, NY: Doubleday.

Lull, J. (1980a). The social uses of television. *Human Communication Research, 6,* 197–209.

Lull, J. (1980b). Family communication patterns and the social uses of television. *Communication Research, 7,* 319–334.

McAnany, E. (1986). *Television and cultural discourses: Latin American and U.S. research as cultural meaning.* Unpublished manuscript, University of Texas-Austin.

Meyrowitz, J. (1985). *No sense of place: The impact of electronic media on social behavior.* New York: Oxford University Press.

Morley, D. (1983). Cultural transformations: The politics of resistance. In H. Davis & P. Walton (Eds.), *Language, image, media.* Oxford, England: Blackwell.

Morgan, M. (1986). Television and the erosion of regional diversity. *Journal of Broadcasting and Electronic Media, 30,* 123–139.

Pacanowsky, M., & Anderson, J. (1982). Cop talk and media use. *Journal of Broadcasting, 26,* 741–755.

Royce, A. (1982). *Ethnic identity: Strategies of diversity.* Bloomington, IN: Indiana University Press.

Schutz, A. (1967). Phenomenology and the social sciences. In J. Kockelmans (Ed.), *Phenomenology: The philosophy of Edmund Husserl and its interpretation.* Garden City, NY: Doubleday.

Traudt, P., & Lont, C. (1986). Media logic-in-use: The family as locus of study. In T. Lindlof (Ed.), *Natural audiences: Qualitative research of media uses and effects.* Norwood, NJ: Ablex Publishing Corp.

Traudt, P., Meyer, T., & Anderson, J. (1985, November). *Unpacking the television experience: A phenomenology of everyday communication and the mass media.* Paper presented before the Speech Communication Association, Mass Communication Division, Denver.

Wolf, M., Meyer, T., & White, C. (1982). A rules-based study of television's role in the construction of social reality. *Journal of Broadcasting, 26,* 813–829.

25

Children, Television, and the Acculturation Process

ALI R. ZOHOORI

State University of New York College at Oneonta

Commonly, television use has been regarded as an antecedent or correlate of changes in children's behavior. In a less traditional way, this study considers television use as *the consequence* of children's acculturation process.

For newcomers to a culture, an essential part of the acculturation process is the adaptation stage (Lee, 1975; Berry, 1980). Adaptation requires, among other things, communication skills for establishing meaningful social interaction with the inhabitants of the new culture as well as acquiring information about the norms and behavior patterns of the host culture. One of the main sources of information about the host culture can be found in its mass media, (Kim, 1982). This study attempts to link theories of acculturation (e.g., Dohrenwend & Smith, 1962; Berry, 1980) with the uses of American television by foreign children residing in the United States.

BACKGROUND

Redfield, Linton, and Herskovits conceptualized acculturation by maintaining that "acculturation comprehends those phenomena which result when groups of individuals having different cultures come into continuous firsthand contact, with subsequent changes in the original cultural patterns of their or both groups" (1936, 149). The authors speculated that, once an individual enters a new cultural context, he or she feels isolated due to the lack of necessary skills amenable to the demands of the new environment. However, the magnitude of such isolation decreases as social contact increases. Whether acculturation is a process or an end product of cultural change, it is likely to consist of series of stages or phases. Indeed, a multitude of schema for the stages of acculturation have been suggested by different scholars (e.g., Dohrenwend & Smith, 1962; Berry, 1980). There is no consensus among scholars, however, with respect to the number, rate, or length of stages involved in the acculturation process.

Scholars have examined communication processes in the adjustment of newcomers to a country. Kim (1982) regarded an individual's prior exposure to the cultural patterns and language of the host society (through mass or interpersonal means) a critical factor in acculturation. Likewise, once in the host culture, the amount of interaction with "native" citizens and their mass media was seen as influencing acculturation success. Kim also emphasized the significance of the acculturation function of the mass media during the initial stage of acculturation; at that time the immigrant often lacks even the minimal competence needed to establish satisfactory interpersonal relationships with members of the host culture.

Studies of acculturation and communication may be classified into two groups: first, those studies which deal with the acculturation of adult immigrants (e.g., DeFleur & Cho, 1957; Chance, 1965; Shibutani & Kwan, 1965; Lee, 1975; Kim, 1977); second, those studies which concentrate on the adjustment process of international students and their mass-media use in a Western country (e.g., Scott, 1956; Markham, 1967; Becker, 1968; Pierce, 1970; Semlak, 1979). The findings of these studies generally support what has been said so far about acculturation and the role of the mass media in that process.

Cross-cultural studies of the uses and gratifications have assessed the use of television by children of different cultures (e.g., Furu, 1971; Greenberg, 1974; Rubin, 1977). Although these studies have shown some differences in children's motivations for watching television, there is no information available about the uses of the mass media by children who are in a new cultural context. However, DeFluer and Cho (1957) pointed out that children can play a crucial role in the assimilation of their parents to the host country. Thus, there is a gap in knowledge with regard to the acculturation of children who travel to a new country, in general, and their mass media use within an acculturation context in particular.

Studies of children watching television in a foreign language have indicated that comprehension of television messages was not hindered by linguistic problems (see, e.g., Gorn, Goldberg, & Kanugo, 1976; Hawkins & Pingree 1980). According to these studies, children extracted meanings from actions portrayed on television. Studies of *Sesame Street* among American children and those of other countries have provided sufficient evidence of television's success in teaching English or another language (Lesser, 1974; Yamamoto, 1976; Salomon, 1976; Diaz-Guerrero, Reyes-Lagunes, Witzke, & Holzman, 1976).

It is evident that nonnative American children residing in the U.S. turn to television because of its accessibility and attractiveness. This in turn enriches their communicative skills and facilitates their adjustment process.

Acculturation theorists stress a period of social isolation among individuals who are in a new cultural environment. The uses and gratifications perspective (e.g., Katz & Foulkes, 1962; Katz, Blumler, & Gurevitch, 1974; McGuire, 1974) suggests that isolated individuals may rely more heavily on the mass media than those already socially integrated. When combining the two perspectives, it might seem reasonable to expect that foreign children residing in the U.S. would make much use of American television, and that, as their acculturation advances, their reliance on television would diminish. Moreover, as the social isolation and language problems of these foreign children diminishes, it might also be expected that they will become more critical of the medium (e.g., less likely to believe TV presentations accurately reflect American society).

In accord with the preceding reasoning, the following hypotheses are proposed:

H.   Overall, the extent to which foreign children are acculturated into American culture will have impact on their uses of American television. Specifically, among foreign children, those less acculturated to American culture will:

1.   use American television more as a source of information about and interaction with others, and as a means of diversion from their social isolation;

2.   be more interested in watching American television programs;

3.   spend more time watching American television;

4.   identify more with American television characters; and

5.   believe more in the reality of American television characters and events.

METHODS[1]

Sample.   Cross-sectional survey data were gathered from the first through fifth grade students attending one public school in a major university community in the midwest. The school was selected because it had the largest enrollment of foreign children in the area. There were 90 foreign children enrolled in that school when this survey was conducted. Seven of these children participated in a pilot test of the questionnaire. The remaining 83 participated in the survey reported here. Inaccessibility to a large sample size of foreign children (due to their geographical dispersion) led to the use of the purposive sampling method. Therefore, limitations regarding representativeness are acknowledged.

The foreign children surveyed were from 33 different countries in Africa,

---

[1] Portions of the method section describing the sample and data collection method have previously appeared in the author's article: A cross-cultural analysis of children's television use, *Journal of Broadcasting & Electronic Media*, 32, 1988, pp. 105–113, and are used here with the permission of the publisher.

Europe, the Middle East, South and East Asia, and Central America.[2] These children varied considerably in how long they had been in America; 14.5% had been here for less than 6 months, 26.5% between 6 and 18 months, 32.5% between 19 and 54 months, and 26.5% more than 54 months. Although these children cannot be regarded as a culturally homogeneous group, they all shared the problem of being in a nonnative/new culture. There were slightly more boys than girls, although both genders were proportionately distributed across age groups. More than half were between 6 and 8 years old.

   Procedure.   Data collection started on Tuesday of each week; Mondays were excluded in order to prevent television exposure differences based on weekday versus weekend viewing.

   Undergraduate students trained for the specifics of this task served as interviewers and monitors for the survey. First-grade children were interviewed individually out of class in a comfortable room. Second through fifth grade children were given self-administered questionnaires to fill out in their classrooms.[3]

   Development of the instrument.   As a result of the research hypothesis and the pilot test, eight different versions of the questionnaire were designed. Each version pertained to a specific subsample of children based on their nationality, gender and grade.

   Operationalization of the variables.   Foreign children were defined as those born in countries other than the U.S. and whose parents were not permanent residents or citizens of the United States.

   Acculturation was measured with six items. The first assessed duration of residency in the United States. The remaining five items assessed preferences thought to be associated with acculturation; specifically, the children were asked about the extent to which they wished to: (a) live in the United States, (b)

[2]Countries represented by the surveyed foreign children were:

Africa	Asia	Middle-East	South America	Eastern Europe
Algeria	Afghanistan	Egypt	Brazil	Romania
Ethiopia	India	Iran	Equador	
Libya	Indonesia	Iraq	Jamaica	
Nigeria	Japan	Saudi Arabia	Mexico	
Tanzania	Malaysia		Panama	
West Africa	Nepal		Puerto Rico	
Zimbabwe	Pakistan		Venezuela	
	South Korea			
	Taiwan			
	Thailand			

[3]The average face-to-face interview for the first graders took about 30 minutes. The second and third graders needed about 40 minutes to answer the questions; fourth and fifth graders needed about 20 minutes to fill out their questionnaires.

return to their home countries, (c) talk in English with their friends, (d) talk in their own home country's language with their family members, and (e) talk in English with their family members. Response choices for each of these five items were: "A lot," "A little," and "Not at all."

Uses of American television were defined in terms of (a) motivations for watching television programs, (b) liking of television programs, (c) patterns of exposure to television, (d) identification with television characters, and (e) assessed reality of television characters and events.

Motivation items used were based on the work of Greenberg (1974), Rubin (1977), and Palmgreen, Wenner, and Rayburn (1980). These studies and a few others (e.g., Greenberg & Dominick, 1969; Rubin, 1979) have demonstrated a consistent pattern of clustering motivation items used in the present study. Thus, the validity and reliability of these items have already been established. Eleven items were measured; these represented five more general clusters of motivations (learning about others, learning about self, social interaction, companionship, and escape). Motivations were measured by asking each child if the item was "a lot like," "a little like" or "not at all like" his or her reason for watching television. Items within each cluster were summed and averaged to create an index. The Cronbach's Reliability Coefficient (Hall & Nie, 1981) of the overall motive index was .72.

Liking of television programs was examined using 29 shows; each had a current rating of at least 10 among children residing in the nearest metropolitan market surveyed by Nielson (1981). For each program, children were asked "Do you like to watch _____ a lot, a little, not at all or don't know?" Four clusters of programs were formed—Educational/Informational, Children's, Adventure, and Other. The first three clusters were consistent with the Nielsen clustering of television programs (Nielson, 1981). An overall index of liking television programs was formed by summing across the raw scores and obtaining the mean value for each of the items answered the respondents. The Cronbach's Reliability Coefficient for the overall liking index was .90.

Television exposure patterns were defined in terms of the number of hours each child indicated watching television on the average weekday and weekend day as well as on the day prior to the survey. A list of television programs broadcasted the previous day was inserted into each questionnaire; each child circled those programs he or she watched. Exposure patterns for the previous morning, afternoon, and evening were computed based on the length of each of the programs watched. The more general weekday viewing patterns were assessed by asking for hours of viewing before school, after school, and after supper. Similarly, weekend viewing patterns were assessed by focusing on weekend morning and afternoon viewing. Overall exposure indices for the previous day, daily viewing, and weekend viewing were generated by adding the scores of each respondent for each viewing time category.

Identification with 13 television characters of different genders, ages, and popularity was assessed . Here, children were asked "When you grow up, how much would you like to be like _____?" Response choices were "a lot," "a little" and "not at all."[4] An identification index was formed by summing and averaging each respondent's scores for the thirteen identification items. The Cronbach's Reliability Coefficient for the identification index was .83.

Finally, reality assessments were made with five measures of television characters and events. Here, children were asked to indicate how much the animals, people, children, places, and events seen on television were like those seen in real life. Response choices were "a lot," "a little" and "not at all." The raw scores for the five perceived reality items were summed and averaged to generate a perceived reality index. The Cronbach's Reliability Coefficient for the perceived reality index was .72.

RESULTS

Acculturation and motivations for watching television.   Duration of residency in the United States was related as predicted with these respondents' motivations for watching American television; children with shorter periods of residency used television more for learning about themselves, learning about others, escape and companionship. The strongest relationship obtained was between duration of residency and watching television to learn how to act with friends ($r = -.38$, $p < .05$). Among the other acculturation measures, wanting to stay in the U.S. also was consistently related in the predicted direction with the motivation clusters. The strongest correlations here were between wishing to stay in the U.S. and using television for learning about one's self and escape. The other acculturation measures were inconsistently related to the motivation items. Generally, then, these data provided some support for hypothesis H1.

Acculturation and liking television programs.   Generally, foreign children with shorter periods of U.S. residency were more interested in watching American television programs. The strongest relationship obtained between duration of residency and liking to watch *Mister Roger's Neighborhood* ($r = -.42$, $p < .05$). The next strongest relationship was between wanting to stay in the U.S. and liking to watch *American Band Stand* ($r = -.33$, $p < .05$). The other acculturation measures varied considerably—both in magnitude as well as directionality. If emphasis is placed on the duration of residency variable, these data provide support for the second hypothesis (i.e., that the less acculturated will be more interested in watching TV.) If, on the other hand, the

---

[4]One of the 13 television characters varied across ages; while third through fifth graders reacted to Willis of "Diff'rent Strokes," first and second graders reacted to Willis's younger brother Arnold. This difference was based on the evidence that younger children usually identify with characters of their own age (see, e.g., Fielitzen & Linne, 1976).

entire set of items assessed acculturation is given equal weight, support for the second hypothesis is much more ambiguous.

Acculturation and television exposure patterns. More acculturated children—anticipated to be more socially integrated—were expected to watch less television. Contrary to expectations, these longer-term children reported watching *more* television on weekdays as well as weekends. They did, however, seem to watch less television the preceding day (e.g., $r = -.34$, $p < .05$, for the relationship between duration of residency and exposure to television the previous evening). Since more specificity was used in the 'previous-day exposure' items, their responses to those items may be more representative of their viewing behavior than the responses obtained with the more general exposure items. One other acculturation measure consistently related to exposure; children more interested in going back to their native lands appeared to watch less television than those expressing more interest in staying in the U.S.

Acculturation and identification with television characters. Once again, the duration of residency related as predicted. Those in the U.S. for shorter periods of time were significantly more likely to identify with 10 of 13 television characters assessed; this relationship was most pronounced with male heroes (e.g., Tarzan, Buck Rogers, and Incredible Hulk). Wanting to talk in English with friends was the only other acculturation measure positively related to identification with TV characters. Aside from the impact of duration of residency, the acculturation items did not appear to play an important or uniform role in identification with television characters. As such, this hypothesis was not supported.

Acculturation and perceived reality of television. Duration of residency was related to four of the five reality items used; children residing in the U.S. for shorter spans of time seemed to accept more strongly in the reality of people, places, and events depicted on television than did their counterparts. These findings were as predicted. However, children who preferred using their native language in family contexts (indicative of lesser acculturation) also were less likely to believe in the televised depictions of reality they encountered. The relationship between the other acculturation items and assessed reality items generally was modest. Overall, then, the relationship between acculturation and perceived reality was neither strong enough nor consistent enough to merit support of the fifth hypothesis.

DISCUSSION

The first hypothesis assessed the impact of acculturation on foreign American children's motivations for watching television. As predicted, children who were less acculturated to American ways seemed to use American television more as a means of escape from their problems and as a source of learning about themselves. While less pronounced, they also used it more for learning about others, including interaction with others. Two acculturation measures, (a) length of residency in the United States and (b) extent of interest in maintaining residency, most frequently related to these motivations.

The results of testing the second hypothesis revealed a limited inverse relationship between acculturation and the interest in watching American television programs. Less acculturated children were more likely to be interested in watching educational-informational, children's, and adventure programs, but less interested in watching other programs. These data provided general support for the hypothesis. Somewhat surprisingly, while the less acculturated children were not strongly motivated to use television as a source of information about others, they were more interested in watching educational-informational programs. One explanation for this apparent contradiction is that motives are different from interests. Among acculturation measures, duration of residency appeared to be the best predictors of foreign children's preferences for watching American television programs.

The third hypothesis predicted an inverse relationship between acculturation and amount of exposure to American television. Counter to this prediction, the less-acculturated children generally spent less time watching American television. Perhaps, as foreign children become more acculturated, they become more avid viewers of the many shows their *American* friends follow.

Hypothesis 4 assessed the relationship between acculturation and identification with American television characters. Here, the data provided ambiguous support for the hypothesis. Only one measure—duration of U.S. residency—related to the identification items as predicted; foreign children in this country for shorter periods of time appeared to identify more with American television characters. Perhaps these children lacked sufficient and effective social contact and thus had more intense parasocial involvement with television characters.

The fifth hypothesis focused on the impact of acculturation on the assessed reality of television. Results for this hypothesis were mixed. Consistent with Hypothesis H.1 through H.4, duration of U.S. residency and the extent of wanting to remain in the U.S. were the best predictors of the reality items. Foreign children with shorter residencies, as well as those less inclined to stay in the U.S., believed more in the reality of American television. However, across the remaining acculturation measures, both less acculturated and more acculturated children were similar in their assessments of television reality.

In short, on the one hand, duration of U.S. residency and wanting to stay in this country had effects in the predicted direction on the uses of American television by foreign children. On the other hand, wanting to return to their home country and/or the language they preferred to use at home generally did not have such effects.

There are rival explanations for the mixed results: (a) foreign children were actually similar to one another in terms of their uses of American television, or (b) with the exception of the duration of U.S. residency and the extent of interest in staying in U.S., the other acculturation measures were not sufficiently on target to pinpoint differences in the uses of American television among foreign children. Considering the level of these children's cognitive skills (Erikson, 1972), the latter seems more explanatory. The duration of residency in the host country is more likely to be a valid predictor of children's uses of television than the other five measures of acculturation used in this study.

The results of this study provided some confirmation of motivations for learning about the host culture through television by children during their acculturation process. The findings are exciting because they help illustrate television's function in the acculturation process. However, more evidence is clearly needed.

Acculturation may, in fact, be better understood through an ethnological approach. In future observational research, one might record, for example, the television behavior of children who reside in a new cultural environment.

REFERENCES

A. C. Nielsen. (1981). *Nielsen station index: Viewers in profile*. Northbrook, IL: Author.

Becker, T. (1968). Patterns of attitudinal changes among the foreign students. *The American Journal of Sociology, 73*, 431–442.

Berry, J. W. (1980). Acculturation of varieties of adaptation. In A. M. Padilla (Ed.), *Acculturation: Theory, models, and some new findings* (pp. 9–25). Boulder, CO: Westview.

Chance, N. A. (1965). Acculturation, self-identification, and personality adjustment. *American Anthropologist, 67*, 372–393.

DeFleur, M. L., & Cho, C.-S. (1957). Assimilation of Japanese-born women in an American city. *Social Problems, 4*, 244–257.

Diaz-Guerrero, R., Reyes-Lagunes, I., Witzke, D. B., & Holtzman, W. H. (1976). Plaza Sesamo in Mexico: An evaluation. *Journal of Communication, 26*(2), 145–154.

Dohrenwend, B. P., & Smith, R. J. (1962). Toward a theory of acculturation. *Southwest Journal of Anthropology, 18*, 30–39.

Erikson, E. H. (1972). Eight ages of man. In C. S. Lavatelli & F. Stenler (Eds.), *Readings in child behavior and development* (pp. 19–30). New York: Harcourt Brace Jovanich.

Fielitzen, C. von., & Linne, O. (1976). Identifying with television characters. *Journal of Communication, 23*(4), 51–55.

Furu, T. (1971). *The function of television for children and adolescents*. Tokyo, Japan: Sophia University.

Gorn, G. T., Goldberg, M. E., & Kanugo, R. N. (1976). The role of educational television in changing the intergroup attitudes of children. *Child Development, 47*, 277–280.

Greenberg, B. S., (1974). Gratifications of television viewing and their correlates for British children. In J. G. Blumlev & E. Katz (Eds.), *The uses of mass communications: Current perspectives on gratifications research* (pp. 71–92). Beverly Hills, CA: Sage.

Greenberg, B. S., & Dominick, J.R. (1969). Racial and social class differences in teen-agers use of television. *Journalism Quarterly, 13*, 3331–3344.

Hawkins, R., & Pingree, S. (1980). Some processes in the cultivation effects. *Communication Research, 1*, 193–226.

Hull, C. H., & Nie, N. (1981). *SPSS update: New procedures and facilities for releases 7–9*. New York: McGraw-Hill.

Katz, E., & Foulkes, D. (1962). On the use of the mass media as escape: Clarification of a concept. *Public Opinion Quarterly, 26,* 377–388.

Katz, E., Blumler, J. G., & Gurevitch, M. (1974). Utilization of mass communication by the individuals. In J. G. Blumler & E. Katz (Eds.), *The Uses of mass communications: Current perspectives on gratifications research* (pp. 19–32). Beverly Hills, CA: Sage.

Kim, Y. Y. (1977). Communication patterns of foreign immigrants in the process of acculturation. *Human Communication Research, 4,* 66–77.

Kim, Y. Y. (1982). Communication and Acculturation. In L. A. Samovar & R. E. Porter (Eds.), *Intercultural communication: A reader* (pp. 359–372). Belmont, CA.: Wadsworth.

Lee, D. C. (1975). *Acculturation of Korean residents in Georgia.* San Francisco, CA: R & E Research.

Lesser, G. S. (1974). *Children and television: Lessons from Sesame Street.* New York: Vintage Books.

Markham, J. W. (1967). *International images and mass communication behavior.* Iowa City, IO: Mass Communication Research Bureau, University of Iowa.

McGuire, W. J. (1974). Psychological motives and communication gratifications. In J. G. Blumler & E. Katz (Eds.), *The Uses of mass communication: Current perspectives on gratifications research* (pp. 167–196). Beverly Hills, CA: Sage.

Palmgreen, P., Wenner, W. A., & Rayburn, J. D. (1980). Relations between gratifications sought and obtained: A study of television news. *Communication Research, 7* (21), 161–192.

Pierce, F. N. (1970). Why foreign students like or dislike American advertising. *Journalism Quarterly, 47,* 560–564.

Redfield, R., Linton, R., & Herskovits, M. J. (1936). Outline for the Study of Acculturation. *American Anthropologist, 38,* 149–152.

Rubin, A. M. (1977). Television usage, attitudes and viewing behaviors of children and adolescents. *Journal of Broadcasting, 21,* 355–369.

Rubin, A. M. (1979). Television use by children and adolescents. *Human Communication Research, 5*(2), 109–120.

Salomon, G. (1976). Cognitive skill learning across cultures. *Journal of Communication, 26*(2), 138–144.

Scott, F. D. (1956). *The American experience of Swedish students.* Minneapolis, MN: University of Minnesota Press.

Semlak, W. D. (1979). Effects of media use on foreign student perception of U.S. political leaders. *Journalism Quarterly, 56,* 153–156, 178.

Shibutani, T., & Kwan, K. M. (1965). *Ethnic stratification: A comparative approach.* New York: MacMillan.

Yamamoto, T. (1976). The Japanese experience. *Journal of Communication, 26*(2), 136–137.

26

The Cultivation of Values by Media*

KARL ERIK ROSENGREN AND BO REIMER
University of Lund, Sweden

INTRODUCTION

Traditionally, research on culture, socialization, and mass communication has been carried out without much mutual contact; however, there is need for a confluence among the three. Gerbner's seminal concepts of cultivation and cultural indicators have served as very useful catalysts in this respect (Melischek, Rosengren, & Stappers, 1984).

Cultural indicators are standardized measures by which to tap the climate of culture, much as economic indicators tap economic development. In America and Europe, cultural indicators research has been carried out (not always under that label) in such different fields and disciplines as sociology, economics, political science, history, literature, linguistics, theology, philosophy, and mass communication. Sometimes the research between areas has been cooperative, and sometimes it has been conducted without much knowledge of relevant research in cognate areas.

Building on consolidation of research already carried out, new integrated research projects, systemically relating to each other various types of economic, social, and cultural indicators will gradually emerge. At the Department of Sociology at the University of Lund and the Unit of Mass Communication at the University of Gothenburg, Sweden, a cooperative research program along these lines has been started: *Interualized Culture*. In this chapter, that program will be presented within the framework of a general overview of research on socialization and culture, cultivation and cultural indicators.

CULTURE

The concept of culture has been used in innumerable ways in different disciplines without consensus. In the cultural indicators tradition, however, it is

* The project presented in this paper, "Internalized Culture," is funded by the Bank of Sweden Tercentenary Foundation. The paper builds also on experiences gained in the research programs *Cultural Indicators: The Swedish Symbol System, 1945–1975* and *Media Panel*. The authors wish to thank the members of all three programs for stimulating cooperation and criticism.

possible to find some common characteristics in the way the concept is treated. First, *culture* is used in the broad, socio-anthropological sense, rather than in the sense of high culture. Second, it is seen as a system of ideas, beliefs, and values manifesting itself in, and in its turn being affected by, actions and artifacts. Third, since culture is a system of ideas, it is abstract. Consequently, it can only be indirectly observed, that is, by means of indicators (Tylor, 1958; Kroeber & Kluckhohn, 1952; Gerbner, 1969; Peterson, 1979; Rosengren, 1985 a).

Societal systems interact with other societal systems, e.g., the interaction among economics, politics, and religion. In this context, mass media may be seen as (horizontal) linkages between the different systems, and as (vertical) linkages between the macro level and the micro level.

Culture may be found and studied at both the macro (societal) level and the micro (individual) level. At both levels, culture may be conceptualized both as structure and process. As structure, it may be regarded as an abstract system of ideas, beliefs, and values. As process, it may be regarded as regularities in behavior and action. Content analysis has been used to study culture as structure at the societal level, and survey analysis has been used to study culture as structure at the individual level. Secondary analysis of behavior data has been the method preferentially used for studies of culture as process (Rosengren, 1985a).

Thus far, studies have as a rule been conducted at one of the two levels, using just one method. To get a more thorough understanding of the complicated processes involved, however, it will be necessary to relate the levels to each other, as well as to study the linkages between the levels. Such an approach demands the combined use of survey analysis, secondary analysis, and content analysis. Gerbner's combination of cultural indicators research and cultivation research represents an important step in that direction (cf. the section on "Cultivation" below).

In our society, as part of the socialization process, the mass media constitute one of the most important linkages between societal and individual culture. It is partly through the differentiated use of the media that individuals—based in their social context—internalize their shared and yet differential sets of cognitions and values: their culture.

The simultaneous study of the two levels of culture and the linkages between them has three components. First, is the macro culture, which is often studied in terms of values expressed in the mass media (see Namenwirth, 1973; Namenwirth & Bibbee, 1976; Weber, 1981; Namenwirth & Weber, 1986). Second, is the vertical media linkages—the effects of the differential use made by individuals of the mass media, as exemplified for instance, by the cultivation analysis of Gerbner and his associates (Gerbner, 1969, 1984). Finally, there is the micro culture, the culture of individuals. This has been studied mainly by researchers not directly associated with the cultural indicators tradition

(Rokeach, 1973, 1974, 1979; cf. Ball-Rokeach, Rokeach, & Grube 1984; Inglehart, 1977, 1984, 1985 a,b).

The Swedish research program *Cultural Indicators: The Swedish Symbol system, 1945–1975 (CISSS)* is an example of study of the macroculture (E. Block, 1984; P. Block, 1984; Goldmann, 1984; Nowak, 1984; Rosengren, 1984, 1985 b). The new research program *Internalized Culture* is a continuation of that program. It is a study of microculture and the mass media. By means of content analysis, which can always be made retrospectively, it will later be possible to relate the microculture to the macroculture supposedly having to a large extent shaped the microculture. The process by which microculture is linked to macroculture is called *socialization*.

SOCIALIZATION

The concept of socialization has become increasingly important in mass communication (Albrecht, Thomas, & Chadwick, 1980; Child, 1969; Goslin, 1968; Halloran, 1976; Zigler & Seitz, 1978) and three issues are relevant: the content, the process, and the agents of socialization.

When discussing the content of socialization, a distinction is often made between, on the one hand, learning and teaching culture-at-large—beliefs, values, and evaluations pertaining not only to social roles and social structure, but to all other domains of the world as well. This distinction is often reflected in the terms *socialization* and *enculturation* (Whiting, 1968, p. 545). In enculturation, knowledge and norms primarily about the self, its society, and the surrounding world are acquired and transferred. In socialization, knowledge, norms, and skills, primarily, in activities pertinent to various positions, roles, and statuses, are acquired and transferred.

The distinction between enculturation and socialization is related to, but not identical with, the distinction between primary and secondary socialization. *Primary socialization* usually refers to the basic and general knowledge, norms, and skills acquired and transferred early in life and related to positions, roles, and, statuses in society; i.e., the parts of the culture more or less common to all. *Secondary socialization* refers to knowledge, norms, and skills related to specific positions in the social structure (Berger & Luckmann, 1967, pp. 129 ff).

A dimension common to both distinctions referred to above (enculturation/socialization, primary/secondary socialization) is generality/specificity. Disregarding other differences, both enculturation and primary socialization are general, while both secondary socialization and socialization, as opposed to enculturation, are specific.

All human societies, including the most undifferentiated ones, have three main agents of socialization: family and/or kin groups, peer groups, and work groups. In more differentiated societies we also find socialization by means of priests (often organized in churches), schools (often cooperating and sometimes competing with the churches), and various law-enforcing agencies. In addition, industrial and postindustrial societies have a number of large organizations with more or less specialized activities (trade unions, more or less institutionalized popular movements, and so on), which also may act as socializing agents. Such societies have another important group of socializing agents: a highly developed media system. In societies such as ours, then, we have at least eight large groups of socializing agents: family, peer groups, work groups, churches, schools, law agencies, organizations, and mass media.

The culture transferred and received in the socialization process in small groups such as the family or the peer group tends to be concrete, specific, implicit, and "lived," while in formal organizations such as the schools it tends to be more abstract, general, explicit, and formalized (disregarding for the moment the hidden curriculum). Small groups such as family, peer, and work groups may develop subcultures of protests and conflict, growing into enclaves of more or less different lifestyles characterized by various combinations of differences and conflicts and deviations (cf. Roe, 1983, p. 169).

The knowledge, norms, and skills mediated by the mass media cover the whole range of culture—from concrete, specific, implicit, lived culture, to abstract, general, explicit,and formalized culture. The mass media of the modern society, therefore, are able to take over large parts of the socialization carried out both in informal and formal organizations. It has often been observed that the mass media to an increasing extent are taking over the functions formerly fulfilled by the family, the churches, and the schools (see Noble, 1975; Postman, 1979; Gerbner, 1984).

The role played by the various socializing agents varies not only between societies and over time, but also over the life span of the individual (Rubin, 1985). In societies such as ours, the most dramatic period of life in this respect—as in so many others—is adolescence, when TV consumption falls rapidly and is replaced by various media of music, mainly transistors and tape recorders (Johnsson-Smaragdi, 1983; Roe, 1983). This thoroughgoing change in media habits reflects the adolescents' development as they turn away from home and parents to peer groups for interaction and mutual socialization.

While some periods of life are more dramatic, the individual is always located in the center of an intricate and dynamic network of mutual relations with a host of socializing agents, in their turn interacting with each other, and with society at large. The characteristics of the networks vary considerably with age, sex and social class, as well as between societies. Nevertheless, there are some general characteristics of such networks. One such characteristic is the importance of the family as a socializing agent; another is the increasingly important role played by the mass media.

CULTIVATION

The relationships between the media and the individual have been studied in a number of research traditions. Two dominant approaches are effects research and uses and gratifications research (Rosengren, Wenner, & Palmgreen, 1985; Bryant & Zillman, 1986). More specific research traditions in the area are diffusion of news research (Rosengren, 1987), agenda-setting research (Mc-Combs & Shaw, 1972; McCombs & Weaver, 1985), spiral of silence research (Noelle-Neumann, 1974, 1983; Taylor, 1982), and cultivation research (Gerbner, 1969, 1984).

Cultivation research is part of a two-pronged research program launched some 20 years ago by George Gerbner, which attempts to describe and explain the content distributed by, and the effects at the micro and macro levels of, television. Systematic, yearly measurements of television content establish the main characteristics of the TV world (the cultural indicators part of the program). Using the results of these content analyses, heavy and light viewers are compared as to their conceptions about themselves, the surrounding society, and the world at large (the cultivation analysis part of the program). Are those people steeped in the TV world more inclined to regard themselves and their environment in a way reminiscent of that world than are people less immersed in the TV world? In the main, the answer given by cultivation analyses is "Yes, TV does indeed shape in significant ways the conceptions and attitudes of various groups of viewers" (Gerbner, 1984; Gross, 1984; Morgan, 1984; Rothschild, 1984; Signorielli, 1984).

In terms of mass-communication research, Gerbner's approach adds new impetus to effects research, being part of a general movement away from specific, short-term effects toward more general and long-term effects. (Other examples of this direction are McComb's agenda-setting research and Noelle-Neumann's spiral of silence research.) In terms of socialization research it represents an attempt to create a coherent framework for systematic studies of TV's role as a dominating agent of socialization, the content transferred in that socialization, and the mechanisms of that type of socialization.

The type of socialization process studied by Gerbner's group—cultivation—represents a special case of enculturation; enculturation by means of television. It was obvious from the beginning that TV's influence is felt with differential strength in different social groupings and within different social strata. Recently, the conditioning influence of other socializing agents than TV has been emphasized increasingly within the Gerbner group (Rothschild, 1984).

Various types of content transferred via cultivation have been made the object of study by Gerbner's group, their followers and critics: conceptions of violence in society (Gerbner, Gross, Signorielli, & Morgan, 1980a), tolerance and intolerance toward blacks and gays (Gross, 1984), beliefs about older people (Gerbner, Gross, Morgan, & Signorielli, 1980b), political attitudes (Gerbner, 1984), role socialization resulting in differential job aspirations (Morgan, 1980; Hedinsson, 1981; Hedinsson & Windahl, 1984; Flodin, 1986). The content analyses carried out within the group adds yet other types of socialization content, for instance, health and medicine (Gerbner, Gross, Morgan, & Signorielli, 1981b), and science (Gerbner, Gross, Morgan, & Signorielli, 1981c).

Cultivation analysis as practiced by Gerbner has been harshly criticized (Hirsch, 1980; Hughes, 1980; compare Gerbner et al., 1981a), as well as replicated and emulated, with somewhat mixed results, in a number of countries other than the United States (compare, for instance, Bouwman, 1984; Hedinsson & Windahl, 1984; Weber, 1984; for an overview, see Hawkins & Pingree, 1984). While some of the criticism no doubt is warranted, it remains a fact that Gerbner's approach represents a major, viable innovation in the research trying to map media linkages of the social fabric. Its weak spots are the representativeness of the media content analyzed in the cultural indicators part of the program, and the techniques of measurements and analysis used in the cultivation part. Also, the dominant variables in the program tend to tap opinions and beliefs more than the values and value orientations which are so central to the concept of culture.

No doubt other research endeavors have been more successful in obtaining representativeness in cultural indicators studies and in developing more reliable measures and techniques of analysis of beliefs, opinions, attitudes and values as affected by media use. The unique asset, on the other hand, of the research program carried out by Gerbner is the systemic juxtaposition of micro studies (cultivation research) and macro studies (cultural indicators research) within the framework of an emerging theory of culture.

The challenge, then, must be to emulate Gerbner's two-pronged research program, using better measurements of representative samples of media content and media users. That challenge equals the task of studying media's role as linkages between culture's two manifestations: culture as a macrophenomenon and culture as a microphenomenon. An additional complication is that, at both levels, culture may be studied either as structure or as process. Also, both cognitive, conative and evaluative aspects of culture must be considered.

VALUES

Culture must of necessity be internalized by individual society members, but what is individual culture? In this context the concept of *value* comes to mind.

The concept of value is not in any way unproblematic (see Blake & Davis, 1964; Frankema, 1965; Meddin, 1975; Archer, 1985; Hutcheon, 1972; Levitin, 1970; Spates, 1983). Kluckhohn (1951) defined values as

> a conception, explicit or implicit, distinctive of an individual or characteristic of a group, of the desirable which influences the selection from available modes, means, and ends of action.

Or, as Rokeach puts it:

> Values are determinants of virtually all kinds of behavior that could be called social behavior—of social action, attitudes and ideology, evaluations, moral judgements and justifications of self and others, comparisons of self with others, presentations of self to others, and attempts to influence others. Boiling all these

down to a more succinct theoretical statement, it can perhaps be stated that values are guides and determinants of social attitudes and ideologies on the one hand, of social behavior on the other. (Rokeach, 1973, p. 27)

Peterson (1979) defines values as choice statements that rank behavior or goals. Norms are the specifications of these values. Beliefs are the justification of both values and norms. Meddin (1975) considers values as concerned with the abstract, while attitudes are the more specific expressions of the values. Opinions focus on concrete issues. The term *value-orientation* is reserved for the most basic values.

As can be deduced from the discussion above, values are considered among the most abstract patterns of thought. Values determine norms, belief, attitudes, and opinions rather than the other way round. It is in this sense the concept of value is used in this chapter.

Definitions such as these do not treat the question of what actually determines values. The distinction between individual and societal values is not made explicit either. In the Internalized Culture program, these two aspects are obviously of great importance, but the classifications just referred to are still useful. Above all, they point towards the boundaries of the study of individual culture.

In the 1970s a breakthrough in the study of individually held values took place. Since then, two main types of value scales have been used in several studies in many countries. These scales were constructed by Rokeach (1973, 1974, 1979; cf. Ball-Rokeach et al., 1984) and Inglehart (1971, 1977, 1984, 1985a,b).

The Rokeach Value Survey measures two sets of human value systems. One set consists of instrumental values; the other consists of terminal values. Together, the two sets cover most of the basic values held by individuals. Analyses of the results from national studies conducted in 1968, 1971, and 1981 suggest that the value hierarchies are stable over time (Rokeach, 1974; Inglehart, 1985b). The value hierarchies differed significantly between categories of sex, age, education, and income. Studies using the Rokeach Value Survey have also been conducted in other countries, notably Australia and Hungary (Braithwaite, 1982; Hankiss, Manchin, Füstös, & Szakolczai, 1984).

The value scale constructed by Inglehart measures the dimension of materialist vs. postmaterialist values. The scale consists of 12 items, six of which are materialist, six are postmaterialist. (In terms of a Maslowian value hierarchy, postmaterialist values are among the highest in the hierarchy, coming after values connected with sheer physical existence, security, etc.) Based on theories of scarcity and socialization, Inglehart's hypothesis is that periods of high prosperity will encourage postmaterialist values, while materialist values will be encouraged by economic decline. His results show an increasing proportion of postmaterialists in Western Europe between 1970 and 1984, especially among younger respondents (Inglehart, 1985a). Inglehart's studies have been replicated and discussed (Marsh, 1975, 1977; Dalton, 1981; Flanagan, 1982;

van Deth, 1983a; Abrams, Gerard, & Timms, 1985; Böltken & Jagodzinski, 1985; Lafferty & Knutsen, 1985; Suhonen, 1985).

The value scales of Inglehart and Rokeach have seldom been related to each other, let alone used in the same studies (the main exception being a panel study of the American public 1974 and 1981; Inglehart, 1985a). In the Internalized Culture project, studies thus far have been conducted with either the Inglehart or the Rokeach value scale. It is our intention in later studies to relate the two scales. Before being able to do that, however, some important methodological decisions have to be made. The next section will treat these problems and also offer some preliminary results from our studies of the relations between mass media use and internalized values as separately measured by Inglehartian and Rokeachean scales.

INTERNALIZED CULTURE

Values are theoretical constructs, latent variables which have to be measured indirectly, by means of one or more indicators, preferably a set of manifest variables measuring the same underlying construct. Quite often, however, just one manifest variable is used to measure the latent variable. This is the case, for instance, with the Rokeach Value Survey, where every item corresponds to one value. Inglehart's postmaterialist–materialist dimension, on the other hand, is measured by means of 12 indicators.

Selecting the best manifest variable(s) is obviously very important, but equally important is the choice of measurement technique. Traditionally, two main techniques have been used: rating and ranking. Both Rokeach and Inglehart use ranking.

The decision about which technique to use must rest on both theoretical and methodological considerations (see Reimer, 1985). The Internalized Culture project includes a number of local surveys and one experimental panel study based on comparisons between results obtained with the two techniques as applied to the two scales. We found the rating technique to be the most powerful of the two (Anshelm, 1986).

These methodological tests may be used also to get a first impression of values in Sweden (see Reimer, 1985; Reimer & Rosengren, 1986; and Anshelm, 1986). Of the Rokeach Value Survey consisting of terminal and instrumental values, some of the values may be characterized as personal (e.g., a sense of accomplishment, self-respect), while others are more "social" (e.g., mature love, true friendship). Our results suggest that Swedish respondents tend to assess social values as more important.

The background variable with the strongest relationship to people's values is age. National security, inner harmony, and salvation typify values held by elderly people. The opposite holds true, especially for a comfortable life, an exciting life, mature love, and happiness. Age also interacts in a complicated way with the variable of education.

One important part of the Internalized Culture project is the relation between the mass media and individually held values. Gerbner's cultivation technique rests on the assumption that the television fare is so homogeneous with respect to values and cognitions that a simple measure of time spent will suffice to show the influence of the medium. While that may be a reasonable assumption to make for American television, it is less plausible for European television, and even less for European daily and weekly press. In our study, no important value differences are found between high and low users of television and newspapers, while significant differences are found when type of content (light vs. heavy content) is introduced into the analysis.

Both with respect to newspapers and television, consumption of light material correlates strongly with the values of a comfortable life, true happiness, and mature love. Even stronger correlations may be found between consumption of heavy material and values such as inner harmony and wisdom, but also for self-respect, equality, and a sense of accomplishment. By and large, these relationships remain after controlling for age and education.

In Rokeachan terms, the over-all-value pattern of a Swedish population is not dissimilar to the one found in American studies, although Swedish people tend to rate social values over personal values more than their American counterparts. The values held are influenced by the social position of the individual, as well as by his or her media use.

The value scale constructed by Inglehart was applied in two local studies. In factor analyses the postmaterialism/materialism dimension regularly turns up as a significant factor. Based on the rating version of the scale, a value index was constructed (cf. Reimer, 1985). The proportion of postmaterialists (some 40%) is higher than has normally been the case in other countries. Due to the rating technique applied here, the descriptive data are not strictly comparable, however.

The proportion of postmaterialists is higher for females than for males. There is a positive relationship between education and postmaterialist values. Elderly people tend to subscribe more to materialist values than young people. By and large, these findings, which are similar to findings in other countries, hold true also after controls for age and education.

As with the Rokeach Value Survey, we can hardly expect a correlation between amount of time spent with different media and postmaterialist values. The interest is directed at the type of media content consumed. Somewhat surprisingly, the proportion of true materialists (extreme values at the end of the scale) is much the same for all categories. At the other end of the continuum, however, there is a larger proportion of true postmaterialists among heavy-content users of TV and morning newspapers. Conversely, people with high consumption of light material are to a lesser degree true postmaterialists. These relations also stay roughly the same after controls for age and education, with one or two exceptions. In the youngest age group, amount of viewing of heavy material on TV is negatively correlated with postmaterialist values; in other age groups, the relationship is positive.

Altogether, we may say that results obtained using the postmaterialist/materialist value scale have shown patterns not unlike those found in other countries. By and large, young people and people with a high level of education tend to have a greater disposition towards postmaterialist values. Results such as these support the underlying theory proposed by Inglehart.

The relationship between media use and values has only been hinted at here. There is a positive correlation between, on one hand, postmaterialist values, and on the other, watching and reading heavy material. There is also a negative correlation between these values and consumption of light material. The correlations, although not strong, remain after control for age and education.

Experiments in the field have shown, among other things, that, under specific conditions, television can and does affect values as measured by the Rokeach scale (Ball-Rokeach et al., 1984). Our results suggest that media at large (not only television), under everyday conditions (not only in specific experimental situations), do indeed affect very basic values internalized by the individual (not only conceptions of, and attitudes about the surrounding society). The full theoretical implications of these results can only be drawn, when they have been confirmed in other studies (see Reimer, 1989; Reimer & Rosengren, 1989.

REFERENCES

Abrams, M., Gerard, D., & Timms, N. (Eds.). (1985). *Values and social change in Britain.* London: Macmillan.

Albrecht, S. L., Thomas D. L., & Chadwick, B. A. (1980). *Social psychology.* Englewood Cliffs, NJ: Prentice-Hall.

Anshelm, M. (1986). *Rangordning eller skattning? En experimentell studie i värdemätning.* [Mimeo] Gothenburg, Sweden: Unit of Mass Communication.

Archer, M. S. (1985). The myth of cultural integration. *The British Journal of Sociology, 36,* 333–353.

Ball-Rokeach, S. J., Rokeach, M., & Grube, J. W. (1984). *The great American values test. Influencing behavior and beliefs through television.* New York: Free Press.

Berger, P. L., & Luckmann, T. (1967). *The social construction of reality.* Garden City, NY: Doubleday.

Blake, J., & Davis K. (1964). Norms, values and sanctions. In R. E. L. Faris (Ed.), *Handbook of modern sociology.* Chicago, IL: Rand McNally.

Block, E. (1984). Freedom, equality etcetera: Values and valuations in the Swedish domestic political debate, 1945–1975. In G. Melischek, K. E. Rosengren, & J. G. Stappers (Eds.), *Cultural indicators: An international symposium.* Vienna, Austria: Akademie der Wissenschaften.

Block, P. (1984). Newspapers' content as a secularization indicator. In G. Melischek, K. E. Rosengren, & J. G. Stappers (Eds.), *Cultural indicators: An international symposium.* Vienna, Austria: Akademie der Wissenschaften.

Böltken, F., & Jagodzinski, W. (1985). Post-materialism in the European Community, 1970–1980: Insecure value orientations in an environment of insecurity. *Comparative Political Studies, 17*, 453–484.

Bouwman, H. (1984). Cultivation analysis: The Dutch case. In G. Melischek, K. E. Rosengren, & J. G. Stappers (Eds.), *Cultural indicators: An international symposium*. Vienna, Austria: Akademie der Wissenschaften.

Braithwaite, V. (1982). The structure of social values: Validation of Rokeach's two-value model. *British Journal of Social Psychology, 21*, 203–211.

Child, I. L. (1969). Socialization. In G. Lindzey (Ed.), *Handbook of social psychology* (Vol. 2, pp. 655–692). Cambridge, MA: Addison-Wesley.

Dalton, R. J. (1981). The persistence of values and life cycle changes. In H. O. Klingemann, M. Kaase, & K. Horn (Eds.), *Politische Psychologie: Sonderheft 12 of Politische: Viertel-jahresschrift* (Vol. 22). Opladen, FRG: Wertdeutscher Verlag.

van Deth, J. W. (1983). The persistence of materialist and post-materialist value orientations. *European Journal of Political Research, 11*, 63–79.

Flanagan, S. C. (1982). Changing values in advanced industrial society. *Comparative Political Studies, 14*, 403–444.

Flodin, B. (1986). *TV och yrkesförväntan.* Lund, Sweden, Studentlitteratur.

Frankema, W. K. (1965). Value and valuation. In P. Edwards (Ed.), *The encyclopedia of philosophy*. New York: Collier Macmillan.

Gerbner, G. (1969). Toward cultural indicators': The analysis of mass mediated public message systems. *AV Communication Review, 17*(2), 137–148.

Gerbner, G. (1984). Political functions of television viewing: A cultivation analysis. In. G. Melischek, K. E. Rosengren, & J. G. Stappers (Eds.), *Cultural indicators: An international symposium*. Vienna, Austria: Akademie der Wissenschaften.

Gerbner, G., Gross L., Signorielli, N., Morgan, M. (1980). Aging with television: Images of television drama, and conceptions of social reality. *Journal of Communication, 30*(1), 137–148.

Gerbner, G., Gross, L., Morgan, M., & Signorielli, N. (1980b). The "mainstreaming" of America: Violence profile no. 11. *Journal of Communication, 30*(3): 10–29.

Gerbner, G., Gross, L., Morgan, M., & Signorielli, N. (1981a). Final Reply to Hirsch. *Communication Research, 8*, 259–280.

Gerbner, G., Gross, L., Morgan, M., & Signorielli, N. (1981b). Health and medicine on television. *New England Journal of Medicine, 305*, 901–904.

Gerbner, G., Gross, L., Morgan, M., & Signorielli, N. (1981c). Scientists on the TV screen. *Society, 18*(4), 41–44.

Goldmann, K. (1984). World politics and domestic culture: Sweden, 1950–1975. In G. Melischek, K. E. Rosengren, & J. G. Stappers (Eds.), *Cultural indicators: An international symposium*. Vienna, Austria: Akademie der Wissenschaften.

Goslin, D. A. (Ed.). (1968). *Handbook of socialization theory and research.* Chicago, IL: Rand McNally.

Gross, L. (1984). The cultivation of intolerance: Television, blacks and gays. In G. Melischek, K. E. Rosengren, & J. G. Stappers (Eds.), *Cultural indicators: An international symposium*. Vienna, Austria: Akademie der Wissenschaften.

Halloran, J. D. (Ed.). (1976). *Mass media and socialization.* Leeds, England: Kavanag & Sons.

Hankiss, E., Manchin, R., Füstös, L., & Szakolczai, A. (1984). Modernization of value systems: Indicators of change in cross-cultural comparisons. In G. Melischek, K. E. Rosengren, & J. G. Stappers (Eds.), *Cultural indicators: An international symposium*. Vienna: Austria: Akademie der Wissenschaften.

Hawkins, R. P., & Pingree S. (1984). The effects of television-mediated culture. In. G. Melischek, K. E. Rosengren, & J. G. Stappers (Eds.), *Cultural indicators: An international symposium*. Vienna, Austria: Akademie der Wissenschaften.

Hedinsson, E. (1981). *TV, family and society.* Stockholm, Sweden: Almqvist & Wiksell International.

Hedinsson, E., & Windahl, S. (1984). Cultivation analysis: A Swedish illustration. In G. Melischek, K. E. Rosengren, & J. G. Stappers (Eds.), *Cultural indicators: An international symposium.* Vienna. Austria: Akademie der Wissenschaften.

Hirsch, P. M. (1980). The scary world of the non-viewer and other anomalies. *Communication Research, 7*(4), 403–456.

Hughes, M. (1980). The fruits of cultivation analysis: A reexamination of some effects of television watching. *Public Opinion Quarterly, 44*(3), 237–302.

Hutcheon, P. D. (1972). Value theory: Towards conceptual clarification. *British Journal of Sociology, 23,* 172–187.

Inglehart, R. (1971). The silent revolution in Europe: Intergenerational change in post-industrial societies. *The American Political Science Review, 65,* 991–1017.

Inglehart, R. (1977). *The silent revolution: Changing values and political styles among western publics.* Princeton, NJ: Princeton University Press.

Inglehart, R. (1984). Measuring cultural change in Japan, Western Europe and the United States. In G. Melischek, K. E. Rosengren, & J. G. Stappers (Eds.), *Cultural indicators: An international symposium.* Vienna, Austria: Akademie der Wissenschaften.

Inglehart, R. (1985a). Aggregate stability and individual-level flux in mass belief systems: The level of analysis paradox. *The American Political Science Review, 79*(1), 97–116.

Inglehart, R. (1985b, August). *Intergenerational change in politics and culture: The decline of traditional values.* Invited Paper for the APSA Conference, New Orleans.

Johnsson-Smaragdi, U. (1983). *TV use and social interaction in adolescence. A longitudinal study.* Stockholm, Sweden: Almqvist & Wiksell International.

Kluckhohn, C. (1951). Values and value orientations in the theory of action. In T. Parsons & E. A. Shils (Eds.), *Towards a general theory of action.* Cambridge, MA: Harvard University Press.

Kroeber, A. L., & Kluckhohn, C. (1952). Culture: A critical review of concepts and definitions. *Harvard University Peabody Museum of American Archeology and Ethnology Papers, 47,* 1.

Lafferty, W. M., & Knutsen, O. (1985). An analysis of the distinctness and congruity of the Inglehart value syndrome in Norway. *Comparative Political Studies, 17,* 411–430.

Levitin, T. (1970). Values. In J. P. Robinson & P. R. Shaver (Eds.), *Measures of social psychological attitudes.* Ann Arbor, MI: ISR, The University of Michigan.

McCombs, M. E., & Shaw, D. (1972). The agenda-setting function of mass media. *Public Opinion Quarterly, 36,* 176–187.

McCombs, M. E., & Weaver, D. (1985). Toward a merger of gratification and agenda-setting research. In K. E. Rosengren, L. A. Wenner, & P. Palmgreen (Eds.), *Media gratifications research: Current perspectives.* Beverly Hills, CA: Sage.

Marsh, A. (1975). The silent revolution, value priorities and the quality of life in Britain. *American Political Science Review, 69,* 21–30.

Marsh, A. (1977). *Protest and political consciousness.* Beverly Hills, CA, and London: Sage.

Meddin, J. (1975). Attitudes, values and related concepts: A system of classification. *Social Science Quarterly, 55*(4), 889–900.

Melischek, G., Rosengren, K. E., & Stappers, J. G. (Eds.). (1984). *Cultural indicators: An international symposium.* Vienna: Austria: Akademie der Wissenschaften.

Morgan, M. (1980). *Longitudinal patterns of TV viewing and adolescent role socialization.* Unpublished doctoral dissertation, Annenberg School of Communications, University of Pennsylvania.

Morgan, M. (1984). Symbolic victimization and real world fear. In G. Melischek, K. E. Rosengren, & J. Stappers (Eds.), *Cultural indicators: An international symposium.* Wien, Austria: Akademie der Wissenschaften.

Namenwirth, J. Z. (1973). Wheels of time and interdependence of value change in America. *Journal of Interdisciplinary History, 3*(4), 649–683.

Namenwirth, J. Z., & Bibbee, R. C. (1976). Change within or of the system: An example from the history of American values. *Quality and Quantity, 10*(2), 145–164.

Namenwirth, J. Z., & Weber, R. P., (1987). *Dynamics of culture.* Winchester, MA: Allen & Unicorn.

Noble, G. (1975). *Children in front of the small screen.* London: Constable.

Noelle-Neumann, E. (1974). The spiral of silence. *Journal of Communication, 24,* 43–51.

Noelle-Neumann, E. (1983). *The spiral of silence.* Chicago, IL: Chicago University Press.

Nowak, K. (1984). Cultural indicators in Swedish advertising, 1950–1975. In G. Melischek, K. E. Rosengren, & J. G. Stappers (Eds.), *Cultural indicators: An international symposium.* Vienna, Austria: Akademie der Wissenschaften.

Peterson, R. A. (1979). Revitalizing the culture concept. *Annual Review of Sociology, 5,* 137–166.

Postman, N. (1979). *Teaching as a conservative activity.* New York: Delaware.

Reimer, B. (1985). *Values and the choice of measurement technique: The rating and ranking of postmaterialism* (Working Paper no. 8). Gothenburg, Sweden: Unit of Mass Communication, University of Gothenburg.

Reimer, B. (1989). Postmodern structures of feeling. Values and life styles in the postmodern age. In J. R. Gibbins (Ed.), *Politics and contemporary culture. New and old politics.* London: Sage.

Reimer, B., & Rosengren, K. E. (1986). *Maps of culture: Macro and micro* [mimeo]. Lung, Sweden: Department of Sociology.

Reimer, B., & Rosengren, K. E. (1989). Cultivated viewers and readers. A life-style perspective. In N. Signorielli & M. Morgan (Eds.), *Advances in cultivation analysis.* Beverly Hills, CA: Sage.

Roe, K. (1983). *Mass media and adolescent schooling: Coexistence or conflict?* Stockholm, Sweden, Almqvist & Wiksell International.

Rokeach, M. (1973). *The nature of human values.* New York: Free Press.

Rokeach, M. (1974). Change and stability in American value systems, 1968–1971. *Public Opinion Quarterly, 38*(2), 222–238.

Rokeach, M. (Ed.). (1979). *Understanding human values.* New York: Free Press.

Rosengren, K. E. (1984). Time and culture: In G. Melischek, K. E. Rosengren, & J. G. Stappers (Eds.), *Cultural indicators: An international symposium.* Vienna, Austria: Akademie der Wissenschaften.

Rosengren, K. E. (1985a). Media linkages of culture and other societal systems. In M. L. McLaughlin (Ed.), *Communication yearbook 9.* Beverly Hills, CA, and London: Sage.

Rosengren, K. E. (1985b). Culture, media and society. *Massa Communicatie, 3–4,* 126–142.

Rosengren, K. E. (1987). The comparative study of news diffusion. *European Journal of Communication, 2,* 227–255.

Rosengren, K. E., Wenner, L., & Palmgreen, P. (Eds.). (1985). *Media gratifications research: Current perspectives.* Beverly Hills, CA: Sage.

Rothschild, N. (1984). Small group affiliation as a mediating factor in the cultivation process. In. G. Melischek, K. E. Rosengren, & J. Stappers (Eds.), *Cultural indicators: An international symposium.* Wien, Austria: Akademie der Wissenschaften.

Rubin, A. M. (1985). Media gratifications through the life cycle. In K. E. Rosengren, L. A. Wenner, & P. Palmgreen (Eds.), *Media gratifications research: Current perspectives.* Beverly Hills, CA: Sage.

Signorielli, N. (1984). The demography of the television world. In G. Melischek, K. E. Rosengren, & J. Stappers (Eds.), *Cultural indicators: An international symposium.* Wien, Austria: Akademie der Wissenschaften.

Spates, J. L. (1983). The sociology of values. *Annual Review of Sociology, 9,* 27–49.

Suhonen, P. (1985). Approaches to value research and value measurement. *Acta Sociologica, 4,* 349–358.

Taylor, D. G. (1982). Pluralistic ignorance and the spiral of silence: A formal analysis. *Public Opinion Quarterly, 46,* 311–335.

Tylor, E. B. (1958). *Primitive culture.* Gloucester, MA: Smith.

Weber, R. P. (1981). Society and economy in the Western world system. *Social Forces, 59*(4), 1130–1148.

Weber, R. P. (1984). Content-analytic cultural indicators. In G. Melischek, K. E. Rosengren, & J. G. Stappers (Eds.), *Cultural indicators: An international symposium.* Vienna, Austria: Akademie der Wissenschaften.

Whiting, J. W. M. (1968). Socialization: Anthropological aspects. In *International encyclopedia of the social sciences* (Vol. 14, pp. 545–551). New York: Collier Macmillan.

Zigler, E., & Seitz, V. (1978). Changing trends in socialization theory and research. *American Behavioral Scientist, 21,* 731–756.

SEX, GENDER, AND FAMILY

27

The Question of a Sexuality of Abuse in Pornographic Films

STEPHEN PRINCE AND PAUL MESSARIS

University of Pennsylvania

In recent years, pornography has often been assessed as an expression of violence against women. This view argues that pornography is characterized by violence, that its character, images, stories and settings are informed by violent attitudes and behavior, and that the targets of this behavior and these attitudes are women. Critics of pornography have regarded it as the visualization of a philosophy of rape (Brownmiller, 1976, p. 443), as the symbolic silencing and murdering of women (Griffin, 1981), and as a medium which encourages real violence against women by portraying it as normal behavior (Barry, 1981, p. 206). It has also been claimed that the male fantasy revealed by pornography "insists that beatings, rape, humiliation and pain turn women on" (Barry, p. 209). These arguments imply that sexual behavior in pornographic films is regularly coupled with violence against women and, in particular, that the frequency of rape and sadomasochism in such films is quite high. Few studies have attempted to investigate these charges systematically and empirically.

This study employs content analysis toward such an investigation. The study is based on a sample of 29 "classic" or top-selling films, covering the years 1972–1985. These are films which are readily available in local video stores. Each film was coded independently by two trained coders, one male and one female.[1] Three units of analysis were employed: characters, sex scenes, and violent actions. Characters were coded for demographic characteristics and variables pertaining to their "love life" and sexual behavior. Sex scenes were coded for the types of sexual activity involved, communication patterns and types of relationships among the participants, and the presence of various categories of violent or abusive behavior. Violent acts, however, were also treated as a separate unit of analysis whenever they occurred in the films, whether as part of a sex scene or not.

In terms of demography 393 characters were coded, of whom 55% were male and 45% female. The modal age category was "young adult" (years 18–40): 75%

[1] The authors would like to express their gratitude to Gail Chalef, Leslie Galan, Ian Gale, Eva Goldfarb, and Amy Jordan for their assistance with the coding.

of the characters fell in this group. Distribution of characters among other age categories was as follows: 8% of characters were coded as "implied adolescent," 15% were coded as "settled adult" (years 41–65), 0% were coded as "older adult" (years 66 and older), and 3% were ambiguous and could not be coded.

With regard to race, characters were overwhelmingly white (94%). Only 2% were black, 2% were oriental, and 1% belonged to some other race.

In terms of socioeconomic status, 75% of characters were "clearly middle," while 8% were "clearly upper" and only 3% "clearly lower." Fifteen percent of characters could not be coded for SES. (These percentages exclude 103 non-speaking characters, for whom an SES judgment was not attempted.) The world of the pornographic feature film is, thus, a world peopled by middle-class, young, white adults.

The mean number of sex scenes per film was eight (range 2–11). The mean number of sex scenes per character was 1.8 (range 0–8). The mean number of male partners for female characters was 2.4 (range 0–15), slightly higher than the mean number of female partners for male characters, which was 1.8 (range 1–10). These data do not support a common criticism which maintains that pornographic films are dominated by a few male characters who are shown having sex with many women. Female characters in our sample were as sexually active as the male characters.

One of the charges often leveled against pornography is that it dehumanizes women by portraying them as exclusively sexual objects. In this view, women exist only as sexual beings in these films and lack important other, social definitions of identity. Interestingly, there is such a class of anonymous characters in pornographic feature films—characters who have neither name nor identity, who deliver no lines of dialogue, and who only appear as sexual performers in a sex scene. However, to a significant degree, these characters were found to be men, not women. Of male characters appearing in a sex scene, 38% were anonymous, compared to only 20% of women characters.

With regard to abusive behavior (including violence) in the films, of a total of 221 sex scenes occurring in our sample, 50 scenes, or 23%, were found to contain some form of abuse. Abusive behavior was coded in terms of the following categories. *Verbal behavior* was coded as *threatening* or *insulting* by virtue of either its *content* or its *intonation*. Seven percent of the sex scenes featured *threats* classified for their *content*, and 5% featured *threats* classified for their *intonation*. Nine percent of the sex scenes featured *insults* classified for their *content*, and 7% featured *insults* classified for their *intonation*. Seven percent of the scenes featured a character *striking, hitting,* or *beating* another. Thirteen percent of the scenes featured some form of *physical restraint* (for example, a male character holding a woman down on a pool table and having sex with her). Four percent featured *coerced sex* (for example, a producer offering an actress a starring role only if she will have sex with him). Eight percent featured some other form of abuse. (These categories were not mutually exclusive. A single instance of abuse might involve several categories.)

With regard to the question of who is abusing whom in the sex scene, 15% of the sex scenes featured male abusers, as compared to only 4% featuring female abusers. (Another 4% of the scenes featured abusers of both sexes.) Eighteen percent of the scenes featured a female victim, as compared to only 3% featuring a male victim. (Additionally, 2% of the scenes featured victims of both sexes.) Taking only those scenes featuring abuse, 68% featured a male abuser, while 80% featured a female victim. Thus, the abuser in these films tends to be male, and the victim tends to be female.

An important variable associated with the presence of abuse is the gender of the character who initiates sexual activity. Initiation—i.e., a prelude to sexual activity—was portrayed in 78% of the sex scenes, and women tended to initiate sex about as often as men: 36% of scenes involving initiation were female-initiated, while 40% were male-initiated. (In the remaining cases, initiation was mutual.) However, the scenes initiated by men had a significantly higher amount of abuse than those initiated by women. Forty percent of male-initiated scenes contained abuse, compared to only 18% of female-initiated scenes. (The corresponding figure for mutually initiated scenes was also 18%, while for scenes involving no initiation it was 9%.) Thus, in these films, the abusive scenes tend to be those featuring male-initiated sex.

Some critics of pornography (e.g., Barry, p. 209; "Pretty Poison," 1977) have asserted that it portrays abusive behavior as being free of consequences. These accounts maintain that pornography normalizes sexually abusive behavior by avoiding a portrayal of the suffering victims. Our coding indicates that, indeed, most scenes which contain abuse do not show an abused character suffering following the abuse. Sixty-five percent of abusive scenes did not include a portrayal of suffering after the abuse.

In addition to abuse coded as part of the sex scene, lethal or nonlethal physical violence was also coded whenever it occurred in the films (whether as part of a sex scene or not). Widespread violent or sadomasochistic behavior was not found. Each film contained a mean of approximately two acts of physical violence. In our sample of 29 films, there were 19 acts of hitting with hands, 8 acts of hitting with an object, 6 rapes, 4 killings, 4 shootings, 3 acts of sexual molestation, 2 suicides, 1 knifing, and 8 acts of other violence, yielding a total of 55 acts of physical violence. To provide a context for these figures, they might be compared to the recent findings reported by Gerbner, Gross, Signiorelli, and Morgan (1986) on the incidence of violent acts in prime-time television programming. Coding for acts of overt physical violence during the 1985–86 television season, they analyzed 62 program hours and reported a total of 421 violent acts and an average occurrence of 6.8 violent acts per hour.

In sum, the data indicate that pornographic feature films are composed of young adult, white, middle-class characters, that men and women have, on the average, a similar number of sexual partners, and that the anonymous sexual characters tend to be men more frequently than women. Seventy-seven percent of the sex scenes in our sample did not contain any form of abuse as coded here. However, in those scenes coded as abusive, the abusers tended to be men, the victims to be women, and the sexual behavior was more likely to have been initiated by men than by women. Furthermore, such portrayals of abusive behavior tended not to include portrayals of a suffering victim.

In conclusion, then, although our data do not support allegations of high frequencies of violent acts in pornographic films, they indicate that, when abuse does occur, its portrayal is consistent with what critics of pornography have claimed: that the instigators are men, the victims women, the consequences few.

REFERENCES

Barry, K. (1981). *Female sexual slavery*. New York: Discus Books.

Brownmiller, S. (1976). *Against our will: Men, women and rape*. New York: Bantam Books.

Gerbner, G., Gross, L., Signorielli, N., & Morgan, M. (1986). *Television's mean world: Violence profile No. 14–15*. Philadelphia, PA: Annenberg School of Communications, University of Pennsylvania.

Griffin, S. (1981). *Pornography and silence*. New York: Harper and Row.

Pretty poison: The selling of sexual warfare. (1977, May 9). *Village Voice*, pp. 18–23.

28

The Boys of Prime Time: An Analysis of "New" Male Roles in Television

JONATHAN DAVID TANKEL
Ithaca College

BARBARA JANE BANKS
Syracuse University

During the 1985–86 prime time television season, popular critics heralded the return of the macho man as that season's trend. These tough-guy characters, many argued, represented a backlash against the sensitive male of the recent television past—the reborn Hawkeye Pierce of *M*A*S*H*'s later years and Frank Furillo of *Hill Street Blues*. The success of *Cheers*, featuring an avowed womanizer in Sam Malone, and the anticipated success of *Moonlighting*'s "hard-boiled" David Addison, were taken as evidence of a return to the patriarchal depiction of gender roles from which, the critics claimed, prime time television had been so recently liberated. This argument contains several flaws in reasoning. Still, this "back to the future" analysis of male roles in prime time invited the public to confuse isolated industry practices with sweeping social movements.

In this chapter, we examine the popular critics's analyses in detail and argue the following: First, popular critics' claims that prime-time television is returning to unreconstructed male roles is not supported by evidence from the prime time lineup as a whole. Second, the critics' interpretation of new-male roles assumes a monolithic ideological focus and fails to account for variable readings of the text. Third, character analysis as presented by these critics is misleading because it isolates traits that constitute only a small part of the larger television context.

THE NEW MACHO MAN COMETH

Peter J. Boyer, writing in the *New York Times* in February 1986, proclaimed that prime-time television was returning to the "hard boiled male"—defined by an "aggressive masculinity." The list of these new male roles included characters as diverse as

> the supercool, super-detached detective of NBC's *Miami Vice*, the lecherous bar proprietor Sam Malone in NBC's *Cheers*, the blunt-spoken newspaper editor

Frank DeMarco in *Mary* and the unreconstructed chauvinist private investigator David Addison in ABC's *Moonlighting*. (Boyer, 1986, p. 1)

(Also mentioned in the article was con-man/detective Remington Steele). Boyer perceived a parallel trend in which existing characters were given a new hard edge—such as Dr. Bobby Caldwell on NBC's *St. Elsewhere*. Most importantly, Boyer offered the thesis that the "some sociologists and some television industry observers suggest that the new man type on television is *partly a reaction to the feminist movement* (p. 29; emphasis added).

Boyer based his analysis partly on an article by Etzioni (1984) which praised characters such as Hawkeye and Captain Furillo. Etzioni saw a trend in "rehabilitated" males, representing a rapprochement between Americans and the institutions these males represented—such as the military and the police. Boyer then turned to Gloria Allred (lawyer and President of the Woman's Equal Rights Legal Defense and Education Fund), who presented a humorless critique—"They are laughing at women, instead of with them." One sociologist and one feminist were thus transformed by Boyer into "some sociologists" and "the feminist movement," and the case for the New Macho Man was made.

Boyer's analysis was published during the 1985–86 television season. The weight of his evidence was the simultaneous existence of six lead male characters in five different prime time television series. Boyer offered quotes from the creators of the series (and sometimes from rival program creators) in which they admitted, in varying degrees, to conscious efforts to bring the unreconstructed male back to television. As an example, *Cheers* co-producer Glen Charles describes Sam Malone as "a spokesperson for a large group of people who thought [the New Male] was a bunch of bull and look with disdain upon people who don't think it was." (Boyer, 1986, p. 29)

It would be easy to dismiss Boyer's argument, since all he did was demonstrate in journalistic fashion the *motivation* of a few individual producers. But Boyer's analysis, or at least analyses similar to Boyer's, gained widespread public attention through the popular press. The most visible of these parallel arguments was Helen Gurley Brown's *TV Guide* article offering advice on "How to Outfox TV's New Breed of Macho Man" (Brown, 1986). The success of ABC's *Moonlighting* resulted in a series of articles in popular periodicals ranging from *Newsweek* to *USA Weekend*, all highlighting David Addison and concluding that the prime-time television audience was ready for the New Macho Male (Collins, 1986; Horowitz, 1986; Waters, 1986).

These articles, taken together, form a public discourse that interprets television texts for viewers, arguing, first, that viewers were tired of liberated heroes such as Hawkeye and Furillo and longed for the return of the macho leading man, and second, that viewers' desires for old-time heroes constituted an antifeminist backlash. One could theorize that these mass-pervasive articles function as a reconstruction of the television text for viewers, but it remains to be seen to what extent viewers participate in or resist this public creation of meaning. Also, while popular critics discerned a radical shift in male TV roles of the 1980s, the truth is that unreconstructed male characters had never really left the air. For example, Archie Bunker, the prototypical unreconstructed male character of the 1960s, overlapped in transmission with the current J. R. Ewing.

THE MACHO MALE IN THE 1980s

Not only had the unreconstructed male never entirely disappeared from prime time, but in 1982–83, 3 years before Boyer discerned his trend, two new shows appeared with such characters in leading roles. When NBC transmitted *Buffalo Bill*, for example, critics could not ignore the sexist nature of the lead character. What is important about *Buffalo Bill* was the show's failure to attract the prime-time television audience. However, at the same time, unreconstructed Sam Malone was solid Top-Twenty material. *Cheers* was a relative success from its inception in 1982. Malone exhibited all the more cliched signifiers of male chauvinism (a little black book, sexual boasting, jock-like demeanor, etc.) but, rather than representing a new antifeminist trend in prime-time television, Malone's sexist behavior was often a target for laughs. As an object of humor, Sam Malone was a poor candidate to lead the postfeminist counterrevolution (Bayles, 1984; Harrington, 1985; Higgins, 1985).

Interestingly, Boyer did not include the most hard-boiled of males in the recent prime-time schedule, Spillaine's detective Mike Hammer. Tom Shales in a January, 1984, *Washington Post* article, asked, "Is Spillaine's detective right for our time?" John J. O'Conner (1984) echoed Shales in the *New York Times*, asking, "Is this supposed age of liberation ready for an unrepentant male chauvinist pig?" And Stacy Keach, who played the detective, referred to the character as an "anachronism" (Shales, 1984).

Keach's assessment of his role provided a third perspective—not Boyer's vision of television's new macho hero, nor the low IQ sexism represented by Sam Malone, but the macho man as a relic of an older society, a man whose sense of displacement becomes the catalyst for humor within a dramatic context. These alternative analyses of male roles exemplify the complexity of interpreting television.

READING TELEVISION: TWO PERSPECTIVES

Scholars of television have been increasingly concerned with the process of reading television, and have suggested that a critic's-eye-view alone ignores contextual factors that influence viewers' interpretations of the television text. Two different perspectives theorizing television provide rationales for an analysis of public criticism as part of the text. One perspective views television as an open text, subject to a variety of readings depending on the circumstances of the text–subject–spectator relationship (Deming, 1985). The television text goes beyond a specific program incorporating the experience of television as a complex of discourses. In constructing the parameters of this text, Deming

(1986, p. 9) includes "how popular press articles, magazines, and program publicity act as textual shifters and position the audience" as one component of television's intertextuality.

Newcomb and Hirsch (1984) see a multilayered television text from a second perspective. The ideological influences of television as practiced in the U.S. are the totality of each individual's experience; the range of possible discourses is *in itself* the raison d'etre of television–the Jeffersonian marketplace of ideas reborn in the prime-time television schedule. And these conflicting discourses need be seen, *not* only within individual programs and whole genres, but also across the entire television schedule.

Thus the public proclamation by popular critics of the existence of a specific character type across the spectrum of prime-time programs—such as the New Macho man—deserves examination (a) to determine the validity of that conclusion, and (b) to theorize the implications of this public analysis for the reading of television texts.

A SURVEY OF UNRECONSTRUCTED MALE ROLES (1985–86)

The prime-time network television schedule (excluding PBS) consists of 66 hours of programming. Across the 1985–86 prime-time schedule, Boyer's designated "new male" characters were seen for 4 hours per week—6% of the prime-time schedule. The programs featuring those characters were not uniformly successful. By season's end, *Moonlighting* and *Miami Vice* were in the Top Ten, *Cheers* in the Top Twenty and *Mary* and *Remington Steele* had been cancelled. (*Steele* was subsequently renewed.) If one includes all programs in the Fall 1985 schedule featuring lead male characters who could be considered "aggressively masculine," (adding at a minimum *Dallas, Airwolf, Hunter, Hardcastle and McCormick, Our Family Honor, The A-Team, Riptide, Simon and Simon,* and *Knightrider*), the percentage increases to 20% (13 hours per week). But some of the programs overlap in the prime time schedule, and no proof exists that large segments of the audience attend solely to these specific programs. And even if they did, it would be precipitate to assume that every viewer shares a single interpretation of the meaning of these programs.

VARIABILITY OF TEXT AND THE CULTURAL FORUM

This crude quantification underscores the difficulty with character analysis as the basis for a dominant reading of television's social matrix. Several more interpretations than those already presented are possible. Consider *The Equalizer* or *Spencer: For Hire*. McCall and Spencer are unabashedly masculine, but "aggressive?" These urbanized knights in armor display a good deal of sensitivity, at least toward their clients (who are usually presented as socially powerless, hence their need for extralegal assistance).

The problem with character analysis is in the construction of television programming—lead characters are conceived in relation to all continuing characters within the series. This proposition is illustrated by Boyer's prime example of the quintessential "hard-boiled male"—David Addison. As recently as October 1986, Bruce Willis, who plays David Addison, was featured on the cover of *Gentleman's Quarterly*, a men's fashion magazine. The persona of Addison described therein was not the hard-boiled male described by Boyer, but his more ineffectual little brother, the "brash boy" (Bayles, 1984; Shales, 1985b). Addison's demotion from man to boy results, not from an interpretation based on him alone, but from David Addison in opposition to the strong-willed Madeline Hayes. As some critics outside the mainstream press have noted, characters such as Addison are not the harbinger of the bad old days redux.

> Are we watching the return of the sexist cutie you thought you had seen the last of in high school? Or worse, some future nightmare where women do all the work and men have all the fun? Not likely. David will go on making clever sexist remarks that unreconstructed and quite a few purportedly reconstructed) men enjoy in the old-fashioned way. But what does it mean if woman viewers laugh louder than men at the presentation of male prowess. And if men in the room with those women have an eerie feeling that the joke, finally, is on them? When you come right down to it, David's got nothing but rhythm, and only a white version at that. Maddie's going somewhere with her life, or trying anyway. (Buhle & Buhle, 1986, p. 41)

Indeed, with the exception of the *Miami Vice* detectives, each of the characters designated by Boyer as one of television's new macho heroes exists in relation to a strong female character: David Addison and Madeline Hayes, Sam Malone and Dianne Chambers, Remington Steele and Laura Holt, and Frank DeMarco and Mary Brenner. These couples seem to exist in a constant state of tension between the unreconstructed male and the woman who isn't having any, thank you. An alternative interpretation of prime-time programs featuring sexist male leads is that these programs function as a forum where the conflict between old and new gender roles is enacted over and over, much as it is in society (Ehrenreich, 1984). Thus we have the traditional world of male privilege being challenged by the new independent woman. And who is winning this battle of the sexes may depend on who is viewing the program.

Critics' opinions about the ideological thrust of prime-time television may form part of the text for some viewers, and so it is important to examine these analyses as close correlates to the text. However, in this particular case of male characters on prime-time television, we suggest that the text itself (TV) does not support the critics' readings. This problem, of course, is further complicated by the fact that critics' interpretation of new-male roles in television precipitously assumes a monolithic ideology and fails to account for variable readings of the text. Finally, current critical interpretations seem to be the result of a truncated focus on a single character or trait in isolation from other characters and contexts of the television experience.

REFERENCES

Bayles, M. (1984, May 3). TV forecast: 'Cheers' and Lion Crow. *Wall Street Journal*, p. 30.
Bayles, M. (1985, September 23). Television: Smooth sleuths. *Wall Street Journal*, p. 28.
Boyer, P. J. (1986, February 16). TV turns to the hard-boiled male. *New York Times*, II, pp. 1,5.
Brown, H. G. (1986). How to outfox tv's new breed of macho man. *TV Guide, 34* (31), 10–12.
Buhle, M. J., & Buhle, P. (1986). Repartee for two. *Village Voice*, pp. 39, 41.
Collins, M. (1986, September 19–21). Three creative wizards who are turning on television. *USA Weekly*, pp. 4–5.
Deming, R. (1985). The spectator-subject. *Journal of Film and Video, 37,* 48–63.
Deming, R. (1986). *Theorizing television text: Text, textuality, intertextuality.* Presented to the Society for Cinema Studies.
Ehrenreich, B. (1984, May 20). A feminist's view of the new man. *The New York Times Magazine*, pp. 36–48.
Etzioni, A. (1984). Nice guys finish first: today's television heroes. *Public Opinion, 7*(14), pp. 16–18.
Harrington, R. (1985, February 15). Of good 'Cheers'. *The Washington Post*, pp. D1, D10.
Higgins, G. V. (1985, December 23). Charge of the light brigade. *Wall Street Journal*, p. 13.
Horowitz, J. (1986, March 30). The madcap behind Moonlighting. *The New York Times Magazine*, pp. 24, 61.
Newcomb, H. M., & Hirsch, P. M. (1984). Television as a cultural forum: implications for research. In W. D. Rowland, Jr., & B. Watkins (Eds.), *Interpreting television: Current research perspectives* (pp. 58–73). Beverly Hills, CA: Sage.
O'Connor, J. (1984, January 27). Stacy Keach stars in Spillaine thriller. *The New York Times* p. C26.
O'Connor, J. (1985, December 11). "A new Mary Tyler Moore." *The New York Times*, p. C30.
Shales, T. (1984, January 29). The tough guy makes a comeback. *The Washington Post*, pp. C1, C9.
Shales, T. (1985a, January 26). Blam! Blam! It's murder. *The Washington Post*, pp. B1, B6.
Shales, T. (1985b, May 2). All new, worn-out gumshoe. *The Washington Post*, pp. G1, G4.
Waters, H. F. (1986, September 8). Sly and sexy: tv's fun couple. *Newsweek*, pp. 46–52.

29

Reagan's America in Television: Return of the Nuclear Family

MARION W. WEISS
Bowie State University

INTRODUCTION

American television has seen many trends come and go in its brief history. These trends have been influenced by a variety of determinants arising from both the medium's internal structure and from those reflecting TV's role in society. The continuing popularity in recent years of *Family Ties, The Cosby Show*, and to a lesser extent, *Cagney and Lacey*, addresses two important questions: What do these shows have in common which may constitute a present trend, and to what determinant(s) do they owe their success?

One answer to the first question is that all the programs focus on the importance of the family in American life, although this theme is more subtle in *Cagney and Lacey*. The second answer is less apparent; these current shows signal a return to traditional values (also reflected in the 1950s with *Father Knows Best* and *Leave It to Beaver*, for example) which Reagan's presidency has come to represent. Embodied in these values is the idea that family is the backbone of American society in providing *stability* and a *moral system* for all its members. The former function is particularly salient in this period of instability with its abundance of wars, terrorism, and unemployment. The focus on family is also especially appropriate when Reagan himself is seen as a father figure, mature in years, full of wisdom and filled with concern for his children.

Family can mean a *nuclear* structure, a *modified* organization including any two or more persons related by blood, marriage, or adoption, or an *extended* unit that may even go beyond blood ties to close bonding associations. Recent TV families follow a similar pattern: the figurative extended unit in *Hill Street Blues* and *Cagney and Lacey*; the modified one in *Who's the Boss* and *Kate and Allie*; and the nuclear one in *Family Ties (FT)* and *The Cosby Show (TCS)*. The 1987 season adds to this list with such shows as *L.A. Law* (extended), *Our House* (modified), and *Married . . . With Children* (nuclear).

This chapter examines how the nuclear unit, represented particularly in *Family Ties* (with references to *The Cosby Show* and *Cagney and Lacey*), celebrates the family as a stabilizing force and as an imparter of traditional values. Episodes viewed were from the Spring 1986 season; primary consideration was given to the thematic thrust of these episodes.

FAMILY AS A STABILIZING FORCE

According to Hansen and Hill (1964), stability in the nuclear family may be measured by (a) how well members handle stress, and (b) how well the unit is organized.

Stress Factors

Any change in family *size* may produce stress, yet the addition of a new baby, Andrew, to *FT* did not lead to a lasting unstable condition within the unit. While the usual problems associated with an infant caused temporary havoc, the solving of these problems (like Jennifer's jealousy and the family's sleepless nights) had a positive cohesive result as members learned to adjust to the new situation.

A change in *status* for any family member can also cause stress, yet Steven Keaton's promotion at the local PBS station did not have an enduring effect on family stability. Initially, his frequent business trips and extra hours at the office *did* produce a modification in family life; however, he decided that the promotion wasn't worth it if he had to lose the intimacy of his family.

Role shifts can also undermine stability, but examples of this in *FT* were ultimately dealt with in a positive manner. Elyse effected a role reversal in three instances which served to challenge the family's concept of what a mother and/or a woman are supposed to be. In one case, both she and Alex enroll in an auto mechanics class, and Elyse does considerably better than her teenage son. When Alex goofs on an assignment, Elyse fixes it, explaining, "What's a mother for." Alex finally admits that "women can do anything a man can do." Thus, while Elyse puts her role as mother first, Alex acknowledges her skill.

In another instance, Elyse decides to try her luck as a singer at a local night club. Jennifer remarks, "How can you be a singer, you're a mother." The children are convinced that she is going through mid-life crisis. Yet, the kids and Steven support her in her endeavor. It is assumed that this experience will be a one-time event for Elyse when she admits she's too old to recapture her youth.

In one last example, Elyse takes a job with an architectural firm, thus giving up her free lance position where she could work at home. She cannot adjust to the office environment and becomes increasingly anxious and overworked. The children resent this, chiding her for being too busy to spend time with them. Elyse finally admits that she was trying to be the "perfect mother and the perfect career girl." Yet the family finally agrees to try and make adjustments without falling victim to her role shift. Thus, stress is reduced or eliminated in these cases when Elyse either decides to give up a role which causes problems or when the family decides to support her.

Conflict from *outside* forces can additionally effect stress within a family. When Alex accepts an invitation to have dinner with his new girl friend's family at a wealthy, restricted club, Elyse and Steven become upset. Steven appears in jeans at the club and demands that Alex come home. Father and son come to terms, however, when, later on, Alex says, "I know you love me, but I'm not you, Dad." They then shake hands and hug each other at the fade-out. Willingness to accept each other's value differences makes it possible for them to maintain a harmonious relationship within the family.

Alex's association with another individual not accepted by his parents also causes conflict. This time, Alex gets involved with a divorced older woman with a child. But the woman breaks off the friendship, telling Elyse that she will abide by the wishes of Alex's parents; thus, continuing stress is avoided. In general, conditions which affect the Keatons' survival are overcome, and the family is stronger for it.

Family Organization

Stability is also influenced by the quality of organization operating within the family. This quality can be determined by how well family members live up to and maintain their particular roles.

Steven manifests well-prescribed traits in his dual role as father and husband. When a promotion interferes with his home life, he gives it up. Although he appears initially somewhat awkward with Andrew, he soon shares parenting chores with Elyse, a nod to the new roles which many fathers now assume. He offers fatherly advice to son, Alex, on a regular basis. As a husband he is consistently patient with his wife and supportive of her endeavors.

Elyse, despite the fact that she has a career in architecture, is first and foremost a mother, giving sound advice to Mallory about sex, caring for a baby, and sewing, and to Jennifer about how to handle a boy–girl birthday party. As a wife, Elyse shows the same loving support and patience for Steven as he does for her.

Alex, in his role of the older brother, advises Mallory on sex and tells his sisters that they must support their parents in stressful times. He even ends an important interview at Princeton to help his sister, who is upset over losing her boyfriend. Alex also becomes a surrogate for Steven when he helps pregnant Elyse, who unexpectedly goes into labor.

The nuclear unit is considered well organized, and thus stable, if members put the family as a whole before individual needs. Several examples from *FT* illustrate adherence to this concept. When Elyse helps a protesting Alex with his auto mechanics project, she tells him, "I want to help you. We're in the same family," suggesting that self-serving competition between them should not be an issue. On a trip to Atlantic City, Elyse gets hooked on black jack.

After an all-night binge, she admits, "I turned away from my family so I could win more money." Acknowledging her remark, the family supports her decision to give the symbolically 'family-destructive' winnings to charity. In another case, Steven puts the family first when he rejects a promotion.

The children also relinquish their personal wishes when, for example, they support Steven with pledge week at his television station. Elyse reminds the children: "This is one of the few things we do as a family . . . your dad works for the family." While the children would rather spend their time elsewhere, Alex, Mallory, and Jennifer do finally appear at the station, with Alex remarking that "We're a family. If it's important to one member, it's important to all of us."

As a result of putting the family first, individual members experience personal growth, thus keeping the family structure organized and stable. Moreover, organization and constancy are maintained through the setting of realistic goals, not only for the family but for individual members. A primary, practical goal in *FT* is that satisfactory solutions to problems be sought, yet with the understanding that problems will not necessarily be solved. The process of mutual collaboration is stressed as central to achieving harmony.

Visual images abound in *FT* to reinforce the idea of stability which result from the handling of stress and the maintaining of organizational structure. In the opening credits, individual cast members are seen in fragmentary shots, but the last shot shows the entire family together. Many episodes end with a similar picture of togetherness—together on a hotel bed in Atlantic City, together at the local jail on Thanksgiving, together at the TV station where Elyse has just given birth, or simply together on the living-room floor on Christmas Day. These shots demonstrate that, no matter *where* the family is or under *what* circumstances, they will always be together. As the opening song indicates, "I bet we've been together for a million years and I'll bet we'll be together for a million more . . ." It is thus suggested that the nuclear family remains intact, avoiding the ravages of time.

FAMILY AS IMPARTER OF VALUES

FT illustrates the role that the nuclear family should take in imparting values, many of which may be deemed traditional and old-fashioned. Respect for one's relatives is especially apparent in episodes dealing with Elyse's brother (Ned), Steven's father, and Elyse's parents. When Ned hides out in the Keaton home, on the run from the authorities, the family offers protection. Steven attempts to reconcile differences with his father, despite a history of conflict between them.

Other values are imparted by Elyse and Steven to their children. Steven cautions Mallory against "using" her friends and family to get into a sorority. Elyse tells Jennifer she should be a strong woman when her daughter wants to buck tradition and invite boys to her birthday party. Both parents admonish Alex for printing the names of students caught cheating; Elyse and Steven also demonstrate the importance of sticking to one's beliefs when they refuse to keep a gun in the house or when they won't sign a statement promising never to demonstrate again. While the social fabric of life may change, certain values remain constant.

THE COSBY SHOW

The Cosby Show (TCS) represents another popular case of the family at work in Reagan's America.

Specific factors accounting for stability in *FT* are not in operation in *TCS*, yet stability exists. The father, Cliff, is an orchestrator in the Huxtable home, a maintainer of the status quo. His seeming unflappability in times of stress provides security and constancy for the family. Claire, the mother, also conveys the idea of a women in control. She seems to experience little internal conflict concerning her roles as mother, wife, and career woman. Thus, unlike Steven and Elyse Keaton, Cliff and Claire Huxtable furnish stability through the force of *personal* strengths.

Within the Huxtable household, individual members recognize and manifest their particular traditional roles. Cliff is firm yet fair; he doles out authority with humor. As the husband, he is responsive to Claire's sexuality and understanding of her independent nature. Claire appears to be a stricter disciplinarian than Cliff and more of a transmitter of values, although Cliff rattles off "instructions" to his kids. Similar to Elyse and Steven, both Claire and Cliff share in decision making and child rearing. The Huxtable children exhibit the kind of typical behavior and relationships with each other that the Keaton children do. When Cliff cannot find one private spot where he can relax because of the children's constant interruptions, one is reminded of a similar situation in *FT*; both sets of parents come to accept this giving up of their individual privacy.

The family unit in *TCS* also serves as a vehicle through which values are imparted: respect for elders is reiterated in episodes dealing with Cliff's parents; the importance of hard work is emphasized when Claire tells Rudy, her youngest child, that she must earn the money for a new doll. Expressions of affection between family members is stressed (like in *FT*) when Cliff and Claire kiss in front of the children. The family survives, with humor and love, with stability and a solid moral foundation.

CAGNEY AND LACEY

While *Cagney and Lacey* started out, according to network publicity, as an adventure series involving two female police officers, it has developed into something much more; it is still a crime show, but it is also about families, including a nuclear unit (Mary Beth Lacey's), an extended one (the police who work together), and, until recently, a modified structure (Chris and her father, Charlie). The program illustrates, among other things, how these various families interconnect; it also demonstrates the endurance of the nuclear family.

Some conflicts arise because Mary Beth sees a difference between her family at work and her family at home, and often her "real" family comes first. Mary Beth says in one episode, "My work is not my job. . .I have a family. I'm going home when my shift ends." For Chris, work is all encompassing, sometimes at the expense of romance. Yet, she unconsciously wishes to be part of a nuclear family herself, so closely does she identify with the birth of Mary Beth's baby. For many of the characters, loyalty to the police family sometimes takes priority over personal ideals. Thus, a close fellow-officer decides to end (temporarily) his boycott from work so that he can help Cagney and Lacey trap a rapist. Additionally, Mary Beth consents to attend her baby shower given by co-workers, despite the fact that she does not want to go.

Often, an episode's theme will be directly related to the various notions of life and death as they affect family units. For example, the taking of a life (a young boy is suspected of killing his grandmother) is juxtaposed with the giving of life (Mary Beth's pregnancy) and the possible ending of life (Charlie's illness and hospitalization).

Despite the ups and downs of Cagney and Lacey's lives, Lacey particularly can depend on her family for support and solace. Co-workers may come and go (and lovers, too, in the case of Cagney), but the nuclear family is enduring.

While recent TV shows have reflected many different kinds of bonding associations, it is *Family Ties, The Cosby Show,* and *Cagney and Lacey* which exemplify the importance of the nuclear family. Such a unit provides the stability and moral system necessary for the maintenance of traditional values in present-day America.

REFERENCE

Hansen, D., & Hill, R. (1964). Families under stress. In H. T. Christensen (Ed.), *Handbook of Marriage and Family* (pp. 782–822). Chicago, IL: Rand McNally.

30

Relationship Development as Represented
in Contemporary American Cinema

BARBARA G. COX
Davis & Elkins College

DAVID W. SEAMAN
Davis & Elkins College

Romance and the movies are intertwined in American culture. A favorite film theme is boy-meets-girl, and movie going remains a popular dating ritual. So it is especially appealing to use movies to carry out scholarly research on interpersonal relationships. This study provides an illustration (in the context of male–female relationships) of Knapp's (1984) five interaction stages and the critical transitional phases between each stage. This focus on movements between plateaus (stages) shifts our attention from the culmination of a relationship to the process of its development.

FILM AS A MEDIUM OF INTERPERSONAL STUDY

Studying the development of interpersonal relationships is problematic. Memories of our own relationships are filled with deletions and corrections, while the laboratory setting is stilted and artificial. Using hidden cameras raises ethical questions, and following people around for weeks or months would be awkward at the very least. Watzlawick, Beavin, and Jackson (1967) solved this problem by using Albee's play, "Who's Afraid of Virginia Woolf?" as their object of study. They contend that this scripted dialogue may be "even more real than reality" and that the limited size of the data, coupled with people's accessibility to it, make this play an ideal example for the study of interaction patterns (p. 150).

We chose to study film for the same reasons, plus an additional consideration. We are interested in verbal as well as nonverbal elements (e.g., physical appearance, movement, and location).

FILM SELECTION

Sixteen films form the basis of this study. They are all American, and only one (*The African Queen*) is not of recent vintage. In each movie there is at least one significant interpersonal relationship that develops, sometimes as the sole action of the story, as in *Same Time Next Year*, but sometimes only incidentally to the central action, as is the case with *Places in the Heart*. All the films are available on videocassette in the mass market and their commercial success reinforces the places they hold as conveyors of contemporary values. See Appendix for film list.

INTERACTION STAGES

Knapp (1984) identified 10 stages in the development of a relationship: initiating, experimenting, intensifying, integrating, bonding, differentiating, circumscribing, stagnating, avoiding, and terminating. The first five constitute *coming together*, and are the focus of this study (pp. 35–39).

Initiating is the briefest and often most difficult stage to observe, as it may last only minutes. Typically, much of the information exchanged is nonverbal (eye contact, posture, distance, clothing). Verbal exchanges are impersonal and highly stylized (Hi, how are you? What's your name?).

Experimenting is characterized by small talk. It gives people a chance to establish common ground and to decide on continuing the relationship. Most relationships, especially in the business setting, remain at this stage.

Self-disclosure increases during the *intensifying* stage. Touching increases, private symbols develop, more sharing takes place. Common experiences and goals are reflected in the use of *we* and *let's*.

Informal commitment can be recognized at the *integrating* stage. The exchange of rings, pins, clothing, or other symbols will signal the establishment of an ongoing relationship to the outside world, which in turn recognizes the relationship by issuing one invitation, sending one gift, and referring to the couple as a team (Let's call Susan-and-John).

Moving from informal to formal commitment occurs at the *bonding* stage. Ceremonies (engagements, weddings) and legal contracts provide structure to the relationship here.

INITIATING

The self-image that people wish to present is emphasized in the initiation stage. In the films in this study, a wide range of initiation possibilities exist for males, including and even promoting the acceptance of drunken and slovenly behavior. While some men present themselves as exemplars of correctness (a military uniform or a nice suit), many of the male protagonists are introduced as grizzle, unruly, and displaying bodily functions (belches and stomach growls, for instance).

Examples of male correctness are found in *An Officer and a Gentleman*, *Same Time Next Year*, and *Carnal Knowledge*. The initial interaction for hese men typically occurs on neutral ground in some formal setting, such as a mixer.

Male slovenliness is more prevalent, with drunkenness appearing in *Arthur*,

The Africa   *ctric Horseman, Tender Mercies,*
High Road   *Big Chill.*

Female   e consistently proper. Even in more
stringent e   as with Sally Field in *Places in the*
Heart, the women display themselves as well kept, tidy, and conventional. Women are also associated with a place, either their home or their work, where they initiate interactions; men typically range from their base and go to the women.

FIRST TRANSITION

One of the first signs of transition from initiating to experimenting is *rule making*. Rule making is an assertion that the relationship is moving to the next stage and that the interaction will be played a certain way.

Women take the first step in rule making. This outcome relates to female properness and to the female's location of the activity. Thus we see the rule making transition defined spatially by females, with actions such as door slamming and hanging up the phone which delimit their territory, and standing with folded arms to close their personal space.

Men typically fight against the rules, and often have their way, too. They call back, push through the doors, and gesticulate wildly.

A transitional scene in *Goodbye Girl* well illustrates both male and female rule making. The female protagonist stands at the door with the guard chain on, hangs up the phone, and shows the male a timer to indicate the limits on his conversation with her. He responds with repeated calls, peeping into the room and eventually marching around the apartment waving his arms and rearranging things. Once this transitional activity is ended, they move to the more placid experimenting stage.

EXPERIMENTING

Men take the lead at the experimenting stage. They are active and typically lean forward, bring gifts, offer help, and, conduct an interview. Females are passive yet receptive. They are willing recipients of the gifts, attentions; they are interviewed.

One of the clearest examples of this occurs in *Falling in Love*, where Robert DeNiro spends most of a lunch-meeting talking to Meryl Streep. When he finally confronts her with her silence, she merely replies, "What do you want to know?" Surprised by her passivity, his response is, "How much do you weigh?"

SECOND TRANSITION

The transition from experimenting to intensifying is characterized by movement. Either the male or the female may make a suggestion to go somewhere else, ranging from "Let's go for a walk," to departure on a cross-country trip.

Two variations of the walk appear in *An Officer and a Gentleman*, when two couples meet at a mixer. One couple trades movements: Richard Gere asks "Do you want to go get a drink?" and then moves with Debra Winger to another room. A short time later, Debra Winger increases the stakes by suggesting they leave the club to find more privacy. A second couple had been dancing closely and, by mutual consent, goes to the beach.

INTENSIFYING

At this level more touching occurs. Penetration of personal space is common. Often, but not always, sex becomes part of the relationship. The couple engages in shared activities such as gardening, cooking, and singing together. Men and women carry out their own customary activities, but with excursions into their partner's territory. In *Places in the Heart*, the lodger helps cook in Sally Field's kitchen, while in *An Unmarried Woman* Jill Clayburgh cooks for Alan Bates in his studio. In *A Star is Born*, Barbara Streisand is pulled on stage to sing at Kris Kristofferson's concert. In *Goodbye Girl*, Richard Dreyfuss goes to Marsha Mason's room to play his guitar.

THIRD TRANSITION

Demonstration of a shared value or attitude signals the transition from intensifying to integrating. Often an extreme situation occurs which tests the person's level of commitment, involving a threat to physical safety or emotional stability. In *Places in the Heart*, the lodger risks his life to protect the girl. Tom Selleck's callous aviator in *High Road to China* nurses his fevered female employer. When Meg Tilly, in *The Big Chill*, asks William Hurt to sleep with her, the drug dealer has to reveal that he is impotent.

INTEGRATING

There are two major indicators of the integration stage. Focus on a third party, often children, is a classic situation. The two people, partners at this point, give their energies over to raising the kids, or caring for an animal. If a child is involved, there is increased touching of the child or an increase in adult–child play. In *Goodbye Girl*, Richard Dreyfuss takes the girl for a carriage ride, and, in *Tender Mercies*, Robert Duvall plays football with the boy.

The second indicator of integration is the taking on a task, quest, or common goal. This can be a geographic journey, as in *High Road to China*, or a symbolic journey into crime, as in *The Postman Always Rings Twice* (though even this involves travel on the highway).

FOURTH TRANSITION

The transition into bonding is made by a formal proposal, often of marriage. This proposal is made exclusively by the men. There certainly exist films in which women suggest marriage, but this does not occur in the films we studied. Further, it is accomplished in less than half of the cases, and even fewer show the event. In *Carnal Knowledge*, for example, Art Garfunkel turns out to have married Candace Bergen, but we learn it only later. Also, men propose marriage indirectly in *Tender Mercies* ("Have you ever thought about getting married again?") and in *Goodbye Girl* ("How about blood tests?").

BONDING

The formal bond is typically marriage, although it could be another type of contract, such as living together. The infrequency of this stage in these films is notable, and leads to speculation about the values of Bonding in American society.

FINDINGS

Open-endedness

The stages of interaction logically culminate in bonding, yet in many of these films bonding does not occur, and the transition into it is not even attempted. This certainly challenges the traditional notion of the happy ending, but failure to bond is not always portrayed negatively. For instance, in *The Electric Horseman*, the relationship ends happily with the separation of the partners, each going his or her own way.

In other films, an "open" conclusion suggests that further interaction will occur. This seems to be a way of suggesting that other satisfactory options exist, giving viewers the right to invent their own ending. It could be that the conclusion is foregone and not worth demonstrating. More likely, however, today's society provides less certainty about how a relationship will proceed. It is hard to judge what presently constitutes a happy ending. In the films in this study, marriage and other forms of bonding are not necessarily seen as desirable conclusions to interpersonal interaction. Also, sexual intercourse is not reserved for the bonding or even integrating stage, but can occur almost anywhere in the interaction sequence.

NEW IMAGES, OLD ROLES

Despite images of women with new clothes, new jobs, and outspoken assertiveness, male control is maintained. Throughout the interaction stages and the transitions, most often the man is the active participant while the woman remains passively receptive or, at best, works at attracting the man.

CONCLUSION

The interaction stages in Knapp's model and others like it have received much attention, but the transitions into these stages are equally important and have not received much notice. If the transitions are not introduced, there is not likely to be movement into the next stage of the sequence. In the films in this study, men exert their control by controlling the transitions. Men are therefore the ones who determine whether the relationship will progress. Women can halt the progress and delay movement, but are less successful at moving things forward.

APPENDIX: FILMS USED IN THIS STUDY

A Star is Born
An Officer and A Gentleman
An Unmarried Woman
Arthur
Carnal Knowledge
Falling in Love
Flashdance
Goodbye Girl

High Road to China
Places in the Heart
Same Time Next Year
Tender Mercies
The African Queen
The Big Chill
The Electric Horseman
The Postman Always Rings Twice

REFERENCES

Knapp, M.L. (1984). *Interpersonal communication and personal relationships*. Boston, MA: Allyn and Bacon.

Watzlawick, P., Beavin, J.H., & Jackson, D.D. (1967). *Pragmatics of human communication: A study of interactional patterns, pathologies and paradoxes*. New York: W.W. Norton.

PART VIII

RETHINKING
COMMUNICATION POLICY

31

Broadcasting Policy:
Competition and Public Service

RICHARD COLLINS
Polytechnic of Central London

Across the nonsocialist world, the provision of resources for, and services by, broadcasters has come from a mixture of state and market allocations. The U.S. uses a state agency, the Federal Communications Commission, to allocate the central resource utilized by broadcasters, a section of the radio spectrum, and provides from the state budgets about 25% of the funds of the Public Broadcasting Service. While West German and the United Kingdom fund public service systems partly through advertising revenue, the U.S. remains one endpoint of the state/market spectrum of mode-of-resource allocation, and the European public service broadcasters (exemplified by the U.K. and West Germany) the other.

In the U.K. a committee of enquiry into the financing of the BBC, (the Peacock Committee, named for its Chairman Professor Alan Peacock,) was established in 1985 and reported in 1986 (Peacock, 1986). Canada's Caplan/ Sauvageau Task Force on Broadcasting Policy reported in the same year with comprehensive proposals (yet to be implemented) for change (Caplan/ Sauvageau, 1986). In France the Socialist and Conservative governments were united in resolving to introduce private capital and competition into broadcasting. Spain looks forward to an era in which radio and television services 'not run directly by the state . . . may be run . . . in a regime of free competition (*Intermedia*, 1985, vol. 13, no. 4/5, p.4), and so on.

The Peacock Committee has received very bad press in Britain. It has pleased few interests. The right wing is disappointed because the report argues for the BBC to remain large so as to resist government pressure, and also that broadcasting requires no moral censorship other than that prescribed in common and statute law. The left is displeased by Peacock's advocacy of the market and consumer sovereignty and its assault on public-sector institutions.

Without choosing sides, it can be argued that the Peacock report is a prodigious attempt to deal with broadcasting policy. Nevertheless, the report too readily overlooks the characteristics of the terrestial broadcast market that make it imperfectly competitive, impervious to consumer influence, and so cheap that it is unlikely to be replaced by pay-per-delivery systems. This chapter examines some of the characteristics of the broadcast market and its political economy and recommends the invention of political institutions and regulatory systems that may realize broadcasting services that deliver both 'American' entertainment and also the 'European' public-service programming of the range, variety, and seriousness that the broadcasting 'publics' are denied when agglomerated into a mass public in an audience-maximizing system.

The universal problem of the mode of allocation of resources for broadcasting is endlessly rehearsed and has, in recent years, been given an unusually explicit attention both in the U.S. and in the homes of the classic European public-sector institutions. Discussion has largely been promoted by critics of the state as allocator.

The FCC has increasingly sought to exercise its jurisdiction by increasing the free play of market forces through promoting competition rather than exercising regulatory power. The deregulation movement that has so strongly marked American communications policy in recent years is not confined to broadcasting. The most important event—the AT&T consent decree (settled in 1982)—resulted in the break-up of the world's largest corporation so as to promote competition and remove the need for regulation, which was (and is) generally perceived in the United States as an unnecessary cost and a brake on innovation.

Because of the perceived inadequacies of regulation and the opportunities for introducing competition into certain telecommunication services (notably long-distance telephony) presented by new transmission technologies (e.g., terrestrial microwave and communications satellites) a telecommunications regime that had endured for more than half a century was dismantled.

A recent exchange between the head of the FCC's Office of Plans and Policy, Peter Pitsch (who served on the Reagan transition team for the Federal Trade Commission in 1981), and Timothy Brennan of the Economic Policy Office of the Department of Justice, signals the political tendencies in play and delineates the intellectual field in question. For Pitsch (1984), technological innovation (VCR and cable) is introducing competition and diminishing the legitimate role of the regulator.

> For most people over-the-air commercial TV is an extremely efficient means of distributing the programming that they desire. (Pitsch, 1984, p.22)

Pitsch does not pause to reflect on the contradiction between these two positions; he sees a diminished, residual role for regulation because of the absence of perfect competition in U.S. commercial broadcasting.

Brennen's (1984) commentary notes a number of recent deregulatory practices of the FCC but argues that a policy model based on a theory of competition and the virtues of the marketplace is inappropriate to broadcasting. Because of the technological barriers to marketplace entry (the finite nature of the radio spectrum), and because there is no direct economic relationship of exchange between viewers and broadcasters, the broadcast-television market is one delineated by the relationships between advertisers and broadcasters, and broadcasters and program producers. Indeed, broadcasting has the characteristics of a public good (though Brennan does not explicitly use this category):

> There is no economical way to keep non-paying viewers from watching. This inability to charge viewers directly prevents broadcasters from profiting on the basis of meeting their audiences' desires, potentially causing an inferior mix of programs. (Brennan, 1984, p.30)

Moreover, the cost of public-good alternatives to broadcast television may be so high as to price the new delivery systems out of the market. This is by no means a purely theoretical concern. The cost of cable subscription is sufficiently high to provoke substantial numbers of U.S. subscribers to disconnect from systems. Cable theft (unauthorized and unpaid for reception of cable signals), in some franchises, constitutes 50% of subscriptions. The burden of Brennan's critique is that, for provision of broadcasting services, a perfect market does not exist. The reasons, in addition to spectrum scarcity, are high initial capitalization requirements, and the high costs of policing alternative delivery methods.

Brennan's view that the competitive-market paradigm is inappropriate for broadcasting is one that will come as no surprise to those socialized in the ethos of public-sector institutions and public-service broadcasting. But competitive market theory may still be an interesting point of departure for broadcasting policy-analysis. For it still remains to be demonstrated that U.S. commercial broadcast TV cannot be said to be:

> for most people . . . an extremely efficient means of distributing the programming that they desire. (Pitsch, 1984, p.22)

It also remains to be demonstrated that public-service broadcasting distributes the programming that most people desire. The BBC's history is replete with examples of audiences preferring alternatives (Radio Luxembourg, Radio Normandy, AFN, ITV, the pirates of the 1960s and 1980s). Canadians watch considerable U.S. or Canadian commercial TV. PBS in the U.S. is the fief of an elite, while mass audiences remain with the networks. Neither commercial broadcasting as practiced in the U.S. nor public-service broadcasting of the European model can confidently be said to maximize consumer welfare. Both modes of broadcasting, whether notionally competitive or regulated, share characteristics that make them extremely unresponsive to consumer demand. It is similarly difficult to assert that high-aggregate consumption corresponds with high-aggregate satisfaction.

> Economic theory suggests that an unregulated competitive marketplace will efficiently provide consumers with what they want, as long as each available product can be bought and sold in a well functioning market. (Brennan, 1984, p.30)

The principle characteristic of a well-functioning market is that it is perfectly competitive, which in turn depends on:

1. Large number of buyers and sellers.
2. Individual transactions being small relative to the total size of the market.
3. The product traded being homogenous and there being substitutes for it readily available.
4. Buyers and sellers enjoying perfect information.
5. Freedom of entry to the market.
    (Conditions drawn from Gellhorn & Pierce, 1982, pp. 30–31).

It is clear that few of these conditions are satisfied in any mass-communication market. Neither in the newspaper or broadcasting industries are there large numbers of sellers in any particular geographical market. Depending on the nature of the transaction studied (e.g., buying a newspaper or a cinema admission ticket), condition two may be satisfied, but, in terms of other transactions (e.g., allocation of radio frequencies as a zero-cost transaction, the purchase of rights to intellectual property, talent or particular spectacles), usually will not be.

Condition three is rarely satisfied. *The Financial Times* is only to a limited extent substitutable for *The Daily Mirror* the *Neue Zürcher Zeitung* or *The Philadelphia Inquirer*. Indeed, the whole point of mass communications is to differentiate each information commodity so that one is not substitutable for another. One watches *Dallas* weekly *because* each episode is different. Similarly, condition four cannot be satisfied if economic exchange is to take place in communication goods. Excluding the deviance of "film buffs" or other hobbyists, consumers customarily purchase information to become informed or experience new gratifications, and it is only after consumption of the information that the buyer is able to determine whether his or her welfare has been augmented by the purchase; whether financial and/or time expenditure was worth it.

Condition five is again satisfied only in rare circumstances. Newspaper production has formidable barriers to entry because of high capitalization required; film and TV-program producers endeavor to raise barriers to entry by the purchase and assertion of intellectual property rights, the development of a star system, and high budget productions and so on; and the scarcity of the radio spectrum and the high cost of alternatives such as cable constitute high barriers to entry in television distribution.

Communications, and broadcasting in particular, is not exceptional in enjoying less than perfectly competitive markets. Such conditions obtain for most economic activity, and Galbraith among others (see, inter alia, Galbraith, 1973) suggests that economics needs a new theoretical paradigm that will cohere around the normative *noncompetitive* market conditions rather than around an increasingly mythical notion of competition. Indeed the durability of the paradigm of the competitive market is a prime support for Galbraith's contention that:

> Economics is not primarily an expository science, it also serves the controlling economic interest. (Galbraith, 1973, p.xii)

Communications poses further problems to neoclassical economic analysis. Not only does the absence of "perfect-competition" conditions exist in the communications industries, but in other areas as well, e.g., the steel or automobile industries. But problems arise out of the specific characteristics of information-as-a-commodity. Unlike steel or shoes, information is not destroyed in consumption; thus, the marginal cost of adding consumers to an information market is characteristically very low in relation to the cost of production of the information commodity. The difference between 'first copy' and 'second and subsequent' copy costs of newspapers well exemplifies this characteristic of information. The first-copy cost includes the salaries and expenses of journalists and photographers, printing and the cost of ink and paper. Second and subsequent copies cost only their material costs in ink, paper, wear on type and presses and so on. The rapid decline in marginal cost of serving additional consumers is even more marked in broadcasting. (At a certain point, the cost of transmission facilities to serve, say, the last 1% of population living in terrain where propagation of signals is poor, far exceeds the proportion of the cost of service borne by each 1% of the 99%.) Thus, there are very considerable entry barriers to new suppliers once well-established enterprises are in place. New entrants to the market are vulnerable to predatory pricing, the costs of which existing suppliers can spread over a wide consumer base. There are, of course, niches in the information market, and there is a class of information where returns can be maximized by high pricing so as to confine the information to relatively few purchasers. Share-tipping newsletters or the *Economist* 'Foreign Report' are relatively public examples of this class of information, where value is dependent, not just on the quality of the product, but on its restricted circulation. Information of this kind also lends itself to being sold in successive markets differentiated by price and time; for early sight of intelligence on, for example, the foreign policy implications of a quarrel in the royal family of Saudi Arabia, subscribers to the *Economist Foreign Report* will pay a premium. The same information will be sold later at a lower price in elite journals like *The Economist* itself, and, later still, by journalists in the daily press who have themselves acquired it from the 'Foreign Report.'

Markets of this kind exist in the stratification of film exhibition between first- and second-run theaters and in the cascading of a particular film property through theatrical exhibition, premium cable, and basic cable channels and broadcast television. There are, then, no categorical differentiations of mass and specific markets for information, only different strategies that may be used to maximize returns on the sale of information.

Information is not the only commodity to exhibit the phenomenon of low marginal costs, but few other commodities exhibit characteristics of imperishability and inexhaustibility in consumption. Again these characteristics may be exploited in different ways, but each has the shared feature of favoring existing enterprises as long as intellectual property rights can be successfully asserted. The continuing interest in Chaplin films or in *I Love Lucy* permits the owners of these intellectual properties to continue to exploit them. Since these goods were not exhausted in their initial consumpion, they remain as actual and potential competitors to new entrants to the information market. New entrants can always be undercut on price, since initial costs for old products have long since been recouped and only the marginal costs of further exhibition remain to be recovered. MGM's recycling of dance segments from its musicals in *That's Dancing*, or the packaging of heterogeneous old movies for television under the Omnibus titles *Nostalgia* or *The Worst of Hollywood*, exemplify these characteristics of the information commodity.

There are, then, specific characteristics of information that ensure that the paradigm of the competitive market applies imperfectly, if at all, to its exchange. To these characteristics (and, following Galbraith, the limited general applicability of the market model) we may add the characteristics of the distribution systems for electronic media goods that render the markets in which they are exchanged imperfectly competitive. Neoclassical economic theory recognizes a class of goods or services that are

> indivisible and non-excludable. National defense, the provision of police and fire services for the community, mosquito abatement, public radio and television, weather forecasts, and clear air are examples of public goods exhibiting these characteristics. They are indivisable in that consumption by one person of the protection offered by the armed forces does not diminish the possibility of its consumption by another. (Gellhorn & Pierce, 1982, p. 18)

Clearly, public goods are divisible and excludable. Private security firms offer their services of crime prevention and suppression only to those who pay; the military, in executing a campaign, may decide to retreat and deny protection to a group of people. But, equally clearly, there is a difference between these services and those—the sale of cabbages or domestic labor, for example—to which the classic competitive market model applies. Broadcasting falls into the category of public goods. The information distributed is, within a given time span and (depending on power and frequency of transmission) geographical location, indivisible. Efforts to assimilate broadcast services to the normative market patterns of consumption, and deny the free-riding characteristics of public goods, have not met with much success. Attempts to remodel the market for broadcasting services to more closely reproduce a classic price system (e.g., through scrambled transmission of signals) has proven an unattractive and excessively costly means of delivering information in the United States.

Wometco Home Theater (WHT), for example, transmitted a single channel of feature films in scrambled form in the greater Philadelphia area from 1982 to 1984. WHT charged subscribers $24.95 per month and an additional $3.95 per month for late-night 'adult' films. Subscribers declined from 20,000 in 1982 to 4,400 in November 1984, when the service was terminated. Such subscription services require, it is estimated, 60,000 subscribers to break even, and in the

1982–84 period 16 such services ceased operation in the United States (*Philadelphia Inquirer*, November 28, 1984, p.91).

Other attempts to introduce competitive market conditions into the public-good provision of broadcasting have adopted new distribution technologies—broadband cable and broadcasting by satellite. Each of these technologies has been seen (see, inter alia, Pitsch, 1984) as abolishing the scarcity in the radio spectrum that has limited the number of broadcasters, which, in turn rendered broadcasting services intrinsically uncompetitive. Certainly, technical change and innovation can create competitive conditions where none existed before: the development of microwave and later satellite transmission in long distance telecommunications has abolished what was previously a natural monopoly. But satellite broadcasting maintains the public-good characteristics of terrestrial broadcasting. Indeed it is arguably possessed of greater public-good characteristics than terrestrial broadcasting television, since it is not as seriously limited by geography as is terrestrial broadcasting. Broadband cable (actually a rather ancient technology dating in the United States from 1949, Canada from 1952, and the U.K. from 1955) has the economic characteristics of a natural monopoly, not a competitive market. That is, it is a business in which economies of scale apply formidably (with existing technologies) so that, in a given geographical area, supply can be performed at minimum cost by a single supplier.

Payment for broadcasting services through a license fee is a form of service through the price system and, here too, the public-good characteristics of broadcasting create a free-rider problem. Avoidance of broadcast-receiving license fees in the U.K. is moderately widespread (in Northern Ireland, endemic) and policing and collection of license fees a significant cost (in 1985, 6.75%).

Some of these arguments are not specific to broadcasting, or indeed to communication industries. Others are specific to information industries or, (like those of scarcity of the spectrum, the public-good characteristics of broadcasting and the imperfectly competitive nature of substitute delivery systems) to television. However, it is a one-finger exercise to demonstrate that broadcasting has characteristics that render it imperfectly susceptible to organization and analysis on a market basis. The question remains *how* imperfect the broadcasting market is, and what the merits and demerits are of operating broadcasting through an admittedly imperfect market regime or through some state-regulated system.

Competition is deemed to optimize economic efficiency in two modes: productive efficiency and allocative efficiency. There seems no reason to doubt that broadcasting is susceptible to competition that will maximize (if indeed competition does maximize) productive efficiency. In the U.S., broadcast television remains dominant even when subjected to competition from alternative delivery systems. In the U.K., there has been virtually no investment in cable systems in spite of the government's encouragement, still less any enthusiasm for new satellite services. Terrestrial broadcasting remains almost the only distribution system for television because of its superior productive efficiency. In program-production, efficiency maximization is probably quite closely related to competition, though with significant advantages for highly-capitalized producers and for those—like the European public-service broadcasters—who enjoy guaranteed access to distribution. The high cost of British television production, and the relative absence of lower-priced competition, is due largely to the absence of competitive pressure for cost reduction, which, in turn, follows from the barriers to entry created by union-closed shops, the vertical integration of producers and distributors, and the structure of the industry's taxation regime.

It is in its allocative efficiency (or lack of it) that the peculiarities of terrestrial television broadcasting inhere. Reception and consumption of television is of public goods, because the benefits of television are nonexcludable and imperfectly sensitive to pressures of consumer demand. In origination and transmission of broadcast TV, competition between television services can only be limited because of the shortage of radio-spectrum capacity (though this shortage bears much more heavily on European states than it does in North America, and they have characteristically allocated spectrum to achieve maximum coverage rather than competition). In the U.K. (with four terrestrial national channels), 99.2% of the population is covered, including all communities of 1,000 or more. The aim is to cover all communities of more than 200 people, and to this end a new transmitter is commissioned every week. But there is clearly competition for viewers' attention and, in systems that are financed wholly or partly by advertising, for advertising revenue, when two or more channels are simultaneously available to viewers. It is this competition that enables advocates of the competitive market to claim that competition is working as indeed it may—in terms of the product assembled by commercial broadcasters, the creation of audiences for advertisements', or the *audience commodity* (Smythe, 1981). However the existence of this competitive market is generally seen by deregulators as maximising allocative efficiency and an agency through which consumer sovereignty is exercised and the audience given what it wants.

There is a partial truth in this argument. If I have established qualifications and limits to the existence of competition in television broadcasting, it is not to argue that audience preference has no place in the determination of television programming and that allocative efficiency is not influenced by the presence or absence of competition in provision of television signals. But I do not think Pitsch's (1984) claim can be sustained:

> For most people over-the-air commercial TV is an extremely efficient means of distributing the programming they desire! (p.22)

If we examine the transaction that takes place between the television audience and broadcaster, we find two resources exchanged by the audience for the gratification it receives from broadcasters. First there is money, in the form of the cost of the receiving apparatus, electricity, etc. expended per unit of programming consumed, and in the form of cost in commodities purchased resulting from the expenditure of the vendor of those commodities on television advertising or the broadcast-receiving license fee. Both these monetary costs are extremely low and have been calculated by Ehrenberg and Barwise (1982) to amount to less than two pence per viewed hour for the U.K. viewer. The second resource exchanged by audiences is time. If we take expenditure of the resources of time and money by audiences, we find that, per hour of leisure activity, television consumption can be performed at an extremely low cost relative to many other leisure activities. Compared, for instances, to eating out, cinema going, dancing, watching professional sport, or driving, television is a very low-cost activity. Because it is a very low-cost activity, it is reasonable to suppose that its consumption is not particularly sensitive to the nature of the product or service it offers.

Competition for the leisure-time expenditure of viewers is one in which we can see the vital criterion of cost of gratifications being very significant. Broadcast-television consumption tends to be high among sections of the audience for whom the cost of television (low in absolute terms though it may be) is high relative to their capacity for leisure expenditure, either through low-disposable income (the poor, the young, the old), much time for leisure activity (the old, the unemployed, the rich), or both. When closely comparable competitors to broadcast television become available (e.g., pay TV), the evidence seems to be that demand for them is extremely price sensitive. It cannot therefore be assumed that there *is* general audience satisfaction with broadcast television, that it gives the audience what it wants. It can only be assumed that it *is* an exceptionally good bargain.

A further limitation on the achievement of maximal allocative efficiency (in respect of the viewer as consumer) by broadcast television inheres in the primary economic exchange taking place, not between viewers and program originators, but between program originators and the funding sources—the state or commercial advertisers. In the case of the state (whether through direct allocations from the general state budget, as in Canada, or through the state employing its powers to tax and raise revenue earmarked for broadcasting, as in the U.K. or the Federal Republic of Germany), the relationship between funder and broadcaster is surprisingly indirect. The Conservative Canadian government of Brian Mulroney has been unable to dislodge one of the preceding Liberal prime minister's closest associates, Pierre Juneau, from the office of President of the CBC, and the BBC's skeptical coverage of the South Atlantic War incurred the wrath of Mrs. Thatcher's government. In these public-service broadcasting orders, broadcasters enjoy substantial autonomy and absence of accountability to audiences or revenue sources. In systems financed by advertising (and the public service systems of the U.K. and Canada secure part of their funding from advertising, as do those of other states such as West Germany or the Netherlands), the economic exchange between broadcasters and advertisers is such that competition to maximize allocative efficiency is exercised in a highly specific manner. Because of the public-good characteristics of television broadcasting, potential viewers cannot be excluded from reception, and differentiated audiences(except in terms of physical location of settlement) cannot be constructed and sold to advertisers. To be sure, some differentiation does take place, but highly specifically differentiated packages of viewers cannot be sold to advertisers with the same degree of precision as, say, magazine journalism can sell an audience of AB males aged 15–25, or directmail advertising can sell an audience of suburban dog owners. Thus, broadcasters do not compete in the sale of audiences to advertisers by constructing highly differentiated audiences but, principally, by constructing large undifferentiated audience packages. Thus CBS competes (or does not) successfully with ABC by offering advertisers a lower cost per 1,000 viewers, which CBS in turn achieves (or does not) by scheduling programming that maximizes gross viewership.

While audience choices between programming offered on different channels at the same time within the same geographical area are significant choices, they are choices within parameters set by a system which does not maximize allocative efficiency (vis-a-vis audiences) whether 'competition' between channels occurs in a state-funded, regulated-broadcasting, or 'commercial'-advertising financed system.

For the reasons adumbrated above, allocative efficiency is not particularly high in any television broadcasting system. What can confidently be said is that audiences can and do express preferences between alternatives available at equivalent costs. The problems of sensibly generalizing on the basis of audience ratings aside, there seems no reason to doubt that, in the U.K. ITV more closely approximates 'what they want' than does Channel 4, or that, in the U.S., of new programs launched in the 1984–85 season, *Miami Vice* is closer to what audiences want than was *Paper Dolls*.

But this expression of preference between given alternatives is hardly more reliable as an index of audience demand than was Bezonian's choice an index of his. Yet such choices are the only indices available to policy makers and analysts when they are concerned with a public good. The introduction, by the FCC, of a more market-oriented broadcasting system in the U.S. is unlikely to serve audiences better, for the same reason that the introduction of broad-band cable in the U.K. (in the unlikely event of investors being found for such a project) is unlikely to give audiences what they want. Neither broadcast television nor cable have the characteristics of competitive markets; and audience reaction to broadcast TV is extremely hard to interpret as an expression of preference, because only very indirect economic exchanges take place between broadcasters and audiences. Nonetheless, such signals that audiences send are ignored by broadcasters and policy makers at their peril, and the preferences expressed between, say, CBS and NBC, CBC and PBS, or ITV and BBC2 are significant preferences. Those who are producing for the television market must take note of audience's consumption patterns. There are no grounds for supposing that higher ratings for *Fame* than *Nova* do not reflect corresponding audience preferences. But it cannot be assumed that *Fame* is necessarily what audiences want, or that existing broadcasting orders deliver efficiently an optimal repertoire of desired programming.

The paradigm of the competitive market is one that is particularly inappropriate to the analysis and organization of broadcast television. The system has characteristics of a monopoly in transmission (whether because of the entry barriers or the high costs for distribution systems) and in reception, in so far as the software consumed has economic characteristics that define and enforce a highly specific market with less-than-perfectly competitive characteristics. It seems, therefore, very unlikely that television broadcasting can ever by successfully deregulated, and that Brennan's (1984), rather than Pitsch's (1984), paradigm is to be preferred.

The pressure by ideologists of the free market, whether in the U.S. (e.g., Pitsch), in the U.K. (Veljanovski & Bishop, 1983) or Canada (e.g., Globerman, 1983) to remove broadcasting from the regulated or state sphere and maximize productive and allocative efficiency seems particularly perverse. There seems little doubt that productive efficiency would rise if program production were more exposed to competitive pressure than it is now. But there can also be little doubt that such a policy would be attended by declining production outside the United States—so great is the competitive advantage enjoyed by U.S. producers (for a contrary view, see Globerman & Vining, 1984).

Broadcasting is an industry that national governments have, from its inception, seen as a vital national interest, and one which—despite concomitant inefficiences—has to be national in character. It is, though, in allocative efficiency, giving the public what it wants, that increases in efficiency, consumer welfare, are less easy to see following the introduction of a more competitive regime.

The public-good characteristics of television broadcasting consumption are such that allocative efficiency is unlikely to be heightened by competition. Yet there seems to be no reason to doubt that, both within public service broadcasting systems—like the U.K. and West Germany—or commercial systems like the U.S., a schizophrenic pattern of audience behavior exists whereby high consumption co-exists with public dissatisfaction. This conundrum can be analytically unravelled by explaining that television viewing is a remarkably inexpensive leisure pursuit and consumption is therefore likely to be highly insensitive to less-than-complete audience satisfaction. But policy makers still have to grapple with the problem of maximizing consumer satisfaction in a situation in which the only real indicator—quantity of consumption measured in the ratings—is highly imperfect. In all television-broadcasting markets, it seems possible to argue that highly contradictory indications of audience satisfaction may co-exist, and that, in a variety of national broadcasting orders, programming is determined by an elite. In the U.S., this elite is committed to maximizing consumer expenditure; in Britain, West Germany, and Canada, elites are committed to the achievement of ideological goals.

The problem, then, is not one that is likely to be solved by deregulation; the nature of broadcast television is such that competitive-market conditions and the maximization of consumer welfare (through increased allocative efficiency) will not likely arise. It is clear, though, that, however well established the historical and theoretical basis for regulation in broadcasting, whichever of the variety of North American or European models of nonmarket allocations are followed, regulation has characteristically been either ineffective (the U.S.) or the instrument of elites who capture the resources of the state sector in broadcasting and use them for their own ends (ends which may or may not command substantial popular support and assent).

The authoritarianism of the Canadian and British models provide no satisfactory answer; the democratic control differently institutionalized in the broadcasting orders of the Netherlands and West Germany have each proven defective in important ways. The organizational form and mechanisms of accountability and response to audience demand remain to be created for broadcast television.

REFERENCES

Brennan, T. (1984, October 8). Limits of the marketplace model. *Broadcasting*, p. 30.
Caplan, J., & Sauvageau F. (chairs). (1986). *Report of the Task Force on Broadcasting Policy*. Ottawa. Minister of Supply and Services Canada.
Ehrenberg, A., & Barwise, T. (1982). *How much does UK television cost?* London: London Business School.
Galbraith, J. K. (1973). *Economics and the public purpose*. Boston, MA: Houghton Mifflin.
Gellhorn, E., & Pierce, R. (1982). *Regulated Industries*. St. Paul, MN: Nutshell Books.
Globerman, S. (1983). *Cultural regulation in Canada*. Montreal, Canada: Institute for Research on Public Policy.
Globerman S., & Vining, A. (1984). *Bilateral cultural free trade: The U.S.-Canadian case*. [mimeo] Faculty of Business Administration, Simon Fraser University, Burnaby.
Intermedia. (1985). Bimonthly. London: International Institute of Communication.
Peacock, A. (Chairman). (1986). *Report of the Committee on Financing the BBC* (Cmnd 9824). London: Home Office, HMSO.
Pitsch, P. (1984, October 22). In defence of the marketplace. *Broadcasting*, p.22.
Smythe, D. (1981). *Dependency road: Communications, capitalism, consciousness and Canada*. Norwood, NJ: Ablex Publishing Corp.
Veljanovski, C., & Bishop, W. (1983). *Choice by cable*. London: Institute of Economic Affairs.

32

The Internationalization of TV Entertainment

MURIEL G. CANTOR
The American University

JOEL M. CANTOR
CRT Associates

This chapter concerns the evolution of overseas-distribution patterns of U.S. television. This distribution process entails such issues as the organization of artistic production, the legal and economic contexts in which programs are produced and distributed, the content of the shows most likely to be seen abroad, and, when possible, the audiences' reactions to those shows. Our main emphases are the economic and political contexts in which shows are distributed and broadcast, and the relationship of economics and politics to culture and cultural change. We do not argue that economics is everything. Rather, we try to show the complex interconnections between the political-economic milieu and the ways in which American culture is adopted (or rejected) in different countries. Specifically, we are questioning the commonly held belief that U.S.-made programs still dominate local cultures in both developed and developing countries. Although the American television industry is the largest worldwide, and American-made programs are seen in practically every country where television exists, it exerts differential power in various countries (Cantor & Cantor, 1986).

A specific concern here is how buyers and sellers of American programs, themselves, understand the distribution patterns and how those patterns might continue to evolve in the near future. This paper does not advance the view that the principal issue involved is neocolonialism—that there is a one-way flow of television programming from the West to other nations (Hamelink, 1983; Mattelart, 1979; Schiller, 1969, 1976; Varis, 1984). Because the model we present is dynamic, not static, our conclusions will also differ. Rather than finding American cultural products dominating overseas markets, our findings confirm those earlier drawn by Katz and Wedell (1977, p. 161) that such a view is "oversimplified." A model more appropriate to the interflow of cultural products among countries is a matrix with multiple sources and overlapping patterns of influence. We find also that, although still popular with audiences in both developed and developing countries, U.S.-made programs must now compete with suppliers who did not exist in the 1950s and 1960s, when overseas markets were first opening.[1]

THE RESEARCH

About 50 persons working at administrative or productions levels in the television industry in six different countries were interviewed. Of these, 43 were involved specifically in the distribution of television programs to overseas markets. Twenty-one interviews were conducted in Europe (Summer 1984) and the others in Los Angeles (Summer 1985). Some of those interviewed had worked in the field since the late 1940s and could be called pioneers—they were among the first to reestablish overseas film markets soon after World War II ended and then include television programs among their wares.

The informants overall were articulate, opinionated and conversant about the controversies concerning the export of U.S. programs, and willing to be taped. Most of the Americans, and a few of the Europeans, had stayed in overseas distribution over the years. Also, each knew, or knew of, each other quite well. Many also recommended overseas associates or business contacts in other countries who had become close friends as well as customers over the years because of frequent meetings over the years at international television markets and film festivals. They could be described as members of small societies or extended social networks.

The group ranged from typical businessmen cynical about the types and quality of programs bought and sold in other countries and amazed that even the worst would be bought, to civil servants with small budgets who had to find programs they could afford for state channels that would be equally popular with both party ideologues and the general public. What all had in common was the responsibility for making or setting up the actual business deals.

According to our informants, three stages can be discerned in the introduction of U.S. television entertainment to other countries and their subsequent development as autonomous centers of production. Each stage expands on and incorporates the earlier ones, so that the final stage for each country becomes a mix of domestic production, some foreign imports and, when possible, export of domestic productions to meet regional (and foreign) needs. Thus, each country that started out importing from the U.S. can itself evolve or has already

---

[1] Our conclusions also question the validity of using the concept of hegemony to understand the motives of those who work in the commercial distribution of entertainment media worldwide. Our data indicate that, both at the administrative and working levels, the participants, buyers, and sellers, domestic and foreign, seem driven more by market forces than by consideration of cultural consequences. The only "ideology" that we could identify was the urge to sell or air more popular television programs than their competitors in the same business.

evolved through such stages.[2] In Stage One, aside from local TV news, sports events and off-the-shelf domestic films, production resources are not sufficient (the infrastructure that is necessary—the producers, writers, directors, actors, financing, studios, etc.) to develop full-time broadcasting schedules for either state or commercial channels. At this stage, inoffensive and affordable foreign programs, whatever the source, are imported from other countries to fill air-time that would otherwise go empty. In the case of commercial channels, longer broadcasting days are essential to attract sponsors. In Stage Two, the infrastructure begins to evolve and local production starts, first with radio formats (such as dramas, lectures, variety, talk shows) adapted to television, and then with original productions. These then gradually replace or displace imported programs which have lost popularity or which station owners think have become too expensive to acquire from outside sources. (As sales in these countries decline, U.S. distributors shift their selling efforts to new countries coming on line in Stage One.) In Stage Three, even countries with full-scale production capability still buy imported programs for domestic viewing which would be cheaper to buy than produce. At this stage, they also try to export programs which might appeal to foreign markets, especially those countries that share their languages and cultural heritages.

Each of these stages can be described in greater detail.

Stage One

The U.S. distributors started with the advantage of large ready-to-ship invento-ries of films already familiar to foreign audiences and television programs of all types which could be made available at minimal cost (editing and dubbing) to foreign markets. They could also be extremely profitable, because their basic cost of production had already been recovered from domestic sales to cinemas and television networks and independent stations as first and reruns. Conse-quently, any fees charged above the basic costs of shipping prints and sales commissions would be just more profit.

Gandy (1980), among others, has suggested that U.S. exporters used this built-in cost/profit advantage to act as a cartel and flood newly opened foreign markets with programs dumped at lower prices to crowd out competition and prevent local production from starting. No one we interviewed claimed that they or any other U.S. distributor ever thought it possible to prevent local production from developing. Some were even puzzled by our questions, be-

---

[2]According to Katz and Wedell (1977, pp. 68–69), there are two phases of institutionalization: an initial phase in which one of five existing "metropolitan" models is chosen for the new broadcasting system; and a second phase, in which the broadcasting systems are adapted "to the social, political and economic context" of each country. They speculate also of a third phase in which the disparate pattern of development will shift toward more homogeneous structures of broadcasting.

cause they saw low pricing as benevolent, not cut-throat, a common-sense business tactic, necessary and realistic for the time. One could not open up sales territories unless one made it easy for potential customers with limited assets to buy sufficient programs to get their stations started and keep them on the air long enough to attract advertisers. To have done otherwise would have put the stations into an impossible bind—they needed programs to attract advertisers, and, without revenue from advertisers, they could not buy programs to attract advertisers to have the revenue, and so forth. The exporters also knew that they would be able to charge higher fees if and when the stations were able to increase their revenues.

Some pointed out that, while their sales strategy helped local television get started, the real opposition came from other local businesses. Cinema and theatre owners lobbied government officials and legislatures to limit broadcast schedules so that they would not lose their audiences to free films. Newspapers encouraged opposition to television because they did not want to lose any advertising income.

Stage Two

Some we interviewed claimed that, without U.S.-business and/or local government subsidies, indigenous production might never have gotten started when it did. With lesser charges, local stations accumulated the investment capital needed to acquire other programs from local producers. In effect, Hollywood subsidized the start of its own future competition. Without using the concepts as such, the respondents also seemed to understand the constraints of ethnocentrism and class-consciousness, because they knew at the outset from their experience in the U.S. market that none of their programs could ever satisfy the demand everywhere for domestic drama based on everyday problems. Therefore, to develop daytime audiences for advertisers, local production would be essential, because soap operas did not "travel" well (their word) between cultures. Also, with certain exceptions, comedy based on local circumstances could not travel. For example, a Johnny Carson opening monologue referring to outdated topical events would not make sense to foreign audiences. One exporter also pointed out that, when you dub into local languages, you cannot dub a play on words.

He summarized the problem as:

> What is funny to the American mentality might be very different from what is funny to the French mentality. The type of hospital comedies that Britons like just wouldn't be funny to Americans. *Sergeant Bilko* can spoof the army in England, but not in Germany, where military uniforms are not allowed on the screen, or in Greece, where the government won't permit fun to be made of the army. Danes do not find British comedies humorous where men dress up as women.

However, if general enough, certain types of comedy, such as situation comedies (sitcoms) can be remade as local productions. *I Love Lucy* has been an outstanding success in almost all countries over the years. Some attribute its appeal to its slapstick comedy which, like circuses, seem to travel easily. Others suggest it was due to good dubbing. Following script outlines, actors from the immediate region can add local slang and emphases which subtly transform the characters into local citizens. (The fact that Desi is Cuban-born or "third-world" makes the transformation even easier.) When they succeeded, the episodes of *I Love Lucy* thus reappeared as "localized."

In almost all countries, local or "localized" productions consistently outdraw those that are imported. Gresham's Law can be applied to television programming—better local programs will crowd out even good imported programs. For example, *Dallas* might have been helped to even greater popularity in France by the established stage actors and actresses who played the characters as "French," and in Germany by the actors and actresses who played them as "German." When it failed miserably in Japan, contributing to the failure might have been the inability of those dubbing, no matter how hard they tried, to "stretch" the characters sufficiently to make them credible as "Japanese." One syndicator suggested it would have failed anyway because (according to Gresham's Law) TV Asahi had foolishly scheduled it opposite a long-running variety show on a national network that had always had high ratings (Lohr, 1982).

Stage Three

According to our informants, there has been a structural shift throughout the world from dependency on American programs toward self-supply and using additional suppliers, especially regional. As one put it:

> If an atom bomb were to wipe out Hollywood today, three countries would never miss us: the U.K., Japan, and Brazil. They produce all the programs they need and are now at the point where they would never ever have to buy another from the U.S.

According to another, such change is inevitable:

> Take Japan, for example. It had to come. Right now (Summer 1985), there are basically no American programs in primetime on any of the six Japanese networks. People want to see their own faces, their own color, their own scenes, their own locales, their own story lines. They don't want to see another story about a man who is a private detective in Santa Monica who goes up and down Wilshire Boulevard, and it is an American actor with a Japanese voice dubbed in. They would prefer to see a detective story set in Yokohama maybe, or Osaka, and the guy is actually speaking Japanese and he is eating Japanese food and is drinking sake with his dinner instead of Scotch.

They also report that any television industry in a country with an advertising base large enough or with a government willing to pay all the costs involved would rarely buy programs from the U.S. Any funding short of full production makes them depend more on lower-cost imported programs.

The U.S. distributors sort their overseas markets into three tiers of customers. The top tier includes Brazil, Japan, and the U.K., all of whom have the option of importing U.S. programs. All other countries, whatever the structure of broadcasting (public, private, or mixed) still depend on outside suppliers to complete their broadcast schedules. The middle tier includes television networks and stations, cable systems, and video outlets in countries such as Canada, Australia, Mexico, France, Germany, Italy, Scandinavia, South Africa, etc., all of which have resources to make some (or most) programs and even export some. However, they still need to import certain types of U.S. programs, those with costly production values difficult to imitate because of the expense involved (for example, *Dallas*) or formats such as action-adventure shows with special effects which they have neither the technology nor training to reproduce. The final tier, the only overseas markets that U.S. exporters can still count on for numerous sales, include the other Central and South American countries, most of Africa, Asia, the Middle East, the Caribbean, and the thousands of independent and pirate stations that have sprung up around the world. This tier also includes the superchannels which are coming online and use satellites to reach viewers in large regional areas.

Why would countries in the middle tier still buy programs from the U.S.? As one exporter explained,

> Everyone else in the world needs us because they do not have the purchasing power through advertisers and agencies to produce enough. A perfect example is Australia. We sell a half-hour of a prime-time network product for $6000. To make something considerably less in production quality (I am not talking about audience appeal—I am talking about production quality) must cost them now $50,000 per half-hour. The only reason they can afford to make those $50,000 half-hour programs is, we subsidize their production at $6000.

Nearly all the countries in the middle tier could eventually join countries in the top tier, because each exports at least some programs somewhere in the world. Over 1,300 television companies from 110 countries registered for the 22nd annual MIP-TV meeting in Cannes in 1985 (Marches des International Programes des Television) to buy and sell television programs. Just six countries supplied nearly 900 companies: the U.S., France, Great Britain, Canada, Australia, and Italy, affirming the position of the U.S. and the U.K. in the top tier and indicating which of the other countries might eventually join them (Dempsey, 1985)[3]

Although most distributors would of course try to sell to all possible buyers,

[3]Because of the convenient location of Cannes in Southern France, the presence of so many companies from France and Italy could indicate that MIP-TV serves them as "domestic" marketplaces for sales within their own countries as well as providing the opportunity to sell in the "international" market.

they know that the easiest sales would be to those markets where viewers share the same historical and cultural traditions. For example, the U.S. distributors know it would be a waste of time to compete head-to-head with Paris distributors for French-Canadian outlets. Besides preferring story-lines and themes based on French, not American, society, French-Canadians prefer the dialogue to be in Parisian French. Consequently, it is sensible for Canadian buyers to buy whatever programs they need directly from Paris. A similar situation exists for U.S. distributors in regard to French-speaking African nations. Because revenues might not offset the entire cost of dubbing, it is simpler to sell programs to the French, who, on dubbing them for domestic use, might then distribute them to the African market.

Besides other outlets, some of these companies buy and sell programs for viewers who migrated to other countries and prefer their own entertainment or formats familiar to them. There are Japanese, Spanish, and Korean channels in the Los Angeles area. Mexico and Brazil have found buyers in Europe for their telenovelas (soap operas). Mexico, with its export channel, SIN (Spanish International Network), has staked out a type of regional control over audiences in the Miami and south Texas areas because its outlets have very high local ratings.

A review by Schement, Gonzalez, Lum, and Valencia (1984) of studies on the flow of television across borders also questions the view that any single nation, even the U.S., is still capable of a worldwide cultural hegemony through television. They also cite Mexico and Brazil as examples of nations who broke their dependency on the U.S. and proceeded to set up neighboring zones of influence, Brazil in Central and South America, and Mexico with SIN throughout the U.S.

CONCLUSION

Our research confirms more recent findings (Schement et al., 1984; Straubhaar, 1984) that the concept of single-source hegemony applied to the commerce of marketing mass media is outdated and inaccurate. The distribution of American television to major broadcasting systems throughout the world did reach a peak in the early 1970s, but since then, depending on the market involved, its influence has either declined permanently or is in continual flux, varying from year to year.[1] There is no denying that U.S.-made television and

---

[1]The drop-off of U.S. programs on Italian television is described in a *Variety* article (Werba, 1986, p. 125):

> Demise of the U.S. series, with the sole exceptions of "Dynasty" and "Dallas" (hanging in with diminished viewerships) is practically total for primetime programming on the commercial webs. . . . holds true for many filmed series. Ratings have slipped to a point where . . . [U.S. series are] still around only in daytime slots and post-post primetime. . . . [the] market will continue to soften. . . . RAI-1 [plans] a ratio of 70% for in-house product and co-ventures and 30% for imports from all foreign markets.

film entertainment is still very popular in most countries. Even in Japan, where no U.S.-made series was bought for prime time in 1985, U.S. films are well attended. However, rather than one nation controlling sales worldwide, the world marketplace has become decentralized into overlapping layers of multi-centered regional spheres of activity. American business no longer finds it easy to "dump" products regardless of price (Wells, 1972). Instead, U.S. distributors report that they have lost sales to two sources of competition: other countries exporting programs to the same markets, and home-grown production. Because of their more expensive look, there will always be markets for U.S. programs overseas. However, even though the number of stations and outlets to buy them will increase world-wide, each increase in local production and export capability also accelerates the decline of American power in the television marketplace.

REFERENCES

Cantor, M. G., & Cantor, J. M. (1986). American television in the international marketplace. *Communication Research, 13*(3), 509–520.

Dempsey, J. (1985, April 17). Private TV fuels MIP program demand. *Variety, 31*, 215.

Gandy, O., Jr. (1980). Market power and cultural imperialism. *Current Research on Peace and Violence, 1*, 47–58.

Hamelink, C. (1983). *Cultural autonomy in global communications.* New York: Longman.

Katz, E., & Wedell, G. (1977). *Broadcasting in the Third World.* Cambridge, MA: Harvard University Press.

Lohr, S. (1982, February 18). *Dallas* strikes no oil on Japanese TV. *New York Times*, p. 30.

Mattelart, A. (1979). *Multinational corporations and the control of culture: The ideological apparatuses of imperialism.* Sussex, England: Harvester Press.

Schement, J. R., Gonzalez, I. N., Lum, P., & Valencia, R. (1984). The international flow of television programs. *Communication Research, 11*, 163–182.

Schiller, H. J. (1969). *Mass communications and American empire.* Boston, MA: Beacon Press.

Schiller, H. J. (1976). *Communication and cultural dominance.* White Plains, NY: M.E. Sharpe.

Straubhaar, J. D. (1984). Brazilian television: The decline of American influence. *Communication Research, 11*, 121–140.

Varis, T. (1984). The international flow of television programs. *Journal of Communication, 34*, 143–152.

Wells, A. (1972). *Picture-tube imperialism? The impact of U.S. television on Latin America.* Maryknoll, New York: Orbis.

Werba, H. (1986, October 15). Italo TV ends its Yank program spree. *Variety*, pp. 125, 146.

33

France Confronts the New Media: Issues in National Communications and Cultural Policy*

JAMES MILLER

Hampshire College

In most nations of the West the crucial relationship between the media of public communications and the state is being reexamined, if not altered in ways that often depart dramatically from past practices. The common pattern is to lessen state-media involvement in favor of corporate, market-oriented decision making. Deregulation, privatization, denationalization, liberalization, all, more or less, describe the same phenomenon. While the ostensible short-term objectives in shifting communications and cultural-policy authority from the public to the private sphere are "economic efficiency" and greater "consumer choice," it is apparent that the long-run issues are matters central to our time: the expanding power of transnational industries, strategies to maintain national growth in a so-called information economy, and the global commodification of contemporary culture.

Various countries respond to these matters differently. In North America, for instance, the United States and Canada follow quite different paths. In Western Europe, the United Kingdom may be more like the U.S. than most of its neighbors. The situation in France is especially intriguing. There, traditions of centralized state-economic planning co-exist with entrepreneurial activity in the newest sectors of communications media. In France one can observe a country in rapid transition: abolishing state monopolies in areas of the cultural realm, while asserting state authority over emerging telematics institutions; building a state-of-the-art national information infrastructure to replace one of the least respected telephone networks in Europe; promoting technological

* Research by the writer on French communications and cultural policy during the past few years has been supported in part by Hampshire College through two faculty development grants, one from the Dana Foundation and the other from the College's National Advisory Council.

I am especially grateful to Thierry Vedel of France's CEVIPOF and CNRS for helping me to begin to understand the French media scene. Numerous other Europeans have been generous as well. None of these persons, of course, is responsible for any errors or misconceptions in this chapter.

325

development to create jobs at home while seeking to dominate international export markets. Until quite recently, at least, a consensus atypical of French politics has seemed to agree, not only on the primacy of communications and cultural policy goals, but on the tactical and strategic means of reaching them.

The uniquenesses of France may make it difficult to argue that the French case is somehow representative of other policy instances in Europe or elsewhere. Yet the very attractiveness of France as a subject for study from a communications and cultural-policy perspective lies in these special qualities, many of which are little known to American researchers and policy planners.

This paper is intended to introduce the American reader to three broad areas of the current French situation: the general structure of policy and politics as they bear on communications and cultural issues, telecommunications and telematics policy authority and activities, and state activities for broadcasting. While a general overview, the paper is necessarily selective, choosing examples to illuminate larger issues and by no means all inclusive or definitive. The paper also tends more toward description than systematic analysis. Finally, as befits a sort of primer, most of the cited references are accessible to the English-speaking reader.

INDUSTRIAL POLICY

The French government has long taken a primary role in determining the country's industrial and economic direction. Until quite recently, Left and Right have agreed on this role in principle, disagreeing mostly on matters of degree of state involvement (see Vernier-Palliez, 1986, p. 1). Because national policies for communications and culture are esssentially industrial policies, it is useful to examine some salient points of this political activity.

It is not uncommon for French policy to be couched in the politics of *projets socials*, or fairly grand schemes for societal betterment. For the Socialists, an important *projet* was stimulating economic growth while distributing its benefits equitably. This entailed increased state control of industry through nationalization. Under Socialist President François Mitterand, the French extended "the public enterprise sector to include about one-third of industrial production." This had the consequence, in the eyes of two observers, of fashioning "a powerful new instrument of international economic competition" (Cohen & Gourevitch, 1982, pp. 183–84) for French industries (see also Aujac, 1986, p. 29). Through extensive nationalization, French industrial policy planners would also be able to designate selected firms within certain industries that would be responsible to develop advanced products or services with the potential to dominate world markets. These high-technology gambles, known as "national champions," are also a part of France's approach to industrial policy. Past experience with them has been mixed, as with the Concorde aircraft, the Bull computer firm and SECAM, the French color television technology. Analyzing the latter example, a case where American technology already dominated an area the French coveted, Crane draws a conclusion that probably pertains to the national champion phenomenon generally and helps frame the recent industrial-policy objectives of the Socialists for communications and culture. "For the French," she writes,

> economic and technological dependence upon the United States portended a threat to their national survival and independence. . . . Political prestige was attached to having a domestic French technology win international adoption. France would gain more global political influence; the [color TV] standard was not only a technical symbol, but also a political symbol projecting the glory of France. (1979, pp. 38, 45)

It is not unreasonable to believe that some areas of the communications and cultural sectors have become, at least implicitly, a national champion during the past several years.

Of course, choosing the "right products" (Cohen & Gourevitch, 1982, p. 184) to become national champions, selecting the best nationalized firms to produce them, and orchestrating industrial policy appropriately are a volatile admixture of practical politics, economic forecasting, and ideology. Thus, it is not surprising that, upon attaining power, French conservatives would reverse the Socialists' nationalizing course and, apparently, begin to shift dramatically certain aspects of communications and cultural policy.

It was announced in July 1986 that some 65 firms would be privatized over the following 5 years. Their sale was expected to raise an estimated $5 billion annually which would be used, it was claimed, to lower French taxes and pay off the national deficit (Lewis, 1986a, 1986b). Mitterand immediately announced his opposition to the plan, both fearing, he said, the loss of direct political control over firms that had long been the beneficiaries of government subsidiaries and worrying that foreign investors would buy into the newly denationalized French businesses.

Despite the powers of the presidency, the conservatives' two-vote majority allowed parliamentary approval of the privatization policy. Under the new law, foreign investment in denationalized firms is limited to 20%. Ten percent of a company's stock will be reserved for purchase by the firm's employees. And the government reserves the right, when judged in the national interest, to deny a foreign investor the right to buy an interest in a firm (Lewis, 1986b).

The first three firms to be sold were a glass manufacturing firm, a leading investment bank, and an insurance company. Their collective worth was estimated at between $7 and $9 billion (Rossant, 1986; Lewis, 1986b), and two of these three had been nationalized in 1981 by the Socialists. This, however, may be just the beginning. It seems likely that socialist and conservative *cohabitation* will become increasingly strained in the near future.

Very much caught in this dramatic shift of political winds are France's telecommunications industry and electronic cultural media. One state-run television channel has been sold, the ambitions of the national cable plan have been reduced, and, in the telecommunications sector, increased competition with transnational firms may be fostered in the domestic market.

Politics of the Center

Although France is a traditionally polarized electorate, the Communists are hardly a factor any longer in deciding elections or influencing policy. And while the extreme Right has made modest gains around such inflammatory issues as the presence of foreign workers in France, the vast middle ground belongs to the several variations of conservatives and the Socialists. Ironically, the election of François Mitterand in 1981 may not have signaled the fundamental policy shifts that many expected. Rather, Cohen and Gurevitch think that in selecting Mitterand "French voters chose an alternative to the left-right face off that has completely dominated French political life . . . for a full generation" (1982, p. 188).

There may be emerging a consensus, at least within groups possessing social power, that the dictates of an increasingly internationalized economy, best indicted by France's membership in the European Community and the constant clamor of US firms to enter European markets, require abandonment of explicitly ideological positions in favor of policy pragmatism. Even at the height of Mitterand's power to make national policy, some analysts questioned the extent to which his government's actions could be recognized as Socialist. This dissolution of sharp differences between major political parties, so familiar to North Americans, may establish practical limits on the range of options available to French policy makers for communications and culture. That is, while Socialist/conservative disagreement over the privatization of one of the three state-owned television stations exists, it was *Mitterand* who earlier introduced privately operated commercial television and radio to France. The policy differences between the Socialist president and conservative premier may be, in effect, two sides of the same political coin.

LA TÉLÉMATIQUE: TELECOMMUNICATIONS AND BEYOND

Policy Authority and Industrial Policy

The French invented the neologism *télématique*, which Americans know as telematics, to express the recent convergence of three previously discrete technologies, the telephone, the computer, and video. During the past decade the French commitment to development of telematics has become so complete that it has been described as "something of a national obsession" (International Institute for Communication, 1981, p. 14). Indeed, as a national champion of industrial policy, telematics has benefitted from a striking political accord: much of the development activity was begun under Giscardians, was implemented by Socialists and continues, under changing conditions, in the context of the current unprecedented power sharing.

France, like most of Europe, vests policy and operational authority for telecommunications in its PTT, the historic monopolist. (For a history of the French PTT, see Bertho, 1981.) A recent change of name suggests France desires to maintain the PTT's centrality in the midst of telematics development: from being the Ministry of Post, Telephone and Telegraph, the PTT became Ministry of Post, Telecommunications and Telediffusion. This name change reflected the new directions in policy and public relations.

Cole and O'Rorke (1983, p. 101) list the French PTT's major responsibilities as including the following: (a) identification of needs, facilities, networks, and services; (b) determination, significantly, of technical standards; (c) establishment of policy for domestic and international purposes; (d) provision of technical assistance to foreign countries; and (e) probably most importantly, telecommunications research and development activities. It is an all-encompassing set of duties and implies preeminent policy power.

Within the PTT a crucial organizational unit is the DGT (*Direction Générale des Télécommunications*), which is responsible for administrating all aspects of French telecommunications, excluding broadcasting but including technological aspects of cable. The DGT's 1983 budget was about $12 million (Vedel, 1984, p. 9). Its revenues are generated primarily through its operation of telecommunications systems. Some 165,000 people were employed in 1983 by the DGT. Its management characteristics, says Vedel, are "more typical of a large public enterprise" than a governmental ministry (1984, p. 9).

TDF (*Télédiffusion de France*) manages the technical side of the country's broadcast television channels. In 1980, following a recommendation by Nora and Minc (1980), the PTT assumed oversight of TDF, removing it from the Ministry of Culture. (The same report called for the separation of postal authority from the PTT, which the analysts regarded as a declining business and one that might inhibit PTT development of such alternative services as electronic mail.) Taking over TDF was seen by some as a major step in the consolidation of PTT policy power. Some regarded this impressive accretion of authority critically. A National Assembly study stated that this action "made the DGT the only center of communications in France," causing an excessive centralization of these instruments of power" (International Institute for Communication, 1981, p. 14)

The National Center for Telecommunications Research (*Centre National d'Études des Télécommunications*, or CNET) is the French PTT's equivalent to America's Bell Labs. Until fairly recently its research was exclusively technical. Now there is a group that investigates questions about the social consequences of introducing new telematics technologies. Altogether CNET employs some 4300 persons (Voge, 1984, p. 5).

For the last decade and a half, the French PTT has worked to put behind its traditional reputation as a slumbering bureaucracy. From 1971 to 1975 the sixth National Plan invested 10 billion francs in telecommunications. The number of lines, the amount of traffic, and the installation of automatic switching grew impressively (Lewis, 1978). The first objective was "to improve the public switched network," which would allow "not only better telephone, telex, etc., but also the more efficient development of videotex, facsimile, the Transpac data network and other new services" (France, 1979). From the start the idea was to provide a single, technologically advanced national network offering a mix of numerous telecommunications services. "Between 1974 and the end of 1979 the national telephone network more than doubled from six million subscribers to 14 million" (International Institute for Communication, 1981, p. 14). In 1976 the DGT moved beyond merely modernizing the telephone system and launched a "telematics offensive" (Mattelart, 1982, p. 25) which, from 1982, included the cabling of France. Transpac, the public packet-switched data network, began service in 1979. By 1985 there were some 25,000 subscribers, with 100,000 predicted by 1990. The French now describe Transpac as the biggest service of its kind in the world (Fortin, 1985, p. 32). Telecom 1, the "telematics satellite," was launched in 1984. Transpac and Telecom 1 offer or will soon offer several services, such as telex, videotex, facsimile, and teletex-with-images, available to mostly business users. Along with broadband cable, they are central to the French objective of single national network, offering multiple services, under the overall control of public authorities. Massive amounts of capital were required for these activities and the PTT became France's largest investor, after the military. Its 1978 investments constitute about 4½% of the nation's total (International Institute for Communication, 1981, p. 14). One report says that between 1978 and 1983 the French spent $4 to $5 billion annually just modernizing the country's telephone network (Cole & O'Rorke, 1983, p. 102).

While French Telecom does not manufacture equipment, it buys about two-thirds of that available domestically from the 40 or so firms that do make French telecommunications hardware. Five companies share about 90% of that market. About one quarter of French-made telecommunications equipment is exported (Voge, 1984, p. 9). France had long kept tight financial controls over, and provided subsidies to, these telecommunications manufacturing firms, when, in 1981, the government of President Mitterand nationalized *Compagnie Général d'Électricité* (CGE), which includes CIT-Alcatel, Thompson-CSF, and others. Mattelart (1982, p. 17) claims that, as of 1982, about 49% of France's "electronic network" comprised nationalized firms. (Thirty percent was foreign, of which 13% belonged to IBM.) The French like to point out, however, that, since the twenties, the PTT has permitted telecommunications users to purchase their own customer premises equipment (CPE), a policy other countries have only recently adopted.

Against this backdrop France has aggressively pursued an industrial policy that emphasizes selected telecommunications and electronics products and services—national champions in the telematics sector. A principal objective has been to make available leading-edge technologies for export to industrialized countries in Europe and North America, and to developing nations in the Third

World. One means for domestic French firms to gain access to lucrative foreign markets is for the state to purchase a majority holding in established companies doing successful business abroad. As long ago as 1980, for example, CGE announced a program of acquisition in the U.S. Said to be looking for both an American minicomputer manufacturer and U.S.-based production facilities for telecommunications equipment, CGE sought to enhance its position in the U.S. office-automation market. In 1985 France's largest electronics firm, the nationalized Thomson Group, moved to buy Mostek Corporation, a U.S. semiconductor-maker that was being shut down for unprofitability by its American owner. The French seemed to be seeking the capacity of Mostek's four chip-making factories and its research center in America. This was said to be part of Thomson's plan to become one of the world's top chip makers; in 1984 the firm had moved from being 25th to 21st in global sales. Furthermore, with a view said to be widely shared in Europe, Thomson's chairman explained such a production position was "a matter of survival" for a firm whose sales were already first in European military electronics and second in consumer electronics. The basic need was to sustain the technological ability to create specialized chips for Thomson's products sold in its primary European markets (Peterson, 1985).

Unquestionably the largest instance of recent French industrial policy action intended to increase that country's dominance of foreign telecommunications equipment markets occured during the summer of 1986, when CGE announced the purchase for $1.5 billion of a 63% share in ITT's telecommunications division. What brought these two giants together was the enormous burden of rapidly increasing research and development costs. France's solution was to take the lead in creating "a truly European consortium" (Sanger, 1986), soon dubbed Eurotel. Eventually, only one Belgian (at 5.7%) and one Spanish national investor (at 1.7%) would join France; the others, including Italy's STET, Germany's Robert Bosch, and the U.K.'s General Electric and Plessey, felt the risks too great. These included paying $902 million in cash plus an additional $350 million toward ITT debt (Lewis, 1987) and sorting out ITT's problematic System 12 digital switch, whose performance was being challenged in several countries. France's particular industrial imperatives and the crowded $19 billion European telecommunications switch industry may have left Alcatel little choice.

Combined, CGE and ITT comprise the second-largest telecommunications equipment supplier in the world; 78% of their sales are in Europe. This move has clearly bought France a huge market share. However, just this strength gave German telecommunications interest pause. In return for its approval of the CGE-ITT deal, Germany demanded that Siemens be assured of the 16% share of the French telephone switch market that France has been negotiating since 1984 to give AT&T-Philips. The demand was couched in disinterested terms: "Siemens was saying Europe has to strengthen forces by keeping the Americans out of the market and promoting a European solution," said one observer. The French chose a neutral solution. They sold *Compagnie Générale de Constructions Téléphoniques* (CGCT), the switch maker, to Ericsson of Sweden (Greenhouse, 1987).

A final recent example of French willingness to buy into foreign telematics markets concerns mainframe computers. In December 1986 the state-owned *Compagnie des Machines Bull* became the world's third largest computer maker. At a cost of $500 million, *Bull* acquired 42.5% of Honeywell, increasing its share to 65 percent within two years. A third investor in this multinational enterprise is the Japanese NEC Corporation (at 15%).

The purchase of ITT and Honeywell and the sale of CGCT underscore the important international dimension of French national policy for telematics.

New Services: *Le Phénomène Minitel*

As the French continue to upgrade their public, switched telephone network to handle ever more sophisticated services, their long-term objective is establishment of an integrated switched digital network (ISDN) that will become the key element in France's telematics infrastructure. A crucial step now being undertaken in that direction is to wire the country with advanced, mostly fiber optic, cable. In the U.S. and elsewhere, cable is closely identified with the mere distribution of conventional television. In France cable's role involves wiring the nation quickly (one third of all households by 1992, according to the original plan) while promoting industrial expertise, creating jobs, fostering cultural expression, and accelerating the effects of Socialist policies to politically decentralize France.

In designing and implementing the Cable Plan, France started from scratch. Vedel (1984, p. 7) reports that, by the mid-'80s, only about .6% of the country was cabled. The star configuration was chosen over the usual tree-and-branch design, so as to foster interactivity. Fiber optic was preferred to coaxial cable for its wider frequency band and capacity for greater number of channels. In at least two major cities, Montpellier and Lille, cable was integrated into urban development projects. (For a discussion see *Le Plan*, 1984.)

In April 1984, when some 130 applications had been made for franchises fairly evenly distributed throughout the country, the regulations governing cable's operation were announced. The PTT would enjoy a monopoly in the construction and maintenance of cable systems, though it would have no involvement in programming. Local entities, known as *Sociétés Locales d'Exploitation Commerciale* (SLECs) would pay for about 30% of the DGT's costs. SLECs would comprise local business and civic interests, excluding newspaper publishers. State authorities imposed a quota with a 30% maximum for imported programming, and announced that about one-third of gross revenues for cable would be spent on producing programs. The PTT would receive half of revenues to pay for system operation. Individual subscribers could expect to pay about 125 frances per month for the service (see Braillard, 1984). Implementation of the plan will be costly; a common estimate is about $6 billion altogether. Consequently, in the fall of 1986, the government scaled back aspects of the Cable Plan.

The one place in France that showcases, on an admittedly small scale, the future that cable planners envision is Biarritz. There, 1500 households, connected by fiber-optic cable, partake in *videophonie*, or a service that, in one instrument, combines a telephone, video screen, and movable video camera. Twelve television channels, including Spanish, Swiss, and British stations, are available. Callers can see one another, their guests, documents, or whatever. There are pay videophone kiosks on the streets of Biarritz. And the *Banque Nationale de Paris* features a branch office whose videophone connects with the main office (Lewis, 1986a).

It will be some time, if ever, and only after great expense, that most French homes and businesses are equipped with videophones. But a related service, using a less sophisticated but similar technology, has been in operation throughout the country since 1981. It is *Télétel*, a videotex service that has become such a great success that the verb *minitelliser*, derived from the name of the telephone/terminal, *minitel*, and meaning to chat using that device, is said to be making its way into everyday speech (Peterson, 1986).

Planning for *Télétel* extends back to 1978 when, ostensibly for cost-cutting reasons, the DGT considered offering an electronic telephone directory service that would be available through "dumb" terminals using the Transpac data network. In May of 1981 an inaugural experiment involving 1500 homes and the *minitel* took place. Paris went on line during the next 2 years. By May 1985 the service was nationally available and some half million terminals had been distributed (Epstein, 1986). Today there are about 2.2 million *minitels* installed (Videotex, 1986–87). The DGT has announced a goal of equipping 30% of France's phone lines for *Télétel* by 1990 (Peterson, 1986). At 30%, or 7 million terminals, authorities expect optimal profitability from the system (Videotex, 1986–87). Central to this strategy of universal availability is giving the basic *minitel* terminals free of charge to residential users. Business users pay a charge of about $11 per month. The DGT spends about $170 to manufacture each basic *minitel*. These have no computer power.

Télétel has not come cheaply. One estimate is that the DGT has spent some $666 million on the project. Yet the DGT confidently predicts recovering these enormous costs within just 4 years, based on increased telephone traffic, cost savings, and income from terminal leasing. If this proves accurate, the remaining period of the terminal's estimated 10-year life span will produce pure profit for the PTT. In 1985 the DGT reported $65 million in *Télétel* revenues; the 1986 estimate is $100 million (Videotex, 1986–87). The number of videotex calls in that year—about half of which are to the electronic directory, one-third of which are to services, and one-fifth among business users—was reportedly four times the previous year's. Overall telephone usage is said to be up 10%. There were some 26 million calls on the system in September 1986 alone (Videotex, 1986–87). In 1984, 200 services were offered to *Télétel* users; some 3,000 were available in 1986. The DGT encourages service growth by generously alloting two-thirds of the $5-per-hour user fee it collects to service providers. In this manner providers made $53 million during the first 6 months of 1986 (Videotex, 1986–87). In addition, *Télétel's* success is claimed to have engendered 5,000 new nongovernmental jobs (Epstein, 1986).

The videotex system is used in a variety of ways. One firm is said to equip its sales force with *minitels* which are then used to check stock and record sales. Consumer finance companies can, within 3 minutes, provide credit checks for the customers of some 9000 retailers (Peterson, 1986). For residential users *Le Kiosque* offers 3,000 services. Among the most popular are those devoted to chatting about sex—dubbed a sort of electronic singles bar by an observer. Gourmet food can be ordered, and psychiatrists are said to offer psychological testing *à la Télétel*. (For a review of user and service data, see the several short articles grouped under *Télétel*, 1986.) About 20 publications offer services, and at least one newspaper reports, as a result, increased circulation and greater name recognition—in addition to earning $300,000 in a single month (Epstein, 1986). The DGT estimates that about two new services are added each day to *Le Kisoque* (Videotex, 1986–87).

The PTT says that it too will soon join the profitable videotex service field, offering electronic mail for the home and locating public terminals in train stations and shopping centers. It has also taken steps to separate *Télétel* traffic from data flows on the Transpac network, following a disastrous overload situation in June of 1985 that brought both to a standstill (Epstein, 1986). In keeping with the broad state strategy of internationally marketing France's high-technology champions, the DGT has established *Intelmatique*, whose job it is to sell *Télétel* and *minitel* abroad. Some 35,000 terminals have thus far been sold to countries in Latin America and Western Europe, as well as to Australia and New Zealand (Epstein, 1986). Honeywell in the U.S. is said to have purchased 2,500 *minitels* to sell as business-to-business communication devices (Peterson, 1986). Infonet now makes available *Télétel* to computer users in the U.S. and Canada, and Amsterdam and Frankfurt will soon have access as well ("In Brief," 1986).

FRENCH RADIO AND TELEVISION

The electronic media the French call *audiovisual* and which Americans know as broadcasting are undergoing fundamental change. To an outsider, compared to the relatively methodical nature of telematics policy, French broadcasting would appear to be in great disorder—changing in such basic ways, at such a rapid rate, and seeming to be without the long-term policy vision that informs decisions for, say, data transmission or videotex—that the purpose and direction of this metamorphosis are not at all clear.

If the policy environment surrounding broadcasting can fairly be described in these terms, it is probably due to three factors. First, unlike telematics, broadcasting is a widely familiar institution. Many constituencies—state policy makers, professional media workers, the national audience—have long-established relations with radio and TV. Change of any sort affects nearly everyone, leading to pulling and hauling over the most minor issue. Secondly, most broadcasting-policy decisions do not primarily involve new technologies. Questions of French sovereignty or glory here are less explicitly a debate over raw economics than a discussion of cultural capital. Finally, and perhaps most significantly, most state actions involving the transformation of French broadcasting have occured within a brief 5-year span, beginning with a 1981 report that recommended rewriting the laws governing broadcasting. The number of successive proposals, reports, and decisions since then would alone be enough to induce a sort of policy vertigo, but all this has been complicated by the 1986 rise to power by the conservatives, who are either accelerating tendencies evident in Socialist policy or who are introducing a radical new policy course, depending on one's point of view.

Organization and Policy Authority

Referring to the system of media which the French term audiovisual, Anthony Smith (1973, p. 156) concluded that France has "created the most unstable set of broadcasting institutions in Europe, if not the world."

The reason, says this British critic, is that "50 years of upheaval" marked by "the series of accidents" that formed French broadcasting have lacked any "enduring principle" (Smith, 1973, p. 156) that might have given direction to either organizational structure or program content. This harsh judgement seems to be borne out by the historical facts. And its suggestion of impulsive policy making is evident in some recent French broadcasting developments.

Pre-World War II French radio stations were operated under private ownership and governmental—PTT—oversight. (Much of the following section draws on Smith, 1973, and Thomas, 1976. See also Kuhn, 1985.) Both commercial advertising and state funds supported these early stations. During the thirties, local management committees, composed of elected holders of the licenses required to own radio sets, supervised station operation. Two fundamental factors determined the administrative structure of post-War radio and later television. One was the establishment in 1941 of *Radiodiffusion Française* by the exile government in London. The other was the pattern of centralized state monopoly characteristic of French radio under the Nazi occupation. Additional historical forces shaped the state-monopoly model of broadcasting. These included the monopoly of the existing French telegraph system, fear of potential advertising revenue loss by newspaper publishers, and the sense, on the one hand, that French high culture ought to be actively promoted and, on the other, that the French state lacked a "center of gravity" that could find a substitute in broadcasting.

Radiodiffusion—télévision Française (or RTF), really a branch of the PTT, was the chief administrative unit of French broadcasting until the mid-sixties, a period of substantial change in the organization and operation of radio and TV in France. The number of television sets climbed from just 1 million in 1959 to 10 million in 1968. This same year saw the establishment of the third channel, meant to serve regional France; a second channel had come about in 1964. In 1965 the government had admitted its status as majority stockholder in the "peripheral" radio stations (popular, commercial stations broadcasting through-out Europe). The RTF had evolved into *L'Office de Radiodiffusion et Télévision Francaise* (ORTF) in 1964. This scheme was intended partly to allow professional broadcasters some autonomy from the habitual intrusions of such politicians as the minister of information. Parliament, however, continued to debate ORTF activities under the aegis of budgetary matters and an Administrative Council, one-half governmental appointees, could remove senior ORTF officials. A series of governmental commissions, studies, statutes, and reforms—in 1968, 1969, 1970, 1971, and 1972—addressed a variety of ills in French broadcasting. They culminated in 1974. Then the ORTF, barely one decade old, was split into seven separate units. Overall there would be the TDF, the national broadcasting authority. *Radio France*, the three TV channels, and another production company would create broadcast programming. And the National Institute for Audiovisual Communication (INA) would provide research, training, and archival assistance.

One of the earliest actions by the Mitterand government was to institute a study that would recommend reforms in the organization and French broadcasting (France, 1982). Following its main recommendations, parliament passed, in July 1982, the landmark Law on Audiovisual Communication which formally ended the state monopoly over program production, though maintained control over the right to broadcast (*Loi sur la*, 1982). Established was a High Authority whose nine members are appointed by the president and the president of the Senate and National Assembly. This body was to act independent of political considerations and make high-level appointments to the broadcasting organizations, and to hear complaints about unfair coverage. Some judge the High Authority to have been, by French standards, surprisingly autonomous (Kuhn, 1985, pp. 65–68). The HA was replaced, in October 1986, by the CNCL (*Commission Nationale de la Communication et des Libertés*), a body still closer to the U.S.-model Federal Communications Commission. (See Labrande, 1986, for a discussion of its powers.)

Policy Activity

Since the Moinot Commission reported to President Mitterand in the fall of 1981, most French policy actions for broadcasting have had the principal objective of breaking the historic monopoly of state-owned radio and television.

One of the first broadcasting policy actions taken by the Socialists in 1981 was to legalize "free radio" stations. These pirates, whose signals where at first jammed by the authorities, competed for some time with the three state-operated, nationally distributed stations, *France-Culture, France-Musique,* and *France-Inter*. Many of these were underground, countercultural outlets. Once made legal, they quickly became established throughout the country. By 1983 there appear to have been 1,000 stations (Vainstein, 1983) and about 15% of the total French radio audience reported listening to them, mostly for the disc jockeys and music (Guigon, 1983). Although certain restrictions seem to have been intended to promote community-oriented radio, the result after just a few years appears to be quite different. As the preferred French terminology to describe these developments has shifted from *free radio* to *local radio* to *private radio*, so have multiple-station ownership, formatted programming, and transnational commercialism come to characterize this new medium. One example of many is the full-page ad in *Libération* promoting *Nostalgie France*, a chain of about 50 stations, including three in Belgium, specializing in a "nostalgia" format (*Nostalgie*, 1986). (For a discussion of this trend internationally, see Miller, 1986; Collin, 1986, offers a critique of the French case.) When commercial television begins to compete for France's scarce advertising revenues, it seems likely that a tendency of this sort will only increase. This apparent outcome in the "liberation" of French radio, however, under both Socialist and conservative policy makers seems not to be a matter of much public concern.

Among the several recent policy actions that have affected French television, four are prominent: establishment of a subscription TV service, *Canal Plus*; two reports recommending ways of proceeding towards the introduction of commercial television; actual approval of the first two commercial TV channels; and the sale of one of the three state-operated channels plus the reassignment of ownership of the commercial channels.

Canal Plus went on the air in November 1984. Within 2 years about 1 million subscribers paid to view its scrambled over-the-air UHF signals. By early 1987 *Canal Plus* was watched by 1.7 million viewers (This is, 1987). Growth in subscribers seemed to taper off with the imminent prospect of "free" commercial television. One observer blamed the nature of *Canal Plus* offerings, describing them as a "rather tired assortment of old cop and comedy series—most of them American—and even older movies" (Williams, 1985). A typical week's schedule, however, reveals a greater, though conventional program variety (see "Radio Television," 1987.) Some analysts believe that, to survive under conditions of widespread commercial TV in France, *Canal Plus* will enter into some sort of cooperative agreement with another media service. Cinema may be the future partner. In September 1986, *Canal Plus* signed a 3-year agreement with a consortium of major American film producers guaranteeing access to 80 U.S. feature films, with the possibility of an additional 40 coming later (French TV, 1986). The largest interest in *Canal Plus*, 25%, is held by Havas, the state-owned advertising agency.

During the summer of 1985, then Prime Minister Laurent Fabius received the Bredin report on the establishment of commercial television, and placed his own stamp on its recommendations. These actions followed Mitterand's own controversial position stating that France could sustain 80 to 85 new local TV stations that would program in concert with national networks. Bredin's estimate was even grander: 133 network-affiliated and 40 independent stations. Bredin called for 62 regional stations responsible for programming during the daytime hours; in the evening they would carry two national commercial networks' programming. Fabius—whose long-term vision foresaw a second *Canal Plus*-like channel, additional networks, and larger regional stations—immediately announced that France would add two commercial channels (Braillard, 1985).

The first of these outlets, *La Cinq*, was awarded in November 1985 to a Franco-Italian partnership whose key member was Silvio Berlusconi, known both for his ties to the French Socialists and for being Italy's leading commercial broadcaster. The situation seemed to promise an American-style commercial operation that triggered a very sharp debate in the French press. Not long after *La Cinq* was given the go-ahead, TV6, a music-video channel, was approved.

The conservatives wasted little time in reshaping audiovisual privatization to their liking. A parliamentary bill was debated in the summer of 1986 to sell one of the three state-operated channels, TF1, and revoke the ownership awarded just months before for *La Cinq* and TV6. Announcement of the impending sale provoked Socialist criticism, the circulation of petitions, a strike among TV journalists, and a march in protest by some 3,000 cultural figures (Bernstein, 1986). In February 1987 the government awarded 25% of *La Cinq* to Robert Hersant, the publisher of the conservative Paris daily *Le Figaro*. Retaining their interest, in 25% and 10% amounts, respectively, were Silvio Berlusconi and Jérome Seydoux. At the same time 25% of TV6 went to the Luxembourg media firm CTL ("Switch Channels," 1987). TF1, which already claims 40% of all French television advertising revenue, was sold in April to Bouygues, a large construction corporation. Holding 25%, Bouygues was joined by the British media baron Robert Maxwell, who also acquired 25% of TF1. Forty percent was sold to the public, while 10% was made available to TF1 employees ("France's TF1," 1987). (For brief, informed accounts of the European transnational broadcasters involved in these moves, see Lhoest, 1986).

Although conservative and Socialist policy makers may disagree heartily on some actions, they do agree on certain fundamentals, such as protecting what they perceive to be the integrity of French popular culture. In September 1986, Prime Minister Jacque Chirac's minister for communications and culture announced that, beginning in 1987, all foreign-produced videos must carry French subtitles. And no less than half the music broadcast by the three state-operated radio stations will, in the future, be French. Private radio stations will not be affected. On this policy issue—with its obvious economic implications—France remains undaunted.

Another related action is the Franco-German direct broadcast satellite (DBS), known in France as TDF 1. Planning goes back to 1980, and its launch has been postponed several times. A four-channel, high-powered satellite, TDF 1 was probably intended to achieve two objectives. On the one hand, there was the desire that the French TV audience would continue to view French television programming until cabling of the country was completed— resisting the temptation to turn to other program sources, such as competing DBS services. On the other, TDF 1 is part of the industrial policy that promotes French hardware. One French official foresaw a European market for DBS antennas growing from 1 million to 10 million in just 4 years (France, 1986, p. 7). France clearly hopes, with DBS, to provide an international distribution system for French TV programming while, at the same time, establishing itself as the manufacturing source for the necessary transmitting and receiving equipment.

CONCLUDING THOUGHTS

From a policy perspective, France's "telematics offensive" may be successful, wiring the country, universally offering affordable services, developing leading-edge technology. The unsettled condition of broadcasting makes its fate less clear, but even so it is quite possible that the French radio and television audience may enjoy a wider choice of programming from local, national, and foreign sources than ever before. Indeed, the French may succeed where other countries have not in integrating telematics and broadcasting services, making that land a model for policy planners elsewhere. The irony is that the determining influence on the French course will probably not be changes in governments or the degree of domestic technological expertise. Rather, the outcome of France's communications and cultural policy will likely be mostly a function of international political economics. If there is insufficient interest, for example, in Third World markets for French industrial and cultural products, the domestic infrastructure may not get built. If a "television without frontiers" comes about among the European Economic Community nations, France may be unable to prohibit foreign programming from its small screens, and this may in turn mean hard times for French production industries. Questions of cultural sovereignty will become moot.

   In this sense the French are not different, whatever their unique historical and political circumstances or the cleverness of their policy planners, from any other modern country. The ultimate effectiveness of any state's communications and cultural policy actions will increasingly be decided by the vagaries of global-trade politics—and by the sheer might of transnational corporations. During the foreseeable future, a crucial period for French national policy development, France will remain the object of even more aggressive marketing attention by American, Japanese, and fellow European purveyors of communications and cultural goods and services, all eager and able to derail the best French intentions.

REFERENCES

Aujac, H. (1986). An introduction to French industrial policy. In W. J. Adams & C. Stoffaes (Eds.), *French industrial policy*. Washington, DC: The Brookings Institution.

Bernstein, R. (1986, June 22). TV station at center of Paris storm. *New York Times*.

Bertho, C. (1981). Télégraphes et téléphones: de Valmy au microprocesseur. Paris: Le Livre de Poche.

Braillard, P. (1984). France: Cable and electronics have a bright future. *InterMedia, 12* (3), 3–4.

Braillard, P. (1985). France: Going commercial. *InterMedia, 13* (4–5), 3.

Cohen, S. S., & Gourevitch, P. A. (1982). Postscript: The Socialists—Major movements in a narrow space. In S. S. Cohen & P. A. Gourevitch (Eds.), *France in the troubled world economy* (pp. 180–189). London: Butterworth Scientific.

Cole, J. E., & O'Rorke, R. J., Jr. (1983). *Telecommunication policies in seventeen countries: Prospects for future competitive access*. Washington, DC: National Telecommunications and Information Administration.

Collin, C. (1986). Radios locales et culture regionale: La grande désillusion. *Mediaspouviors, 3*, 34–48.

Crane, R. J. (1979). *The politics of international standards: France and the color TV war*. Norwood, NJ: Ablex Publishing Corp.

Epstein, N. (1986, March 9). Et Voila! Le Minitel. *The New York Times Magazine*, pp. 46, 48–49, 69.

Fortin, P. (1985, April). 1985 Transpac: Un réseau au service des entreprises. *Revue Française des Télécommunications*, pp. 32–41.

France: Integrated Videotex. (1979). *InterMedia, 7* (5), 4.

France: The Socialist reforms. (1982). *InterMedia, 10* (1), 3–5.

France: Whose dishes on the rooftops? (1986). *InterMedia, 14* (1), 6–7.

France's TF1 moves to private side. (1987, April 13). *Broadcasting*, p. 39.

French TV to get American films. (1986, September 19). *News from France, 86*, 17.

Greenhouse, S. (1987, April 30). French defeat for AT&T. *New York Times*.

Guigon, C. (1983). Radio libres: l'Onde de choc. Vieille radio, Nouvelles radios. *Problèmes Audiovisuels, 16*, 33–35.

In Brief. (1986). *French Advances in Science and Technology, 1* (1), 2.

International Institute of Communications. (1981). France: La Télématique: The technological bubble. *InterMedia, 9* (1), 12-16.

Kuhn, R. (1985). France: The end of the government monopoly. In R. Kuhn (Ed.), *The politics of broadcasting* (pp. 47–82). New York: St. Martin's.

Labrande, C. (1986). CNCL: Un état dans l'état? *De Visu, 7*, 15–18.

Le Plan Câble á Paris et Montpellier. (1984). *Revue Française des Télécommunications, 53*, 24–35.

Lewis, P. (1986a, July 17). French vote due on sale by state. *New York Times*.

Privatization move by the French. (1986b, September 11). *New York Times*.

French-ITT joint venture predicts $260 million profit for year. (1987, January 8). *New York Times*.

Lewis, R. (1978). Impacts of computerization in France. *Telecommunications Policy, 2* (4), 336–337.

Lhoest, H. (1986). *Les multinationales de l'audiovisuel en Europe*. Paris: Les Pressés Universitaires de France.

Loi sur la communication audiovisuelle. (1982). *Assemblée Nationale no. 754*. Paris: La Documentation Française.

Mattelart, A. (1982). *Communications in socialist France or the difficulties of articulating technology and democracy*. Paper presented to the International Association for Mass Communication Research. Paris.

Miller, J. (1986). Is there a future for genuinely local services? Some lessons from community radio. *Le Bulletin de l'IDATE, Les Services de Communication du Futur, 25*, 718–30.

Nora, S., & Minc, A. (1980). *The computerization of society*. Cambridge, MA: MIT Press.

Nostalgie France. (1986, November 19). *Libération*, p. 37.

Peterson, T. (1985, November 11). Why Thompson is hungry for UTC's lemon. *Business Week*, pp. 35–36.

Why the French are in love with videotex. (1986, January 20). *Business Week*, pp. 84–85.

Radio Television. (1987, March 1–2). *Le Monde Supplement* no. 13901

Rossant, J. Come one, come all to the great French sell-off. (1986, September 2). *Business Week*, p. 46.

Sanger, D. (1986, July 3). ITT in $1.8 billion sale of business to France. *New York Times*.

Smith, A. (1973). *The shadow in the cave*. Urbana, IL: University of Illinois Press.

Switch channels, same programme? (1987, February 28). *The Economist*, pp. 80–81.

Télétel au quotidien. (1986). *Revue Française des Télécommunications*, 59, 36–51.

This is the CBS Evening News with Dan Rather . . . in France. (1987) *News from France*, 87 (6), 7.

Thomas, R. (1976). *Broadcasting and democracy in France*. London: Bradford University Press.

Vainstein, G. (1983). Presentation du dossier. Vieille radio, Nouvelles radios. Problémes Audiovisuels, 16, 1–3.

Vedel, T. (1984, July). *Local wiring policies in France: From Biarritz to Paris*. Paper presented at the Research Forum on Advanced Wired Cities, Washington, DC.

Vernier-Palliez, B. (1986). Preface. In W. J. Adams & C. Stoffaes (Eds.), *French Industrial Policy* (p.1). Washington, DC: The Brookings Institution.

Videotex: A big success with a small screen. (1986–87). *French Advances in Science and Technology*, 1 (3), 4–5.

Voge, J. (1984, April-May). *Survey of French regulatory policy*. Research Workshop on Economic Policy Towards Telecommunications, Information and Media Activities in Industrialized Countries, Washington, DC.

Williams, R. M. (1985, September-October). France: A revolution in the making. *Channels*, pp. 60–61.

34

Participant Observation and the Study of African Broadcast Organizations

LOUISE M. BOURGAULT
Northern Michigan University

INTRODUCTION

During the heady days of the 1960s, mass media was believed to hold much promise for the development of Third World nations. Mass media was regarded by Lerner (1958) and others as a key factor in the creation of upward individual and social mobility (Schramm, 1964; Rao, 1968; McClelland, 1961). In the same era, Oshima (1967) and de Sola Pool (1966) lobbied for the promotion of economic growth through these media.

By the 1970's many great hopes of the early development had been greatly tempered. Where social and economic progress had been predicted, urban migration and crime had grown (Schramm, 1976, p. 2). Where national and social integration had been forecast, there was increased psychical and social instability (Bretton, 1973, pp. 220–224; Schramm, 1976, p. 2). And by the mid-1970s development scholars had begun to rethink and recast some of their earlier assumptions.[1]

Katz and Wedell (1977) note that many of the failures of the early 'mass communication cum development' projects were predictable—that development-communication scholars had, in fact, warned that attention should be given to the social contexts of surrounding development projects. But in the rush to establish systems of modernization, they argue, little heed was paid to this advice either by the countries giving aid or by the nations accepting it.

Writing as early as 1972, Benge (1972) lashed out at the range of development-communication theories, calling them reductionist and based on pseudoscientific methods.

Inspired, no doubt, less by Benge than by the so-called ferment in the field,

---

[1] See Schramm and Lerner (1976). This work contains published proceedings of a meeting of development scholars who convened at the East-West Center in Honolulu in the mid-1970s to assess development communication projects of the 1960s and early 1970s, and to derive improved development strategies suitable for the late twentieth century.

discussions of shortcomings of communication projects in Third World nations have in the 1970s and 1980s become fashionable. Crowley's (1982) reappraisal of communication theory provides one good example. It tackles, among other questions, the issue of development communication (pp. 148–157). Crowley notes that many of the early development communication models failed because their focus was on *information*, the narrow level of message content, rather than on *communication*. Here, he provides a definition of *communication*:

> the social, organizational, and psychological dynamics of human message transmission and reception, that is the processes which describe information flows as well as their effects on senders and receivers, and the processes whereby meanings themselves are changed.

Crowley's reappraisal of development theory urges those concerned with the processes of development to adopt methods which enable scholars to study communication as he has defined it, notably through the use of ethnography. Citing the work of Hymes (1973), Crowley points out that ethnography allows the scholar more easily to take note of the range of sociological and psychological differences among Third World communities of communication (pp. 155–156).

A corollary to the extension of mass media to Third World societies has been the exportation of western technological and managerial systems, and presumably an accompanying set of professional norms required to operate these systems. As few development scholars focused on this problematic aspect of development communication, we have perhaps been blessed by a dearth of studies in this area, studies which Mody has called "globalistic, scientific studies which disregard situational patterns, stressing (rather) the development of universal laws across settings" (1985, p. 138).

Sensitive to some of the currents of criticism in the field discussed above, Katz and Wedell (1977) studied broadcast organizations in 12 countries, using a case-study technique. Their investigation of Third World broadcast organizations describes some of the strains which have resulted from the failure to create local professional norms and practices in line with the sociopolitical circumstances of the countries in question.

Elliott and Golding (1979) also used the case-study and participant-observer techniques. Their research on Nigeria notes strains between traditional behavior and values, and the need to establish a professional set of operating norms. Golding (1979) is concerned with need for Third World Media organizations to create standards of professionalism untinged with imported First or Second World ideologies.

In this discussion of these issues, Mody's counsel, though addressed to the topic of development communication, is appropriate. Mody (1985, p. 138) urges researchers to regard "differential adaptations in different Third World environments as the natural product of local interaction rather than as distortions or substandard adoptions of a Western norm."

Applying Mody's mandate to systems of media diffusion and professionals who operate them, this calls for a view of media institutions in Third World countries as products of the interaction (or in some cases collision) of traditional and modern modes of operation, and the attendant social and psychological correlates thereof.

Participant Observation

Much has been said about traditional social patterns and norms in the Third World and how these may clash with modern systems inherent in the development process. Yet precious little has been written about these questions as they relate to the operation of modern media management in the Third World. These traditional patterns must necessarily be explored if we are to come to a fuller understanding of how they operate within the context of media organizations, how they impact upon the day to day professional behavior of media workers, and how they figure in the formation of professional norms and identities.

Traditional patterns should be examined specifically *within* the context of these modern media organizations, so that the pattern of overgeneralization, so typical of the early development-communication theories, will not be repeated in the investigation of Third World media management.

Such a position calls for, at the outset, an extensive series of case studies of the organizations in question. The case-study/participant-observer technique is the recommended mode of inquiry, because it provides the researcher with the best opportunity to explore the situation (organization) at hand. It allows for the fuller discovery of unexpected social/organizational value patterns, patterns often at considerable variance with those in the West. Moreover, it helps to discourage the researcher from the use of codes, concepts, or frames of analysis devised from western models of management, many of which may be incongruent with Third World situations, and which could serve to obfuscate further the already complex interworkings in operation.

This chapter is drawn from an extensive series of participant observations made in Nigerian broadcasting houses.[2] It considers management practices,

---

[2]As Senior Consultant/Managing Director for the Media Development Consultants, Ltd., the author provided in-service training in the following television stations of the Nigerian Television Authority: Kano, Kaduna, Jos, Bauchi, and Maiduguri. The author also collaborated with The Federal Radio Corporation of Nigeria by providing a number of short courses outside the stations. This included a seminar on broadcast management conducted with general managers from all the roughly twenty federally operated stations. Media Development Consultants, Ltd., a Nigerian based consultancy firm, offers a full range of media services including in-service training for media professionals in radio, television, print, and educational media. The author's experience in Nigeria also included 2 years of full-time university level teaching in the Department of Mass Communication, Bayero University, Kano. Before living in Nigeria, the author worked for the UNESCO in the Ivory Coast Educational Television Project.

social relationships, professional behavior, and values, linking these to the backdrop of traditional African life.

It would seem that such study should be preliminary to consideration of the larger issues with which Third World media scholars are concerned, namely the question of cultural imperialism as related to Third World media management ideology and the development of alternative (i.e., Third World) models of media professional practice.

THE SOCIAL AND PSYCHOLOGICAL COMPONENTS OF THE NIGERIAN BROADCAST ORGANIZATION

In the mid-1970s Golding and Elliott (1979, p. 89) conducted a study of news production in three nations: Sweden, Ireland, and Nigeria. Their report bears a rich descriptive style, lush with contextual detail. The Nigerian portion of the study is replete with references to the apparent chaos of Nigerian broadcast organizations. These examples are typical: "A Chief Sub Editor fishes in a compendious drawer for a Visnews Stock Slide . . ."—The newsroom is filled with "incessant chatter."—To better catch the "scratchy fade and boom of the BBC short wave bulletin, someone has switched off the AP Wire. Today, as frequently, nobody remembers to switch it on again."

Despite these asides, Elliott and Golding conclude that, beyond obvious differences in style, the "cultural product" (news) produced in the Nigerian newsroom is quite similar to that of Sweden and Ireland. They write:

> At the end of the day in each newsroom there's an air of satisfaction. A neat tidy bulletin with an unequivocally important main story, well prepared and well presented. (1979, p. 90)

While Elliott and Golding's conclusions are sound, they leave the reader with gnawing questions: (a) Why are these Nigerian organizations so apparently chaotic? (b) How, out of this seeming confusion, do these cultural products manage to be produced?

The answer to the first question lies in part to the existence of a number of traditional social structures, structures which all too often seem at variance with the functional exigencies of the modern broadcast organization. These include social systems of lineage, hierarchical stratification, and patronage. These social systems, moreover, have strong psychological/value components which also appear dysfunctional to the efficient operation of modern broadcasting. Each of these social and value systems, and their apparent effect on the organization, is detailed below.

Lineage Relationships
A *lineage* is defined as a group of persons who, depending on their cultural background, trace common ancestry through either male or female descent and which actually establishes kinship (Robinson, 1986, pp. 134–135).

Traditionally, lineage heads have had corporate duties and rights. They may oversee marriages, and regulate use of property and access to land; they may assume collective liability if one of their members is harmed.

In modern Africa, lineage relationships play an important role in the distribution of benefits from the modern, Western, economic and political structure. Western authors have been quick to note that the persistence of lineage/kin relationships among individuals engaged in the modern sector have given rise to at least two conditions known to be the bane of modern African development: nepotism and corruption.

Nepotism is the result of enormous pressure on lineage members employed in the modern sector to give preferential treatment in hiring and promotion to kin. *Corruption* (graft, bribe taking) is the natural answer to financial demands made on successful lineage members to provide monetary assistance to the ever-expanding African family network.

But results of lineage-group importance extend far beyond these two rather obvious considerations. In every phase and aspect of the broadcast organization, lineage relationships interpose over "normal" (i.e., Western) working affairs.

Kinship can influence decisions not only about hiring and firing, but also far more mundane matters: preferential allocation of broadcast facilities, times, schedules, news beats, and any number of perks and privileges, such as on-the-job training or much sought after subventions to institutions of higher education, particularly those abroad.

An equally compelling, though much less documented, demand is placed by the lineage group on the *time* of the modern African elite. Family obligations and the long-distance travel to rural areas they necessitate also compete for the time of the modern media manager. A highly dedicated and well-respected NTA (Nigerian Television Authority) general manager, lamenting over his "out-of-station responsibilities," gave a running account of his 9-day absence from his post as head of the station. Four days had been spent officiating at the turbaning (coronation) and attendant ceremony of a local traditional chief; 3 days had been spent rescuing a cousin from an attempted suicide, arranging for psychiatric care, and placing the cousin under proper medical supervision; and 2 days had been spent enrolling his own children in elementary school.

The obvious deleterious effects such as absence would have in a Western organization is enormous. In Nigeria, it is further compounded by the hierarchical and authoritarian nature of these organizations, wherein much administrative power, particularly the power of the purse, rests solely with the general manager.

Hierarchical Relationships

Some of the larger African tribal groupings, by the 19th century, had long been organized along hierarchical lines, among them, two major Nigerian ethnic groups, the Hausa and the Yoruba (LeVine, 1971, pp. 171–181, 186–189).

In hierarchical societies, lineages, even today, are divided along caste lines, and traditional professions are ascriptively inherited (Ames, 1973). Persons belonging to low-status lineages often join the modern sector, including the mass media, for purposes of social mobility (Elliott & Golding, 1979, p. 173). Nevertheless, it would be erroneous to assume that, once a Nigerian joins a broadcast organization, he or she leaves his or her traditional notions of hierarchy/concern-for-status at the doorstep. Far from it.

Hierarchical structures abound within the Nigerian broadcast organization. This gives rise to a top-heavy management whose role seems the endless, establishment, dissolution, and recreation of policy decisions. Managers appear typically to see themselves and be seen as above the day-to-day operations of broadcasting. Elliott and Golding (1979, p. 87) describe the manager of news, for example, as "locked in combat with the telephone 'doing administrative tasks'."[3]

Indeed, there, is a tendency for management to be isolated from everyday activities of Nigerian broadcast operations. Typically, the large bureaucratic arm of the organization is removed by several floors or building wing from the studios; in one organization, the administrative complex was located in a separate building on the other side of a medium-sized city (about 50,000 people), even though traffic jams abound and telephones were almost always inoperative.

Managers are not the only employees of the broadcast station concerned with hierarchical relationships; they are simply most successful at creating them. New producers/directors of television programs often find themselves mired in dysfunctional hierarchical webs as they attempt to cue camera operators, sound recorders, and studio hands during routine production work. This author has witnessed, on numerous occasions, intransigent crew personnel refusing to carry out production commands because of the real or imagined low status of the director in command of the program.[4]

Patron/Client Relationships

In some stratified traditional African societies, patron/client relationships permitted social mobility to those not born into wealth or status. The lowly-born could pledge their allegiance to an individual of higher caste who competed with others within his or her social group for power. Where a patron was successful, some of the spoils would accrue to the client (Levine, 1971, pp. 177–178; Robinson, 1986, p. 134–135). Patron/client relationships have persisted in modern Africa and are regarded by sociologists and political scientists as one major cause of factionalism in modern African politics (Robinson, 1986, p. 141).

---

[3]This may involve patron/client relationships. See below.
[4]The status question is complicated by a number of factors, some traditional some modern: inherited social status, years of experience, seniority within the broadcast organization, civil service ranking, age, and perceived importance of function within the media organization.

Patron/client relationships exist both within the Nigerian broadcast organization and between key members of the broadcast organization and the society at large.

Within the broadcast organization, they operate to align weaker individuals behind key management personnel vying for power within the local or the government broadcast authority. The patron/client relationship traditionally demonstrates "placing a premium on loyalty, obedience, sensitivity to the demands of those in authority, and undermining the values of excellence, independence, originality, and goal orientation" (Levine, 1971, p. 178). Undoubtedly, this explains how less talented, caring, and/or industrious individuals, who are not tied by lineage groupings to key managers, make their way up the professional ladder. Patron/client relationships between management personnel and forces outside the station raise important conflict-of-interest questions.

Station managers may serve as both patrons and clients vis-a-vis the economic and political sectors of the country, handing out lucrative equipment contracts in the one case, providing favorable political coverage in the other. Clearly, an enforceable code of ethics is needed to regulate these matters.

That conflict of interest should arise within a modern setting is hardly surprising. What is striking about the Nigerian broadcast organization is the extent to which such extraprofessional relationships may actually crowd out the normal functioning of the organization. A manager, entombed and not to be disturbed for hours in his inner office with would-be "clients," is commonplace and surprises no one but the participant observer.

The foregoing subsection highlights social structures operating in the broadcast organization in Nigeria. This second portion of the report focuses on the attendant value component which accompanies the African social world.

African Values: Pluralism and Harmony

Chernoff (1979) describes African sensibility as one which is profoundly *pluralistic*. He means, by this, that African sensibility is primarily group oriented, that the locus of individual identity depends upon important attachments to the social group. The existential dilemma of the African, where it occurs, derives from an inability to establish group ties, i.e., to find meaning within a social network. The contrast between African sensibility and that of the highly individualistic Westerner is marked. Existential angst of the latter, by opposition, defines itself ultimately in questions of *personal* self definition and *personal* self-worth.

Corresponding to the pluralistic lifeworld of the African is a highly valued sense of social harmony, one which leads to the placement of group needs over those of the individual.

Chernoff notes that the values of pluralism and social harmony are not mere hallmarks of some rather pristine and romantically simple African village life.

Rather they operate in modern Africa among large social groupings. In any case, he argues, both contemporarily and historically, African social life has been enmeshed in a complex and often contradictory network of social relations. Certainly, the modern broadcast organization is as good an arena as any to examine the operation of these values. Indeed values of communalism permeate the life of the organization.

It was noted earlier that kin and lineage relationships and their attendant obligations make for high absenteeism within the organization. What has been observed for management is equally true for workers at all levels: production staff, news reporters, engineering staff, and even the providers of custodial services. But absenteeism is only one small effect of communalism, one which is potentially reparable through the engagement/training of supplementary personnel.

Management meetings, as noted above, take up the lion's share of upper-level management, leaving little remaining time for the more routine day-to-day administrative functions: maintenance of schedules, processing of paperwork, commissioning of repairs, and ordering of ever-needed spare parts, for example. Management meetings owe much in form to their traditional village equivalent—the communal palaver of elders under the proverbial baobab tree. These ever-frequent management meetings at Nigerian broadcast stations can easily last 4 hours of a working day which is seldom 8 hours long. Each individual is expected to participate and proffer opinions on topics discussed.

In Africa, the oral tradition has made discussion an art form. The form engenders a hyperbolic speaking style punctuated by rhetorical flourishes: proverbs, maxims, references to history, and dydactic object lessons. Like other oral-culture expressive traditions, the public meeting style is highly redundant.

To a great extent, the purpose of these meetings, as in the West, is problem solving. But the focus tends to be on the human aspect of a problem rather than on its technical solution. If Studio A becomes inoperative, for example, the problem at hand will, in all likelihood, be defined as how to coax the staff of Production Studio B to allow access to Studio A's operatives. Ong (1982, pp. 42–43) would describe this focus of analysis as "close to the humanlifeworld." Fernandez would note the value of this art form in imposing social order (1973, pp. 207–208).

These management meetings undoubtedly foster a process of group decision making by upper-level management and serve as a useful counterweight to some of the stratified authority structures within the system. As Elliott and Golding remark, "they mediate the inevitable into the desirable" (1979, p. 89). They also account, in part, for the great spillover of management function noted by these two authors (1979, p. 71).

Chernoff's (1979, p. 158) analysis, one which strongly highlights the plurality of the African situation, parallels the role of conversation (and hence the meeting, by extension) to the role of music in African life.

They expect dialogue, and most significantly, they stay very much open to influence. The many ways one can change a rhythm, by cutting it with different rhythms is parallel to the many ways one can approach or interpret a situation or a conversation. And there is always an in-between, always a place to add another beat. A musical occasion, like any other social occasion, is therefore beyond any one perspective a person can bring to it, and people in Africa are usually realistic enough not to try to impose a single point of view on the larger contest in which they are playing a part.

The communal model of management finds many parallels in other operations of the broadcast organization. Elliott and Golding (1979) make repeated references to the noise level and apparent confusion of the newsroom. This state of affairs obtains equally in the control room, where hapless television directors attempt to direct live broadcasts while any number of "assistants" wander in and out to greet, chat with, and offer gratuitous commands to the working control-room staff. The final product of such endeavor is, of course (much more so than in its western equivalent), a communal success or failure, rather than the result of the clear interlocking or interworking of individual efforts combined into a smooth whole.

In his analysis of oral societies, Ong (1982, pp. 41–42) observes that communal orientations foster a highly conservative or traditional world view. He argues that conservatism is engendered by the very difficulty with which knowledge is acquired in these oral cultures, i.e., through painstaking memorization. The literate mind, in contrast, released by writing from the need to commit ideas to memory, is free to engage in speculation.

This author noted, among production staff members in Nigerian broadcasting organizations, an apparently curious practice which becomes comprehensible in the light of explanations offered by Ong and Chernoff.

TV-production staff members, particularly the least senior and the least educated, had a strong propensity to routinize random (to this author) occurrences and to incorporate them into regular practice. For example, a great deal of studio training in Nigeria occurs on the job, particularly for lower-level production personnel. Since relatively little status or importance is attached to these positions, training is done haphazardly, often by persons with little more skill than the trainee. When this author was invited to conduct in-service training at NTA stations, she often met with resistance when attempting to institute new studio procedures (such as proper camera focusing). The resistance was not as surprising as the reasons given to justify it. Attempting to validate a particular (often incorrect) procedure, young cameramen with as little as 2 or 3 months on the job would explain, "This is the way we always do it!"

Production personnel were equally reticent to engage in crew-rotational schemes used typically in American television production classes. Sound men had to be coaxed to assume camera positions in crew-training sessions, and cameramen were of necessity cajoled into assuming the role of audio operator.

This reticence was compounded where crew rotation involved the added variable of breached hierarchy, as when directors were asked to play studio assistant.

Although this traditionalism was most prevalent among the lower-level personnel, it was not limited to them. One general manager, for example invited the author to use on-site television facilities for production training courses but mandated that neither the sets, nor the props, nor the lighting be moved—a requirement which quite strongly undermined the course value.

Chernoff (1979, p. 161) argues that externalized (ritualized) institutional procedures and roles are important to Africans, because they "provide a framework and help them to know what is happening and get into it." The ritualizations and conventions are the means through which the African connects to the larger social world around him.

Ong would argue that finding one's identity through ritualization is a hallmark of oral culture. Its opposite in the literate world is the search for self-knowledge through solitary introspection. In oral cultures, participation, since it is externalized, is also situational. So are concepts, including self-concepts. Denatured, analytical, abstractive processes required for concept formation are alien to the oral culture. These points explain the apparently curious attitudes many Nigerians seemed to hold vis-a-vis their jobs in broadcasting.

This author was surprised by the limited degree to which media professionals at all levels identified with the calling. Elliott and Golding (1979, pp. 173–184) made similar observations. Equally amazing was the often serendipitous manner though which Nigerians had come to take posts in the NTA, and the serendipity which might propel them to leave. It comes as no surprise that such practical attractions as higher salaries or easier opportunities for promotion elsewhere could and did attract individuals to other sectors. What did, however, give pause, was the imagined (or perhaps unimagined) ease with which many employees expected to transfer professional identities. When questioned on these matters, many revealed only the haziest abilities at self-analysis or job-skill analysis in the abstract. Many reported being unhappy with their jobs, but only those with concrete practical reasons (low pay, no foreign scholarships, for example) could articulate the source of their dissatisfaction. Many of these individuals would create elaborate fantasies projecting themselves into (what appeared to the author to be) professions for which they appeared profoundly unsuited.[5] On the other hand, some individuals equally unsuited by temperament or natural ability to their present media occupation might express high levels of satisfaction and a belief that they were doing a good job. Rewards from management, ostensibly for work well done, often appeared just as serendipitous.

[5] Painfully honest and shy men would imagine future careers as dealers of Nigerian art works/curios, for example. This calls for roughly the same personal qualities as are required conventionally for used-car salesmen in the United States.

The source of these tendencies, it seems, resides partly in the oral culture, a culture which inhibits abstraction and self-analysis. Professional role concepts in this context tends to be but vaguely understood, and almost always situationally assumed.

These observations are also true for upper-level management. And the importance of proper skill assessment and recognition of native abilities have important ramifications on recruitment and training of staff. Indeed Katz and Wedell (1977, pp. 231–238) make similar observations as they call for improved recruitment procedures in Third World Broadcast Personnel.

SUMMARY, CONCLUSIONS, SUGGESTIONS

This chapter has discussed some of the African social structures which permeate the modern Nigerian broadcast organization. Specifically, it has noted the operation of lineage/kin group structures, hierarchical structures, and patron/client relationships. It has also highlighted some of the psychological orientations which derive from the African social values of plurality and harmony. Many of these orientations are at odds with Western concepts of modern media management.

The points raised here may seem irrelevant to some academics. One reason behind such an assessment may be the legacy of colonialism—both among those who endured it and those who imposed it. The most comprehensive accounts of the postcolonial social situation have come from those authors not plagued with the legacy, namely Myrdal (1968), a Swede, and Andreski (1968), a Pole. Colonialist mentality would not suggest that comparative scholarship of this sort takes recourse in African values and African social systems to explain events and procedures observed. Colonialists would brand certain practices as "incorrect" or dysfunctional and simply seek to correct them.

Clearly, the observations made in this report arise only from long-term, direct observation and interaction with the individuals and systems implicated. The era of colonialism has passed. And for this, most Africans heave a sigh of relief. The ear of neocolonial transportation models of mass communication development research has also passed. At this, the ethnographers and participant-observers may also breathe more freely.

Now Africans must devise their own systems for managing media organizations. Katz and Wedell (1978, pp. 101–102) conclude that the dominant Western model of Third World broadcast organization is frequently out of step with local customs and practices.

The time is now ripe for a serious assessment by scholars, especially African scholars, but more importantly by African media managers, of the contributions local and situationally based African social systems and social values can make to their media organizations. The aim should be to determine what works and what does not within specific *local contexts*. A similar assessment must proceed with regard to the Western management models heretofore imported. And again, caution is advised against the use of imported theory and research paradigms in making these assessments.

REFERENCES

Ames, D. (1973). A sociocultural view of Hausa musical activity. In W. L. d'Azevedo (Ed.), *The traditional artist in African societies* (pp. 128–160). Bloomington, IN: Indiana University Press.

Anderski, S. (1968). *The African predicament*. London: Michael Joseph Ltd.

Benge, R. (1972). *Communication and identity*. Hampden, CT: Linnet Books.

Bretton, H. L. (1973). *Power and politics in Africa*. Chicago, IL: Aldine Publishing Co.

Chernoff, J. M. (1979). *African rhythm and sensibility: Aesthetics and social action in African musical forms*. Chicago, IL: University of Chicago Press.

Crowley, D. J. (1982). *Understanding communication: The signifying web*. New York: Gordon and Breach.

de Sola Pool, I. (1966). Mass media and politics in the modernization process. In L. Pye (Ed.), *Communication and political development*. Princeton, NJ: Princeton University Press.

Elliott, P., & Golding, P. (1979). *Making the news*. London: Longman Group Ltd.

Fernandez, J. (1973). The exposition and imposition of order: Artistic expression in Fang culture. In W. L. d'Azevedo (Ed.), *The traditional artist in African societies* (pp. 194–217). Bloomington, IN: Indiana University Press.

Golding, P. (1979). Media professionalism in the Third World: The transfer of an ideology. In J. Curran, M. Gurevitch, & J. Woollacott (Eds.), *Mass communication and society*. Beverly Hills & London: Sage.

Hymes, D. (1973). On the origins and foundations of inequality among speakers. *Daedalus, 102* (3), 59–86.

Katz, E., & Wedell, G. (1977). *Broadcasting in the Third World: Promise and performance*. London: Macmillan Press Ltd.

Levine, R. A. (1971). Dreams and deeds: Achievement motivation in Nigeria. In R. Melson & H. Wolpe (Eds.), *Nigeria: Modernization and the politics of communalism*. East Lansing, MI: Michigan State University Press.

Lerner, D. (1958). *The passing of traditional society*. Glencoe, IL: The Free Press.

McClelland, D. (1961). *The achieving society*. New York: Van Nostrand.

Mody, B. (1985). First World communication technologies in Third World contexts. In E. Rogers & F. Balle (Eds.), *The media revolution in America & Western Europe*. Norwood, NJ: Ablex Publishing Corp.

Myrdal, G. (1968). *Asian drama: An inquiry into the poverty of nations*. New York: Twentieth Century Fund.

Ong, W. J. (1982). *Orality and literacy: The technologizing of the word*. London and New York: Methuen.

Oshima, H. T. (1967). The strategy of selective growth. In W. Schramm & D. Lerner (Eds.), *Communication and change in developing nations* (pp. 76–91). Honolulu, HI: East-West Center Press.

Pye, L. (1967). Communication , institution building, and the reach of authority. In W. Schramm & D. Lerner (Eds.), *Communication and change in the developing countries* (pp. 37–56). Honolulu, HI: East-West Center Press.

Rao, Y. V. L. (1964). *Communication and development: A study of two Indian villages*. Minneapolis, MN: University of Minnesota Press.

Robinson, P. (1986). Conflicts. In A. Mazrui & T. Levine (Eds.), *The Africans: A reader* (pp. 133–143). New York: Praeger.

Schramm, W. (1964). *Mass media and development*. Palo Alto, CA: Stanford University Press.

Schramm, W. (1976). Overview. In W. Schramm & D. Lerner (Eds.), *Communication and Change—The last ten years and the next* (pp. 1–14). Honolulu, HI: University of Hawaii Press.

Author Index

A

Abercrombie, N., 56, 68
Abrahams, R.D., 228, 235
Abrams, M., 272, 274
Aburdene, P., 154
Agar, M., 136, 140
Albrecht, S.L., 267, 274
Alexander, A., 237, 241, 243
Alison-Broomhead, M., 11, 14
Allaire, Y., 151, 154
Allen, R., 229, 234, 235
Anshelm, M., 274
Altheide, D., 34, 51
Ames, D., 347, 353
Anderski, S., 352, 353
Anderson, J., 250, 253, 254
Ang, I., 231, 235
Anthos, A.G., 143, 154
Archer, M.S., 270, 274
Ascherson, N., 44, 45, 46, 49, 51
Ash, T.G., 46, 47, 48, 49, 51
Aujac, H., 340
Austin, D.J., 140, 140
Austin, N., 149, 154

B

Bachrach, P., 68
Baker, E.L., 143, 154
Baker, W.E., 201, 206
Balane, J.I., 131, 133
Ball-Rokeach, S., 54, 55, 68, 174, 179, 267, 271, 274, 274
Baratz, M., 68
Baritz, L., 26, 29, 32
Barrett, L.E., 117, 123, 126
Barry, J., 196
Barry, K., 281, 284
Barteniedd, I., 129, 133
Barthes, R., 167
Bartlett, F.C., 102, 114
Barwise, T., 313, 316
Bascom, W., 92, 93, 97
Batscha, R., 34, 42, 51, 51
Bayles, M., 287, 289, 290

Beaufre, A., 11, 14
Beavin, J.H., 297, 302
Becker, T., 256, 263
Benger, R., 342, 353
Benet, L., 134, 140
Bennett, T., 55, 68, 230, 235
Benton, W., 190, 192, 196
Berger, P.L., 267, 274
Bernstein, R., 338, 340
Berry, G., 250, 251, 253
Berry, J.W., 255, 263
Bertho, C., 340
Bibbee, R.C., 266, 277
Bird, D.A., 227, 235
Bishop, W., 315, 316
Blake, J., 270, 274
Block, E., 267, 274
Block, P., 267, 274
Blumler, J.G., 256, 264
Bodman, J., 103, 114
Bolter, J.D., 198, 200, 206
Böltken, F., 272, 275
Boot, A., 123, 126
Bouwman, H., 270, 275
Boyer, P.J., 286, 290
Braillard, P., 332, 338, 340
Braithwaite, V., 271, 275
Brennan, T., 306, 307, 315, 316
Bretton, H.L., 342, 353
Briones, C.G., 131, 133
Brooks, L., 231, 235
Brooks, T., 196
Brown, C.W., 11, 15
Brown, H.G., 286, 290
Brown, S., 15
Brownmiller, S., 281, 284
Brumberg, A., 45, 51
Brunsdon, C., 229, 235
Buckholdt, D., 70, 81
Buerkel-Rothfuss, N.L., 237, 243
Buhle, M.J., 289, 290
Buhle, P., 289, 290
Burgoon, M., 247, 253
Burke, K., 125, 126

Marsh, E., 196
Martel, H., 181, 184
Marvin, C., 194, 196
Marwell, G., 171, 172, 173
Mason, D., 47, 49, 53
Mason, R., 220, 222
Mattelart, A., 22, 24, 317, 324, 330, 341
Mayer, A., 217, 222
Mayes, S., 237, 243
McAnany, E., 252, 254
McClelland, D., 342, 353
McCombs, M.E., 269, 276
McFadden, D., 196
McGuire, W.J., 256, 264
McLuhan, M., 168, 208, 214
Meddin, J., 270, 271, 276
Meijer, J., 124, 126
Melischek, G., 265, 276
Merrill, J., 55, 68
Merton, R., 68
Meyer, P., 55, 68
Meyer, T., 250, 253, 254
Meyrowitz, J., 226, 235, 251, 254
Miles, G.L., 151, 155
Miller, J., 337, 341
Miller, L., 89, 90
Mills, C.W., 79, 82
Minc, A., 329, 341
Mishler, E.G., 74, 82
Mitchell-Kernan, C., 250, 251, 253
Mizutani, N., 89, 90
Mizutani, O., 89, 90
Mody, B., 343, 353
Monaco, J., 157, 168
Morgan, M., 251, 254, 269, 270, 275, 276, 283, 284
Morley, D., 248, 254
Morris, G.H., 75, 82
Moses, P., 126
Muller, J., 14, 15, 16
Muller, P., 14, 15
Myrdal, G., 352, 353

N

Naisbitt, J., 151, 154
Namenwirth, J.L., 266, 277
Newcomb, H.M., 288, 290
Nemeth, C.J., 175, 179
Nettleford, R., 117, 126, 134, 140
Newcomb, H.M., 225, 234, 235
Nicolson, M., 201, 202, 203, 204, 205, 207
Nie, N., 259, 263
Nielson, A.C., 259, 263

Nixon, R.M., 27, 33
Noble, G., 268, 277
Noelle-Neumann, E., 269, 277
Nofke, C., 6, 10, 15
Nora, J.J., 152, 154
Nora, S., 329, 341
Nowak, K., 267, 277
Nowak, S., 49, 53

O

O'Connor, J., 287, 290
Odell, J., 55, 68
Omard, D., 134, 140
Ong, W.J., 349, 350, 353
O'Rorke, R.J., 329, 330, 340
Oshima, H.T., 342, 353
Owen, M., 70, 82
Owens, J., 117, 126

P

Pacanowsky, M., 253, 254
Palmgreen, P., 259, 264, 269, 274
Panofsky, E., 168
Parsons, 170, 171, 173
Pascale, R.T., 143, 152, 154
Pattison, R., 210, 214
Peacock, A., 305, 316
Pelton, R., 134, 140
Persky, S., 49, 52
Peters, T.J., 143, 146, 149, 150, 154
Peterson, R.A., 266, 271, 277
Peterson, S., 22, 24
Peterson, T., 331, 333, 334, 340, 341
Phillips, D., 15
Pierce, F.N., 256, 264
Pierce, R., 308, 310, 316
Pines, J., 123, 124, 126
Pingree, S., 237, 243, 256, 263, 270, 275
Pitsch, P., 306, 307, 311, 312, 315, 316
Polanyi, L., 86, 90
Porter, B., 51
Posner, B.Z., 147, 154
Postman, N., 268, 277
Potel, J., 52
Prince, A.V., 140, 140
Pringle, K., 194, 196
Prokesch, S., 151, 155
Propp, V., 158, 168
Pye, L., 353

R

Rabinow, P., 56, 68
Radway, J., 196, 229, 235

Subject Index

Lens culture, 199
  development of, 199–204, 205
Levi-Strauss, C., 157–58
Liberalization, *see* Deregulation
Life magazine, 193, 194, 209
Lifestyles of the Rich and Famous
      (television program), 226
Lineage, in Nigeria, 345–47
Linguistics, 57, 59
  see also Language
Listeners
  role in narratives, 85–87, 88–90
  see also Audiences
Literature, development of, 211–13
L'Office de Radiodiffusion et Télévision
      Française (ORTF), 336
Logical positivism, 57
  and journalism, 55
Lollards, 210–11
Lorimar Productions, 231–32
Lucas, G., 158

M
M*A*S*H (television program), 285
Mack, Mr., 134, 137, 138–40
Madonna (entertainer), 160–61
Magazines, *see* Periodicals, popular
Males, *see* Men
Malone, Sam (character), 285, 286, 287,
      289
Management theories, and corporate
      culture, 144
Mandela, Nelson, 13
Marches des International Programes des
      Television (MIP-TV), 322
"Marketing media", defined, 158
Marley, Bob, 118, 124–25
Married . . . With Children (television
      program), 291
Marriott Corp., 149
Marriott, J. Willard, Jr., 149
Marvell, A., 203
Marx, K., 10
Marxism
  and linguistic theory, 57
  and Soviet cinema, 181–82
Mary Kay Cosmetics, 149
Mary (television program), 286, 288
Mason, Marsha, 300
Mass media, *see* Communications media;
      News media; Newspapers; Radio;
      Television

Maurolycus, F., 201
Maxwell, Robert, 338
Maytag Corp., 149
McDonald's Corp., 146, 149
McLuhan, M., 208, 209, 212
Media, *see* Communications media
Media Development Consultants, Ltd.,
      344n.
Medium, defined, 213n.
Meetings, in organizations, 148
Memos, in organizations, 148, 149
Men
  in movies, 298–99, 300, 301, 302
    pornographic, 282, 283, 284
  in television programs, 285–87, 288–89
  relationships with women, 299–302
  see also Families
Merrill Lynch & Co., 146
Meta-commodities, 156
Metaphors, 17–18
  in news stories, 18–21, 22–23
Mexico
  in news stories, 22–23
  television in, 253, 322
Miami Vice (television program), 285, 288
Microscope, importance of, 203, 204
Middle East
  Newsweek coverage of, 37
  television in, 322
Miller, G., 158
Ministry of Post, Telecommunications and
      Telediffusion (PTT), France, 329–30,
      332, 334
Minitel, 333–34
Minnesota Mining and Mfg. Co., 146, 147
MIP-TV (Marches des International
      Programes des Television), 322
Mister Roger's Neighborhood (television
      program), 260
Mitterand, François, 326, 327, 328, 336,
      337–38
Montage
  in advertisements, 183–84
  in movies, 181, 182
Moonlighting (television program), 285,
      286, 288
Morality, fears about TV and, 193–95
Morton Thiokol, 151
Mostek Corp., 331
Movement for the Defense of Human and
      Civil Rights (ROP-CIO), 44
Movie stars, *see* Celebrities

Nigeria
  broadcasting in, 343–45, 346, 347, 348,
    349, 352–53
  social systems in, 345–48
  television in, 345, 350–52
  see also Africa
Nightclubs, music videos in, 163–64
Nixon, Richard, 27, 32
No Hot Water Tonight (Bodman and
    Lazano), 103
  conversation about, 104–12
"No Woman, No Cry" (song), 118–20
  music, 122–24
  text analyzed, 120–22
Norms, 271
Nostalgia (television program), 310
Novels, *see* Fiction

O

Officer and a Gentleman, An (moving
    picture), 298, 300
Olszowski, Stefan, 43
Oracles, 209
Organizational cultures, 143–44, 152
  changes in, 151–54
  characteristics, 146–47
  environment, 144–45
    "bet your company," 144–45, 147, 148,
      150
    "macho," 144, 147, 148, 149–50
    "process," 145, 147, 148–49, 150
    "work hard," 144, 147, 148, 150
  heroes in, 149–50
  leaders in, 149
  lifecycle of, 151
  networks in, 150–51, 152, 154
  rituals in, 148–49
  structure, 145–47
    bureaucratic, 145
    innovative, 145
    supportive, 145
  values, 147–48
ORTF (L'Office de Radiodiffusion et
    Télévision Française), 336
Osaka, Japan
  talk show in, 87–88
  see also Japan
Our Family Honor (television program),
    288
Our House (television program), 291

P

Parents magazine, 193
"Parole" (speech), 56, 158
Participatory management, 145, 146
Pay television, 191, 307, 313
  in France, 337
PBS (Public Broadcasting Service), 305, 307
Peacock Committee, 305
Peckinpah, S., 182
Penny press, 62
People magazine, 226
Pepys, S., 203
Periodicals, popular
  on male TV characters, 286–87
  on television, 188–89, 190, 192–95
Personality journalism, *see* Gossip
Perspective, in drawing, 200–201
Phaedrus (Plato), 209–10
Phenomenology, and communication, 249–
  50
Philippines, dance in, 128–33
"Photographic culture," 199
Photography
  invention of, 204–5
  precursors of, 199, 201
Pierce, Hawkeye (character), 285, 286
Places in the Heart (moving picture), 298,
    299, 300
Plastics company, change in culture, 153
Plato, 210
Pluralism, as African value, 348–49
Poland
  Catholic Church in, 44, 45
  Communist Party in, 42
  Newsweek coverage of, 34–51
    amount, 36–38
    in cover stories, 38, 39
    thematic emphases, 38–45
Polish United Workers' Party (PUWP), 39,
    40, 41, 42–43
Political linguistics, 59
Pornography
  violence and, 281, 283
  see also Moving pictures
Positivism, in journalism, 63–65
Postman Always Rings Twice, The (moving
    picture), 300
"Postplay" (sales), 171–72
Potemkin (moving picture), 181–82
Power, aspects of, 58–59
Power, H., 203